Italian
FOR
DUMMIES®
2ND EDITION

Italian
FOR
DUMMIES®
2ND EDITION

by Teresa Picarazzi, Francesca Romana Onofri, and Karen Möller

WILEY

John Wiley & Sons, Inc.

Italian For Dummies®, 2nd Edition

Published by
John Wiley & Sons, Inc.
111 River St.
Hoboken, NJ 07030-5774
www.wiley.com

WILEY

About the Authors

Teresa Picarazzi graduated with a BA from Skidmore College and an MA/PhD in Italian Literature from Rutgers University. For many years she taught Italian language, literature, and culture at several universities, including The University of Arizona, Wesleyan University, and Dartmouth College. She also directed the Italian language and study abroad programs at some of these. For the past six years, she has taught Italian at The Hopkins School in New Haven, Connecticut.

In her spare time, Teresa likes to cook and read. She lives in Fairfield, Connecticut, with her daughter, her husband, Toby the dog, and Mittens and Governor the cats. The family spends every summer in Ravenna, Italy.

After her university studies in linguistics and Spanish and English language and literature, **Francesca Romana Onofri** lived several years abroad to better her understanding of the cultures and languages of different countries. In Spain and Ireland she worked as an Italian and Spanish teacher, as well as a translator and interpreter at cultural events. In Germany she was responsible for communication and special events in a museum of modern art, but even then she never gave up on her passion for languages: She was an Italian coach and teacher at the Opera Studio of the Cologne Opera House, and did translations — especially in the art field. Back in Italy, Francesca has edited several Berlitz Italian books and is working as a translator of art books, as well as a cultural events organizer and educator.

Karen Möller is currently studying Italian and English linguistics, literature, and culture. Before entering academia, Karen worked in the field of public relations and wrote articles for all kinds of fashion magazines and newspapers. Recently she has had occasion to work with Berlitz Publishing on German-Italian projects, including verb, vocabulary, and grammar handbooks, and Italian exercise books.

Dedication

I would like to dedicate this book to my parents, Mary and Domenico.

—Teresa Picarazzi

Author's Acknowledgments

I would like to thank my husband Giancarlo and daughter Emilia for their patience and support while I was working on this book, and my students, present and past, for their curiosity and love for all things Italian. I would also like to thank the people at Wiley for making this book come true: acquisitions editor Michael Lewis for contacting me; project editor Susan Hobbs for carefully guiding me step by step through the process, and technical editors Alicia Vitti and Christiana Thielmann for making me look at some aspects of Italian language and culture through a different lens.

—Teresa Picarazzi

Publisher's Acknowledgments

We're proud of this book; please send us your comments at http://dummies.custhelp.com.
For other comments, please contact our Customer Care Department within the U.S. at 877-762-2974,
outside the U.S. at 317-572-3993, or fax 317-572-4002.

Some of the people who helped bring this book to market include the following:

Acquisitions, Editorial, and
Media Development

Project Editor: Susan Hobbs

Acquisitions Editor: Michael Lewis

Copy Editor: Susan Hobbs

Assistant Editor: Erin Calligan Mooney

Editorial Program Coordinator: Joe Niesen

Technical Editors: Alicia Vitti,
Christiana Thielmann

Editorial Manager: Jennifer Ehrlich

Editorial Supervisor and Reprint Editor:
Carmen Krikorian

Editorial Assistants: David Lutton,
Jennette ElNaggar

Art Coordinator: Alicia B. South

Cover Photos: © iStockphoto.com / stevedangers

Cartoons: Rich Tennant
(www.the5thwave.com)

Composition Services

Project Coordinator: Nikki Gee

Layout and Graphics: Claudia Bell, Carl Byers,
Nikki Gately, Joyce Haughey,
Corrie Socolovitch, Christin Swinford

Proofreaders: Laura Albert, Susan Moritz,
Mildred Rosenzweig

Indexer: Potomac Indexing, LLC

Publishing and Editorial for Consumer Dummies

    Kathleen Nebenhaus, Vice President and Executive Publisher

    Kristin Ferguson-Wagstaffe, Product Development Director

    Ensley Eikenburg, Associate Publisher, Travel

    Kelly Regan, Editorial Director, Travel

Publishing for Technology Dummies

    Andy Cummings, Vice President and Publisher

Composition Services

    Debbie Stailey, Director of Composition Services

Contents at a Glance

Introduction 1

Part 1: Getting Started 7
Chapter 1: Saying It Like It Is 9
Chapter 2: Jumping Into the Basics of Italian 21
Chapter 3: Buongiorno! Salutations! 43
Chapter 4: Getting Your Numbers and Time Straight 63

Part II: Italian in Action 83
Chapter 5: Casa dolce casa (Home Sweet Home) 85
Chapter 6: Where Is the Colosseum? Asking Directions 103
Chapter 7: Food Glorious Food — and Don't Forget the Drink 119
Chapter 8: Shopping, Italian Style 139
Chapter 9: Having Fun Out on the Town 151
Chapter 10: Taking Care of Business and Telecommunicating 173
Chapter 11: Recreation and the Outdoors 191

Part III: Italian on the Go 207
Chapter 12: Planning a Trip 209
Chapter 13: Money, Money, Money 221
Chapter 14: Getting Around: Planes, Trains, Taxis, and Buses 233
Chapter 15: Finding a Place to Stay 255
Chapter 16: Handling Emergencies 271
Chapter 17: Small Talk, Wrapping Things Up 293

Part IV: The Part of Tens 313
Chapter 18: Ten Ways to Pick Up Italian Quickly 315
Chapter 19: Ten Things Never to Say in Italian 319
Chapter 20: Ten Favorite Italian Expressions 323
Chapter 21: Ten Phrases to Say So That People Think You're Italian 327

Part V: Appendixes 331

Appendix A: Verb Tables 333

Appendix B: Dictionaries 347

Appendix C: About the CD 359

Appendix D: Answer Keys..361

Index 369

Table of Contents

Introduction 1
  About This Book.. 1
  Conventions Used in This Book... 1
  Foolish Assumptions... 3
  How This Book Is Organized 3
    Part I: Getting Started... 3
    Part II: Italian in Action... 3
    Part III: Italian on the Go 4
    Part IV: The Part of Tens 4
    Part V: Appendixes 4
  Icons Used in This Book 4
  Where to Go from Here... 5

Part 1: Getting Started 7

Chapter 1: Saying It Like It Is 9
  You Already Know Some Italian!...9
    Cognates..11
    Popular expressions 11
  Mouthing Off: Basic Pronunciation 12
    The Alphabet 13
    Vowels 13
    Consonants 15
  Stressing Words Properly...19
  Using Gestures 20

Chapter 2: Jumping Into the Basics of Italian 21
  Setting Up Simple Sentences 21
  Coping with Gendered Words (Articles, Nouns, and Adjectives) 22
    Nouns and gender...22
    The indefinite articles 23
    Definite articles 24
    Adjectives 25
  Talking about Pronouns 26
    Personal pronouns 27
    Saying "you": Formal and informal...27

Verbs 28
Introducing regular and irregular verbs 28
Idiomatic uses of avere 32
Having to, wanting to, being able to................................37
Presenting the Simple Tenses: Past, Present, and Future....................38

Chapter 3: Buongiorno! Salutations! 43
Looking at Common Greetings and Good-byes 43
Deciding between formal or friendly 45
Replying to a greeting 45
Specifying your reuniting..46
Making Introductions..47
Introducing yourself 47
Introducing other people 50
Getting Acquainted..53
Finding out whether someone speaks Italian................53
Talking about where you come from 54
Extending and responding to invitations......................60

Chapter 4: Getting Your Numbers and Time Straight 63
Counting Numbers..63
Times of Day and Days of the Week 66
Using the Calendar and Making Dates 68
Making dates..69
Telling time..70
Chatting about the Weather..72
Familiarizing Yourself with the Metric System......................77
Length and Distance..78
Weight 78

Part II: Italian in Action 83

Chapter 5: Casa dolce casa (Home Sweet Home) 85
Ordering Ordinals..85
Inhabiting Your Home..87
Hunting for an apartment 87
Sprucing up your apartment 92
Furnishing your new pad 93
Housekeeping in style 95
Cooking and cleaning 98
Doing household chores 100

Chapter 6: Where Is the Colosseum? Asking Directions **103**

Finding Your Way: Asking for Specific Places 103
    Mapping the quarters and following directions 105
Verbs on the Move 109
Locations You May Be Looking For 113

Chapter 7: Food Glorious Food — and Don't Forget the Drink **119**

Eating, Italian Style 119
Drinking, Italian Style 119
    Expressing your love for espresso 120
    Beverages with even more of a kick 121
The Start and End of Dining Out 123
    Making reservations 124
    Paying for your meal 125
Having Breakfast 126
Eating Lunch 127
Enjoying Dinner 129
Shopping for Food 132
    Al macellaio (ahl mah-chehl-lahy-oh) (at the butcher's) 132
    Pesce (fish) (peh-sheh) 133
    At the panetteria (breadshop) 134

Chapter 8: Shopping, Italian Style **139**

Clothing Yourself 139
    Deciding between department stores and boutiques 139
    Sizing up Italian sizes 143
    Talking definitely and indefinitely 144
    Coloring your words 145
    Accessorizing 147
    Stepping out in style 148

Chapter 9: Having Fun Out on the Town **151**

Acquiring Culture 151
    Going to the movies 154
    Going to the theater 156
    Going to a museum 160
    Going to a local festival 161
    Going to a concert 162
Inviting Fun 164

Chapter 10: Taking Care of Business and Telecommunicating **173**

Phoning Made Simple 173
    Connecting via cellphones, texts, and Skype 174
    Calling for business or pleasure 176
Making Arrangements over the Phone 178
Asking for People and Getting the Message 179

What Did You Do Last Weekend? — Talking about the Past 182
Discussing Your Job 186
    The human element 187
    Office equipment 187

Chapter 11: Recreation and the Outdoors 191
Taking a Tour 191
Speaking Reflexively 195
Playing Sports 196
Talking about Hobbies and Interests 200

Part III: Italian on the Go 207

Chapter 12: Planning a Trip 209
Deciding When and Where to Go 209
Taking a Tour 211
Booking a Trip/Traveling to Foreign Lands 213
Arriving and Leaving: The Verbs "Arrivare" and "Partire" 216
Going to the Beach and Spa 217
Using the Simple Future Tense 217

Chapter 13: Money, Money, Money 221
Going to the Bank 221
Changing Money 224
Using Credit Cards 226
Looking at Various Currencies 228

Chapter 14: Getting Around: Planes, Trains, Taxis, and Buses 233
Getting through the Airport 233
    Checking in 234
    Dealing with excess baggage 236
    Waiting to board the plane 237
    Coping after landing 238
Going through Customs 240
Losing Luggage 241
Renting a Car 243
Navigating Public Transportation 245
    Calling a taxi 245
    Moving by train 246
    Going by bus or tram 249
    Reading maps and schedules 251
Being Early or Late 253

Chapter 15: Finding a Place to Stay **255**

Choosing a Place to Stay.. 255
Reserving a Room.. 256
Checking In.. 259
Personalizing pronouns.. 262
This or these: Demonstrative adjectives and pronouns..............263
Yours, mine, and ours: Possessive pronouns 263
Bending Others to Your Will: Imperatives 267

Chapter 16: Handling Emergencies. **271**

Talking to Doctors 272
Describing what ails you..273
Understanding professional medical vocabulary....................277
Getting what you need at the pharmacy...................................277
Braving the dentist 279
Reporting an Accident to the Police 280
I've Been Robbed! Knowing What to Do and
Say When the Police Arrive 281
Dealing with Car Trouble.. 285
When You Need a Lawyer: Protecting Your Rights....................... 287
Reporting a Lost or Stolen Passport 288

Chapter 17: Small Talk, Wrapping Things Up **293**

Discovering Interrogative Pronouns 293
Asking simple questions 295
Taking care of basic needs 296
Talking About Yourself and Your Family — Possessives Part 2 300
Speaking Reflexively.. 305
Talking shop 307
Discussing your job 307

Part IV: The Part of Tens... **313**

Chapter 18: Ten Ways to Pick Up Italian Quickly. **315**

Read Italian Food Labels.. 315
Ask for Food in Italian 316
Listen to Italian Songs 316
Read Italian Publications.. 316
Watch Italian Movies... 316
Tune in to Italian Radio and TV Programs 317
Listen to Italian Language Tapes... 317
Share Your Interest 317
Surf the Net.. 318
Cook!... 318

Chapter 19: Ten Things Never to Say in Italian.............319
Ciao-ing Down 319
Don't Be Literal 320
Five Fickle "False Friends" 320
Food Faux Pas 321
The Problem with "Play" 321
Being Careful of "False Friends" 321

Chapter 20: Ten Favorite Italian Expressions 323
Mamma mia! 323
Che bello! 323
Uffa!..324
Che ne so!/Boh! 324
Magari!......................................324
Ti sta bene! 324
Non te la prendere!..........................324
Che macello! 325
Non mi va! 325
Mi raccomando!..............................325

Chapter 21: Ten Phrases to Say So That
People Think You're Italian 327
In bocca al lupo!.............................327
Acqua in bocca!..............................328
Salute!......................................328
Macché!.....................................328
Neanche per sogno! 328
Peggio per te!...............................328
Piantala! 329
Vacci piano! 329
Eccome!.....................................329
Lascia perdere!..............................329

Part V: Appendixes 331

Appendix A: Verb Tables 333
Italian Verbs 333
Irregular Italian Verbs.......................336
Italian –IRE Verbs with a Special Pattern (-isc-) 343
Common Irregular Past Participles 345

Appendix B: Dictionaries 347

Appendix C: About the CD. 359

    Track Listing..359
    Customer Care 360

Appendix D: Answer Keys 361

Index.. *369*

Introduction

• •

As society becomes more global, knowing how to say at least a few words in other languages opens doors to communication. Carrying on a brief conversation in an immersion situation can enrich your experience. You may be planning a trip to Italy for business or pleasure. You may have friends and neighbors who speak other languages, or you may want to get in touch with your heritage by learning a little bit of the language that is spoken today in the place your ancestors came from.

Whatever your reason for wanting to learn some Italian, *Italian For Dummies* can help. Two experts at helping readers develop knowledge — Berlitz, experts in teaching foreign languages; and John Wiley & Sons, Inc., publishers of the best-selling *For Dummies* series — have teamed up to produce a book that gives you basic Italian language skills. We're not promising fluency here, but basic communicative competency that will allow you to be understood. If you need to greet someone, purchase a ticket, or order off a menu in Italian, you need look no further than *Italian For Dummies*.

About This Book

This is not a class that you have to drag yourself to twice a week for a specified period of time. You can use *Italian For Dummies* however you want to, whether your goal is to learn some words and phrases to help you get around when you visit Italy, or you just want to be able to say "Hello, how are you?" to your Italian-speaking neighbor. Go through this book at your own pace, reading as much or as little at a time as you like. You don't have to trudge through the chapters in order, either; just read the sections that interest you.

Note: If you've never taken Italian before, you may want to read the chapters in Part I before you tackle the later chapters.

Conventions Used in This Book

To make this book easy for you to navigate, we've set up a few conventions:

✔ Italian terms are set in **boldface** to make them stand out.

✔ Pronunciations are set in normal type with stressed syllables in *italics*. English translations are also set in italics.

✔ Verb conjugations (lists that show you the forms of a verb) are given in tables in this order of six persons: "I," "you" (singular, informal), "he/she/it/you" (formal), "we," "you" (plural/informal), and "they/you" (plural, formal) form. Pronunciations follow in the second column. Following is an example using **parlare** (pahr-*lah*-reh) (*to speak*). The translations in the third column have all three forms, but for the sake of space, I only give you the first:

Conjugation	Pronunciation	Translation
io parlo	*ee*-oh *pahr*-loh	*I speak, I do speak, I am speaking*
tu parli	tooh *pahr*-lee	*You (informal) speak*
lei/lui/lei parla	ley/*looh*-ee/lehy *pahr*-lah	*She/he/you (formal) speak*
noi parliamo	noi pahr-lee-*ah*-moh	*We speak*
voi parlate	voi parl-*lah*-teh	*You (plural informal) speak*
loro parlano	*loh*-roh *pahr*-lah-noh	*They/you (plural formal) speak*

Language learning is a peculiar beast, so this book includes a few elements that other *For Dummies* books do not. Following are the new elements you'll find:

✔ **Talkin' the Talk dialogues:** The best way to learn a language is to see and hear how it's used in conversation, so we include dialogues throughout the book under the heading "Talkin' the Talk." Listen to and repeat these dialogues as often as you like. In both the CD and the text, they will help you approximate authentic pronunciation.

✔ **Words to Know blackboards:** Identifying key words and phrases is also important in language learning, so we collect the important words in a chapter (or section within a chapter) in a chalkboard, with the heading "Words to Know."

✔ **Fun & Games activities:** You can use the Fun & Games activities to reinforce some chapter concepts you've learned. These word games are fun ways to gauge your progress.

Also note that because each language has its own ways of expressing ideas, the English translations that we provide for the Italian terms may not be exactly literal. We want you to know the gist of what's being said. For example, the phrase **Mi dica** (mee *dee*-kah) can be translated literally as the formal imperative "Tell me," but the phrase really means "(How) Can I help you?"

Foolish Assumptions

To write this book, we had to make some assumptions about who you are and what you want from a book called *Italian For Dummies.* These are the assumptions we made:

- ✔ You know no Italian — or if you took it back in school, you don't remember much.

- ✔ You're not looking for a book that will make you fluent in Italian; you just want to know some words, phrases, and sentence constructions so that you can communicate basic information in Italian.

- ✔ You don't want to have to memorize long lists of vocabulary words or a bunch of boring grammar rules.

- ✔ You want to have fun and learn a little bit of Italian at the same time.

If these statements apply to you, you've found the right book!

How This Book 1s Organized

This book is divided by topic into parts, and then into chapters. The following sections tell you what types of information you can find in each part.

Part 1: Getting Started

This part lets you get your feet wet by giving you some Italian basics: how to pronounce your ABCs, numbers, words, and so on. We even boost your confidence by reintroducing you to some Italian words that you probably already know. Finally, we outline the basics of Italian grammar that you may need to know when you work through later chapters in the book.

Part 11: Italian in Action

In this part, you begin learning and using Italian. Instead of focusing on grammar points as many language textbooks do, this part focuses on everyday situations, such as shopping, dining, going out, asking for directions, and being home.

Part III: Italian on the Go

This part gives you the tools you need to take your Italian on the road, whether it's planning a trip or excursion, navigating public transportation, finding a room, or handling an emergency.

Part IV: The Part of Tens

If you're looking for small, easily digestible pieces of information about Italian, this part is for you. Here, you can find ten ways to learn Italian quickly, ten useful Italian expressions to know, ten things never to say in Italian, and more.

Part V: Appendixes

This part of the book includes important information that you can use for reference. We include verb tables, which show you how to conjugate regular and irregular verbs. We also provide a listing of the tracks that appear on the audio CD that comes with this book so that you can find out where in the book those dialogues are and follow along. We give you a mini-dictionary in both Italian-to-English and English-to-Italian formats. If you encounter an Italian word that you don't understand, or you need to say something in Italian, you can look it up here. You can also find the answers to the Fun and Games sections here.

Icons Used in This Book

You may be looking for particular information while reading this book. To make certain types of information easier for you to find, we've placed the following icons in the left-hand margins throughout the book:

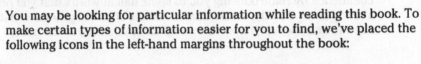

This icon highlights tips that can make learning Italian easier.

To ensure that you don't forget important information, this icon serves as a reminder, like a string tied around your finger.

Languages are full of quirks that may trip you up if you're not prepared for them. This icon points to discussions of these weird grammar rules.

If you're looking for information and advice about culture and travel, look for these icons.

The audio CD that comes with this book gives you the opportunity to listen to real Italian speakers so that you can get a better understanding of what Italian sounds like. This icon marks the Talkin' the Talk dialogues that you can find on the CD. This is a great way to practice your own speaking.

Where to Go from Here

Learning a language is all about jumping in and giving it a try (no matter how bad your pronunciation is at first). So make the leap! Start at the beginning, pick a chapter that interests you, or pop the CD into your stereo or computer and listen to a few dialogues. Skip over the parts that distract you and take you away from Italian (such as the pronunciation spellings and translations after you've been through them once): The more you think in Italian, the more natural it will come to you. Before long, you'll be able to respond, "Sì!" when people ask, "Parla italiano?"

Part I
Getting Started

The 5th Wave   By Rich Tennant

Magnifico!

Molto bello!

"I insisted they learn some Italian. I couldn't stand the idea of standing in front of the Trevi Fountain and hearing, 'gosh', 'wow', and 'far out.'"

In this part . . .

Ciao! See? You already understand some Italian, although you may think we're saying good-bye before we even say hello. The truth is that **ciao** means both "hello" and "goodbye."

These first four chapters introduce you to the basics of the Italian language: Chapter 1 gets you going with pronunciation, Chapter 2 helps you with basic Italian grammar. You learn how to say "hello" and "goodbye" as well as how to introduce yourself and others in Chapter 3. And you learn how to tell time, put dates in your calendar, and ask for phone numbers in Chapter 4. So Andiamo! (ah-*dyah*-moh) (Let's go!)

Chapter 1

Saying It Like It Is

In This Chapter

▶ Taking note of the little Italian you know

▶ Looking at popular expressions and cognates

▶ Learning basic Italian pronunciation

▶ Using gestures

You probably know that Italian is a Romance language, which means that Italian, just like Spanish, French, Portuguese, and some other languages, is a "child" of Latin. There was a time when Latin was the official language in a large part of Europe because the Romans ruled so much of the area. Before the Romans came, people spoke their own languages, and the mixture of these original tongues with Latin produced many of the languages and dialects still in use today.

If you know one of these Romance languages you can often understand bits of another one of them. But just as members of the same family can look very similar but have totally different personalities, so it is with these languages. People in different areas speak in very different ways due to historical or social reasons, and even though Italian is the official language, Italy has a rich variety of dialects. Some dialects are so far from Italian that people from different regions cannot understand each other.

Despite the number of different accents and dialects, you will be happy to discover that everybody understands the Italian you speak and you understand theirs. (Italians don't usually speak in their dialect with people outside their region.)

You Already Know Some Italian!

Although Italians are very proud of their language, they have allowed some English words to enter it. They talk, for example, about gadgets, jogging, feeling and shock; they often use the word okay; and since computers have entered their lives, they say **"cliccare sul mouse"** (kleek-*kah*-reh soohl mouse) (to click the mouse). Finally, there's **lo zapping** (loh *zap*-ping), which means switching TV channels with the remote. These are only a few of the flood of English words that have entered the Italian language.

In the same way, many Italian words are known in English-speaking countries. Can you think of some?

How about . . .

- **pizza** (*peet*-tsah)

- **pasta** (*pahs*-tah)

- **spaghetti** (spah-*geht*-tee)

- **tortellini** (tohr-tehl-*lee*-nee)

- **mozzarella** (moht-tsah-*rehl*-lah)

- **espresso** (ehs-*prehs*-soh)

- **cappuccino** (kahp-pooh-*chee*-noh)

- **panino** (pah-*nee*-noh): For one sandwich: for two or more, the word is **panini** (pah-*nee*-nee)

- **biscotti** (bees-*koht*-tee) (cookies): One cookie is a **biscotto** (bees-*koht*-toh)

- **tiramisù** (tee-rah-mee-*sooh*)

Incidentally, did you know that tiramisù literally means "pull me up"? This refers to the fact that this sweet is made with strong Italian espresso.

You may have heard words from areas other than the kitchen, such as the following:

- **amore** (ah-*moh*-reh): This is the word "love" that so many Italian songs tell about.

- **avanti** (ah-*vahn*-tee): You use this word as "come in!" and also "come on!" or "get a move on!"

- **bambino** (bahm-*bee*-noh): This is a male child. The female equivalent is **bambina** (bahm-*bee*-nah).

- **bravo!** (*brah*-voh): You can properly say this word only to one man. To a woman, you must say **"brava!"** (*brah*-vah), and to a group of people, you say **"bravi!"** (*brah*-vee) unless the group is composed only of women, in which case you say **"brave!"** (*brah*-veh).

- **ciao!** (chou): **Ciao** means "hello" and "goodbye."

✔ **scusi** (*skooh*-zee): This word stands for "excuse me" and "sorry" and is addressed to persons you don't know or to whom you speak formally. You say **"scusa"** (*scooh*-zah) to people you know and to children.

You've heard at least some of these words, haven't you? This is just a little taste of all the various words and expressions you'll get to know in this book.

Cognates

In addition to the words that have crept into the language directly, Italian and English have many cognates. A cognate is a word in one language that has the same origin as a word in another one and may sound similar. You can get an immediate picture of what cognates are from the following examples:

✔ **aeroporto** (ah-eh-roh-*pohr*-toh) (*airport*)

✔ **attenzione** (aht-tehn-*tsyoh*-neh) (*attention*)

✔ **comunicazione** (koh-mooh-nee-kah-*tsyoh*-neh) (*communication*)

✔ **importante** (eem-pohr-*tahn*-teh) (*important*)

✔ **incredibile** (een-kreh-*dee*-bee-leh) (*incredible*)

You understand much more Italian than you think you do. Italian and English are full of cognates. To demonstrate, read this little story with some Italian words and see how easy it is for you to understand.

It seems **impossibile** (eem-pohs-*see*-bee-leh) to him that he is now at the **aeroporto** (ah-eh-roh-*pohr*-toh) in Rome. He always wanted to come to this **città** (cheet-*tah*). When he goes out on the street, he first calls a **taxi** (*tah*-ksee). He opens his bag to see if he has the **medicina** (meh-dee-*chee*-nah) that the **dottore** (doht-*toh*-reh) gave him. Going through this **terribile traffico** (tehr-*ree*-bee-leh *trahf*-fee-koh), he passes a **cattedrale** (kaht-teh-*drah*-leh), some **sculture** (skoohl-*tooh*-reh), and many **palazzi** (pah-*laht*-tsee). He knows that this is going to be a **fantastico** (fahn-*tahs*-tee-koh) journey.

Popular expressions

Every language has expressions that you use so often that they almost become routine. For example, when you give something to somebody and he or she says, "Thank you," you automatically reply, "You're welcome!" This type of popular expression is an inseparable part of every language. When you know these expressions and how to use them, you're on the way to really speaking Italian.

The following are some of the most common popular expressions in Italian (Track 2):

- **Accidenti!** (ahch-chee-*dehn*-tee) (*Wow!/Darn it!*)
- **Andiamo!** (ahn-*dyah*-moh) (*Let's go!*)
- **Che c'è?** (keh cheh) (*What's up?*)
- **D'accordo? D'accordo!** (dahk-*kohr*-doh) (*Agreed? Agreed!*)
- **E chi se ne importa?** (eh kee seh neh eem-*pohr*-tah) (*Who cares?*)
- **È lo stesso.** (eh loh *stehs*-soh) (*It's all the same; It doesn't matter.*)
- **Fantastico!** (fahn-*tahs*-tee-koh) (*Fantastic!*)
- **Non fa niente.** (nohn fah nee-*ehn*-teh) (*Don't worry about it. It doesn't matter.*) You say **"Non fa niente"** when someone apologizes to you for something.
- **Non c'è di che.** (nohn cheh dee keh) (*You're welcome.*)
- **Permesso?** (pehr-*mehs*-soh) (*May I pass/come in?*) Italians use this expression every time they cross a threshold entering a house or when passing through a crowd.
- **Stupendo!** (stoo-*pehn*-doh) (*Wonderful!; Fabulous!*)
- **Va bene!** (vah *beh*-neh) (*Okay!*)

Mouthing Off: Basic Pronunciation

Italian provides many opportunities for your tongue to do acrobatics. This is really fun, because the language offers you some new sounds. In this section, I give you some basic pronunciation hints that are important both for surfing through this book and for good articulation when you speak Italian. First, I'd like to make a deal with you. Next to the Italian words throughout this book you find the pronunciation in parentheses. In the following sections, I give you some helpful hints about how to read these pronunciations — that is, how to pronounce the Italian words. The deal is that you and I have to agree on which letters refer to which sounds. You have to follow this code all through this book.

In the pronunciations, I separate the syllables with a hyphen, like this: **casa** (*kah*-zah) (*house*). Furthermore, I italicize the stressed syllable, which means that you put the stress of the word on the italicized syllable. (See the section "Stressing Words Properly," later in this chapter, for more information about stresses.) If you learn the correct pronunciation in this chapter, starting with the alphabet, you may even forego the pronunciation spelling provided, and read it like a real Italian.

The Alphabet

What better way is there to start speaking a language than to familiarize yourself with its alphabet! Table 1-1 shows you all the letters as well as how each sounds. It's essential to learn how to pronounce the Italian alphabet so that you'll be able to pronounce all of the new words you will be learning. Listen to and repeat the CD (Track 1) as many times as you need to in order to get down the right sounds. In the long run, this will help you be understood when you communicate in Italian. Note that there are only 21 letters in the Italian alphabet: missing are j, k, w, x, and y (which have crept into some Italian words now used in Italy).

Table 1-1		The Italian Alphabet (ahl-fah-*beh*-toh)	
Letter	**Pronunciation**	**Letter**	**Pronunciation**
a	ah	b	bee
c	chee	d	dee
e	eh	f	*ehf*-feh
g	jee	h	*ahk*-kah
i	ee	j	
k		l	*ehl*-leh
m	*ehm*-meh	n	*ehn*-neh
o	oh	p	pee
q	kooh	r	*ehr*-reh
s	*ehs*-seh	t	tee
u	ooh	v	vooh
w		x	
y		z	*dzeh*-tah

Vowels

I'll start with the tough ones: vowels. The sounds are not that new, but the connection between the written letter and the actual pronunciation is not quite the same as it is in English.

Italian has five written vowels: a, e, i, o, and u. The following sections tell you how to pronounce each of them.

The vowel "a"

In Italian, the letter a has just one pronunciation. Think of the sound of the a in the English word father. The Italian a sounds just like that.

To prevent you from falling back to the other a sounds found in English, I transcribe the Italian a as (ah), as shown earlier in **casa** (*kah*-zah) (*house*). Here are some other examples:

- **albero** (*ahl*-beh-roh) (*tree*)
- **marmellata** (mahr-mehl-*lah*-tah) (*jam*)
- **sale** (*sah*-leh) (*salt*)

The vowel "e"

Try to think of the sound in the French word gourmet (you don't pronounce the t). This sound comes very close to the Italian e. In this book, I transcribe the e sound as (eh). For example:

- **sole** (*soh*-leh) (*sun*)
- **peso** (*peh*-zoh) (*weight*)
- **bere** (*beh*-reh) (*to drink*)

The vowel "i"

The Italian i is simply pronounced (ee), as in the English word see. Here are some examples:

- **cinema** (*chee*-neh-mah) (*cinema*)
- **bimbo** (*beem*-boh) (*little boy*)
- **vita** (*vee*-tah) (*life*)

The vowel "o"

The Italian o is pronounced as in the English (from the Italian) piano. I therefore list the pronunciation as (oh). Try it out on the following words:

- **domani** (doh-*mah*-nee) (*tomorrow*)
- **piccolo** (*peek*-koh-loh) (*little; small*)
- **dolce** (*dohl*-cheh) (*sweet*)

The vowel "u"

The Italian u sounds always like the English (ooh), as in zoo. Therefore, I use (ooh) to transcribe the Italian u. Here are some sample words:

- ✔ **tu** (tooh) (*you*)
- ✔ **luna** (*looh*-nah) (*moon*)
- ✔ **frutta** (*frooht*-tah) (*fruit*)

Pronunciation peculiarities

You will come across some sounds and spellings that are not so familiar, for example:

- ✔ oi as in oink: **noi** (noi) (*we*)
- ✔ ahy as in ice: **dai** (dahy) (*you give*)
- ✔ ee as in feet: **diva** (*dee*-vah) (*diva*)
- ✔ ey as in aid: **lei** (ley) (*she*)
- ✔ ou as in out: **auto** (*ou*-toh) (*car*)

Consonants

Italian has the same consonants that English does. You pronounce most of them the same way in Italian as you pronounce them in English, but others have noteworthy differences. I start with the easy ones and look at those that are pronounced identically:

- ✔ **b:** As in **bene** (*beh*-neh) (*well*)
- ✔ **d:** As in **dare** (*dah*-reh) (*to give*)
- ✔ **f:** As in **fare** (*fah*-reh) (*to make*)
- ✔ **l:** As in **ladro** (*lah*-droh) (*thief*)
- ✔ **m:** As in **madre** (*mah*-dreh) (*mother*)
- ✔ **n:** As in **no** (noh) (no)
- ✔ **p:** As in **padre** (*pah*-dreh) (*father*)
- ✔ **t:** As in **treno** (*treh*-noh) (train) Make certain to exaggerate the **t** when it's doubled, like in the word **spaghetti** (spah-*geht*-tee) as in the last name Getty.
- ✔ **v:** As in **vino** (*vee*-noh) (*wine*)

Finally there are some consonants that do not really exist in Italian except in some foreign words that have entered the language.

- ✔ **j:** Exists mostly in foreign words such as jogging, junior, and jeans, and sounds like the *y* in *yam*.
- ✔ **k:** The same as *j*; you find it in words like *okay*, *ketchup*, and *killer*.
- ✔ **w:** As with *j* and *k*, you find it in some foreign words (for the most part English words), like *whisky*, *windsurf*, and *wafer*.
- ✔ **x:** As with *j*, *k*, and *w*, *x* doesn't really exist in Italian, with the difference that "x words" derive mostly from Greek. Examples include **xenofobia** (kseh-noh-foh-*bee*-ah) (*xenophobia*) and **xilofono** (ksee-*loh*-foh-noh) (*xylophone*).
- ✔ **y:** The letter *y* normally appears only in foreign words, like *yogurt*, *hobby*, and *yacht*.

Now, on to the consonants that are pronounced differently than they are in English.

The consonant "c"

The Italian c has two sounds, depending on which letter follows it:

- ✔ **Hard c:** When *c* is followed by *a*, *o*, *u*, or any consonant, you pronounce it as in the English word *cat*. I transcribe this pronunciation as (k). Examples include **casa** (*kah*-sah) (*house*), **colpa** (*kohl*-pah) (*guilt*), and **cuore** (*kwoh*-reh) (*heart*).

  To obtain the "k" sound before *e* and *i*, you must put an *h* between the c and the e or i. Examples include **che** (keh) (what), **chiesa** (*kyeh*-zah) (*church*), and **chiave** (*kyah*-veh) (*key*).

- ✔ **Soft c:** When *c* is followed by *e* or *i*, you pronounce it as you do the first and last sound in the English word church; therefore, I give you the pronunciation (ch). Examples include **cena** (*cheh*-nah) (*dinner*), **cibo** (*chee*-boh) (*food*), and **certo** (*chehr*-toh) (*certainly*).

  To obtain the "ch" sound before *a*, *o*, or *u*, you have to insert an *i*. This *i*, however, serves only to create the "ch"" sound; you do not pronounce it. Examples include **ciao** (chou) (*hello; goodbye*), **cioccolata** (chok-koh-*lah*-tah) (*chocolate*), and **ciuccio** (*chooh*-choh) (*baby's pacifier*).

This pronunciation scheme sounds terribly complicated, but in the end, it's not that difficult. Here I present it in another way, which you can take as a little memory support:

Follow a scheme like this:

C + i, e = "ch"

C+ h, o, u, a, cons = "k"

The consonant "g"

The Italian *g* behaves the same as the *c*. Therefore, I present it the same way:

- ✔ **Hard g:** When *g* is followed by *a*, *o*, *u*, or any consonant, you pronounce it as you pronounce the *g* in the English word good. I transcribe this pronunciation as (*g*). Examples include **gamba** (*gahm*-bah) (*leg*), **gomma** (*gohm*-mah) (*rubber*), and **guerra** (*gwehr*-rah) (*war*).

  To obtain the "g" sound before *e* or *i*, you must put an h between the letter g and the *e* or *i*. Examples include **spaghetti** (spah-*geht*-tee) (*spaghetti*), **ghiaccio** (*gyahch*-choh) (*ice*), and **ghirlanda** (geer-*lahn*-dah) (*wreath*).

- ✔ **Soft g:** When g is followed by *e* or *i*, you pronounce it as you do the first sound in the English word job; therefore, I write the pronunciation as (*j*). Examples include **gentile** (jehn-*tee*-leh) (*kind*), **giorno** (*johr*-noh) (*day*), and **gelosia** (jeh-loh-*zee*-ah) (*jealousy*).

  To obtain the "j" sound before *a*, *o*, or *u*, you have to insert an *i*. The *i* serves only to indicate the proper sound; you do not pronounce it. Examples include giacca (*jahk*-kah) (*jacket*), gioco (*joh*-koh) (*game*), and giudice (*jooh*-dee-cheh) (*judge*). Here's another little pattern to help you remember these pronunciations:

gamba	gomma	guerra	ghiaccio	spaghetti	= g
gentile	giorno	giacca	gioco	giudice	= j

The consonant "h"

The consonant *h* has only one function: namely, to change the sound of c and *g* before the vowels e and *i*, as described earlier. It also appears in foreign expressions such as hostess, hit parade, and hobby, and in some forms of the verb **avere** (ah-*veh*-reh) (*to have*), but it's <u>always</u> silent.

The consonant "q"

Q exists only in connection with u followed by another vowel; that is, you always find *qu*. The q is pronounced like (k), and *qu* is, therefore, pronounced (*kw*). Examples include **quattro** (*kwaht*-troh) (*four*), **questo** (*kwehs*-toh) (*this*), and **quadro** (*kwah*-droh) (*picture*).

The consonant "r"

The Italian *r* is not pronounced with the tongue in the back, as it is in English, but trilled at the alveolar ridge, which is the front part of your palate, right behind your front teeth. You have to practice it. In the beginning, you may not find this pronunciation manageable, but practice makes perfect!

Here are some words to help you practice:

- **radio** (*rah*-dee-oh) (*radio*)
- **per favore** (pehr fah-*voh*-reh) (*please*)
- **prego** (*preh*-goh) (*you're welcome*)

The consonant "s"

S is sometimes pronounced as the English *s*, as in so. In this case, I give you the pronunciation (*s*). In other cases, it's pronounced like the English *z*, as in *zero*; in these cases, I list (*z*) as the pronunciation. Examples include **pasta** (*pahs*-tah) (*pasta*), **solo** (*soh*-loh) (*only*), **chiesa** (*kyeh*-zah) (*church*), and **gelosia** (jeh-loh-*zee*-ah) (*jealousy*).

The consonant "z"

A single *z* is pronounced (*dz*) — the sound is very similar to the English *z* in zero, with a *d* added at the beginning, as in **zero** (*dzehr*-oh) (*zero*). Just try it. When the *z* is doubled, you pronounce it more sharply, like (*t-ts*), as in **tazza** (*taht*-tsah) (*cup; mug*). Furthermore, when *z* is followed by the letter *i*, it also has a ts sound, like in the word **nazione** (nah-*tsyoh*-neh) (*nation*).

Double consonants

When you encounter double consonants in Italian, you have to pronounce each instance of the consonant or lengthen the sound. The difficult part is that there's no pause between the consonants.

Doubling the consonant usually changes the meaning of the word. So, to make sure that your Italian is understandable, emphasize doubled consonants well. To make you pronounce words with double consonants correctly, I write the first consonant at the end of one syllable and the other one at the beginning of the following one, as in these examples:

- **nono** (*noh*-noh) (*ninth*)
- **nonno** (*nohn*-noh) (*grandfather*)
- **capello** (kah-*pehl*-loh) (*hair*)
- **cappello** (kahp-*pehl*-loh) (*hat*)

Try it once again:

- **bello** (*behl*-loh) (*beautiful*)
- **caffè** (kahf-*feh*) (*coffee*)
- **occhio** (*ohk*-kyoh) (*eye*)
- **spiaggia** (*spyahj*-jah) (*beach*)

Consonant clusters

Certain consonant clusters have special sounds in Italian. Here they are:

- **gn** is pronounced as the English "ny." The sound is actually the same as in a Spanish word I'm sure you know: **señorita** (seh-nyoh-*ree*-tah) (*miss*), or better yet, an Italian word like **gnocchi** (*nyohk*-kee).

- **gl** is pronounced in the back of the throat like the English word million in words like **gli** (lyee) (*the*) and **famiglia** (fah-*mee*-lyah) (*family*.) You should not say anything like the English *g*.

- **sc** follows the same rules of the soft and hard "c" from the previous section. It is pronounced as in the English scooter when it comes before *a*, *o*, *u*, or *h* — that is, as in **scala** (*skah*-lah) (*scale*), **sconto** (*skohn*-toh) (*discount*), and **scuola** (*scwoh*-lah) (*school*). Before *e* and *i*, it is pronounced like the *sh* in **cash**. Examples of this pronunciation include **scena** (*sheh*-nah) (*scene*), **scesa** (*sheh*-sah) (*descent*), and **scimmia** (*sheem*-mee-ah) (*monkey*).

Stressing Words Properly

Stress is the audible accent that you put on a syllable as you speak it. One syllable always gets more stress than all the others. (A reminder: In this book I *italicize* the syllable to stress.)

Some words give you a hint as to where to stress them: They have an accent grave (ˋ) or acute (ˊ) above one of their letters. Here are some examples:

- **caffè** (kahf-*feh*) (*coffee*)
- **città** (cheet-*tah*) (*city*)
- **lunedì** (looh-neh-*dee*) (*Monday*)
- **perché** (pehr-*keh*) (*why*)
- **però** (peh-*roh*) (*but*)

> ✔ **università** (ooh-nee-vehr-see-*tah*) (*university*)
>
> ✔ **virtù** (veer-*tooh*) (*virtue*)

Only vowels can have accents, and in Italian all vowels at the end of a word can have this accent (`). If there's no accent in the word, you're unfortunately left on your own. A rough tip is that Italian tends to have the stress on the penultimate (the next-to-last) syllable. But there are too many rules and exceptions to list them all here!

> ✔ The accent tells you where to stress the word.
>
> ✔ Fortunately, only a few words have the same spelling and only an accent to distinguish them. But it can be a very important distinction, as in the following example:
>
> **e** (eh) and **è** (eh) (*he/she/it is*) are distinguished only by the accent on the vowel.

Using Gestures

Italians love to emphasize their words with gestures. For example, there are gestures to express the following feelings: **Ho fame** (oh *fah*-meh) (*I'm hungry*), **Me ne vado** (meh neh *vah*-doh) (*I'm leaving*), and **E chi se ne importa?** (eh kee seh neh eem-*pohr*-tah) (*Who cares?*). Needless to say, a flood of rude gestures exist as well.

Unfortunately, describing the gestures in words is too difficult, because Italian body language is a science and is hard for non-Italians to copy. You also have to make the right facial expressions when performing these gestures. These gestures generally come naturally and spontaneously, and you're sure to see some as you observe Italian life. Still, I won't let you go off without some of the practical, useful gestures that you might make when with Italians. Greeting and saying goodbye, for example, are accompanied by a common gesture — hugging and kissing. Italians seek direct contact when greeting one another. When you're not very familiar with a person, you shake hands. But when you know a person well or you have an immediate good feeling, you kiss cheek to cheek; that is, you don't really touch with your lips, but only with your cheek.

Chapter 2

Jumping Into the Basics of Italian

. . . .

In This Chapter

▶ Introducing simple sentence construction

▶ Dealing with masculine and feminine words

▶ Discovering the use of pronouns

▶ Using the right "you"

▶ Exploring regular and irregular verbs

▶ Uncovering the present tense

. . . .

This chapter takes a look at some basic Italian grammar and leads you through the building blocks of sentences. Consider these blocks as challenging scaffolding that helps you to construct your sentences, piece by piece. In this chapter, I walk you through gender and number, as well as how to conjugate enough verbs to get you immediately on the road to communicating in Italian.

Setting Up Simple Sentences

Becoming a fluent speaker of a foreign language takes a lot of work. Simply communicating or making yourself understood in another language is much easier. Even if you only know a few words, you can usually communicate successfully in common situations such as at a restaurant or a hotel.

Forming simple sentences is, well, simple. The basic sentence structure of Italian is subject-verb-object — the same as in English. Nouns in Italian are gender specific. In the following examples, you can see how this structure works:

> ✔ **Carla parla inglese.** (*kahr*-lah *pahr*-lah een-*gleh*-zeh) (*Carla speaks English.*)

> ✔ **Pietro ha una macchina.** (pee-*eh*-troh ah *ooh*-nah *mahk*-kee-nah) (*Pietro has a car.*)

> ✔ **L'Italia è un bel paese.** (lee-*tahl*-ee-ah eh oohn behl pah-*eh*-zeh) (*Italy is a beautiful country.*)

Coping with Gendered Words (Articles, Nouns, and Adjectives)

Gender drives the construction of definite and indefinite articles, nouns, and adjectives. It is essential to learn the gender of nouns as soon as you encounter them, because that will determine what article and adjective you're going to use with them — these are all interconnected. Luckily most of this grammar follows some very cool schemata which you can plug in anywhere once you have it down. The more you commit these to memory, the easier it will be to effectively create sentences.

Nouns and gender

All nouns have a specific gender (masculine and feminine) and number (singular and plural). You need to know what those are in order to create (and understand) sentences, have verb agreement, and add on articles and adjectives. The good news is that nouns follow a predictable pattern. The following shows you how to form the singular and plural of masculine and feminine nouns. See if you can infer the rules just by looking at the chart.

Feminine nouns singular	a (ah)	**una casa** (*ooh*-nah *kah*-zah) (*one house*)
Feminine nouns plural	e (eh)	**due case** (*dooh*-eh *kah*-zeh) (*two houses*)
Masculine nouns singular	o (oh)	**un libro** (oohn *lee*-broh) (*one book*)
Masculine nouns plural	i (ee)	**due libri** (*dooh*-eh *lee*-bree) (*two books*)
Masculine/feminine nouns singular	e (eh)	**un esame** (m) (oohn eh-*zah*-meh) (*one exam*)
Masculine/feminine nouns plural	i (ee)	**due esami** (*dooh*-eh eh-*za*-mee) (*two exams*)/una lezione (f.) (*ooh*-nah lets-*yoh*-neh) due lezioni (*dooh*-eh lets-*yoh*-nee)

So the rules are:

- ✔ Feminine nouns usually end in **a** in the singular and **e** in the plural.
- ✔ Masculine nouns usually end in **o** in the singular and **i** in the plural.
- ✔ There are masculine and feminine nouns that end in **e** in the singular end in **i** in the plural. You need to memorize their gender the first time you encounter them.

Here's a tip. Anything ending in **–ione** (like **nazione** [nahts-*yoh*-neh]) is feminine.

That was pretty painless, wasn't it? Are you ready for some exceptions in the way of invariable nouns? These nouns only have one form: that is, they are the same in both the singular and plural forms. See if you can guess the rules for these as you go through the following bullets.

- **un caffè** (m) (oohn kahf-*feh*)   **due caffè** (*dooh*-eh kahf-*feh*)
  one coffee,   *two coffees*

- **un bar** (m) (oohn bahr)   **due bar** (*dooh*-eh bahr)
  one bar,   *two bars*

- **una bici** (f) (*ooh*-nah *bee*-chee) **due bici** (*dooh*-eh *bee*-chee)
  one bike,   *two bikes*

- **uno zoo** (m) (*ooh*-noh zoh)   **due zoo** (*dooh*-eh zoh)
  one zoo,   *two zoos*

The rules for the three main types of invariable nouns follow:

1. Nouns that end in an accented final vowel, such as **caffè** and **città** (cheet-*tah*) (*city*), are invariable.

2. Nouns that end in a consonant (these are rare!), such as **bar** and **film** (feelm) (*film, movie*) are invariable.

3. Nouns that are abbreviations, such as **zoo**, **bici**, **radio** (*rah*-dee-oh) and **cinema** (*chee*-neh-mah) (*cinema, movie-house*) are invariable.

The indefinite articles

Did you happen to notice the indefinite articles for "one" or "a/an" that precede all of the previously mentioned nouns? They are always singular. Also, Italian indefinite articles agree in gender. And the one you choose also has to take into account the first letter of the noun that it precedes. Table 2-1 shows you the indefinite articles plus some examples.

Table 2-1	Indefinite articles (Gli articoli indeterminativi) (lyee ahr-tee-*koh*-lee een-deh-tehr-meen-ah-*tee*-vee)
Feminine Femminili (fehm-meen-ee-lee)	**Masculine Maschili (mahs-kee-lee)**
una ragazza (*ooh*-nah rah-*gahts*-tsah) (*a girl*)	**un ragazzo** (oohn rah-*gahts*-tsoh) (*a boy*)
un'amica (oohn-ah-*mee*-kah) (*a (girl) friend*)	**un amico** (oohn ah-*mee*-koh) (*a (boy) friend*)
una zia (*ooh*-nah dzee-ah) (*an aunt*)	**uno zio** (*ooh*-noh dzee-oh) (*an uncle*)
una studentessa (*ooh*-nah stooh-dehn-tehs-sah) (*a (female) student*)	**uno studente** (*ooh*-noh stooh-*dehn*-teh) (*a (male) student*)

Did you make a special note of the letters that the nouns begin with? So the rules for indefinite articles go something like this:

una before all feminine nouns beginning with a consonant

un' before all feminine nouns beginning with a vowel

un before all masculine nouns beginning with vowels and consonants

uno before all masculine nouns beginning with the **s impura** (s+ consonant), **z, gn, ps, st: zio** (*dzee*-oh) (*uncle*); **gnomo** (*nyoh*-moh) (*gnome*); **psicologo** (psee-*kohl*-oh-goh); **studente** (stooh-*dehn*-teh) (*student*)

Definite articles

Of course, you don't go around talking about singular things all the time. Italian is one of those languages that require a definite article before the noun in most cases. For example, if you want to say "Sicily is interesting," you need to precede Sicily with an article, such as "**La Sicilia è interessante**" (lah see-*chee*-lee-ah eh een-tehr-ehs-*sahn*-teh). The same goes for the following noun: "Love is blind" (**L'amore è cieco**) (lah-*moh*-reh eh *cheh*-koh).

Table 2-2 shows a list of articles that you should try to commit to memory. Italian definite articles agree in number and gender with the nouns they precede. Just like with the indefinite articles, the letter that heads the noun also determines what article to use.

Table 2-2	Definite Articles (Articoli determinative) (ahr-*tee*-koh-lee deh-tehr-mee-nah-*tee*-vee)		
Feminine		**Masculine "the"**	
Singular	Plural	Singular	Plural
l' (*l*)		**lo** (*loh*)	
la (*lah*)	**le** (*leh*)	**l'**	**gli** (*lyee*)
		il (*il*)	**i** (*ee*)

Here are some examples of definite articles. Can you identify a pattern?

la casa/le case (lah *kah*-zah/leh *kah*-zeh) (*house, houses*)

l'amica/le amiche (lah-*mee*-kah, leh ah-*mee*-keh) (*friend, friends*)

il libro/i libri (il *lee*-broh, ee *lee*-bree) (*book, books*)

lo zio/gli zii, (loh *dzee*-oh, lyee zee) (*uncle, uncles*) **lo studente, gli studenti** (loh stooh-*dehn*-teh, lyee stooh-*dehn*-tee) (*student, students*)

Here are two examples. Note how the article does not appear in the translation, but is necessary in Italian:

> **Gli amici vengono a cena** (lyee ah-*mee*-chee *vehn*-goh-noh ah *cheh*-nah) (*Friends are coming for dinner.*)

> **Mi piacciono le lasagne!** (mee *pyahch*-choh-noh leh lah-*zah*-nyeh) (*I like lasagna!*)

Adjectives

The gender feature of nouns extends to other grammatical categories, including pronouns and adjectives. First, I take a look at the adjectives.

An adjective is a word that describes a noun — whether a person, a thing, or whatever — with a quality or characteristic. (You can read more about these in Chapters 3, 8 and 16.) There are two types of adjectives in Italian: The first type has four endings, and the second type has two.

The first type matches in both number and gender with the noun it is modifying, and, therefore, ends in **o, a, i, e**, as follows with the adjective **italiano** (ee-tahl-ee-*ah*-noh) (*Italian*):

> ✔ **il ragazzo italiano** (il rah-*gahts*-tsoh ee-tah-lee-*ah*-noh) (*the Italian boy*)

> ✔ **i ragazzi italiani** (ee rah-*gahts*-tsee ee-tah-lee-*ah*-nee) (*the Italian boys*)

> ✔ **la ragazza italiana** (lah rah-*gahts*-tsah ee-tah-lee-*ah*-nah) (*the Italian girl*)

> ✔ **le ragazze italiane** (leh rah-*gahts*-tseh ee-tah-lee-*ah*-neh) (*the Italian girls*)

Other typical adjectives with the four endings include **spagnolo** (spahn-*yoh*-loh) and **giallo** (*jahl*-loh) (*yellow*).

The second type only agrees in number (and not gender), and ends in **e** in the singular and **i** in the plural. The adjective **grande** (*grahn*-deh) (*big*) is one of those adjectives. These adjectives are valid for both feminine and masculine nouns. In the plural of both genders, change the -e to an -i — for example, **grandi** (*grahn*-dee) (*big*). Other adjectives that only agree in number include **francese** (frahn-*cheh*-zeh) (*French*) and **verde** (*vehr*-deh) (*green*).

> ✔ **l'esame facile** (leh-*zah*-meh *fah*-chee-leh) (*the easy exam*)

> ✔ **gli esami facili** (lyee eh-*zah*-mee *fah*-chee-lee) (*the easy exams*)

> ✔ **la prova facile** (lah *proh*-vah *fah*-chee-leh) (*the easy test*)

> ✔ **le prove facili** (leh *proh*-veh *fah*-chee-lee) (*the easy tests*)

In Italian, the position of the adjective is not as rigid as it is in English. In most cases, the adjective follows the noun. Nevertheless, there are some adjectives which can stand before the noun, such as **bello** (*behl*-loh) (*beautiful*), **buono** (*bwoh*-noh) (*good*), and **cattivo** (kaht-*tee*-voh) (*bad*).

Words to Know

esame (m)	eh-<u>zah</u>-meh	exam
prova (f)	<u>proh</u>-vah	test
ragazzo/a (m/f)	rah-<u>gats</u>-tsoh	boy
studente (m)	stooh-<u>dehn</u>-teh	student (male)
studentessa (f)	stooh-dehn-<u>tehs</u>-sah	student (female)
casa (f)	<u>kah</u>-zah	house
libro (m)	<u>lee</u>-broh	book
amica (f/sing.)	ah-<u>mee</u>-kah	girl-friend
amiche (f/pl.)	ah-<u>mee</u>-keh	girl-friends
amico (m/sing)	ah-<u>mee</u>-koh	friend (male)
amici (m/pl)	ah-<u>mee</u>-chee	male friends or mixed gender firends.
caffè (m)	kahf-<u>feh</u>	coffee
bici (f)	<u>bee</u>-chee	bike

Talking about Pronouns

A pronoun replaces, as the word itself says, a noun. When you talk about Jim, for example, you can replace his name with **he**. You often use pronouns to avoid repetition.

Personal pronouns

Several types of personal pronouns exist. The most important ones for you are the subject pronouns, which refer to *I, you, he, she, it, we,* or *they.* Every verb form refers to one of these pronouns, as the following section points out. Table 2-3 lists the subject pronouns.

Table 2-3	Subject Pronouns	
Pronoun	*Pronunciation*	*Translation*
io	ee-oh	*I*
tu	tooh	*you*
lui	*looh-ee*	*he*
lei	ley	*she*
noi	noi	*we*
voi	voi	*you*
loro	*loh-roh*	*they*

Italians often drop subject pronouns because the verb ending shows what the subject is. Use a personal pronoun only for contrast, for emphasis, or when the pronoun stands alone.

- Contrast: **Tu tifi per il Milan, ma io per la Juventus.** (tooh *tee*-fee pehr il *mee*-lahn mah ee-oh pehr lah yooh-*vehn*-toohs) (*You're a fan of Milan, but I'm a fan of Juventus.*)

- Emphasis: **Vieni anche tu alla festa?** (*vyeh*-nee *ahn*-keh tooh *ahl*-lah fehs-tah) (*Are you coming to the party, too?*)

- Isolated position: "**Chi è?**" "**Sono io.**" (kee eh *soh*-noh ee-oh) ("*Who's there?*" "*It's me.*")

Saying "you": Formal and informal

You probably already know that many foreign languages contain both formal and informal ways of addressing people. If you didn't know before, now you do! In Italian, you need to respect this important characteristic. Use the informal pronoun **tu** (tooh) (*you*) with good friends, young people, children, and your family members. When, however, you talk to a person you don't know well (a superior, shopkeeper, waiter, teacher, professor, and so on), you should address him or her formally — that is, with **lei** (ley) (*you*). When you become more familiar with someone, you may change from formal to informal. According to custom, the elder person initiates the use of **tu**.

Tu requires the verb form of the second person singular — for example, **tu sei** (tooh sey) (*you are*). **Lei** calls for **lei è** (ley eh) (*you are* [formal singular]).

The following examples show the forms of you:

- Informal singular: **Ciao, come stai?** (chou *koh*-meh stahy?) (*Hi, how are you?*)

- Formal singular: **Buongiorno, come sta?** (bwohn-*johr*-noh *koh*-meh stah) (*Good morning, how are you?*)

- Informal plural: **Ciao, come state?** (chou *koh*-meh *stah*-teh) (*Hi, how are you?* (Speaking here to a group of people.)

Verbs

There seems to be an infinite number of verbs in Italian. These truly are the glue to bind the different parts of speech together. Some people try to get by using only infinitives (the verbs before you conjugate them), but I want you to make sense and feel confident when speaking, so learn the regular and irregular verbs patterns in this chapter (and also Appendix A), and you'll be on your way to talking in the present, past, and future tenses. Getting a good handle on them gives you a solid basis from which to build your sentences, communicate, and be understood!

Introducing regular and irregular verbs

What's the difference between regular and irregular verbs? Regular verbs follow a certain pattern in their conjugation: They behave the same way as other verbs in the same category. Therefore, you can predict a regular verb's form in any part of any tense. On the other hand, you cannot predict irregular verbs in this way — they behave a bit like individualists.

Regular verbs

You can divide Italian verbs into three categories, according to their ending in the infinitive form. They are, -are, as in **parlare** (pahr-*lah*-reh) (*to speak*); -ere, as in **vivere** (*vee*-veh-reh) (*to live*); and -ire, as in **partire** (pahr-*tee*-reh) (*to leave*). Verbs in these categories can be regular as well as irregular. Notice the subject pronouns that go with the verbs: We place them here to remind you which verb form you need.

These translate in the present tense as, for example: I speak, I do speak, I am speaking, I'm going to speak (if it's not too much in the future) — it depends on the context. I translate the first person of all of the verbs that follow: the other persons follow suit.

The following shows you the conjugation of three regular verbs:

Conjugation	Pronunciation	Translation
parlare	pahr-*lah*-reh	*to speak*
io parlo	*ee*-oh *pahr*-loh	*I speak, I do speak, I'm speaking, I'm going to speak*
tu parli	tooh *pahr*-lee	
lui/lei parla	*looh*-ee/ley *pahr*-lah	
noi parliamo	noi pahr-*lyah*-moh	
voi parlate	voi pahr-*lah*-teh	
loro parlano	*loh*-roh *pahr*-lah-noh	
vivere	*vee*-veh-reh	*to live*
io vivo	*ee*-oh *vee*-voh	*I live, I do live, I'm living*
tu vivi	tooh *vee*-vee	
lui/lei vive	*looh*-ee/ley *vee*-veh	
noi viviamo	noi vee-*vyah*-moh	
voi vivete	voi vee-*veh*-teh	
loro vivono	*loh*-roh *vee*-voh-noh	
partire	pahr-*tee*-reh	*to leave, to depart*
io parto	*ee*-oh *pahr*-toh	*I leave, I do leave, I am leaving*
tu parti	tooh *pahr*-tee	
lui/lei parte	*looh*-ee/ley *pahr*-teh	
noi partiamo	noi pahr-*tyah*-moh	
voi partite	voi pahr-*tee*-teh	
loro partono	*loh*-roh *pahr*-toh-noh	

You can apply these patterns to every regular verb, such as **mangiare** (mahn-*jah*-reh) (*to eat*), **giocare** (joh-*kah*-reh) (*to play*), **ripetere** (ree-*peh*-teh-reh) (*to repeat*), **prendere** (*prehn*-deh-reh) (*to have or take as in a restaurant*) and **aprire** (ah-*pree*-reh) (*to open*). Some regular verbs behave a bit differently, but this doesn't render them irregular. In some cases — for example, some -ire verbs — you insert the letters -isc- between the root and the ending (in all persons except the **noi** and **voi**), as in this example of **capire** (kah-*pee*-reh) (*to understand*):

Conjugation	Pronunciation	Translation
io capisco	*ee*-oh kah-*pees*-koh	*I understand,* *I do understand,* *I am understanding*
tu capisci	tooh kah-*pee*-shee	
lui/lei capisce	*looh*-ee/ley kah-*pee*-sheh	
noi capiamo	noi kah-*pyah*-moh	
voi capite	voi kah-*pee*-teh	
loro capiscono	*loh*-roh kah-*pees*-koh-noh	

Other verbs that follow this pattern are **finire** (fee-*nee*-reh) (*to finish, end*) and **preferire** (preh-feh-*ree*-reh) (*to prefer*). For more verbs that follow this **isc** pattern, check out Appendix A, and for lots more on Italian verbs in general, pick up a copy of my *Italian Verbs For Dummies* (John Wiley & Sons, Inc.).

Irregular verbs

Two important verbs, which you often use as auxiliary verbs, are irregular — **avere** (ah-*veh*-reh) (*to have*) and **essere** (ehs-seh-reh) (*to be*).

Conjugation	Pronunciation	Translation
avere	ah-*veh*-reh	*to have*
io ho	*ee*-oh oh	*I have, I do have*
tu hai	tooh ahy	
lui/lei ha	*looh*-ee/ley ah	
noi abbiamo	noi ahb-*byah*-moh	
voi avete	voi ah-*veh*-teh	
loro hanno	*loh*-roh *ahn*-noh	
essere	ehs-seh-reh	*to be*
io sono	*ee*-oh *soh*-noh	*I am*
tu sei	tooh sey	
lui/lei è	*looh*-ee/ley eh	
noi siamo	noi see-*ah*-moh	
voi siete	voi see-*eh*-teh	
loro sono	*loh*-roh *soh*-noh	

Talkin' the Talk

Cindy is visiting Florence for the first time. She's gotten lost, and so she asks a traffic cop, a vigile urbano (*vee*-jee-leh oohr-*bah*-noh), how to find her hotel. (Track 3)

Cindy: **Scusi, ho una domanda.**
skooh-zee oh *ooh*-nah doh-*mahn*-dah
Excuse me, I have a question.

Parla inglese?
pahr-lah een-*gleh*-zeh
Do you speak English?

Vigile: **No ma lei parla italiano!**
noh mah ley *pahr*-lah ee-tahl-ee-*ah*-noh
No, but you speak Italian!

Cindy: **Parlo poco ma capisco di più.**
pahr-loh *poh*-koh mah kah-*pees*-koh dee pyooh
I speak a little but I understand more.

Mi sono persa.
mee *soh*-noh *pehr*-sah
I'm lost.

Vigile: **Dove deve andare?**
doh-veh *deh*-veh ahn-*dah*-reh
Where do you need to go?

Cindy: **Non posso trovare il mio albergo.**
nohn *pohs*-soh troh-*vah*-reh il *mee*-oh ahl-*behr*-goh
I can't find my hotel.

Vigile: **Ha una piantina di Firenze?**
ah *ooh*-nah pyahn-*tee*-nah dee fee-*rehn*-zeh
Do you have a map of Florence?

Cindy: **Si eccola qua.**
see *ehk*-koh-lah kwah
Yes, here it is.

Ecco! (*ehk*-koh) Here you go! Here it is! is used only when pointing something out. You can attach a direct object pronoun to **ecco** if you like: **"Dov'è la mia borsa?" "Eccola!"** (doh-*veh* lah *mee*-ah *bohr*-sah *ehk*-koh-lah) (*Where's my bag? Here it is!*) **"Gigio, dove sei?" "Eccomi!"** (*jee*-joh *doh*-veh sey *ehk*-koh-mee) (*"Giorgio, where are you?" "Here I am!"*).

You frequently hear this expression in a hotel: **Ecco la sua chiave** (*ehk*-koh lah *sooh*-ah *kyah*-veh) (*Here is your key*), and in a bar: **Ecco i due cappuccini!** (*ehk*-koh ee *dooh*-eh kahp-pooh-*chee*-nee) (*Here are the two cappuccinos!*)

Idiomatic uses of avere

Even though the verb **avere** means *to have*, it is frequently used in circumstances when we would use the verb to be in English (such as to be hungry, to be thirsty, to be hot, to be cold, to be a certain age). In Italian, these terms literally mean to have hunger, to have thirst, to have heat, to have years. Table 2-4 lists some common idiomatic expressions with **avere**.

Table 2-4	Idiomatic Uses of Avere	
Expression	*Pronunciation*	*Translation*
avere fame	ah-*veh*-reh *fah*-meh	*to be hungry*
avere sete	ah-*veh*-reh *seh*-teh	*to be thirsty*
avere caldo	ah-*veh*-reh *kahl*-doh	*to be hot*
avere freddo	ah-*veh*-reh *frehd*-doh	*to be cold*
avere sonno	ah-*veh*-reh *sohn*-noh	*to be sleepy*
avere voglia di	ah-*veh*-reh *vohl*-yah dee	*to feel like, have a craving for*
avere bisogno di	ah-*veh*-reh bee-*zoh*-nyoh dee	*to need*
avere torto	ah-*veh*-reh *tohr*-toh	*to be wrong*
avere ragione	ah-*veh*-reh rah-*joh*-neh	*to be right*
avere anni	ah-*veh*-reh *ahn*-nee	*to be a certain age*

Other common irregular verbs are **andare** (ahn-*dah*-reh) (*to go*), **venire** (veh-*nee*-reh) (*to come*), **dire** (*dee*-reh) (*to say or tell*), **fare** (*fah*-reh) (*to do or make*), **dare** (*dah*-reh) (*to give*), and **uscire** (ooh-*shee*-reh) (*to go out*):

Conjugation	Pronunciation	Translation
andare	ahn-_dah_-reh	_to go_
io vado	_ee_-oh _vah_-doh	_I go, I do go, I'm, going_
tu vai	tooh vahy	
lui/lei va	_looh_-ee/ley vah	
noi andiamo	noi ahn-_dyah_-moh	
voi andate	voi ahn-_dah_-teh	
loro vanno	_loh_-roh _vahn_-noh	
venire	veh-_nee_-reh	_to come_
io vengo	_ee_-oh _vehn_-goh	_I come, to do come, I'm coming_
tu vieni	tooh _vyeh_-nee	
lui/lei viene	_looh_-ee/ley _vyeh_-neh	
noi veniamo	noi veh-_nyah_-moh	
voi venite	voi veh-_nee_-teh	
loro vengono	_loh_-roh _vehn_-goh-noh	
dire	_dee_-reh	_to say or tell_
io dico	_ee_-oh _dee_-koh	_I say, I do say, I'm saying_
tu dici	tooh _dee_-chee	
lui/lei dice	_looh_-ee/ley _dee_-cheh	
noi diciamo	noi dee-_chah_-moh	
voi dite	voi _dee_-teh	
loro dicono	_loh_-roh _dee_-koh-noh	
fare	_fah_-reh	_to do or make_
io faccio	_ee_-oh _fahch_-choh	
tu fai	tooh fahy	
lui/lei fa	_looh_-ee/ley fah	
noi facciamo	noi fahch-_chah_-moh	
voi fate	voi _fah_-teh	
loro fanno	_loh_-roh _fahn_-noh	

Like the verb **avere**, Table 2-5 shows that the verb **fare** (to do or to make) has some interesting idiomatic uses that don't translate word for word.

Table 2-5	Idiomatic Uses of Fare	
Expression	*Pronunciation*	*Translation*
fare domanda	*fah*-reh doh-*mahn*-dah	*to apply for a job or to a university*
fare una domanda	*fah*-reh *ooh*-nah doh-*mahn*-dah	*to ask a question*
fare una passeggiata	*fah*-reh *ooh*-nah pahs-sehj-*jah*-tah	*to take a walk*
fare una pausa	*fah*-reh *ooh*-nah *pou*-zah	*to take a break*
fa bel/cattivo tempo	fah behl kaht-*tee*-voh *tehm*-poh	*to be nice/ugly out (weather)*
fa caldo/freddo	fah *kahl*-doh *frehd*-doh	*to be hot or cold out*
fare un giro	*fah*-reh oohn *jee*-roh	*to take a ride*
fare fotografie	*fah*-reh *foh*-toh-grah-*fee*-eh	*to take pictures*

Then there are other very common, very irregular verbs, which are best to commit to memory.

Conjugation	*Pronunciation*	*Translation*
dare	*dah*-reh	*to give*
io do	doh	*I give, I do give, I'm giving*
tu dai	dahy	
lui/lei dà	*looh*-ee/ley dah	
noi diamo	noi dee-*ah*-moh	
voi date	voi *dah*-teh	
loro danno	*loh*-roh *dahn*-noh	

So, too, does the verb **dare** (*to give*) have some idiomatic uses, and so it also means to take when you're taking an exam: **dare un esame** (*dah*-reh oohn eh-*zah*-meh)

Conjugation	Pronunciation	Translation
uscire	ooh-*shee*-reh	*to go out, to exit, to leave the house*
io esco	*ee*-oh *ehs*-koh	
tu esci	tooh *ehsh*-ee	
lui/lei esce	*looh*-ee/ley *ehsh*-eh	
noi usciamo	noi ooh-*shah*-moh	
voi uscite	voi ooh-*shee*-teh	
loro escono	*loh*-roh *ehs*-koh-noh	

Talkin' the Talk

Fabio has just called Giacomo to chat and catch up on things.
(Track 4)

Fabio:	**Ciao Giacomo, sono Fabio.** chou *jah*-koh-moh *soh*-noh *fah*-byoh Hi Giacomo, it's Fabio.
Giacomo:	**Uè Fabio, come va?** ooh-*eh fah*-byoh *koh*-meh vah Hey, Fabio, how's it going?
Fabio:	**Benone! Studio molto in questi giorni.** beh-*noh*-neh *stooh*-dee-oh *mohl*-toh in *kwehs*-tee *johr*-nee Great! I'm studying a lot these days.
Giacomo:	**Dai l'esame di filosofia lunedì?** dahy leh-*zah*-meh dee fee-loh-soh-*fee*-ah looh-neh-*dee* Are you taking the philosophy exam on Monday?
Fabio:	**Si, e ho ancora 120 pagine da leggere.** see eh oh ahn-*koh*-rah *chehn*-toh-*vehn*-tee *pah*-gee-neh dah *lehj*-jeh-reh Yes, and I still have to read 120 pages.

Ma ho bisogno di fare una pausa, di uscire.
mah oh bee-*zoh*-nyoh dee *fah*-reh *ooh*-nah *pou*-zah
dee ooh-*shee*-reh
But I need to take a break, to go out.

Cosa fai stasera?
koh-zah fahy stah-*seh*-rah
What are you doing tonight?

Giacomo: **Esco con Anna.**
ehs-koh kohn *ahn*-nah
I'm going out with Anna.

Fabio: **Dove andate?**
doh-veh ahn-*dah*-teh
Where are you going?

Giacomo: **Se fa bello, andiamo a mangiare in collina.**
seh fah *behl*-loh ahn-*dyah*-moh ah mahn-*jah*-reh
in kohl-*lee*-nah
If it's nice out, we're going to go eat in the country.
(Lit: the hills)

Perchè non venite anche tu e Daniela?
pehr-*keh* nohn veh-*nee*-teh *ahn*-keh tooh eh
dahn-*yeh*-lah
Why don't you and Daniela come?

Fabio: **Buon'idea!**
bwohn-ee-*dey*-ah
Good idea!

Vedo cosa dice Daniela e ti richiamo fra mezz-ora.
veh-doh *koh*-zah *dee*-cheh dahn-*yeh*-lah eh tee ree-
kyah-moh frah medz-*dzoh*-rah
I'll see what Daniela says and call you back in a
half hour.

Giacomo: **D'accordo – ciao a dopo!**
dahk-*kohr*-doh chou ah *doh*-poh
Okay, talk to you later!

Fabio: **Ciao!**
chou
Bye!

Having to, wanting to, being able to

Three modal verbs — **dovere** (doh-*veh*-reh) (*to have to, must, to need to, ought to*), **volere** (voh-*leh*-reh) (*to want*), **potere** (poh-*teh*-reh) (*to be able to, can*) — are kind of like helping verbs. You conjugate them and then the verb that follows is the infinitive. For example:

Devo fare la spesa. (*dey*-voh *fah*-reh lah *speh*-zah) *I need to go (food) shopping.*

Voglio dormire! (*vohl*-yoh dohr-*mee*-reh) *I want to sleep!*

Posso andare a bere? (*pohs*-soh ahn-*dah*-reh ah *beh*-reh) *May I go get a drink?*

Conjugation	Pronunciation	Translation
dovere	doh-*veh*-reh	*to have to, must, ought to, need to*
io devo	io *dey*-voh	*I must, I should, I ought to, I need to*
tu devi	tooh *dey*-vee	
lui/lei deve	*looh*-ee/ley *dey*-veh	
noi dobbiamo	noi dohb-*byah*-moh	
voi dovete	voi doh-*veh*-teh	
loro devono	*loh*-roh *deh*-voh-noh	
volere	voh-*leh*-reh	*to want*
io voglio	io *vohl*-yoh	
tu vuoi	tooh vwoi	
lui/lei vuole	*looh*-ee/ley *vwoh*-leh	
noi vogliamo	noi vohl-*yah*-moh	
voi volete	voi voh-*leh*-teh	
loro vogliono	*loh*-roh *vohl*-yoh-noh	
potere	poh-*teh*-reh	*to be able to, can, may*
io posso	*ee*-oh *pohs*-soh	
tu puoi	tooh pwoi	
lui/lei può	*looh*-ee/ley pwoh	
noi possiamo	noi pohs-*syah*-moh	
voi potete	voi poh-*teh*-teh	
loro possono	*loh*-roh *pohs*-soh-noh	

Presenting the Simple Tenses: Past, Present, and Future

Clearly, people don't use just one tense. Sometimes you need to report what you did yesterday or outline what you're going to do tomorrow. These three tenses (past, present, and future) are not high grammar — just basic stuff.

- ✔ **Ieri ho mangiato un gelato.** (*yeh*-ree oh mahn-*jah*-toh oohn jeh-*lah*-toh) (*Yesterday I ate an ice-cream.*)

- ✔ **Mangio un gelato.** (*mahn*-joh oohn jeh-*lah*-toh) (*I am eating/eat an ice cream.*)

- ✔ **Domani mangerò un gelato.** (doh-*mah*-nee mahn-jeh-*roh* oohn jeh-*lah*-toh) (*Tomorrow I'm going to eat an ice cream.*)

You find more on these tenses in Chapter 12 (future) and Chapter 10 (present perfect).

Talkin' the Talk

Emilia and Cristina are two middle-school-aged girls who are walking home from the first day at their new school.

Cristina: **Ho una nuova bici rossa!**
oh *ooh*-nah *nwoh*-vah *bee*-chee *rohs*-sah
I have a new red bike!

Emilia: **La mia è sempre quella veccchia.**
lah *mee*-ah eh *sehm*-preh *qwehl*-lah *vehk*-kyah
I still have my old one.

Cristina: **Quella azzurra? È carina.**
kwehl-lah adz-*dzooh*-rah eh kah-*ree*-nah
The blue one? It's nice.

Mi piacciono i miei nuovi insegnanti.
mee *pyach*-choh-noh ee myey *nwoh*-vee
in-sehn-*yahn*-tee
I like my new teachers.

Emilia: **Quanti anni ha la tua nuova insegnante di matematica?**
qwahn-tee *ahn*-nee ah lah *tooh*-ah *nwuoh*-vah
in-seh-*nyahn*-teh dee mah-teh-*mah*-tee-kah
How old is your new math teacher?

Cristina: **Non lo so. Forse quaranta.**
nohn loh soh *fohr*-seh qwah-*rahn*-tah
I don't know. Maybe 40.

È brava!
eh *brah*-vah
She's good!

Emilia: **Anch'io sono contenta della nuova scuola.**
ahn-*kee*-oh *soh*-noh kohn-*tehn*-tah *dehl*-lah
nwuoh-vah *skwoh*-lah
I'm happy, too, with the new school.

Vuoi fare un giro in centro?
vwoi *fah*-reh oohn *gee*-roh in *chehn*-troh
Do you want to take a ride down-town?

Cristina: **Si ma dobbiamo metterci il casco.**
see mah dohb-*byah*-moh *meht*-tehr-chee il *kahs*-koh
Yes, but we have to wear our helmets.

Emilia: **Va bene.**
vah *beh*-neh
Okay.

Ce l'ho qua.
cheh loh kwah
I have it here.

Cristina: **Dove andiamo?**
doh-veh ahn-*dyah*-moh
Where are we going?

Emilia: **Ho fame! Pizza o gelato?**
oh *fah*-meh *peets*-tsah oh geh-*lah*-toh
I'm hungry! Pizza or ice cream?

Cristina: **Gelato, naturalmente!**
geh-*lah*-toh nah-tooh-rahl-*mehn*-teh
Ice cream, of course!

Emilia: **Andiamo!**
ahn-*dyah*-moh
Let's go!

Words to Know

albergo	ahl-_behr_-goh	hotel
piantina	pyahn-_tee_-nah	map
mi sono persa	mee _soh_-noh _pehr_-sah	I'm lost
casco	_kahs_-koh	helmet
gelato	jeh-_lah_-toh	ice-cream
insegnante	in-seh-_nyahn_-teh	teacher
va bene	vah _beh_-neh	okay
d'accordo	dahk-_kohr_-doh	okay, agreed
ciao	chou	hi/bye
mi piace	mee _pyah_-cheh	I like (something singular)
mi piacciono	mee _pyahch_-choh-noh	I like (something plural)
anch'io	ahn-_kee_-oh	I also, me too
pausa	_pou_-za	break
domanda	doh-_mahn_-dah	question
stasera	stah-_seh_-rah	tonight
dove	_doh_-veh	where
quanti anni ha	_kwahn_-tee _ahn_-nee ah	how old is . . . ?

Fun and Games

The following contains several Italian words that I introduced in this chapter. Just find and circle the words from the list! See Appendix D for the answer key.

```
A  R  Q  D  R  P  U  F  C  M  N  D
V  O  L  E  R  E  A  A  T  G  H  O
E  S  A  D  H  C  O  M  L  Z  E  V
R  S  D  B  I  F  E  E  S  A  M  E
E  O  I  L  P  A  R  T  I  R  E  R
T  B  E  W  E  R  N  R  D  I  R  E
O  D  A  L  B  E  R  G  O  E  S  T
Z  S  M  Q  C  F  V  G  V  S  L  R
I  C  I  B  A  X  E  T  E  S  U  M
O  A  C  S  R  Z  K  R  D  E  B  O
T  P  A  U  S  A  E  U  P  R  A  D
U  I  T  A  L  I  A  N  O  E  J  L
F  R  A  G  A  Z  Z  A  N  T  K  A
Y  E  N  D  Q  U  A  L  R  I  L  C
```

albergo	facile
amica	fame
avere	fare
bici	italiano
caldo	partire
capire	pausa
dire	ragazza
dove	rosso
dovere	sete
esame	volere
essere	zio

Chapter 3

Buongiorno! Salutations!

. . . .

In This Chapter

▶ Greetings and good-byes

▶ Deciding when to be formal or friendly

▶ Responding to a greeting

▶ Asking whether someone speaks English

▶ Describing places, nationalities, and where you come from

▶ Introducing yourself and others

. . . .

Buongiorno! (bwohn-*johr*-noh) (*Hello!*)

Have you ever counted the number of times you say hello in a single day? You probably say it more often than you realize. When you interact with people, you usually begin with a greeting — and that greeting can have an impact on the first impression you give. This chapter explains how to say hello and good-bye as well as how to supplement a greeting with some basic small talk.

Looking at Common Greetings and Good-byes

Italians like to have social contact and meet new people. Generally, they're easygoing and receptive to people trying to speak their language. At the same time, they tend to be very respectful and polite.

To give you a good start in greeting people in Italian, we want to familiarize you with the most common greetings and good-byes, followed by examples.

✔ **Ciao**	chou	Hello and good-bye: informal
Ciao Claudio	chouh *klou*-dee-oh	Hi, Claudio! Bye, Claudio!
✔ **Salve**	*sahl*-veh	Hello and good-bye: neutral, but more formal than **Ciao**!
Salve ragazzi!	*sahl*-veh rah-*gaht*-tsee	Hi, folks!, or Hey, guys!

Salve is a relic from Latin. In Caesar's time; the Romans used it a lot.

✔ **Buongiorno**	bwohn *johr*-noh	Good morning (Literally: Good day) formal,
Buongiorno Signora Bruni!	bwohn *johr*-noh see-*nyoh*-rah *brooh*-nee	Good morning, Mrs. Bruni!

Buongiorno is the most formal greeting. Whenever you're in doubt, use this word (if it is before 2:00 p.m.). You frequently hear it when you leave an Italian shop.

✔ **Buonasera**	*bwoh*-nah-*seh*-rah	Good afternoon; good evening: formal
Buonasera signor Rossi!	*bwoh*-nah-*seh*-rah see-*nyohr* rohs-see	Good afternoon/evening Mr. Rossi!

You use **buonasera** after 2 p.m. to say both hello and good-bye. Just mind the time of day!

✔ **Buonanotte**	*bwoh*-nah-*noht*-teh	Good-night! (Use only when parting for the night and going to bed)
Buonanotte ragazzi!	*bwoh*-nah-*noht*-teh rah-*gaht*-tsee	Good night, guys!
✔ **Buona giornata!**	*bwoh*-nah johr-*nah*-tah	Have a good day!

You often use this phrase when you're leaving somebody or saying goodbye on the phone.

✔ **Buona serata!**	*bwoh*-nah seh-*rah*-tah	Have a good evening!

Like **buona giornata**, you use **buona serata** when you're leaving someone or saying good-bye on the phone, if that person is your friend. The difference is that you use **buona serata**, according to Italian custom, after 2 p.m.

✔ **Arrivederci**	ahr-ree-veh-*dehr*-chee	Good bye.
Arrivederci signora Eva!	ahr-ree-veh-*dehr*-chee see-*nyoh*-rah eh-vah	Good-bye, Mrs. Eva!

Deciding between formal or friendly

In Chapter 2 you saw some of the differences between using the **tu**, **voi**, **Lei**, and **Loro** pronouns and verbs when you want to say "you."

An important feature of Italian culture is that there are two different ways of addressing people.

✔ You generally use the formal form of address — **Lei** (ley) (*you*: formal singular) — with adults you don't know: businesspeople (waiters, shopkeepers), officials, and persons of higher rank, such as supervisors, teachers, professors, older people, and so on. (With children or among young people you use the informal **tu**.)

✔ When you get to know someone better, depending on your relationship, you may switch to the informal form of address — **tu** (tooh) (*you,* informal singular). You also use the informal with members of your family, friends, and, as already mentioned, with children.

Replying to a greeting

When you reply to a greeting in English, you often say "How are you?" as a way of saying "Hello" — you don't expect an answer. In Italian, however, this is not the case; you respond with an answer. Following are common ways to reply to particular greetings.

Formal greeting and reply

Greeting:

Buongiorno signora, come sta?

bwohn-*johr*-noh see-*nyoh*-rah *koh*-meh stah

Hello, ma'am, how are you?

Reply:

Benissimo, grazie, e Lei?

beh-*nees*-see-moh *grah*-tsee-eh eh ley

Very well, thank you, and you?

Informal greeting and reply

Greeting:

Ciao, Roberto, come stai?

chou roh-*behr*-toh *koh*-meh stahy

Hi, Roberto, how are you?

Reply:	**Bene, grazie, e tu?**
	beh-neh *grah*-tsee-eh eh *tooh*
	Fine, thanks, and you?

Another typical, rather informal, greeting and reply

Greeting:	**Come va?**
	koh-me *vah*
	How are things?
Reply:	**Non c'è male.**
	nohn cheh *mah*-leh
	Not bad.

Specifying your reuniting

Sometimes, you want to say more than just good-bye and specify your next meeting. The following expressions are common and also can be used as good-byes on their own:

A presto! (ah *prehs*-toh) (*See you soon!*)

A dopo! (ah *doh*-poh) (*See you later!*)

A domani! (ah doh-*mah*-nee) (*See you tomorrow!*)

Ci vediamo! (chee veh-*dyah*-moh) (*See you!*)

You can combine **Ci vediamo** with other phrases. For example:

Ci vediamo presto! (chee veh-*dyah*-moh *prehs*-toh)
(*See you soon!*)

Ci vediamo dopo! (chee veh-*dyah*-moh *doh*-poh)
(*See you later!*)

Ci vediamo domani! (chee veh-*dyah*-moh doh-*mah*-nee)
(*See you tomorrow!*)

Using body language

In Italy, people who are familiar with each other, such as family and friends, commonly hug and kiss on both cheeks.

Italians kiss twice: once right, once left.

Another common physical greeting is the more formal handshake. You shake hands with people you meet for the first time and with those you don't know well.

Making Introductions

It's important to be able to introduce yourself to someone, and to answer questions about who you are and where you're from.

Whether to use first or last names as well as formal and informal registers are important considerations. In a job situation, you usually use last names, whereas at private functions, people are more likely to tell you their first names. The fact that someone gives you his or her first name, however, does not necessarily mean that you should use the informal **tu** (tooh) (*you*); using a person's first name with the formal form of address is quite common. Usually, the older person proposes making the switch to the informal form.

Introducing yourself

We want to familiarize you with an important reflexive verb, **chiamarsi** (kyah-*mahr*-see) (*to call oneself*), which you use to introduce yourself and to ask others for their names. Here is the present tense of this important verb: word missing)

Conjugation	Pronunciation	Meaning
mi chiamo	mee *kyah*-moh	*My name is*
ti chiami	tee *kyah*-mee	*Your name is*
si chiama	see *kyah*-mah	*Your/ his,/her/its name is*
ci chiamiamo	chee kyah-*myah*-moh	*Our names are*
vi chiamate	vee kyah-*mah*-teh	*Your names are*
si chiamano	see kyah-*mah*-noh	*Their names are*

So that you can get the ring of the verb **chiamarsi**, practice these easy examples. Just change your intonation and word order, and you can ask someone's name instead of telling them.

- ✔ **Ciao (or Buongiorno), mi chiamo Eva.** (*chou/bwohn*-johr-*noh* mee *kyah*-moh *eh*-vah) (*Hello, my name is Eva.*)

- ✔ **E tu come ti chiami?** (eh too *koh*-meh tee *kyah*-mee) (*And what's your name?*)

- ✔ **Lei, come si chiama?** (ley *koh*-meh see *kyah*-mah) (*What's your name?*)

- ✔ **Piacere!** (pyah-*cheh*-reh) (with a quick hand-shake) is one way of saying: *Nice to meet you!*

Incidentally, as in English, you can also introduce yourself simply by saying your name: **Io sono Pietro** (*ee*-oh *soh*-noh pee-*eh*-troh) (*I'm Pietro*). Finally, you can just simply state your name, without the "Mi chiamo" (*My name is*) or "Sono," (*I am*) as in the sample dialogue that follows.

Talkin' the Talk

The people in this dialogue are colleagues assigned to work on the same project. They introduce themselves to each other.

Mr. Messa: **Carlo Messa. Piacere!**
               kahr-loh *mehs*-sah pyah-*cheh*-reh
               Carlo Messa, nice to meet you!

Mr. Rossi: **Piacere, Marco Rossi.**
               pyah-*cheh*-reh *mahr*-koh *rohs*-see
               Nice to meet you, Marco Rossi.

Ms. Pertini: **Piacere, sono Paola Pertini.**
               pyah-*cheh*-reh *soh*-noh *pah*-oh-lah pehr-*tee*-nee
               Nice to meet you, I'm Paola Pertini.

Ms. Salvi: **Lieta di conoscerla. Anna Salvi.**
               lee-*eh*-tah dee koh-*noh*-shehr-lah *ahn*-nah *sahl*-vee
               Pleased to meet you, Anna Salvi.

Mr. Melis: **Mi chiamo Carlo Melis, piacere.**
               mee *kyah*-moh *kahr*-loh *meh*-lees pyah-*cheh*-reh
               My name is Carlo Melis, nice to meet you.

Mr. Foschi: **Molto lieto, Silvio Foschi.**
               mohl-toh lee-*eh*-toh *seel*-vee-oh *fohs*-kee
               Very pleased to meet you, Silvio Foschi.

Children and young people forego ceremony and introduce themselves more casually, though still politely — something like this:

Ciao! Sono Giulio.
chou *soh*-noh *jooh*-lee-oh
Hello! I'm Giulio.

E io sono Giulia, piacere.
eh *ee*-oh *soh*-noh *jooh*-lee-ah pyah-*cheh*-reh
And I'm Giulia, nice to meet you.

The following example offers a very informal introduction, used only in a very casual situation, such as on the beach or at a club:

>**Come ti chiami?**
>*koh*-meh tee-*kyah*-mee
>*What's your name?*

>**Chiara. E tu?**
>*kyah*-rah eh tooh
>*Chiara, and yours?*

>**Amedeo.**
>ah-meh-*deh*-oh
>*Amedeo.*

Talkin' the Talk

Now listen to two young people introducing each other in a less formal setting. Mario enters the café and comes up to a table occupied by another person, Patrizia.

Mario:	**È libero?** eh *lee*-beh-roh Is it free?
Patrizia:	**Sì.** see Yes.
Mario:	**Grazie. Scusa, ma non sei la sorella di Gianni?** *grah*-tsee-eh *skooh*-za mah nohn sey lah soh-*rehl*-lah di *giahn*-nee Thank you. Excuse me, but aren't you Gianni's sister?
Patrizia:	**Sì.** see Yes.
Mario:	**Mi chiamo Mario.** mee *kyah*-moh *mah*-ree-oh My name is Mario.
	Gioco a calcio con Gianni. *joh*-koh ah *kahl*-choh kohn *jahn*-nee I play soccer with Gianni.

Patrizia:	**Ciao, io sono Patrizia.**
	chou *ee*-oh *soh*-noh pah-*tree*-tsee-ah
	Hello, I'm Patrizia.
Mario:	**Ti disturbo?**
	tee dees-*toohr*-boh
	Am I bothering you?
Patrizia:	**No, per niente.**
	Noh pehr nee-*ehn*-teh.
	No, not at all.
	Sto aspettando due amici.
	stoh ahs-peht-*tahn*-doh *dooh*-eh ah-*mee*-chee
	I'm waiting for two friends.

Introducing other people

Sometimes you not only have to introduce yourself, but also introduce someone to your friends or to other people.

The following vocabulary may be helpful in making introductions. With it, you can indicate the relationship between you and the person you're introducing. Gesturing toward the person and simply saying **mio fratello** means, quite simply, "This is my brother."

✔ **mio fratello** (*mee*-oh frah-*tehl*-loh) (*my brother*)

✔ **mia sorella** (*mee*-ah soh-*rehl*-lah) (*my sister*)

✔ **mia figlia** (*mee*-ah *fee*-lyah) (*my daughter*)

✔ **mio figlio** (*mee*-oh *fee*-lyoh) (*my son*)

✔ **mio marito** (*mee*-oh mah-*ree*-toh) (*my husband*)

✔ **mia moglie** (*mee*-ah *mohl*-yeh) (*my wife*)

✔ **mia madre** (*mee*-ah *mah*-dreh*)* (*my mother*)

✔ **mio padre** (*mee*-oh *pah*-dreh*)* (*my father*)

✔ **la mia amica/il mio amico** (lah *mee*-ah ah-*mee*-kah eel *mee*-oh ah-*mee*-koh) (*my friend [m]*) Sometimes this also means girlfriend or boyfriend.

✔ **la mia ragazza/il mio ragazzo** (lah *mee*-ah rah-*gat*-tsah/eel *mee*-oh rah-*gat*-tsoh) (*my girlfriend/my boyfriend*)

✔ **la mia fidanzata/il mio fidanzato** (lah *mee*-ah fee-dahn-*zah*-tah/eel *mee*-oh fee-dahn-*zah*-toh) (*my fiancée/fiancé*)

✔ **il mio collega** (eel *mee*-oh kohl-*leh*-gah) (*my colleague [m]*)

✔ **la mia collega** (lah *mee*-ah kohl-*leh*-gah) (*my colleague [f]*)

To make life easier I give you here the verb **presentare** (preh-zehn-*tah*-reh) (*to introduce*). (See Chapter 2 for more on ___ARE verb conjugations.)

Ti presento mia moglie, Teresa.	(tee preh-*zehn*-toh *mee*-ah *mohl*-yeh teh-*reh*-sah) (*Let me introduce you (informal) to my wife, Teresa.*)
Le presento mia suocera, Mary.	(leh preh-*zehn*-toh *mee*-ah swoh-chehr-ah) (*Let me introduce you (formal) to my mother-in-law, Mary.*)

Talkin' the Talk

The following dialogue, which represents a formal occasion, contains some typical expressions used during introductions. Here, Mrs. Ponti introduces a new colleague to one of her co-workers. Note the abbreviation for signora. (Track 5)

Sig.ra Ponti: **Buonasera signora Bruni . . . Signora Bruni, Le presento il signor Rossi.**
bwoh-nah-*seh*-rah see-*nyoh*-rah *brooh*-nee see-*nyoh*-rah *brooh*-nee leh preh-*zehn*-toh eel see-*nyohr rohs*-see
Good afternoon, Mrs. Bruni . . . Mrs. Bruni, I'd like to introduce you to Mr. Rossi.

Sig.ra Bruni: **Lieta di conoscerla.**
lee-*eh*-tah dee koh-*noh*-shehr-lah
Pleased to meet you.

Sig. Rossi: **Il piacere è tutto mio!**
eel pyah-*cheh*-reh eh *tooht*-toh *mee*-oh
The pleasure is all mine!

Talkin' the Talk

Of course, friends can be informal with one another, as the next conversation shows. Here Teresa bumps into her old friend Marinella. Both are married now and introduce their husbands.

Marinella:	**Ciao, Teresa, come stai?** chou teh-*reh*-zah *koh*-meh stahy Hello, Teresa. How are you?
Teresa:	**Bene, grazie.** *beh*-neh *grah*-tsee-eh. Well, thank you.
	Sono contenta di vederti! *soh*-noh con-*tehn*-tah dee veh-*dehr*-tee I'm happy to see you!
	Marinella, ti presento mio marito Giancarlo. mahr-een-*ehl*-lah tee preh-*zehn*-toh *mee*-oh mah-*ree*-toh jahn-*kahr*-loh Marinella, I'd like to introduce you to my husband, Giancarlo.
Marinella:	**Ciao, Giancarlo.** chou jahn-*kahr*-loh Hello.
Giancarlo:	**Piacere.** pyah-*cheh*-reh Nice to meet you.
Marinella:	**E questo è Gianni.** eh *kwehs*-toh eh *jahn*-nee And this is Gianni.
Gianni:	**Piacere.** pyah-*cheh*-reh Nice to meet you.

Getting Acquainted

Introducing yourself is the first step in getting to know someone. If you get a good feeling about the person and want to speak more, a conversation usually follows the introduction. This section tells you about the different topics you might talk about to get to know each other.

Finding out whether someone speaks Italian

Of course you will want to practice your Italian as soon as you get to Italy. You have an opportunity to try out your newly acquired smattering of Italian.

Parla italiano?/	(*pahr*-lah/*pahr*-lee	*Do you speak Italian?*
Parli italiano?	ee-tahl-ee-*ah*-noh)	(Formal/Informal))
Parla inglese?/	(*pahr*-lah/*pahr*-lee	*Do you speak English?*
Parli inglese?	een-*gleh*-seh)	(Formal/Informal))

A possible response to these questions is:

Parlo un po'.	(*pahr*-loh oohn poh)	*I speak a little bit.*

Talkin' the Talk

Ilaria and Carmen have recently gotten to know each other. Because Carmen is not Italian, although she lives in Italy, Ilaria is curious to know how many languages she speaks.

Ilaria: **Quante lingue parli?**
kwahn-teh *leen*-gweh *pahr*-lee
How many languages do you speak?

Carmen: **Tre: italiano, spagnolo e tedesco.**
treh ee-tah-lee-*ah*-noh spah-*nyoh*-loh eh
teh-*dehs*-koh
Three: Italian, Spanish, and German.

Ilaria: **E qual è la tua lingua madre?**
eh *kwah*-leh lah *tooh*-ah *leen*-gwah *mah*-dreh
And which is your mother tongue?

Carmen:	**Lo spagnolo.**
	loh spah-*nyoh*-loh
	Spanish.
Ilaria:	**Tua madre è spagnola?**
	tooh-ah *mah*-dreh eh spah-*nyoh*-lah
	Is your mother Spanish?
Carmen:	**Sì. E mio padre è austriaco.**
	see eh *mee*-oh *pah*-dreh eh ous-*tree*-ah-koh
	Yes, and my father is Austrian.

Talking about where you come from

You know how interesting meeting people from other countries and nationalities can be. Two common questions are useful to remember:

- ✔ **Da dove viene?** (dah *doh*-veh vee-*eh*-neh) (*Where do you come from? Where are you coming from; in this instance, where are you from?*) Formal

- ✔ **Da dove vieni?** (dah *doh*-veh vee-*eh*-nee) (*Where are you from?*) Informal

- ✔ **Di dov'è?** (dee *doh*-veh) (*Where are you from?*) Formal

- ✔ **Di dove sei?** (dee *doh*-veh sey) (*Where are you from?*) Informal

The answers are, respectively:

- ✔ **Vengo da . . .** (*vehn*-goh dah) (*I come from/I'm from*)
- ✔ **Sono di . . .** (*soh*-noh dee) (*I'm from . . .*)

Now you can play with these phrases. You can insert the names of continents, countries, cities, or places.

Talkin' the Talk

Il signor Dadina is sitting in his favorite café in Ravenna drinking his coffee and notices somebody at the next table who is examining a map of the city's Byzantine churches. Il signor Dadina is a curious person:

Sig. Dadina:	**Non è di qui, vedo. Di dov'è?**
	nohn eh dee kw-ee *veh*-roh di doh-*veh*
	I can see you're not from here: where are you from?

Sig. Tarroni:	**Sono di Perugia.**
	soh-noh dee peh-*rooh*-jah
	No, I'm from Perugia.

Sig. Belli:	**Una bella città!**
	ooh-nah *behl*-lah cheet-*tah*
	A beautiful town!

Sig. Verdi:	**Sì, è piccola ma molto bella.**
	see eh *peek*-koh-lah mah *mohl*-toh *behl*-lah
	Yes, it is small but very beautiful.

If you want to talk about provenance, the adjectives denoting nationalities come in handy. As you say in English, "Are you American?" you say the same in Italian:

✔ **È americano/a?** (eh ah-meh-ree-*kah*-noh/nah) (*Are you American?*) Formal

✔ **Sei americano/a?** (sey ah-meh-ree-*kah*-noh/nah) (*Are you American?*) Informal

After you know the basics for such a situation, you're ready to chat.

Talkin' the Talk

Il signor Bennati, meets a Canadian, Mr. Walsh. Because they are strangers, their exchange is in the formal form.

Sig. Bennati:	**Di dov'è?**
	dee doh-*veh*
	Where are you from?

Mr. Walsh:	**Sono canadese.**
	soh-noh kah-nah-*deh*-zeh
	I'm Canadian.

Sig. Bennati:	**Di dove esattamente?**
	dee *doh*-veh eh-zaht-tah-*mehn*-teh
	From where, exactly?

Mr. Walsh: **Di Montreal. Lei è italiano?**
dee *mohn*-treh-ahl ley eh ee-tah-lee-*ah*-noh
From Montreal. Are you Italian?

Sig. Bennati: **Sì, di Firenze.**
see dee fee-*rehn*-tseh
Yes, from Florence.

In English, you must put the pronoun (I, you, he, she, we, and so on) in front of the verb. You may have noticed that this is not the case in Italian. Because the verb form is different for each pronoun, you can easily leave out the pronoun — you understand who is meant from the verb ending and from the context. You use the pronoun only when the subject isn't clear enough or when you want to emphasize a fact — for example, **Loro sono americani, ma io sono italiano** (*loh*-roh *soh*-noh ah-meh-ree-*kah*-nee mah *ee*-oh *soh*-noh ee-tahl-*yah*-noh) (*They are American, but I am Italian*).

Use adjectives ending in *-o* (singular) and *-i* (plural) to refer to males, and adjectives ending in *-a* (singular) and *-e* (plural) to refer to females. Adjectives that end in *-e* in the singular refer to both males and females and end in the plural with *-i*.

Some adjectives indicating nationality end with *-e:* This form is both feminine and masculine. Table 3-1 gives some examples.

Table 3-1	Some Nationalities and Countries	
Nationality/Country	*Pronunciation*	*Translation*
albanese/i	ahl-bah-*neh*-zeh/zee	*Albanian/Albanians*
Albania	ahl-bah-*nee*-ah	*Albania*
canadese/i	kah-nah-*deh*-zeh/zee	*Canadian/Canadians*
Canada	*kah*-nah-dah	*Canada*
cinese/i	chee-*neh*-zeh/zee	*Chinese* (sing.pl.)
Cina	*chee*-nah	*China*
francese/i	frahn-*cheh*-zeh/zee	*French* (sing./pl.)
Francia	*frahn*-chah	*France*
giapponese/i	jahp-*poh*-neh-zeh/zee	*Japanese* (sing/pl.)
Giappone	jahp-*poh*-neh	*Japan*
inglese/i	een-*gleh*-zeh/zee	*English* (sing./pl.)
Inghilterra	een-geel-*tehr*-rah	*England*

Nationality/Country	Pronunciation	Translation
irlandese/i Irlanda	eer-lahn-*deh*-zeh/zee eer-*lahn*-dah	*Irish* (sing./pl.) *Ireland*
olandese/i olanda	oh-lahn-*deh*-zeh/zee oh-*lahn*-dah	*Dutch* (sing./pl.) *Holland*
portoghese/i Portogallo	pohr-toh-*geh*-zeh/zee pohr-toh-*gahl*-loh	*Portuguese* (sing./pl.) *Portugal*
senegalese/i Senegal	seh-neh-gahl-*eh*-zeh/zee *seh*-neh-gahl	*Senegalese* (sing./pl.) *Senegal*
svedese/i Svezia	sveh-*deh*-zeh/zee *sveh*-tsee-ah	*Swedish* (sing./pl.) *Sweden*

In other cases, nationalities have feminine, masculine, plural feminine, and plural masculine forms, and end in **a, o, e, i**, as Table 3-2 shows.

Table 3-2   Gender-Specific Nationalities and Countries

Nationality/ Country	Pronunciation	Translation
americana/o/e/i Stati Uniti d'America	ah-*meh*-ree-kah-nah/noh/ neh/nee *stah*-tee ooh-*nee*-tee dah-*meh*-ree-kah	*American/Americans* *America*
australiana/o/e/i Australia	ou-strahl-*yah*-nah/noh/ neh/nee ou-strahl-*yah*	*Australian/Australians* *Australia*
brasiliana/o/e/i Brasile	brah-see-*lyah*-nah/noh/ neh/nee brah-see-leh	*Brazilian/Brazilians* *Brazil*
greca/o/greci/greche Grecia	*greh*-koh/*greh*-kah/*greh*-chee/*gre*-keh *greh*-chah	*Greek/Greeks* *Greece*
italiana/o/e/i Italia	ee-*tah*-lee-ah-nah/noh/ neh/nee ee-*tah*-lee-ah	*Italian/Italians* *Italy*
marocchina/o/e/i Marocco	mah-rohk-*kee*-nah/noh/ neh/nee mah-*rohk*-koh	*Moroccan/Moroccans* *Morocco*

(continued)

Table 3-2 *(continued)*

Nationality/ Country	Pronunciation	Translation
messicano/a/e/i Messico	meh-see-*kah*-nah/noh/ neh/nee mehs-see-koh	*Mexican/Mexicans* *Mexico*
polacco/a/polacchi/ polacche Polonia	poh-*lah*-koh/kah/kee/keh poh-*loh*-nee-ah	*Polish* (sing./pl.) *Poland*
rumeno/a/i/e Romania	rooh-*meh*-nah/noh/neh/nee roh-mah-*nee*-ah	*Romanian/Romanians* *Romania*
russa/o/e/i Russia	*roohs*-sah/soh/seh/see *roos*-see-ah	*Russian/Russians* *Russia*
spagnola/o/e/i Spagna	spah-*nyoh*-lah/loh/leh/lee spah-nyah	*Spanish* (sing./pl.) *Spain*
svizzera/o/e/i Svizzera	*sveet*-tseh-rah/roh/reh/ree *sveet*-tseh-rah	*Swiss* (sing./pl.) *Switzerland*
tedesca/o/tedesche/ tedeschi Germania	teh-*dehs*-kah/koh/keh/kee jehr-*mah*-nee-ah	*German/Germans* *Germany*

Instead of saying **sono americano** (*soh*-noh ah-meh-ree-*kah*-noh) (*I'm American*), you can also say **vengo dall'America** (*vehn*-goh dahl-lah-*meh*-ree-kah) (*I'm from America*). The same is true for all countries.

The following examples give you more practice with this construction.

- **Veniamo dall'Italia.** (veh-nee-*ah*-moh dahl-lee-*tah*-lee-ah) (*We come from Italy/we're from Italy.*)

- **Vengono dalla Spagna.** (*vehn*-goh-noh *dahl*-lah spah-nyah) (*They come from Spain.*)

- **Vengo dal Giappone.** (*vehn*-goh dahl jahp-*poh*-neh) (*I come from Japan.*)

- **Veniamo dal Canada.** (veh-nee-*ah*-moh dahl *kah*-nah-dah) (*We come from Canada.*)

- **Veniamo dagli U. S. A.** *(or Stati Uniti)* (veh-nee-*ah*-moh *dah*-lyee ooh-zhah/*stah*-tee ooh-*nee*-tee) (*We come from the U. S. A. or United States*)

If you travel to Italy and make new friends, you may be asked these informal questions:

- ✔ **Ti piace l'Italia?** (tee *pyah*-cheh lee-*tah*-lee-ah) (*Do you like Italy?*)
- ✔ **Sei qui per la prima volta?** (say kwee pehr lah *pree*-mah *vohl*-tah) (*Is this your first time here?*)
- ✔ **Sei qui in vacanza?** (say kwee een vah-*kahn*-tsah) (*Are you on vacation?*)
- ✔ **Quanto rimani?** (*kwahn*-toh ree-*mah*-nee) (*How long are you staying?*)

Talkin' the Talk

In the following dialogue, you can catch some typical expressions for describing a city.

Tokiko: **Ti piace Venezia?**
tee *pyah*-cheh veh-*neh*-tsee-ah
Do you like Venice?

Dolores: **Sì, è molto romantica.**
see eh *mohl*-toh roh-*mahn*-tee-kah
Yes, it's very romantic.

Tokiko: **È bellissima! Io sono giapponese.**
eh behl-*lees*-see-mah. *ee*-o *soh*-noh jahp-poh-*neh*-zeh
It's very beautiful! I am Japanese.

Dolores: **Com'è Tokio?**
kohm-*eh toh*-kee-oh
What's Tokyo like?

Tokiko: **È grandissima, moderna.**
eh grahn-*dees*-see-mah moh-*dehr*-nah
It's huge, modern.

Extending and responding to invitations

You may be asked to join an Italian friend for a meal in a restaurant, or even at his/her home after you've become friends. When you want to invite someone to dinner, you can use the following phrases:

✔ **Andiamo a cena insieme?** (ahn-*dyah*-moh ah *cheh*-nah een-*syeh*-meh) (*Should we go to dinner together?*)

✔ **Posso invitarti stasera?** (*pohs*-soh een-vee-*tahr*-tee stah-*seh*-rah) (*Can I invite you for this evening?*) This usually means that the person asking is going to be treating.

To accept an invitation, you can use the following expressions:

✔ **Volentieri, grazie!** (voh-lehn-*tyeh*-ree *grah*-tsee-eh) (*I'd like to, thank you!*)

✔ **Con piacere, grazie!** (kohn pyah-*cheh*-reh *grah*-tsee-eh) (*With pleasure, thank you!*)

Of course, you can't accept every invitation you receive. Following are expressions you can use to decline an invitation:

✔ **Mi dispiace ma non posso.** (mee dees-*pyah*-cheh mah nohn *pohs*-soh) (*I'm sorry, but I can't.*)

✔ **Magari un'altra volta, grazie.** (mah-*gah*-ree oohn-*ahl*-trah *vohl*-tah *grah*-tsee-eh) (*Perhaps another time, thank you.*)

✔ **Mi dispiace, ho già un altro impegno.** (mee dees-*pyah*-cheh oh jah oohn *ahl*-troh eem-*peh*-nyoh) (*I'm sorry, but I already have another appointment.*)

Talkin' the Talk

Francesca talks to Giovanni to get the particulars for their date that evening.

Francesca: **Ci vediamo per cena questa sera?**
chee veh-*dyah*-moh pehr *cheh*-nah *kwehs*-tah *seh*-rah
Shall me meet for supper tonight?

Giovanni: **Si, perchè no? Offro io, però.**
see pehr-*keh* noh. *ohf*-froh ee-oh pehr-*oh*
Yes, why not? It's my treat, though.

Fun & Games

• •

A chance meeting leads to a quick introduction in the short dialogue. Fill in the blanks in the Italian, using the following phrases. See Appendix D for the answer key.

le presento, il piacere, e lei, come sta, conoscerla

Gayle: **Buonasera, signora Frederick. _____?**

Good afternoon, Ms. Frederick. How are you?

Ms. Frederick **Benissimo, grazie, _____?**

Very well, thank you, and you?

Gayle: **Bene, grazie. _____ il mio amico, George.**

Fine, thanks. I'd like to introduce my friend, George.

George: **Lieta di _____, signora.**

Pleased to meet you, Ma'am.

Ms. Frederick: **_____ è mio.**

The pleasure is mine.

• •

Chapter 4

Getting Your Numbers and Time Straight

In This Chapter

▶ Counting numbers

▶ Telling time

▶ Using the calendar and making dates

▶ Reviewing the metric system

*N*umbers are a basic part of any language, so we've included numbers early on in this chapter. You can't get away without knowing numbers, even in small talk. Somebody may ask you how old you are, how many days you're visiting, or whatever. You can see how numbers are used throughout this book, for example in Chapters 7 and 13.

Counting Numbers

Every language follows a certain scheme to formulate higher numbers. When you know the basics — the numbers from one to ten — you're halfway there.

In the Italian scheme, as in English, the higher value precedes the lower one, so that to say "22," you first say **venti** (*vehn*-tee) (*twenty*) and then **due** (*dooh*-eh) (*two*) and simply put them together: **ventidue** (*vehn*-tee-*dooh*-eh) (*twenty-two*). The same is true for higher numbers — like **trecentoventidue** (treh-*chehn*-toh-*vehn*-tee-*dooh*-eh) (*three hundred and twenty-two*) and **duemilatrecentoventidue** (*dooh*-eh-*mee*-lah-treh-*chehn*-toh-*vehn*-tee-*dooh*-eh) (*two thousand three hundred and twenty-two*).

One thing merits some further explanation: When two vowels meet (this happens frequently with **uno** [*ooh*-noh] [*one*] and **otto** [*oht*-toh] [*eight*]) you eliminate the first vowel as in **vent**(**i**)**uno** (vehn-*tooh*-noh) (*twenty-one*) and **quarant**(**a**)**otto** (*kwah*-rahn-*toht*-toh) (*forty-eight*). So far so good.

Every rule has exceptions, and there are some irregular numbers, which you simply have to memorize. The numbers from 11 to 19 follow their own rules: **undici** (*oohn*-dee-chee) (*eleven*), **dodici** (*doh*-dee-chee) (*twelve*), **tredici** (*treh*-dee-chee) (*thirteen*), **quattordici** (kwaht-*tohr*-dee-chee) (*fourteen*), **quindici** (*kween*-dee-chee) (*fifteen*), **sedici** (*seh*-dee-chee) (*sixteen*), **diciassette** (dee-chahs-*seht*-teh) (*seventeen*), **diciotto** (dee-*choht*-toh) (*eighteen*), and **diciannove** (dee-chahn-*noh*-veh) (*nineteen*).

In Italian you cannot express a decade in just one word — you use a phrase. When you want to say "in the sixties," you have to say **negli anni sessanta** (*neh*-lyee *ahn*-nee sehs-*sahn*-tah), which literally means "in the years sixty." You form all the other decades using this method also. To say "the seventies" (without the "in the") you simply say "**gli anni settanta**" (lyee *ahn*-nee seht-*tahn*-tah).

One other thing to keep in mind is that the plural of **mille** (*meel*-leh) (*one thousand*) is **mila** (*mee*-lah), as in **duemila** (*dooh*-eh-*mee*-lah) (*two thousand*).

Table 4-1 gives you enough numbers so that you can form the ones on your own not included here.

Table 4-1	Numbers	
Italian	*Pronunciation*	*Number*
From 1 to 30		
zero	*dzeh*-roh	0
uno	*ooh*-noh	1
due	*dooh*-eh	2
tre	treh	3
quattro	*kwaht*-troh	4
cinque	*cheen*-kweh	5
sei	sey	6
sette	*seht*-teh	7
otto	*oht*-toh	8
nove	*noh*-veh	9
dieci	*dyeh*-chee	10
undici	*oohn*-dee-chee	11
dodici	*doh*-dee-chee	12
tredici	*treh*-dee-chee	13
quattordici	kwaht-*tohr*-dee-chee	14

Italian	Pronunciation	Number
quindici	*kween*-dee-chee	15
sedici	*seh*-dee-chee	16
diciassette	dee-chahs-*seht*-teh	17
diciotto	dee-*choht*-toh	18
diciannove	dee-chahn-*noh*-veh	19
venti	*vehn*-tee	20
ventuno	vehn-*tooh*-noh	21
ventidue	vehn-tee-*dooh*-eh	22
ventitré	vehn-tee-*treh*	23
ventiquattro	vehn-tee-*kwaht*-troh	24
venticinque	vehn-tee-*cheen*-kweh	25
ventisei	vehn-tee-*sey*	26
ventisette	vehn-tee-*seht*-teh	27
ventotto	vehnt-*oht*-toh	28
ventinove	vehn-tee-*noh*-veh	29
trenta	*trehn*-tah	30
Numbers 40 to 100		
quaranta	kwah-*rahn*-tah	40
cinquanta	cheen-*kwahn*-tah	50
sessanta	sehs-*sahn*-tah	60
settanta	seht-*tahn*-tah	70
ottanta	oht-*tahn*-tah	80
novanta	noh-*vahn*-tah	90
cento	*chen*-toh	100
Numbers from 200 to 900		
duecento	*dooh*-eh-*chehn*-toh	200
trecento	treh-*chehn*-toh	300
quattrocento	*kwaht*-troh-*chehn*-toh	400
cinquecento	*cheen*-kweh-*chehn*-toh	500
seicento	*sey*-*chehn*-toh	600
settecento	*seht*-teh-*chehn*-toh	700
ottocento	*oht*-toh-*chehn*-toh	800
novecento	*noh*-veh-*chehn*-toh	900

(continued)

Table 4-1 (continued)

Italian	Pronunciation	Number
Higher numbers		
mille	*meel*-leh	1,000
duemila	*dooh*-eh-*mee*-lah	2,000
un milione	oohn mee-*lyoh*-neh	1,000,000
due milioni	*dooh*-eh mee-*lyoh*-nee	2,000,000
un miliardo	oohn mee-*lyahr*-doh	1,000,000,000

Common usage for numbers that denote the centuries are:

Manzoni scrisse nell'Ottocento. (mahn-*zoh*-nee *skrees*-seh nehl-*oht*-toh-*chehn*-toh). (*Manzoni wrote in the 1800s.*)

Il Rinascimento fu nel '400 e '500 (nel Quattrocento e nel Cinquecento). (eel ree-*nahsh*-ee-*mehn*-toh fooh nehl *kwaht*-troh-*chehn*-toh eh nehl *cheen*-kweh-*chehn*-toh.) (*The Renaissance was in the 15th and 16th centuries — literally, 1400s and 1500s.*)

Times of Day and Days of the Week

Arranging your social life — whether you want to go to a performance or invite someone to a party — requires knowing the days of the week and times of the day. Table 4-2 gives you the days of the week and the abbreviations for them. You can hear the days of the week on Track 8 on the CD.

You don't capitalize the days of the week or the months in Italian as you do in English.

Table 4-2	Days of the Week	
Italian/Abbreviation	*Pronunciation*	*Translation*
domenica/do.	doh-*meh*-nee-kah	*Sunday*
lunedì/lun.	looh-neh-*dee*	*Monday*
martedì/mar.	mahr-teh-*dee*	*Tuesday*
mercoledì/mer.	mehr-koh-leh-*dee*	*Wednesday*
giovedì/gio.	joh-veh-*dee*	*Thursday*
venerdì/ven.	veh-nehr-*dee*	*Friday*
sabato/sab.	*sah*-bah-toh	*Saturday*

Here are terms for *today*, *tomorrow*, *day after tomorrow*, and *yesterday*: **oggi** (*oj*-jee), **domani** (doh-*mah*-nee), **dopodomani** (*doh*-poh-doh-*mah*-nee), and **ieri** (*yeh*-ree).

There's a great song, "Domani il 21 aprile" that most of Italy's greatest contemporary singers put together in support of the people of Abruzzo after the earthquake of 2009. You can do an online search for the title of the song, and sing along with it. This is a fun way to practice your pronunciation!!

Talkin' the Talk

Note the following teacher/student exchange in Italian 101:

Teacher: **Se oggi è lunedì, che giorno è domani?**
seh *oj*-jee eh looh-neh-*dee* keh *johr*-noh eh doh-*mah*-nee
If today is Monday, what day is tomorrow?

Student: **Domani è martedì.**
doh-*mah*-nee eh mahr-teh-*dee*
Tomorrow is Tuesday.

Teacher: **Bravo. Oggi è giovedì: che giorno è domani?**
brah-voh. *ohj*-jee eh joh-veh-*dee*. keh *johr*-noh eh doh-*mah*-nee
Good job. Today is Thursday: what day is tomorrow?

Student: **Domani è venerdì.**
doh-*mah*-nee eh veh-nehr-*dee*
Tomorrow is Friday.

Now the teacher is talking to her colleagues.

Colleague: **Quando parti per le vacanze?**
kwahn-doh *pahr*-tee pehr leh vah-*kahn*-zeh
When are you leaving for vacation?

Teacher: **Sabato, dopodomani.**
sah-bah-toh *doh*-poh-doh-*mah*-nee
Saturday, day after tomorrow.

You may find the Italian expression for "the day before yesterday" interesting. It is **l'altro ieri** (*lahl*-troh *yeh*-ree), which literally means "the other yesterday." Some of the ways you might use these expressions are:

✔ **Il concerto è martedì sera.** (eel kohn-*chehr*-toh eh mahr-teh-*dee seh*-rah) (*The concert is on Tuesday evening.*)

✔ **Dov'eri ieri pomeriggio?** (doh-*veh*-ree *yeh*-ree poh-meh-*reej*-joh) (*Where were you yesterday afternoon?*)

✔ **Il concerto c'è stato l'altro ieri. L'hai perso!** (eel kohn-*chehr*-toh cheh *stah*-toh *lahl*-troh *yeh*-ree lahy *pehr*-soh) (*The concert was the day before yesterday. You missed it!*)

Using the Calendar and Making Dates

 Table 4-3 lists the months that you need in order to plan a vacation, organize your life, remember your friends' birthdays, and also talk about your favorite holidays and seasons. You can hear the days of the year on Track 9 on the CD.

Table 4-3	Months	
Italian	*Pronunciation*	*Translation*
gennaio	gehn-*nahy*-oh	*January*
febbraio	fehb-*brahy*-oh	*February*
marzo	*mahr*-tsoh	*March*
aprile	ah-*pree*-leh	*April*
maggio	*mahj*-joh	*May*
giugno	*jooh*-nyoh	*June*
luglio	*looh*-lyoh	*July*
agosto	ah-*gohs*-toh	*August*
settembre	seht-*tehm*-breh	*September*
ottobre	oht-*toh*-breh	*October*
novembre	noh-*vehm*-breh	*November*
dicembre	dee-*chehm*-breh	*December*

Here is a useful rhyme that most Italians learn some version of. This might help you to remember and pronounce some of the months and numbers. You can listen and repeat as much as you want!

Trenta giorni ha novembre con aprile, giugno e settembre. Di ventotto ce n'è uno. Tutti gli altri ne han trentuno.

(*trehn*-tah *johr*-nee ah noh-*vehm*-breh kohn ah-*pree*-leh *jooh*-nyoh eh seht-*tehm*-breh. Dee vehn-*toht*-toh cheh neh *ooh*-noh. *Tooht*-tee lyee *ahl*-tree neh ahn *trehn*-tooh-noh.)

(Thirty days have November, April, June, and September. With 28 there is but one. All the rest have thirty-one.)

Making dates

To ask for the date you say:

Che giorno è oggi? (keh *johr*-noh eh *ohj*-jee) *(What is the date today?/What day is today?)* This is also the same way to ask for the day. Or

Quanti ne abbiamo oggi? (*kwahn*-tee neh *ahb*-byah-moh *ohj*-jee) (What is today's date?) Here is an important difference between saying the date in English and in Italian. The word order is reversed in Italian. To say the date you use this order: **è** (eh) (it's) + **il** (eel) (the)+ number + month + (year, if necessary). Here's a sample.

Oggi è il dieci febbraio duemilaundici. (*ohj*-jee eh eel *dyeh*-chee fehb-*brahy*-oh *dooh*-eh-mee-lah-*oohn*-dee-chee) *(Today is February 10, 2011.)*

To ask when something is occurring, just use the word **quando** (*qwahn*-doh) *(when)*.

Quando parti per la Sicilia? (*kwahn*-doh *pahr*-tee pehr lah see-*cheel*-ee-ah) *(When are you leaving for Sicily?)*

. . . and to answer

Parto l'8 agosto. (*pahr*-toh *loht*-toh ah-*gohs*-toh) *(I'm leaving August 8th.)*

Or to ask when someone was born:

Quando sei nata? (*kwahn*-doh sey *nah*-tah) *(When were you born?)*

. . . and to respond

Sono nata il sette novembre millenovecentosessantuno. (*soh*-noh *nah*-tah eel *seht*-teh noh-*vehm*-breh *meel*-leh-*noh*-veh-*chehn*-toh-sehs-sahn-*tooh*-noh) *(I was born in '61.)*

Note: I gave the past participle a feminine ending **nata**. If you're speaking to or about a male, the word should be **nato** (ending in the "**o**".)

Telling time

When you write the time in Italian, you go from 1.00 to 24.00 (or 00.00). But generally when you speak, you use just 1 to 12, and if there's a doubt about a.m. or p.m., you can add **di mattina** (dee maht-*tee*-nah) (*in the morning*), **di pomeriggio** (dee poh-meh-*reej*-joh) (*in the afternoon*) or **di sera** (dee *seh*-rah) (*in the evening*).

Asking for the time

You can ask for the time in two interchangeable ways:

1. **Che ora è?** (keh *oh*-rah eh) (*What time is it?*)

2. **Che ore sono?** (keh *oh*-reh *soh*-noh) (*What time is it?*)

Another way of asking politely for the time follows:

Scusi, mi può dire l'ora, per favore? (*skooh*-zee mee pwoh *dee*-reh *loh*-rah pehr fah-*voh*-reh) (*Excuse me, can you please tell me the time?*)

If the hour is *singular*, you answer with the singular verb:

È l'una. (eh *looh*-nah) (*It's one o'clock.*) **È mezzanotte.** (eh *medz*-ah-*noht*-teh) (*It's midnight.*)

È mezzogiorno. (eh *medz*-oh-*johr*-noh) (*It's noon.*)

If the time is plural (i.e., more than one), just change your verb from "**è**" (eh) (it is) to "**sono**" (*soh*-noh) ("*they are*," literally, to reflect the plural **ore** [*oh*-reh] — hours.)

Sono le due. (*soh*-noh leh *dooh*-eh). (*It's two o'clock.*)

Sono le diciotto. (*soh*-noh leh deech-*oht*-toh) (*It's six p.m.*)

Did you notice the use of military time in the previous example? In Italy, the 24-hour clock is used all the time, from movie times to plane and train schedules.

You can also add on when necessary some specifics, such as the examples that follow:

e un quarto (eh oohn *qwahr*-toh) (*a quarter past*)

e mezzo (e *mehdz*-oh) (*half past*)

e tre quarti (eh treh *kwahr*-tee) (*three-quarters past*)

e tredici (eh *treh*-dee-chee) (*thirteen past*)

Asking what time something begins

Of course, sometimes you'd like to take the conversation about time a little farther. Frequently we ask what time something begins. Just add the preposition "a" onto the above questions and answers for telling time. Look here:

A che ora inizia la partita? (ah keh *oh*-rah ee-*neets*-ee-yah lah pahr-*tee*-tah) (*What time does the game begin?*)

And to answer . . .

All'una. (ahl-*looh*-nah) (*At one.*)

Alle dieci. (*ahl*-leh *dyeh*-chee) (*At ten.*)

A mezzogiorno. (ah *medz*-oh-*johr*-noh) (*At noon.*)

(Note that the preposition "a" contracts with the definite article that precedes the number.)

Let's take a look at some of these terms in everyday usage.

Using the 24-hour clock

All schedules and posted time in Italy use a 24-hour clock, from trains and planes, to movies to concerts. It's a good idea to review how the 24-hour clock works, especially when you're at a train or bus station. The word for clock and watch is **orologio** (oh-roh-*loh*-joh). So from midnight to 12:00 noon the hours are the same, but at 1:00 p.m. it becomes 13 hours, or **le tredici** (leh *treh*-dee-chee). 2:00 p.m. becomes **le quattordici** (leh kwaht-*tohr*-dee-chee), and so on.

So let's say you arrive at the train station and want to know what time the trains heading down to Naples are. Here are some options: **6:37 (le sei e trentasette)** (leh sey eh *trehn*-tah-*seht*-teh) (*6:37 a.m.*); **17:23 (le diciassette e ventitrè)** (leh *deech*-ahs-*seht*-teh eh *vehn*-tee-treh) (*5:23 p.m.*). And the same system goes for shop and museum hours, buses, and movie and theater times.

Talkin' the Talk

Giancarlo and Daniele, two Roman university students, are in the piazza chatting about a concert tomorrow being held at the Circus Maximus.

Giancarlo: **Sai a che ora c'è il concerto dei Pink Floyd domani?**
sahy ah keh *oh*-rah cheh eel kon-*chehr*-toh dehy Pink Floyd doh-*mah*-nee
Do you know what time the Pink Floyd concert is tomorrow?

Daniele: **Certo! Inizia alle 10 di sera.**
chehr-toh ee-n*eets*-ee-ah *ahl*-leh *dyeh*-chee dee *seh*-rah.
Of course! It starts at 10:00 p.m.

Giancarlo: **A proposito, che ore sono adesso?**
ah proh-*poh*-zee-toh keh *oh*-reh *soh*-noh ah-*dehs*-soh
By the way, what time is it now?

Daniele: **Sono le due e mezzo in punto.**
soh-noh leh *dooh*-eh eh *medz*-oh een *poohn*-toh
It's 2:30 on the dot.

Giancarlo: **O dio! Sono in ritardo per l'esame!**
oh *dee*-oh *soh*-noh een ree-*tahr*-doh pehr leh-*zah*-meh
Oh God! I'm late for the exam!

Chatting about the Weather

Whenever you're in conversational trouble and don't know what to say, you can always talk about the weather: "It's very hot today, isn't it?" Or, you can ask, "Is Spring your rainy season?" Talking about the weather can save your conversation in many situations!

Because the weather is such an important topic, you must be armed with the necessary vocabulary. In this section, we talk about the **quattro stagioni** (*kwaht*-troh stah-*joh*-nee) (*four seasons*).

Weather wise

Italy is a fortunate country, at least as far as weather is concerned. During at least three of the four seasons, it has a mild climate and gets a lot of sun.

The summers are for the most part warm — sometimes *too* hot. The winters can be very cold, but snow is rare, except for primarily in the mountains of north and central Italy, but as far south as Calabria.

Summer in the cities is generally terribly hot, so most Italians take their vacation in August and flee to cooler places: the sea or the lakes or the mountains. As a matter of fact, in August, it is hard to find actual residents in the big cities. The only people you find there are likely to be tourists and those Italians who have to work.

The fact that both the famous concertos by Antonio Vivaldi (ahn-*toh*-nee-oh vee-*vahl*-dee) and an oh-so-good pizza are named Quattro stagioni is no accident. Both are subdivided into four parts, and each part refers to one season. (Track 7)

- ✔ **primavera** (pree-mah-*veh*-rah) (*spring*)
- ✔ **estate** (ehs-*tah*-teh) (*summer*)
- ✔ **autunno** (ou-*toohn*-noh) (*autumn; fall*)
- ✔ **inverno** (in-*vehr*-noh) (*winter*)

Talkin' the Talk

Mr. Brancato and Ms. Roe, seatmates on a plane, are talking about the weather.

Ms. Roe: **Le piace Milano?**
leh *pyah*-cheh mee-*lah*-noh
Do you like Milan?

Sig. Brancato: **Sì, ma non il clima.**
see mah nohn eel *klee*-mah
Yes, but not its climate.

Ms. Roe:	**Fa molto freddo?**
	fah *mohl*-toh *frehd*-doh
	Is it very cold?

Sig. Brancato:	**In inverno sì.**
	een een-*vehr*-noh see
	In winter it is.

Ms. Roe:	**E piove molto, no?**
	eh *pyoh*-veh *mohl*-toh noh
	And it rains a lot, doesn't it?

Sig. Brancato:	**Sì, e c'è sempre la nebbia.**
	see eh cheh *sehm*-preh lah *nehb*-bee-ah
	Yes, and there is always fog.

Ms. Roe:	**Com' è il clima a Palermo?**
	kohm-*eh* eel *klee*-mah ah pah-*lehr*-moh
	What's Palermo's climate like?

Sig. Brancato:	**Temperato, mediterraneo.**
	tehm-peh-*rah*-toh meh-dee-tehr-*rah*-neh-oh
	Temperate, Mediterranean.

Ms. Roe:	**Non fa mai freddo?**
	nohn fah mahy *frehd*-doh
	Is it never cold?

Sig. Brancato:	**Quasi mai.**
	kwah-zee mahy
	Almost never.

An expression that shows a difference between cultures is: **Una rondine non fa primavera** (*ooh*-nah-*rohn*-dee-neh nohn fah pree-mah-*veh*-rah) (*One swallow does not a summer make*). Note the difference; in English, the expression refers to summer; in Italian it refers to spring. This difference may be due to the fact that the birds come earlier in Italy and later to other countries.

Talkin' the Talk

Our friends Il signor Brancato and Ms. Roe, airplane seatmates, are still talking about the weather.

Ms. Roe:	**E l'estate a Milano com'è?**
	e lehs-*tah*-teh ah mee-*lah*-noh cohm-*eh*
	What's the summer like in Milan?

Sig. Brancato:	**Molto calda e lunga.**
	mohl-toh *kahl*-dah eh *loohn*-gah
	Very hot and long.

Ms. Roe:	**E la primavera?**
	eh lah pree-mah-*veh*-rah
	And the spring?

Sig. Brancato:	**La mia stagione preferita.**
	lah *mee*-ah stah-*joh*-neh preh-feh-*ree*-tah
	My favorite season.

Ms. Roe:	**Davvero?**
	dahv-*veh*-roh
	Really?

Sig. Brancato:	**Sì, perché è mite.**
	see pehr-*keh* eh *mee*-teh
	Yes, because it's mild.

Ms. Roe:	**Come l'estate in Canada.**
	koh-meh lehs-*tah*-teh een *kah*-nah-dah
	Like the fall in Canada.

When you're talking about the weather, the following expressions, which are very idiomatic, will make you sound like a heritage speaker!

✔ **Fa un caldo terribile!** (fah oohn *kahl*-doh tehr-*ree*-bee-leh) (*It's terribly hot!*)

✔ **Oggi il sole spacca le pietre!** (*ohj*-jee eel *soh*-leh *spahk*-kah leh *pyeh*-treh) (*The sun today is breaking the stones!*)

✔ **Fa un freddo cane!** (fah oohn *frehd*-doh *kah*-neh) (*It's terribly cold!*)

✔ **Fa un freddo/un caldo da morire!** (fah oohn *frehd*-doh/oon *kahl*-doh dah moh-*ree*-reh) (*It's deadly cold/warm!*)

Da morire (dah moh-*ree*-reh) (*deadly*) is a typical expression used for emphasis in Italian. You can use it in all kinds of situations: For example, **sono stanco da morire** (*soh*-noh *stahn*-koh dah moh-*ree*-reh) (*I'm dead tired*) or **ho una sete da morire** (oh *ooh*-nah *seh*-teh dah moh-*ree*-reh) (*I'm so thirsty I could die*).

Talkin' the Talk

Back in the plane, there is more small talk about the weather as the plane goes in for its landing.

Voice over the loudspeaker:	**Signore e Signori!** see-*nyoh*-reh eh see-*nyoh*-ree Ladies and gentlemen!
Sig. Brancato:	**Che succede?** kee sooh-*cheh*-deh What's up?
Voice:	**Stiamo atterrando a Milano Malpensa.** stee-*ah*-moh aht-tehr-*rahn*-doh ah mee-*lah*-noh mahl-pehn-sah We're landing now at Milan Malpensa.
Sig. Brancato:	**Meno male!** *meh*-noh *mah*-leh Thank goodness!
Voice:	**Il cielo è coperto.** eel *cheh*-loh eh koh-*pehr*-toh The sky is overcast.
Ms. Roe:	**Come al solito!** *koh*-meh ahl *soh*-lee-toh As usual!
Voice:	**E la temperatura è di cinque gradi.** eh lah tehm-peh-rah-*tooh*-rah eh dee *cheen*-kweh *grah*-dee And the temperature is five degrees.

You probably know that in Europe the Celsius scale is used to measure temperature. So, in the preceding dialogue, "five degrees" converts to 41 degrees Fahrenheit.

Words to Know

come al solito	koh-meh ahl soh-lee-toh	as usual
umido	ooh-mee-doh	humid
tempo incerto [m]	tehm-poh een-chehr-toh	uncertain weather
nebbia [f]	nehb-bee-ah	fog
mite	mee-teh	mild
visibilità	vee-zee-bee-lee-tah	visibility
gradi	grah-dee	degrees
piove	pyoh-veh	It's raining

Piove sul bagnato (*pyoh*-veh soohl bah-*nyah*-toh) (Literally: *it rains on the wet*) is an idiomatic expression that Italians use when something positive happens to someone who doesn't really need it. For example, if a millionaire wins the lottery, you may say **piove sul bagnato** to indicate your feeling that you should have won instead.

There's a lovely song about rain, called "Piove," by Jovanotti. Find the song online, listen to it, and sing along to practice your Italian!!

Familiarizing Yourself with the Metric System

The whole world uses the metric system, with the exception of the United States, Liberia, and Burma, so it's a good idea to review this very common system of measurement. You'll need it to understand directions, order bread and cheese at a market, understand your pharmacy prescription, and even figure out how to make your favorite Italian dishes if you're watching Italianfoodnet.com.

Length and Distance

Measures of length go up incrementally as follows. I'm only putting the main ones in, and you can find scores of conversion sites on-line if you'd like to take this farther:

millimetro (meel-*lee*-meh-troh) (*millimeter*); **centimetro** (chehn-*tee*-meh-troh) (*centimeter*); **metro** (*meh*-troh) (*meter*); **chilometro** (kee-*loh*-meh-troh) (*kilometer*)

To ask how far something is, you may say, "**Quanto dista il Colosseo?**" (*kwahn*-toh *dees*-tah eel koh-lohs-*sey*-oh) (*How far is the Colosseum?*)

A typical response could be: "**Duecento metri a destra.**" (*dooh*-eh-*chehn*-toh *meh*-tree ah *dehs*-trah) (*200 meters on the right.*)

Weight

If you're worried about how much weight you're gaining, you can easily pop into a pharmacy in Italy and weigh yourself on one of their scales. (This usually costs **cinquanta centesimi** (cheen-*qwahn*-tah chehn-*teh*-zee-mee) (*50 cents*). You will get your weight in **chili** (*kee*-lee) (*kilos*), which you then have to multiply by 2.2, if you're from the United States and the above-mentioned other two countries. Similarly, if you decide you need to buy some very expensive dried **funghi porcini** (*foohn*-gee pohr-*chee*-nee) (*porcini mushrooms*) or **tartufi** (tahr-*tooh*-fee) (*truffles*), you will ask for those by weight, in this case, **grammi** (*grahm*-mee) (*grams*).

So, incrementally, measures of weight go as follows:

milligrammo (meel-lee-*grahm*-moh) (*milligram*); **grammo** (*grahm*-moh) (*gram*); **ettogrammo** (*eht*-toh-*grahm*-moh) (*hectogram*); **chilogrammo** (kee-loh-*grahm*-moh) (*kilogram*); **quintale** (kwin-*tah*-leh) (*quintal*); **tonnellata** (tohn-nehl-*lah*-tah) (*ton*).

Then there are the **millilitro** (meel-lee-*lee*-troh) (*milliliter*) and **litro** (*lee*-troh) (*liter*) with **mezzo litro** (*medz*-zoh *lee*-troh) (*half liter*) also thrown in here for those individual-serving water bottles.

Talkin' the Talk

Sarah, an American high school student with two years of Italian, is doing a home stay with an Italian family in Castellaneta this year. Here is a piece of her first dinner conversation with her new host family: They are getting to know each other. Is she glad she learned her numbers!

Host Mom: **Sarah, quanti fratelli hai?**
sah-rah *kwahn*-tee frah-*tehl*-lee ahy
Sara, how many brothers and sisters do you have?

Sarah: **Ho un fratello e due sorelle.**
oh oohn *frah*-tehl-loh eh *dooh*-eh soh-*rehl*-leh
I have one brother and two sisters.

Host Mom: **Quanti anni hanno?**
kwahn-tee *ahn*-nee *ahn*-noh
How old are they?

Sarah: **Mio fratello David ha dodici anni.**
mee-oh frah-*tehl*-loh David ah *doh*-dee-chee *ahn*-nee
My brother David is 12.
Mia sorella Rebecca ne ha diciannove, e mia sorella Naomi ne ha 21.
mee-ah soh-*rehl*-lah Rebecca neh hah *deech*-ahn-*noh*-veh eh *mee*-ah soh-*rehl*-lah Naomi neh ah vehn-*tooh*-noh.
My sister Rebecca is 19 and my sister Naomi is 21.

Host Mom: **E quando è il tuo compleanno?**
eh *kwahn*-doh eh eel *tooh*-oh kohm-pleh-*ahn*-noh
And when is your birthday?

Sarah: **Il ventidue maggio.**
eel *vehn*-tee-*dooh*-eh *mahj*-joh
May 22.

Host Mom: **Quanto dista casa tua da New York?**
kwahn-toh *dees*-tah *cah*-sah *tooh*-ah dah New York?
How far is your house from New York?

Sarah: **Centoventi chilometri più o meno.**
chehn-toh-*vehn*-tee kee-*loh*-meh-tree pyooh oh *meh*-noh
120 kilometers, more or less.
O che bel cane! Che razza è?
oh keh behl *kah*-neh. keh *rats*-tsah eh
Oh, what a beautiful dog! What kind of dog is he?

Host Mom: **è un pastore maremmano.**
eh oohn pahs-*toh*-reh mah-rehm-*mah*-noh
He's a Maremma Shepherd.

Sarah: **Quanto pesa?**
kwahn-toh *peh*-zah
How much does he weigh?

Host Mom:	**Cinquanta chili.**
	cheen-*kwahn*-tah *kee*-lee
	50 kilos.

Words to Know

a proposito	ah proh-<u>poh</u>-zee-toh	by the way
anni	<u>ahn</u>-nee	years
chilo	<u>kee</u>-loh	kilo
compleanno	kohm-pleh-<u>ahn</u>-noh	birthday
giorno	<u>johr</u>-noh	day
mese	<u>meh</u>-zeh	month
numero	<u>nooh</u>-mehr-oh	number
pastore	pahs-<u>toh</u>-reh	shepherd
quanti	<u>kwahn</u>-tee	how many
quando	<u>kwahn</u>-doh	when
quanto	<u>kwahn</u>-toh	how much

Fun and Games

Take a look at this picture and name the four seasons. For a more challenging task, name the months that comprise each of the seasons. See Appendix D for the answer key.

Part II
Italian in Action

The 5th Wave   By Rich Tennant

"Honey, can you look in the phrase book and tell me how 'scrambled' is pronounced in Italian?"

In this part . . .

These chapters help you with everyday activities, such as:

- ✔ Doing household chores
- ✔ Asking directions
- ✔ Eating and drinking, Italian style
- ✔ Shopping for clothes and shoes
- ✔ Going to concerts, museums, and other cultural events
- ✔ Making and taking phone calls
- ✔ Enjoying some outdoor recreation

So choose your interest and put your Italian into action!

Chapter 5

Casa dolce casa
(Home Sweet Home)

- -

In This Chapter

▶ Looking for an apartment

▶ Decorating your home

▶ Cleaning your house

▶ Navigating the kitchen

- -

This chapter introduces you to the different vocabulary and situations associated with the house, from renting an apartment to furnishing it to setting the table and eating in it. Just as Italy leads the way in the fashion industry, so too does it enjoy a well-deserved reputation for its fine furnishings and interior spaces.

This chapter walks you through some essential household chores like cleaning and setting the table, and supplies you with the vocabulary for some everyday utensils and appliances. I even give you a quick cooking lesson for some pasta later in the chapter.

Ordering Ordinals

When giving and receiving directions to your home as well as when talking about the different floors of a building, you need a command of **numeri ordinali** (*nooh*-meh-ree ohr-dee-*nah*-lee) (*ordinal numbers*). Because ordinal numbers are adjectives, they agree with the noun they describe. For example, you use the feminine forms when referring to **via** (*vee*-ah) or **strada** (*strah*-dah) (*street*), which are feminine nouns, and the masculine form when talking about a **piano** (*pyah*-noh) (*floor*). Table 5-1 includes the ordinal numbers in the singular masculine form followed by the singular feminine form.

Table 5-1	Ordinal Numbers	
Italian	*Pronunciation*	*Translation*
il primo/la prima	eel *pree*-moh/lah *pree*-mah	the first
il secondo/la seconda	eel seh-*kohn*-doh/lah seh-*kohn*-dah	the second
il terzo/la terza	eel *tehr*-tsoh/lah *tehr*-tsah	the third
il quarto/la quarta	eel *kwahr*-toh/lah *kwahr*-tah	the fourth
il quinto/la quinta	eel *kween*-toh/lah *kween*-tah	the fifth
il sesto/la sesta	eel *sehs*-toh/lah *sehs*-tah	the sixth
il settimo/la settima	eel *seht*-tee-moh/lah *seht*-tee-mah	the seventh
l'ottavo/l'ottava	loht-*tah*-voh/loht-*tah*-vah	the eighth
il nono/la nona	eel *noh*-noh/lah *noh*-nah	the ninth
il decimo/la decima	eel *deh*-chee-moh/lah *deh*-chee-mah	the tenth
il tredicesimo/la tredicesima	eel *treh*-dee-*cheh*-zee-moh	the thirteenth
il ventesimo/la ventesimo	eel vehn-*teh*-zee-moh	the twentieth
il quararantottesimo/la quarantottesima	eel qwah-rahn-toht-*teh*-zee-moh	the forty-eighth

After tenth, you take the whole number, drop the final vowel, and add **esimo/a/e/i** (*ehz*-ee-moh/ah/eh/ee).

These examples show you how to use ordinal numbers in sentences:

È la terza strada a sinistra. (eh lah *tehr*-tsah *strah*-dah ah see-*nees*-trah) (*It's the third street on the left.*)

Abitiamo al nono piano. (ah-bee-*tyah*-moh ahl *noh*-noh *pyah*-noh) (*We live on the ninth floor.*)

Non so se abitino all'undicesmo o al dodicesimo piano. (nohn soh seh *ah*-bee-tee-noh ahl-loohn-dee-*cheh*-zee-moh oh ahl doh-dee-*cheh*-zee-moh *pyah*-noh) (*I don't know if they live on the eleventh or twelfth floor.*)

All Italian buildings begin on the **pianterreno** (pyahn-tehr-*reh*-noh) or ground floor. So the first floor (**il primo piano**) (eel *pree*-moh *pyah*-noh) corresponds to a North American second floor, a second floor (**il secondo piano**) (eel seh-*kohn*-doh *pyah*-noh) corresponds to a North American third floor, and so on.

Types of Italian housing

In Italy, there are different types of dwellings where people live, the most common being the **appartamento** (ahp-pahr-tah-*mehn*-toh). An apartment is usually in a **condominio** (kohn-doh-*meen*-ee-oh) (condominium building) or an old refurbished **palazzo** (pah-*lats*-soh). A **villa** (*veel*-lah) is a free-standing house, usually in the country or by the sea. The **villa** is generally someone's second home. Some people opt to live **in campagna** (een kahm-*pahn*-yah) (the countryside). This is not the same as living in the suburbs in the United States. As a matter of fact, **periferia** (peh-ree-fehr-*ee*-ah) (suburbs which are neither country nor city) has a negative connotation in Italy.

Inhabiting Your Home

Italians usually speak of **la casa** (lah *kah*-zah) (*the house; the home*), even though they often mean **l'appartamento** (lahp-pahr-tah-*mehn*-toh) (*the apartment*). Italians of all social strata live in apartment buildings in small towns and large cities rather than in single-family dwellings or in the suburbs. Houses can be rented as **monolocali** (*moh*-noh-loh-*kah*-lee) (*studio apartments*), **bilocali** (*bee*-loh-*kah*-lee) (*two-room apartments*), or as an **appartamento** with a specified number of **camere da letto** (*kah*-meh-reh dah *leht*-toh) (*bedrooms*).

Hunting for an apartment

When you're looking for an apartment or a house to rent for the summer, you need to know about the rooms in the house and the size of the apartment. The size is given in square meters.

You can find an apartment or a house on your own through newspaper **annunci** (ahn-*noohn*-chee) (*advertisements*), or you can turn to **un'agenzia immobiliare** (oohn-ah-jehn-*tsee*-ah eem-moh-bee-*lyah*-reh) (*a real estate agency*) for help. You can also find housing by searching online.

You need to know if the **casa** is **ammobiliata** (ah-moh-beel-*yah*-tah) (*furnished*), as most short-term rentals are. If you're renting for the long term, many times the house will be completely empty, devoid of even a fridge. **L'aria condizionata** (*lah*-ree-ah kohn-deets-ee-ohn-*ah*-tah) (*air conditioning*) is an important feature to look for in the summer months, although many places don't have it.

These words can help you specify your wishes concerning the number and types of rooms and as well as location and amenities.

✔ **l'ascensore** (lah-shehn-*soh*-reh) (*the elevator*)

✔ **l'angolo cottura** (*lahn*-goh-loh koht-*tooh*-rah) (*cooking area, such as in a studio apartment*)

✔ **il bagno** (eel *bah*-nyoh) (*the bathroom*)

✔ **il balcone** (eel bahl-*koh*-neh) (*the balcony*)

✔ **la camera da letto** (lah *kah*-meh-rah dah *leht*-toh) (*the bedroom*)

✔ **la cantina** (lah kahn-*tee*-nah) (*the cellar*)

✔ **la cucina** (lah kooh-*chee*-nah) (*the kitchen*)

✔ **la doccia** (lah *doch*-chah) (*the shower*)

✔ **la finestra** (lah fee-*nehs*-trah) (*the window*)

✔ **il garage** (eel gah-*raj*) (*the garage*)

✔ **la mansarda** (mahn-*sahr*-dah) (*the attic*)

✔ **la piscina** (lah pee-*shee*-nah) (*the pool*)

✔ **il soggiorno** (eel sohj-*johr*-noh) (*the living room*)

✔ **la stanza** (lah *stahn*-tsah) (*the room*)

✔ **la sala da pranzo** (lah *sah*-lah dah *prahn*-zoh) (*the dining room*)

✔ **lo studio** (loh *stooh*-dee-oh) (*the office or study*)

✔ **la vasca da bagno** (lah *vahs*-kah dah *bahn*-yoh) (*the bath tub*)

Using the verb "to rent" may be somewhat confusing. The confusion comes from this: As in English, both **i padroni di casa** (ee pah-*droh*-nee dee *kah*-sah) (*landlords*) and **gli inquilini** (lyee een-kwee-*lee*-nee) (*tenants*) use the verb **affittare** (ahf-feet-*tah*-reh) (*to rent*). To avoid misunderstandings, landlords sometimes say **dare in affitto** (*dah*-reh een ahf-*feet*-toh) and tenants use **prendere in affitto** (*prehn*-deh-reh een ahf-*feet*-toh). Other useful verbs for these types of actions might include: **subaffittare** (soohb-ahf-fee-*tah*-reh) (*to sublet*), **traslocare** (trahs-loh-*kah*-reh) (*to change houses*), and **trasferirsi** (trahs-feh-*reer*-see) (*to move from one city to another*).

Talkin' the Talk

Flaminia is looking for an apartment, and Pietro helps her read through the newspaper ads. After a few minutes, Pietro thinks he's found something interesting.

Pietro: **Affittasi appartamento zona centro.**
             ahf-*feet*-tah-see ahp-pahr-tah-*mehn*-toh *dzoh*-nah *chehn*-troh
             Apartment for rent, central area.

Flaminia: **Continua!**
             kohn-*tee*-nooh-ah
             Go on!

Pietro: **Due stanze, balcone, garage.**
             dooh-eh *stahn*-tseh bahl-*koh*-neh gah-*rahj*
             Two rooms, balcony, garage.

Flaminia: **Perfetto!**
             pehr-*feht*-toh
             Perfect!

Pietro: **Tranquillo, in Via Treviso.**
             trahn-*kweel*-loh een *vee*-ah treh-*vee*-zoh
             Quiet, on Treviso Street.

Flaminia: **Chiamo subito. Non è molto centrale.**
             kyah-moh *sooh*-bee-toh. Nohn eh *mohl*-toh chehn-*trah*-leh
             I'll call immediately. It's not very central.

Pietro: **No, ma costa sicuramente meno.**
             noh mah *kohs*-tah see-kooh-rah-*mehn*-teh *meh*-noh
             No, but it's surely cheaper.

Flaminia: **È vero.**
             eh *veh*-roh
             It's true!

Pietro: **Chiama!**
             kyah-mah
             Call!

When you see a newspaper ad that interests you, reacting immediately is always best — **Chi prima arriva macina** (kee *pree*-mah ahr-*ree*-vah *mah*-chee-nah) (*First come first served.*) You don't want to hear **Mi dispiace, è già affittato** (mee dees-*pyah*-cheh eh jah ahf-feet-*tah*-toh) (*I'm sorry, it's already rented.*)

You may want to know the following words when searching for an apartment (and any other time you are considering making a purchase). **Caro** (*kah*-roh) means "expensive," and **economico** (eh-koh-*noh*-mee-koh) means "cheap," although Italians seldom use the word **economico**. Rather, most people say **costa poco** (*kohs*-tah *poh*-koh) (*it costs little*) or **non è caro** (nohn eh *kah*-roh) (*it's not expensive*). When you want to compare costs, you say **costa meno** (*kohs*-tah *meh*-noh) (*it costs less*) or **costa di più** (*kohs*-tah dee pyooh) (*it costs more*). Other questions you might want to ask include: **A che piano è?** (ah keh *pyah*-noh eh) (*What floor is it on?*) and **Cè l'ascensore?** (cheh lah-shehn-*soh*-reh) (*Is there an elevator?*)

Talkin' the Talk

Flaminia calls the number given in the ad to find out more about the apartment.

Landlord: **Pronto!**
prohn-toh
Hello!

Flaminia: **Buongiorno, chiamo per l' annuncio. Quant'è l'affitto?**
bwohn-*johr*-noh *kyah*-moh pehr lahn-*noohn*-choh kwahn-*teh* lah-*fit*-toh
Good morning! I'm calling about the ad. How much is the rent?

Landlord: **600 euro al mese.**
sehy-*chehn*-toh eh-ooh-roh ahl *meh*-zeh
Six hundred euros per month.

Flaminia: **Riscaldamento e acqua sono compresi?**
rees-kahl-dah-*mehn*-toh eh *ahk*-wah *soh*-noh kohm-*preh*-zee
Are heat and water included?

Landlord: **No, sono nelle spese di condominio.**
noh *soh*-noh *nehl*-leh *speh*-zeh dee kohn-doh-*mee*-nee-oh
No, they are included in the maintenance.

Flaminia: **Sono alte?**
soh-noh ahl-teh
Are they high?

Landlord: **Dipende dal consumo, come l'elettricità.**
dee-pehn-deh dahl kohn-sooh-moh koh-meh
leh-leht-tree-chee-tah
It depends on your consumption, the same
as electricity.

Flaminia: **Quando lo posso vedere?**
kwahn-doh loh pohs-soh veh-deh-reh
When can I see it?

Landlord: **Subito, se vuole.**
sooh-bee-toh seh vwoh-leh
Immediately, if you want.

You'll probably have many other questions if you decide to rent an apartment. Table 5-2 lists some of the more common questions, and some possible answers.

Table 5-2 Common House-Hunting Questions and Answers

Questions	Possible Answers
È occupato? eh ohk-kooh-pah-toh *Is it occupied?*	**No, è libero.** noh eh lee-beh-roh *No, it's vacant.* **Sì, per il momento.** see pehr eel moh-mehn-toh *Yes, at the moment.* **È libero fra sei mesi.** eh lee-beh-roh frah say meh-zee. *It will be vacant in six months.*
Bisogna lasciare un deposito? bee-zoh-nyah lah-shah-reh oohn deh-poh-zee-toh *Is it necessary to put down a deposit?*	**Sì, un mese d'affitto.** see oohn meh-zeh dahf-feet-toh *Yes, one month's rent.* **Sì, la cauzione** see lah kow-tsee-oh-neh. *Yes, we require a security deposit.*
Paghi molto per la casa? pah-gee mohl-toh pehr lah kah-sah *Do you pay a lot for your house?*	**No, l'affitto è veramente basso.** noh lahf-feet-toh eh veh-rah-mehn-teh bahs-soh *No, the rent is really low.*
La casa è tua? lah kah-sah eh tooh-ah *Do you own your home?*	**No, sono in affitto.** noh soh-noh een ahf-feet-toh *No, I rent.* **Sì, l'ho comprata l'anno scorso.** see loh kohm-prah-tah lahn-noh skohr-soh *Yes, I bought it last year.* **Ho fatto un mutuo.** oh faht-toh oohn mooh-tooh-oh *I took out a mortgage.*

Sprucing up your apartment

When you finally find an apartment, you probably want to furnish it beautifully.
The following dialogues show you some Italians talking about their furniture.

Talkin' the Talk

Valerio has found a new, **non ammobiliato** (nohn ahm-moh-bee-
lyah-toh) (*unfurnished*) apartment. His friend Eugenia is asking
him what he needs.

Valerio:	**Ho trovato un appartamento! Devo comprare dei mobili.**
	oh troh-*vah*-toh oohn ahp-pahr-tah-*mehn*-toh *deh*-voh kohm-*prah*-reh dehy *moh*-bee-lee
	I just found an apartment! I have to buy some furniture.
Eugenia:	**Tutto?**
	tooht-toh
	(Do you need) everything?
Valerio:	**No, per la camera da latto il letto e l'armadio.**
	noh pehr lah *kah*-meh-rah dah *leht*-toh eel *leht*-toh eh lahr-*mah*-dee-oh
	No, for the bedroom a bed and a wardrobe.
Eugenia:	**Nient'altro?**
	nee-ehnt-*ahl*-troh
	Anything else?
Valerio:	**Ho due comodini e una cassettiera.**
	oh *dooh*-eh koh-moh-*dee*-nee eh *ooh*-nah kahs-seht-*tyeh*-rah
	I have two bedside tables and a chest of drawers.
Eugenia:	**E per il soggiorno?**
	eh pehr eel sohj-*johr*-noh
	Do you have furniture for the living room?
Valerio:	**Ho una poltrona. Mi mancano ancora il divano e un tavolino.**
	oh *ooh*-nah pohl-*troh*-nah mee *mahn*-kah-noh ahn-*koh*-rah eel dee-*vah*-noh eh oohn tah-voh-*lee*-noh
	Only one chair. I still need a couch and a coffee table.

La signora Giorgetti wants to buy secondhand furniture. She reads an interesting ad:

Vendesi (*vehn*-deh-see) (*For sale*): **tavolo e due sedie** (*tah*-voh-loh eh *dooh*-eh seh-dee-eh) (*table and two chairs*) **stile Liberty** (*stee*-leh *lee*-behr-tee) (*Liberty style*)

"Quello che cercavo!" (*kwehl*-loh keh chehr-*kah*-voh) ("*Just what I was looking for!*"), she exclaims. She immediately calls the number on the ad. Of course, she needs answers to some questions:

Sono autentici? (*soh*-noh ou-*tehn*-tee-chee) (*Are they authentic?*)

Sì, comprati ad un' asta. (see kohm-*prah*-tee ahd oohn-*ahs*-tah) (*Yes, [they were] bought at an auction.*)

Sono in buono stato? (*soh*-noh een *bwoh*-noh *stah*-toh) (*Are they in good condition?*)

Venga a vederli! (*vehn*-gah ah veh-*dehr*-lee) (*Come and see them!*)

Furnishing your new pad

Table 5-3 divides the different pieces of **i mobili** (ee *moh*-bee-lee) (*furniture*) and other items according to the rooms.

Table 5-3	Room Furniture Translation	
il soggiorno/il salotto (eel soj-johr-noh) (eel sah-loht-toh)	*the living room*	
	il divano (eel dee-*vah*-noh)	*the couch*
	la poltrona (lah pohl-*troh*-nah)	*the arm-chair*
	il tappeto (eel tahp-*peht*-toh)	*the rug*
	lo scaffale (loh skahf-*fah*-leh)	*the book-shelf*
la cucina (lah kooh-chee-nah)	*the kitchen*	
	il frigorifero (eel free-goh-ree-*fehr*-oh)	*the refrigerator*
	il grembiule (el grehm-*byooh*-leh)	*apron*

(continued)

Table 5-3 (continued)

la cucina (lah kooh-chee-nah)	the kitchen	
	la lavastoviglie (lah lah-vah-stoh-veel-yeh)	the dishwasher
	il lavello (eel lah-vehl-loh)	the sink
	le sedie (leh seh-dee-eh)	the chairs
	il tavolo (eel tah-voh-loh)	the table
	la credenza (lah creh-dehn-zah)	the credenza
	i pensili (ee pehn-see-lee)	cabinets
la camera da letto (lah kah-meh-rah dah leht-toh)	the bedroom	
	il letto (eel leht-toh)	bed
	il comodino (eel koh-moh-dee-noh)	nightstand
	l'armadio (lahr-mah-dee-oh)	armoire
	il comò (eel koh-moh)	dresser
	i cuscini (ee kooh-shee-nee)	pillows
	la lampada (lah lahm-pah-dah)	lamp
	il lenzuolo/le lenzuola (eel lehn-zwoh-lo/leh lehn-zwoh-lah)	sheet/sheets
	le tende (leh tehn-deh)	curtains
il bagno (eel bahn-yoh)	bathroom	
	Il bidet (eel bee-deh)	bidèt
	la tazza (lah tats-sah)	toilet bowl
	la doccia (lah doch-chah)	shower
	l'asciugamano/gli asci-umagmani (lah-shooh-gah-mah-noh) (lyee ah-shooh-gah-mah-nee)	towel/s
	Il lavandino (eel lah-vahn-dee-noh)	sink
	la doccia (lah doch-chah)	shower
	la vasca da bagno (lah vahs-kah dah bahn-yoh)	bathtub

Words to Know

accanto	ahk-<u>kahn</u>-toh	next to
davanti a	dah-<u>vahn</u>-tee ah	in front of
dietro	dee-<u>eh</u>-troh	behind
sopra	<u>soh</u>-prah	on top of
sotto	<u>soht</u>-toh	under
di lato	dee <u>lah</u>-toh	on its side
dentro	<u>dehn</u>-troh	inside
fuori	<u>fwoh</u>-ree	outside

Housekeeping in style

Italians do love their **elettrodomestici** (eh-*leht*-troh-doh-*mehs*-tee-chee) (*household appliances*), and there are many sleek Italian brands for these things. Dryers are very rare in Italy because of the enormous amount of electricity they consume, but many households now have dishwashers. Some essential **elettrodomestici** include:

l'aspirapolvere	lahs-*pee*-rah-*pohl*-veh-reh	*vacuum cleaner*
la lavatrice	lah *lah*-vah-*tree*-cheh	*washing machine*
la lavastoviglie	lah *lah*-vah-stoh-*veel*-yeh	*the dishwasher*
il frullatore	eel froohl-ah-*toh*-reh	*blender*
il tostapane	eel *tohs*-tah-*pah*-neh	*toaster*
il frigorifero	eel free-goh-*ree*-fehr-oh	*the refrigerator*
i fornelli	ee fohr-*nehl*-lee	*stove-top (burners)*
il forno	eel *fohr*-noh	*oven*
il microonde	eel *mee*-kroh-*ohn*-deh	*microwave oven*

Talkin' the Talk

A mother and son are preparing for dinner. She asks him to set the table and sweep the floor in the **sala da pranzo** (*sah*-lah dah *prahn*-zoh) (dining room) before their guests arrive.

Mamma:	**Salvatore, per favore, passa la scopa prima che arrivino gli ospiti.**
	sahl-vah-*toh*-reh pehr fah-*voh*-reh *pahs*-sah lah *skoh*-pah *pree*-mah keh ahr-*ree*-vee-noh lyee *ohs*-pee-tee
	Salvatore, please sweep before the guests arrive.
Salvatore:	**Va bene, mamma.**
	vah *beh*-neh *mahm*-mah
	Okay, Mom.
	Che altro?
	keh *ahl*-troh
	What else?
Mamma:	**Apparecchia il tavolo, caro.**
	ahp-pah-*rek*-kyah eel *tah*-voh-loh *kah*-roh
	Set the table, dear.
Salvatore:	**Cosa ci metto?**
	koh-zah chee *meht*-toh
	What should I put out?
Mamma:	**Metti la tovaglia con i limoni con i suoi tovaglioli.**
	meht-tee lah toh-*vah*-lyah kohn ee lee-*moh*-nee kohn ee swoi toh-vahl-*yoh*-lee
	Put out the tablecloth with the lemons and the matching napkins.
Salvatore:	**Quali piatti?**
	kwah-lee *pyaht*-tee
	What dishes?
Mamma:	**Quelli di Faenza, il piano e il fondo.**
	kwehl-lee dee fahy-*enz*-ah eel *pyah*-noh eh eel *fohn*-doh
	The ones from Faenza, the flat ones and the bowls.
	Non dimenticare forchette, coltelli, e cucchiai per il brodetto.
	nohn dee-mehn-tee-*kah*-reh fohr-*keht*-teh kohl-*tehl*-lee eh koohk-*kyahy* pehr eel broh-*deht*-toh
	Don't forget forks, knives and spoons for the fish stew.

Salvatore: **Mamma, Non bastano i bicchieri per l'acqua.**
mahm-mah nohn *bahs*-tah-noh ee beek-*kyeh*-ree
pehr *lahk*-wah
Mom, there aren't enough water glasses.

Mamma: **Non importa, li ho qui nella lavastoviglie.**
nohn eem-*pohr*-tah lee oh kwee *nehl*-lah
lah-vah-stoh-*veel*-yeh
That's okay. I have them here in the dishwasher.

Aggiungiamo anche i bicchieri da vino. Grazie.
aj-joohn-*jah*-moh *ahn*-keh ee beek-*kyeh*-ree dah
vee-noh *grah*-tsee-eh
Let's add wine glasses, too. Thanks.

Words to Know

apparecchiare	ahp-pahr-ehk-kyah-reh	to set the table
bicchiere/i	beek-kyeh-reh/ee	glass/glasses
coltello/i	kohl-tehl-loh/ee	knife/knives
cucchiaio/chucchiai	koohk-kyahy-oh/ee	spoon/s
il (piatto) fondo	eel fohn-doh	bowl (for soup or pasta)
forchetta/e	fohr-keht-tah/eh	fork/s
il (il piatto) piano	eel pyah-noh	flat dish
piatto/i	pyaht-toh/ee	dish/dishes
scopa	skoh-pah	broom
sparecchiare	spah-rehk-kyah-reh	to clear the table
tovaglia	toh-vahl-yah	table-cloth
tovagliolo/i	toh-vahl-yoh-loh/lee	napkin/s

Did you know that some of the most beautiful ceramics are produced all over Italy? Many are hand-painted works of art unto themselves. Some towns well-known for their ceramics include Faenza (Emilia Romagna), Deruta (Umbria), Vietri (Amalfi Coast), and Caltagirone (Sicily). It might be hard to go into one of these towns and not buy some ceramics to bring back home.

Cooking and cleaning

If you love to **cucinare** (kooh-chee-*nah*-reh) (*cook*) you will certainly have fun buying your ingredients in an Italian market or supermarket. Maybe you're enrolled in an Italian cooking school in Tuscany this summer. But even if you're not in Italy and like to practice your Italian by listening to Italian cooking channels, you're going to need some essential kitchen words.

Talkin' the Talk

Listen to the following recipe by Amedeo, chef for the **Italiani in cucina** food network. This is only part of the recipe, but enough to get you started on some important kitchen terminology. (Track 10)

Amedeo: **Buongiorno e benvenuti a "Italiani in cucina." Oggi prepariamo le penne all'arrabbiata per quattro persone.**
bwohn *johr*-noh eh behn-veh-*nooh*-tee a ee-tahl-ee-*ah*-nee een kooh-*chee*-nah *ohj*-jee preh-pah-ree-*ah*-moh leh *pehn*-neh ahl-lahr-rahb-*byah*-tah pehr *kwaht*-troh pehr-*soh*-neh
Hello, and welcome to Italians in the Kitchen. Today we will be preparing penne all'arrabbiata for four people.

Gli ingredienti sono:
lyee een-greh-dee-*ehn*-tee *soh*-noh
The ingredients are:

500 grammi di pomodori
cheen-kweh-*chehn*-toh *grahm*-mee dee poh-moh-*doh*-ree
500 grams of tomatoes

Mezzo chilo di penne
medz-oh *kee*-loh dee *pehn*-neh
Half a kilo of penne

Un cucchiaio di peperonicino
oohn koohk-*kyahy*-oh dee pe-pehr-ohn-*chee*-noh
One tablespoon of hot pepper

Olio d'oliva extra vergine
ohl-yoh doh-*lee*-vah *ehxs*-trah *vehr*-jee-neh
Extra-virgin olive oil

Quattro spicchi di aglio
kwaht-troh *speek*-kee dee *ahl*-yoh
Four cloves of garlic

Un mazzetto di prezzemolo
oohn mats-*tseht*-toh dee prehts-*ehm*-oh-loh
A small bunch of parsley

Inoltre, avrete bisogno di:
een-*ohl*-treh ah-*vreh*-teh bee-*zoh*-nyoh dee
Furthermore, you will need:

una pentola grande per la pasta
ooh-nah *pehn*-toh-lah *grahn*-dah pehr lah *pahs*-tah
A large pot for the pasta

una padella grande per la salsa
ooh-nah pah-*dehl*-lah pehr lah *sahl*-sah
A large pan for the sauce

Sale e pepe
sah-leh eh *peh*-peh
Salt and pepper

Inanzitutto fai bollire una pentola grande di acqua per la pasta.
een-ahn-zee-*tooht*-toh fahy bohl-*lee*-reh *ooh*-nah *pehn*-toh-lah *grahn*-deh dee *ahk*-wah pehr lah *pahs*-tah
First of all, put a large pot of water for the pasta on to boil.

Doing household chores

Italians do like to keep a spic and span house. I don't know anyone who likes to clean house, but if you've found an Italian roommate and you're going to be dividing the chores, you may as well know how to say some of these things.

Talkin' the Talk

Jenny and Lucia are two new roommates who have just moved in together while attending the University of Bologna. They are dividing the household shores, or **faccende di casa** (fahch-*chehn*-deh dee *kah*-zah).

Jenny:	**Allora, come vogliamo dividere le faccende di casa?** ahl-*loh*-rah *koh*-meh vohl-*yah*-moh dee-*vee*-deh-reh leh fach-*chehn*-deh dee *kah*-zah So how should we divide the chores?
Lucia:	**Facciamo a settimane alternate.** fach-*chah*-moh ah seht-tee-*mah*-neh ahl-tehr-*nah*-teh Let's do alternating weeks.
Jenny:	**Una buon'idea.** *ooh*-nah *bwohn*-ee-*dey*-ah Good idea.
	Questa settimana io porto fuori la spazzatura e pulisco il bagno e la cucina. *kwehs*-tah seht-tee-*mah*-nah ee-oh *pohr*-toh *fwoh*-ree lah spats-ah-*tooh*-rah eh pooh-*lees*-koh eel *bahn*-yoh e la kooh-*chee*-nah This week I'll bring out the garbage and clean the bathroom and kitchen.
Lucia:	**Ed io passo la scopa e l'aspirapolvere e spolvero tutta la casa.** ehd ee-oh *pahs*-soh lah *skoh*-pah eh lahs-pee-rah-*pohl*-veh-reh eh *spohl*-veh-roh *tooht*-tah lah *kah*-zah And I'll sweep, vacuum, and dust the whole house.

Words to Know

camera	kah-meh-rah	room
lavare i pavimenti	lah-vah-reh ee pah-vee-mehn-tee	to wash the floors
mettere in ordine	meht-teh-reh een ohr-dee-neh	to straighten up
ognuno	ohn-yooh-noh	each person
passare l'aspirapolvere	pahs-sah-reh lahs-pee-rah-pohl-veh-reh	to vacuum
passare la scopa	pahs-sah-reh lah skoh-pah	to sweep
portare fuori la spazzatura	pohr-tah-reh fwoh-ree lah spats-ah-tooh-rah	to take out the garbage
pulire	pooh-lee-reh	to clean
spolverare	spohl-veh-rah-reh	to dust

Fun & Games

This is an easy one! Identify the various rooms and items marked with a solid, numbered line with their Italian names. For extra credit, keep on naming as many items as you can! See Appendix D for the answer key.

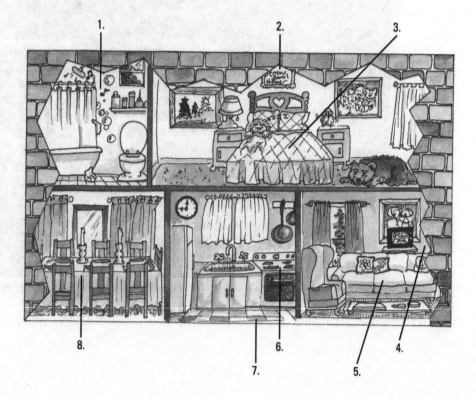

Chapter 6

Where Is the Colosseum? Asking Directions

· ·

In This Chapter

▶ Asking for directions

▶ Giving directions

▶ Understanding directions

· ·

Have you ever been lost in a foreign city or country? If so, you realize how helpful it is when you know enough of the native language to be able to ask for directions. Knowing the language also enables you to understand the answer. In this chapter, we give you some helpful conversational tips that make it easier to find your way around.

Finding Your Way: Asking for Specific Places

When asking for directions, it's always polite to start your question with one of the following expressions (which are friendly forms of the imperative or command tense):

Mi scusi. (mee *skooh*-zee) (*Excuse me, you singular, formal*)

Scusi. (*skooh*-zee) (*Excuse me, you singular, formal*)

Mi scusino. (mee *skooh*-zee-noh) (*Excuse me, you plural, formal*)

Scusa. (*skooh*-zah) (*Excuse me, you singular, informal*)

Scusate. (skooh-*zah*-teh) (*Excuse me, you plural, informal*)

or

Per favore. (pehr fah-*voh*-reh) (*Please.*)

Un'informazione. (oohn een-fohr-mahts-*yoh*-neh) (*I need some information.*)

Then you can continue with your questions, something like the following:

- **Dov'è il Colosseo?** (doh-*veh* eel koh-lohs-*seh*-oh) (*Where is the Colosseum?*)

- **È questa via Garibaldi?** (eh *kwehs*-tah *vee*-ah gah-ree-*bahl*-dee) (*Is this via Garibaldi?*)

- **Per la stazione?** (pehr lah stah-*tsyoh*-neh) (*How do I get to the station?*)

- **Può indicarmi la strada per il centro?** (pwoh een-dee-*kahr*-mee lah *strah*-dah pehr eel *chehn*-troh) (*Can you show me the way downtown?*)

- **Dove siamo adesso?** (*doh*-veh see-*ah*-moh ah-*dehs*-soh) (*Where are we now?*)

- **Mi sono perso. Dov'è il duomo?** (mee *soh*-noh *pehr*-soh. doh-*veh* eel *dwoh*-moh) (*I'm lost; where is the cathedral?*)

- **È qui vicino La Fontana di Trevi ?** (eh kwee vee-*chee*-noh lah fohn-*tah*-nah dee *treh*-vee) (*Is the Fountain of Trevi nearby?*)

Some possible answers, and not in any particular order (mix and match according to context!), to the preceding questions are:

- **Si è proprio qui vicino!** (see eh *proh*-pree-oh kwee vee-*chee*-noh) (*Yes, it is very close!*)

- **Segua la strada principale fino al centro.** (*seh*-gwah lah *strah*-dah preen-chee-*pah*-leh *fee*-noh ahl *chehn*-troh) (*Follow the main street to the center of the city.*)

- **Vada sempre dritto.** (*vah*-dah *sehm*-preh *dreet*-toh) (*Go straight ahead.*)

- **Dopo il semaforo giri a destra.** (*doh*-poh eel seh-*mah*-foh-roh *jee*-ree ah *dehs*-trah) (*After the traffic light, turn right.*)

- **È in fondo a sinistra.** (eh een *fohn*-doh ah see-*nees*-trah) (*It's at the end, on the left side.*)

- **È vicino alla posta.** (eh vee-*chee*-noh *ahl*-lah *pohs*-tah) (*It's next to the post office.*)

- **Attraversi il ponte, poi c'è una piazza e lì lo vede.** (aht-trah-*vehr*-see eel *pohn*-teh poi cheh *ooh*-nah *pyahts*-tsah eh lee loh *veh*-deh) (*Cross the bridge, then there's a square and there you see it.*)

- **È la terza strada a sinistra.** (eh lah *tehr*-tsah *strah*-dah ah see-*nees*-trah) (*It's the third street on the left.*)

- **È dopo il terzo semaforo a destra.** (eh *doh*-poh eel *tehr*-tsoh seh-*mah*-foh-roh ah *dehs*-trah) (*It's after the third light, on the right.*)

- **Ha sbagliato strada.** (ah sbah-*lyah*-toh *strah*-dah) (*You're on the wrong road.*)

Talkin' the Talk

Anna Maria and Robert are looking for the Trevi Fountain. They are on Rome's via del Corso, and stop to ask a Carabiniere (a type of police officer) for directions. Note that here the Carabiniere has used the Loro polite imperative form because he is speaking to two other adults whom he doesn't know.

Anna Maria:	**Scusi, è qui vicino La Fontana di Trevi?**
	skooh-zee eh kwee vee-*chee*-noh lah fohn-*tah*-nah dee *treh*-vee
	Excuse me, is the Fountain of Trevi nearby?
Carabiniere:	**Sì, è proprio qui vicino! Si girino a destra in Via delle Muratte e proseguano per all'incirca 200 metri.**
	see eh proh-*pree*-oh kwee vee-*chee*-noh. see *gee*-ree-noh ah *dehs*-trah een *vee*-ah *dehl*-leh mooh-*raht*-teh eh *proh*-seh-*gwah*-noh pehr ahl-leen-*cehr*-cah *dooh*-eh *chehn*-toh *meh*-tree
	Why yes, it's very close. Take a right at via delle Muratte and then keep going for about 200 meters.
Anna Maria:	**Molte grazie.**
	mohl-teh *grah*-tsee-eh
	Many thanks.
Carabiniere:	**Non c'e di che.**
	nohn cheh dee keh
	Don't mention it.

Mapping the quarters and following directions

Four orientations you already know are the cardinal points of the compass: north, south, east, and west. The four directions are especially helpful to know when you use a map. The following are **i quattro punti cardinali** (ee *kwaht*-troh *poohn*-tee kahr-dee-*nah*-lee) (*the four cardinal points*):

- ✔ **nord** (nohrd) (*north*)
- ✔ **est** (ehst) (*east*)

- ✔ **sud** (soohd) (*south*)
- ✔ **ovest** (*oh*-vehst) (*west*)

You may hear the directions used in sentences like the following:

- ✔ **Trieste è a nord-est.** (tree-*ehs*-teh eh ah nohrd-*ehst*) (*Trieste is to the northeast.*)
- ✔ **Napoli è a sud.** (*nah*-poh-lee eh ah soohd) (*Naples is to the south.*)
- ✔ **Roma è a ovest.** (*roh*-mah eh ah *oh*-vehst) (*Rome is to the west.*)
- ✔ **Bari è a sud-est.** (*bah*-ree eh ah soohd-*ehst*) (*Bari is to the southeast.*)

Some lovely city centers, such as the ones in Verona and Ravenna, are closed off to traffic, so you really need to go around by foot. It's important to know how to orient yourself in relation to people and buildings when following or giving directions. Italians also frequently use meters to describe distances on foot:

- ✔ **davanti a** (dah-*vahn*-tee ah) (*in front of*)
- ✔ **dietro a** (dee-*eh*-troh ah) (*behind*)
- ✔ **vicino a** (vee-*chee*-noh ah) (*beside; next to*)
- ✔ **di fronte a** (dee-*frohn*-teh ah) (*opposite*)
- ✔ **dentro** (*dehn*-troh) (*inside*)
- ✔ **fuori** (*fwoh*-ree) (*outside*)
- ✔ **sotto** (*soht*-toh) (*under; below*)
- ✔ **sopra** (*soh*-prah) (*above*)

You also need to know relationships between distance and **la direzione** (lah dee-reh-*tsyoh*-neh) (*the direction*):

- ✔ **dritto** (*dreet*-toh) (*straight*)
- ✔ **sempre dritto** (*sehm*-preh *dreet*-toh) (*straight ahead*)
- ✔ **fino a** (*fee*-noh ah) (*to; up to*)
- ✔ **prima** (*pree*-mah) (*before*)
- ✔ **dopo** (*doh*-poh) (*after*)
- ✔ **a destra** (ah *dehs*-trah) (*on the right*)
- ✔ **a sinistra** (ah see-*nees*-trah) (*on the left*)
- ✔ **dietro l'angolo** (dee-*eh*-troh *lahn*-goh-loh) (*around the corner*)
- ✔ **all'angolo** (ahl-*lahn*-goh-loh) (*at the corner*)
- ✔ **all'incrocio** (ahl-leen-*kroh*-choh) (*at the intersection*)

More vocabulary you can use for giving and receiving directions:

- **la calle** (lah *kahl*-leh) (*narrow Venetian street*; term found only in Venice)
- **il largo** (eel *lahr*-goh) (*wide square*)
- **il marciapiede** (eel mahr-chah-*pyeh*-deh) (*sidewalk*)
- **la piazza** (lah *pyahts*-tsah) (*square*)
- **il ponte** (eel *pohn*-teh) (*bridge*)
- **il sottopassaggio** (eel *soht*-toh-pahs-*sahj*-joh) (*underpass*)
- **la strada** (lah *strah*-dah) (*road; street*)
- **la via** (lah *vee*-ah) (*road; street*)
- **la via principale** (lah *vee*-ah preen-chee-*pah*-leh) (*main street*)
- **il viale** (eel vee-*ah*-leh) (*avenue*)
- **il vicolo** (eel *vee*-koh-loh) (*alley; lane*)

Talkin' the Talk

Laurie is visiting Florence from Oregon and has just finished a mid-morning coffee break in Piazza della Repubblica. She asks the man standing near her how to get to the post office.

Laurie: **Scusi, dov'è l'ufficio postale?**
skooh-zee doh-*veh* loohf-*feech*-oh poh-*stah*-leh
Excuse me, where is the post office?

Enzo: **È dietro l'angolo, là, sotto i portici. L'accompagno?**
eh dee-*eh*-troh *lahn*-goh-loh lah *soht*-toh ee *pohr*-tee-chee. lah-kohm-*pahn*-yoh
It's around the corner, over there there, underneath the porticoes. Shall I accompany you?

Laurie: **Grazie, No grazie, vado da sola.**
grah-tsee-eh. noh *grants*-ee-eh *vah*-doh dah *soh*-lah
Thank you. No thank you, I can go by myself.

La strada and **la via** are synonymous, but you always use **via** when the name is specified:

- **È una strada molto lunga.** (eh *ooh*-nah *strah*-dah *mohl*-toh *loohn*-gah) (*It's a very long road.*)
- **Abito in via Merulana.** (*ah*-bee-toh een *vee*-ah meh-rooh-*lah*-nah) (*I live in Via Merulana.*)

I thought you might want to know the translation and pronunciation of a famous Italian proverb you may have heard:

Tutte le strade portano a Roma. (*tooht*-teh leh *strah*-deh *pohr*-tah-noh ah *roh*-mah) (*All roads lead to Rome.*)

Talkin' the Talk

Mary is in **Bologna** *(boh-loh-*nyah*)* for the first time. She has visited the city and walked a lot, and now she wants to go back to the train station. Because she can't remember the way, she asks an older man. (Track 12)

Mary:	**Scusi?** *skooh*-zee Excuse me?
Man:	**Sì?** see Yes?
Mary:	**Dov'è la stazione centrale?** doh-*veh* lah stah-*tsyoh*-neh chehn-*trah*-leh Where is the central station?
Man:	**Prenda la prima a destra.** *prehn*-dah lah *pree*-mah ah *dehs*-trah Take the first right.
Mary:	**Poi?** poi Then?
Man:	**Poi la terza a sinistra.** poi lah *tehr*-tsah ah see-*nees*-trah Then the third left.
Mary:	**Sì?** see Yes?
Man:	**Poi la seconda, no la prima . . .** poi lah seh-*kohn*-dah noh lah *pree*-mah Then the second, no the first . . .

Mary: **Grazie: Prendo un taxi!**
grah-tsee-eh *prehn*-doh oohn *tah*-ksee
Thank you: I'll take a taxi!

Words to Know

la strada principale [f]	lah <u>strah</u>-dah <u>preen-chee-pah</u>-leh	main street
il semaforo [m]	eel seh-<u>mah</u>-foh-roh	traffic light
il ponte [m]	eel <u>pohn</u>-teh	bridge
la piazza [f]	lah <u>pyahts</u>-tsah	square
il centro [m]	eel <u>chehn</u>-troh	downtown; city center
la stazione [f]	lah stah-<u>tsyoh</u>-neh	station
il duomo [m]	eel <u>dwoh</u>-moh	cathedral
l'ufficio postale [f]	loh-<u>fee</u>-choh pohs-<u>tah</u>-leh	post office
la rotonda (f)	lah roh-<u>tohn</u>-dah	rotary

Verbs on the Move

You need to know certain verbs when trying to understand directions. Some of the verbs you'll find handy for finding your way include:

✔ **andare** (ahn-*dah*-reh) (*to go*)

✔ **girare a destra/a sinistra** (jee-*rah*-reh ah *dehs*-trah/ah see-*nees*-trah) (*to turn right/left*)

✔ **prendere** (*prehn*-deh-reh) (*to take*)

✔ **proseguire** (proh-seh-*gwee*-reh) (*to continue on*)

✔ **seguire** (seh-*gwee*-reh) (*to follow*)

✔ **tornare indietro** (tohr-*nah*-reh een-dee-*eh*-troh) (*to go back*)

Imperatives are useful verb forms to know in a variety of situations, including when you're trying to get around in unfamiliar territory. This list shows the informal verb form (**tu**), the formal verb form (**Lei**), the informal pl. form (**voi**) and the formal plural form (**Loro**). Check out Chapter 2 for help on deciding when to use formal or informal forms.

Appendix A provides you with the conjugations of some regular and irregular verbs.

✔ **Va/Vada/Andate/Vadano!** (vah/*vah*-dah/ahn-*dah*-teh/*vah*-dah-noh) (*Go!*)

✔ **Gira/Giri/Girate/Girino!** (*jee*-rah/*jee*-ree/ jee-*rah*-teh/ *jee*-ree-noh) (*Turn!*)

✔ **Prendi/Prenda/Prendete/Prendano!** (*prehn*-dee/*prehn*-dah/prehn-*deh*-teh/prehn-*dah*-noh) (*Take!*)

✔ **Prosegui/Prosegua/Proseguite/Proseguano!** (proh-*seh*-gwee/proh-*seh*-gwah/ proh-seh-*gwee*-teh/ proh-*seh*-gwah-noh) (*Go on!*)

✔ **Segui/Segua/Seguite/Seguano!** (*seh*-gwee/*seh*-gwah/ seh-*gwee*-teh/*seh*-gwah-noh) (*Follow!*)

✔ **Torna/Torni/Tornate/Tornino!** (*tohr*-nah/*tohr*-nee/tohr-*nan*-teh/*tohr*-nee-noh) (*Go back!*)

✔ **Attraversa/Attraversi/Attraversate/Attraversino!** (aht-trah-*vehr*-sah/ aht-trah-*vehr*-see/aht-trah-vehr-*sah*-teh/ aht-trah-*vehr*-see-noh) (*Cross!*)

Notice that the endings of these verbs vary, apparently without any consistent pattern. These aren't typing mistakes — they're determined by the ending of the infinitive form of the verb (-are, -ere, or -ire), and also whether or not these verbs are regular or irregular. The easiest way about this is to simply believe us and memorize the verbs and their endings. You may want to know how near or far you are from your destination. Some typical questions and responses are:

✔ **Quant'è lontano?** (kwahn-*teh* lohn-*tah*-noh) (*How far is it?*)

✔ **È molto lontano?** (eh *mohl*-toh lohn-*tah*-noh) (*Is it very far?*)

✔ **Quanto dista?** (*kwahn*-toh *dees*-tah) (*How far is it?*)

✔ **Saranno cinque minuti.** (sah-*rahn*-noh *cheen*-kweh mee-*nooh*-tee) (*About five minutes.*)

✔ **Circa un chilometro.** (*cheer*-kah oohn kee-*loh*-meh-troh) (*About one kilometer.*)

✔ **Non saranno più di 150 metri.** (Nohn sah-*rahn*-noh pyooh dee *chehn*-toh-cheen-*qwahn*-tah *meh*-tree). (*It's no more than 150 meters away.*)

✔ **No, un paio di minuti.** (noh oohn *pah*-yoh dee mee-*nooh*-tee) (*No, a couple of minutes.*)

✔ **Posso arrivarci a piedi?** (*pohs*-soh ahr-ree-*vahr*-chee ah *pyeh*-dee) (*Can I walk there?*)

✔ **Certo, è molto vicino.** (*chehr*-toh eh *mohl*-toh vee-*chee*-noh) (*Sure, it's very close.*)

✔ **È un po' lontano.** (eh oohn poh lohn-*tah*-noh) (*It's a bit far away.*)

✔ **È proprio a due passi.** (eh *proh*-pree-oh ah *dooh*-eh *pahs*-see) (*It's very close.* Literally: Just a couple of steps away.)

✔ **È all'incirca 20 metri di distanza.** (eh ahl-leen-*cheer*-kah *vehn*-tee *meh*-tree dee dees-*tahn*-zah) (*It's about 20 meters away.*)

Talkin' the Talk

Jenny and Lucy are visiting Rome and would like to walk to their favorite pizzeria in Trastevere from the converted monastery where they are staying. They ask the woman at the front desk how to get there.

Jenny: **Scusi, un'informazione, per favore.**
skooh-zee oohn een-fohr-mah-*tsyoh*-neh pehr fah-*voh*-reh
Excuse me, we'd like some information, please.

Woman: **Prego!**
preh-goh
How can I help you?

Jenny: **Quanto dista la pizzeria Ai marmi?**
kwahn-toh dees-tah lah peets-tseh-*ree*-ah ahy mahr-mee
How far is the pizzeria Ai marmi?

Woman: **È vicino, potete andarci a piedi facilmente.**
eh vee-chee-noh poh-teh-teh ahn-dahr-chee ah pyeh-dee fah-cheel-mehn-teh
It's close, you can get there easily on foot.

Woman:	**Quando uscite dall'albergo girate a destra, e all'incrocio girate ancora a destra. Proseguite in Viale Trastevere per all'incirca 100 metri e vedrete la pizzeria a sinistra.**
	qwahn-doh ooh-*shee*-teh *dahl*-lahl-*behr*-goh gee-*rah*-teh ah *deh*-strah eh ahl-leen-*kroh*-choh gee-*rah*-teh ahn-*koh*-rah ah *deh*-strah. proh-seh-*gwee*-teh in vee-*ah*-leh trah-*steh*-veh-reh pehr ahl-leen-*cheer*-kah *chehn*-toh *meh*-tree eh veh-*dreh*-teh lah peets-tsehr-ee-ah ah see-*nee*-strah
	When you leave the hotel take a right and then at the intersection take another right. Go down viale Trastevere for about 150 meters and you'll see the pizzeria on the left.
Lucy:	**Scusi, non ho capito, può ripetere più lentamente, per favore?**
	skooh-zee nohn oh kah-*pee*-toh. pwoh ree-*peh*-teh-reh pyooh *lehn*-tah-mehn-teh pehr fah-*voh*-reh
	I'm sorry, but I didn't understand. Would you please repeat a bit more slowly?
Woman:	**Certo! Allora, esci dall'albergo e giri a destra. Va bene?**
	chehr-toh ahl-*lohr*-ah ehsh-ee *dah*-lahl-*behr*-goh eh *gee*-rah *dehs*-trah vah *beh*-neh
	Of course. You leave the hotel and turn right. Okay?

What to say when you don't understand

Occasionally, maybe frequently, you may not understand the directions someone gives you. For those times, you need some useful polite expressions to ask the other person to repeat their directions.

✔ **Come, scusi?** (*koh*-meh *skooh*-zee) (*I beg your pardon?*) (formal)

✔ **Come, scusa?** (*koh*-meh *skooh*-zah) (*I beg your pardon?*) (informal)

✔ **Mi scusi, non ho capito.** (mee *skooh*-zee nohn oh kah-*pee*-toh) (*I'm sorry, I didn't understand.*)

✔ **Può ripetere più lentamente, per favore?** (pwoh ree-*peh*-teh-reh pyooh lehn-tah-*mehn*-teh pehr fah-*voh*-reh) (*Would you please repeat it more slowly?*)

When someone does you a favor — explaining the way or giving you directions — you probably want to thank him or her, and that's the easiest task: **Mille grazie!** (*meel*-leh *grah*-tsee-eh) (*Thank you very much!*)

Words to Know

numero [m]	<u>nooh</u>-meh-roh	number
minuto [m]	mee-<u>nooh</u>-toh	minute
lentamente	lehn-tah-<u>mehn</u>-teh	slowly
autobus [m]	<u>ou</u>-toh-boohs	bus
fermata [f]	fehr-<u>mah</u>-tah	bus stop
macchina [f]	<u>mahk</u>-kee-nah	car

Locations You May Be Looking For

When you're searching for a specific place, these sentences can help you ask the right questions.

- ✔ **Mi sa dire dov'è la stazione?** (mee sah *dee*-reh doh-*veh* lah stah-*tsyoh*-neh) (*Can you tell me where the station is?*)

- ✔ **Devo andare all'aeroporto. Quale strada devo prendere?** (*deh*-voh ahn-*dah*-reh *ahl*-lah-eh-roh-*pohr*-toh. *kwah*-leh *strah*-dah *dey*-voh *prehn*-deh-reh) (*I have to go to the airport. What road should I take?*)

- ✔ **Sto cercando il teatro Valle.** (stoh chehr-*kahn*-doh eel teh-*ah*-troh *vahl*-leh) (*I'm looking for the Valle theater.*)

- ✔ **Dov'è il cinema Astoria, per favore?** (doh-*veh* eel *chee*-neh-mah ahs-*toh*-ree-ah pehr fah-*voh*-reh) (*Where is the Astoria cinema, please?*)

- ✔ **Come posso arrivare al Museo Etrusco?** (*koh*-meh *pohs*-soh ahr-ree-*vah*-reh ahl mooh-*zeh*-oh eh-*trooh*-skoh) (*How can I get to the Etruscan Museum?*)

- ✔ **La strada migliore per il centro, per favore?** (lah *strah*-dah mee-*lyoh*-reh pehr eel *chehn*-troh pehr fah-*voh*-reh) (*The best way to downtown, please?*)

- ✔ **Che chiesa è questa?** (keh *kyeh*-zah eh *kwehs*-tah) (*What church is this?*)

✔ **Quale autobus va all'ospedale?** (*kwah*-leh *ou*-toh-boohs vah ahl-lohs-peh-*dah*-leh) (*Which bus goes to the hospital?*)

✔ **Come faccio ad arrivare all'università?** (*koh*-meh *fach*-choh ahd ahr-ree-*vah*-reh ahl-*looh*-nee-vehr-see-*tah*) (*How can I get to the university?*)

Talkin' the Talk

Peter wants to meet with a friend at a restaurant on via Torino. After getting off the bus, he asks a girl for directions. (Track 11)

Peter:	**Scusa?** *skooh*-zah Excuse me?
Girl:	**Dimmi.** *deem*-mee Yes, can I help you?.
Peter:	**Sto cercando via Torino.** stoh chehr-*kahn*-doh *vee*-ah toh-*ree*-noh I'm looking for via Torino.
Girl:	**Via Torino!?** *vee*-ah toh-*ree*-noh Via Torino!?
Peter:	**È qui vicino, no?** eh kwee vee-*chee*-noh noh It's close to here, isn't it?
Girl:	**No, è lontanissimo.** noh eh lohn-tah-*nees*-see-moh No, it's very far away.
Peter:	**Oddio, ho sbagliato strada!** ohd-*dee*-oh oh sbah-*lyah*-toh *strah*-dah Oh, heavens, I went the wrong way!
Girl:	**Devi prendere il 20 verso il centro.** *deh*-vee *prehn*-deh-reh eel *vehn*-tee *vehr*-soh eel *chehn*-troh You have to take the [bus number] 20 to the city center.

Talkin' the Talk

Amy Jo is spending her junior year abroad in Florence, and living with a family near the Boboli Gardens. She is at the Piazza Duomo and has to meet her roommate Oona at the Uffizi Gallery, but she is a little disoriented. (See Figure 6-1.) She asks a young street musician how to get there.

Amy Jo: **Scusa, un'informazione, per favore. Sono un po' persa.**
skooh-zah oohn-*een*-fohr-mah-*tsyoh*-neh perh fah-*voh*-reh. *soh*-noh oohn poh *pehr*-sah
Excuse me, I need some information please: I'm a little lost.

Musician: **Dimmi!**
deem-mee
Shoot!

Amy Jo: **Come posso arrivare alla Galleria degli Uffizi?**
koh-meh *pohs*-soh ahr-ree-*vah*-reh *ahl*-lah gahl-lehr-ee-ah *deh*-lyee ooh-*fee*-tsee
How can I get to the Uffizi Gallery?

Musician: **Non è lontano. Vai sempre dritto in Via dei Calzaiuoli finchè arrivi alla Piazza della Signoria. Guarda un po' in giro quando arrivi.**
nohn eh lohn-*tah*-noh. vahy *sehm*-preh *dreet*-toh een *vee*-ah dey *kahl*-tsahy-*woh*-lee feen-*keh* ahr-*ree*-vee *ahl*-lah *pyahts*-sah *dehl*-lah see-nyoh-*ree*-ah. *gwahr*-dah oohn poh in *gee*-roh *qwahn*-doh ahr-*ree*-vee
It's not far. Just go straight down Via dei Calzaiuoli until you get to the Piazza della Signoria. Look around when you get there.

Amy Jo: **Quanti minuti ci vogliono a piedi?**
kwahn-tee mee-*nooh*-tee chee *vohl*-yoh-noh ah *pyeh*-dee
How many minutes away is it on foot?

Musician: **Una decina.**
oohn-ah dech-*ee*-nah
About 10.

Amy Jo: **Grazie!**
grah-tsee-eh
Thank you!

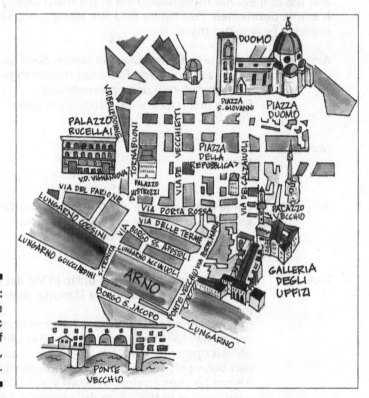

Figure 6-1:
Map of the
historic
district of
Florence,
Italy.

Words to Know

a destra	ah <u>dehs</u>-trah	to the right
a sinistra	ah see-<u>nees</u>-trah	to the left
stazione [f]	stah-<u>tsyoh</u>-neh	station
aeroporto [m]	ah-eh-roh-<u>pohr</u>-toh	airport
teatro [m]	teh-<u>ah</u>-troh	theater
cinema [m]	<u>chee</u>-neh-mah	cinema
chiesa [f]	<u>kyeh</u>-zah	church
ospedale [m]	ohs-peh-<u>dah</u>-leh	hospital
ponte (m)	<u>pohn</u>-teh	bridge

Fun & Games 1

Take a look at Figure 6.1, the map of Florence's city center, and provide the following information. See Appendix D for the answer key.

1. Palazzo Rucellai is in via _____.

2. Two bridges on this map are the _____ and the
_____.

3. The river that runs through Florence is called the _____.

4. A building that is attached to the Galleria degli Uffizi is the
_____.

5. The Duomo sits on what two piazzas? _____.

6. The roads running alongside the Arno have what word in common in their
names? _____

7. _____ looks like the main piazza in Florence's center.

Chapter 7

Food Glorious Food — and Don't Forget the Drink

• •

In This Chapter

▶ Eating, Italian style

▶ Ordering at the bar

▶ Reserving a table and paying for your meal

▶ Getting three meals a day (at least)

▶ Shopping for food

• •

You are probably familiar with a good amount of Italian food, such as spaghetti, ravioli, espresso, pizza, and pasta. Reading the sections in this chapter, you'll find a lot of information about food and drink, from marketing to dining out. This chapter invites you to take a closer look at some of the variations that make Italian food so famous. "Buon appetito!" (bwohn ahp-peh-*tee*-toh)! (*Enjoy!*)

Eating, Italian Style

Italians have three main meals: **la (prima) colazione** (lah *pree*-mah koh-lah-tsyoh-neh) (*breakfast*), **il pranzo** (eel *prahn*-zoh) (*lunch*), and **la cena** (lah *cheh*-nah) (*dinner*). **Uno spuntino** (*ooh*-noh spoohn-*tee*-noh) (*a snack*) is taken when you're hungry between main meals. **La merenda** (lah meh-*rehn*-dah) is snack-time that most children enjoy daily.

Drinking, Italian Style

This section talks about many sorts of drink, starting, obviously, with good Italian coffee, but covering also water, tea, and some spirits.

Expressing your love for espresso

You may have to order an espresso at your favorite coffee emporium back home, but in Italy, you get the same drink by asking the **barista** (bah-*rees*-tah) (*bar person*) or **il cameriere** (eel kah-meh-*ryeh*-reh) (*the waiter*) for just **un caffè** (oohn kahf-*feh*) (*a coffee*).

Italy's national drink: Espresso

Use the following terms exactly as you see them when ordering your coffee at the **bar** (caffè), and you will definitely be understood!

✔ **Un Caffè Hag** (oohn kahf-*feh* ahg) is a popular brand of instant decaffeinated coffee — every Italian knows it.

✔ Un **caffè** (kahf-*feh*): When you order **caffè**, you automatically get an espresso.

✔ Un caffè **ristretto** (ree-*streht*-toh): Very strong and concentrated espresso.

✔ un caffè **doppio** (*dohp*-pyoh): Double espresso.

✔ Un caffè **lungo** (*loohn*-goh): Espresso with more water to make it less concentrated.

✔ Un caffè **corretto** (kohr-*reht*-toh): Espresso with a bit of cognac or other liquor.

✔ Un **cappuccino** (kahp-pooh-*chee*-noh): Espresso with frothed milk.

✔ Un **caffelatte** (*kahf*-feh-*laht*-teh): Espresso with plenty of milk.

✔ Un caffè **macchiato** (mahk-*kyah*-toh): Espresso with a touch of milk.

✔ Un **latte macchiato** (*laht*-teh mahk-*kyah*-toh): Hot milk with just a touch of espresso.

✔ Un **caffè americano** (kahf-*feh* ah-meh-ree-*kah*-noh): American coffee but stronger — this type of coffee has become a new fashion.

✔ Un caffè **decaffeinato** (deh-kahf-feh-ee-*nah*-toh): Decaffeinated coffee.

✔ Un **caffè d'orzo** (kahf-*feh dohr*-zoh): Coffee substitute made from germinated, dried, and roasted barley. You can have it strong or light.

✔ **caffè freddo/shakerato** (kahf-*feh* frehd-doh/ sheh-keh-*rah*-toh): Iced espresso shaken like a martini with cane syrup and ice

And here are some tips to help you order your Italian coffee.

✔ Super-size coffee portions don't exist in Italy, and there is one size for a cappuccino and a caffelatte.

✔ Italians generally have their coffee while standing at the bar. The concept of coffee "to go" is one used primarily by tourists.

✔ Italians don't drink cappuccino after breakfast (11ish at the latest).

✔ And beware! A latte is precisely what it says — milk. If you're hankering for a glass of warm milk, say "Un bicchiere di latte tiepido (oohn bee-*kyeh*-reh dee *laht*-teh *tyeh*-pee-doh).

In addition to **caffè**, you can enjoy a nice cup of **cioccolata calda** (chohk-koh-*lah*-tah *kahl*-dah) (*hot cocoa*; cold chocolate milk doesn't exist in Italy); **tè** or **tè freddo** (teh *frehd*-doh) (*cold or iced tea*); infusi (een-*fooh*-zee) (*herbal teas*) with a **camomilla** (kah-moh-*mee*-lah), the perfect bed-time infusion; **succhi di frutta** (*soohk*-kee dee *frooht*-tah) (*fruit juices*); **spremute** (spreh-*mooh*-teh) (*fresh-squeezed fruit juice*); and a wide selection of water (*ah*-kqwah).

Not many Italians anywhere in Italy drink tap water. Most Italians drink **acqua minerale** (*ah*-kwah mee-neh-*rah*-leh) (*mineral water*), which can be **acqua gassata/gasata** (*ah*-kwah gas-*sah*-tah/gah-*zah*-tah) (*sparkling water*) also called **acqua frizzante** (*ah*-kwah freez-*zahn*-teh), or **acqua liscia** or **naturale** (*ah*-kwah *lee*-shah or nah-tooh-*rah*-leh) (*still water*).

In **estate** (ehs-*tah*-teh) (*summer*), you will seek **ghiaccio** (*gyahch*-choh) (*ice*) wherever you go because most bars will part with only one small piece.

When you order a drink in Italy, you may need to specify how much you want, such as a whole bottle, a carafe, or just a glass. Use the following words:

- **Una bottiglia di. . .** (*ooh*-nah boht-*tee*-lyah dee) (*A bottle of. . .*)

- **Un bicchiere di. . .** (oohn beek-*kyeh*-reh dee) (*A glass of . . .*)

- **Una caraffa di. . .** (*ooh*-nah kah-*rahf*-fah dee) (*A carafe of. . .*)

- **Mezzo litro di . . .** (*mehdz*-oh *lee*-troh dee) (*half a liter of . . .*)

- **Un quartino di . . .** (oohn kwahr-*tee*-noh dee) (*a quarter of a liter*)

When do you pay for your drinks in an Italian coffee bar? It depends. Normally, you have your coffee or whatever first and pay afterward. In little Italian bars, where just one or two people work behind the bar, you simply tell the cashier what you had and pay then. In bigger bars, and especially in large cities with many tourists, you first pay at the register, get a sales slip called a **scontrino** (skohn-*tree*-noh), and take that sales slip over to the **barista**.

Beverages with even more of a kick

Italy is also famous for its **vini** (*vee*-nee) (*wines*) and other fermented beverages, like the popular after-dinner drinks limoncello (lee-mohn-*chehl*-loh) and grappa (*grahp*-pah). Each region has its own many varieties of wine, so make certain you try some of the wines of the regions you visit.

Talkin' the Talk

Friends eating a casual meal in a trattoria (traht-tohr-ee-ah) are ordering wine to have with their meal. They are in Tuscany and have ordered **pappa al pomodoro** (pahp-pah ahl poh-moh-*doh*-roh) (a Tuscan bread soup) and one **bistecca alla fiorentina** (bee-*stehk*-kah *ahl*-lah fyohr-ehn-*tee*-nah) (a huge steak for two or more people).

Server:	**Ecco la lista dei vini.**
	ehk-koh lah *lees*-tah dey *vee*-nee
	Here's the wine list.
Laura:	**Che cosa ci consiglia?**
	keh *koh*-za chee kohn-*see*-lyah
	What do you recommend?
Server:	**Abbiamo un ottimo Chianti della casa.**
	ahb-b*yah*-moh oohn *oht*-tee-moh kee-*ahn*-tee
	dehl-lah *kah*-sah
	We have some great house Chianti.
Silvio:	**Prendiamo un po' di vino rosso, allora, con la bistecca.**
	prehn-*dyah*-moh oohn poh dee *vee*-noh rohs-soh
	ahl-*loh*-rah kohn lah bee-*stehk*-kah
	Let's get some red wine, then, to have with our steak.
Laura:	**Si, Quello della casa?**
	see. *kwehl*-loh *dehl*-lah *kah*-sah
	Yes. The house wine?
Silvio:	**Perfetto!**
	pehr-*feht*-toh
	Perfect!

In Italy, the **aperitivo** (ah-pehr-ah-*tee*-voh), or before-dinner drink, is usually taken at the bar, either standing or seated at a **tavolino** (tah-voh-*lee*-noh) (*small table*). **Campari** and **prosecco** (*a dry sparkling wine*) are two major aperitivi, but you can also get alcohol-free aperitivi like **un Crodino** or **un Sanbitter**. The aperitivo is frequently served with a delectable assortment of free munchies.

Talkin' the Talk

Teresa and Laura are meeting around 7:00 p.m. before going out to dinner. They are at a table outdoors.

Server (Remo):   **Ditemi!**
dee-teh-mee
How can I help you?

Teresa: **Io prendo un Bitter Campari con una fetta di arancia.**
ee-oh prehn-doh oohn bee-tehr kahm-pah-ree kohn ooh-nah feht-tah dee ah-rahn-chah
I'll have a Campari with a slice of orange

Laura: **Per me un prosecco, grazie.**
pehr meh oohn proh-sehk-koh grah-tsee-eh
For me a prosecco, thank you.

Remo: **Altro?**
ahl-troh
Anything else?

Teresa: **Avete delle noccioline?**
ah-veh-teh dehl-leh noch-choh-lee-neh
Do you have any peanuts?

Remo: **No, mi dispiace, sono finite.**
noh mee dees-pyah-cheh soh-noh fee-nee-teh
I'm sorry, we're all out.

You may prefer to get a birra (beer-rah) (beer) grande or piccola (grahn-deh or peeh-koh-lah), either in a bottiglia (boht-tee-lyah) (bottle) or alla spina (ahl-lah spee-nah) (draft beer).

The Start and End of Dining Out

One of the more enjoyable (if potentially fattening) ways to explore a new culture is to sample the native cuisine. People interested in Italian cuisine are lucky — Italian-style restaurants are plentiful in North America. You can eat in a pizza joint, or enjoy a traditional, multi-course meal in a classy restaurant. And, if you're fortunate enough to actually travel to Italy, your taste buds are in for a real treat! Just be aware that pizza and pasta are different in Italy than in the United States.

This section discusses the beginning and endings of meals — from making reservations to paying the tab.

Making reservations

Unless you're going to a pizzeria or the **trattoria** (traht-toh-*ree*-ah) (*little restaurant*) down the street, you may need to reserve a table in a nice Italian restaurant.

Talkin' the Talk

Mr. Di Leo calls for reservations at his favorite restaurant. (Track 13)

Waiter:
Pronto. Ristorante Roma.
prohn-toh rees-toh-*rahn*-teh *roh*-mah
Hello! Roma Restaurant.

Sig. Di Leo:
Buonasera. Vorrei prenotare un tavolo.
bwoh-nah-*seh*-rah *vohr*-rey preh-noh-*tah*-reh oohn *tah*-voh-loh
Good evening! I would like to reserve a table.

Waiter:
Per stasera?
pehr stah-*seh*-rah
For this evening?

Sig. Di Leo:
No, per domani.
noh pehr doh-*mah*-nee
No, for tomorrow.

Waiter:
Per quante persone?
pehr *kwahn*-teh pehr-*soh*-neh
For how many people?

Sig. Di Leo:
Per due.
pehr *dooh*-eh
For two.

Waiter:
A che ora?
ah keh *oh*-rah
At what time?

Sig. Di Leo:	**Alle nove.**
	ahl-leh *noh*-veh
	At nine.
Waiter:	**A che nome?**
	ah keh *noh*-meh
	In whose name?
Sig. Di Leo:	**Di Leo.**
	dee *leh*-oh
	Di Leo.

Words to Know

tavolo [m]	tah-voh-loh	table
cameriere [m]	kah-meh-ryeh-reh	waiter
domani [m]	doh-mah-nee	tomorrow
prenotazione [f]	preh-noh-tah-tsyoh-neh	reservation
stasera [f]	stah-seh-rah	this evening

Paying for your meal

You don't need to use cash in all restaurants. There are many, mostly higher-end ones, where you can pay with your credit card, too.

No one tips in Italy; truly, not even in an elegant restaurant. You always pay **pane e coperto**, (*pah*-neh eh koh-*pehr*-toh), a cover or service charge, just to sit down.

When you want the bill **il conto** (eel *kohn*-toh) you ask the server "to bring" it to you. She will never bring it to you unless you ask for it. Use the verbs **portare** (pohr-*tah*-reh) or **fare** (*fah*-reh) and say:

Ci porta/fa il conto, per favore? (chee *pohr*-tah eel *kohn*-toh perh fah-*voh*-reh) (*Will you please bring us the bill?*) (formal)

Or simply

Il conto, per favore! (eel *kohn*-toh pehr fah-*voh*-reh) (*The bill please.*)

Save that sales slip

Be sure to keep **lo scontrino** (loh skohn-*tree*-noh) (*the sales slip*), at least until you leave an Italian bar or any kind of shop or restaurant. This is important in Italy because **la Guardia di Finanza** (lah *gwahr*-dee-ah dee fee-*nahn*-tsah) (*Financial Guard*) often checks. If you leave without a sales slip and are caught, you and the owner of the establishment have to pay a fine.

Having Breakfast

Your first meal of the day is always **la prima colazione** (lah *pree*-mah koh-lah-*tsyoh*-neh) (*breakfast*).

Some Italians begin the day with **un caffè** (oohn kahf-*feh*) (*espresso*) at home, but many stop for breakfast in **un bar** (oohn bahr) on their way to work. Breakfast consists of coffee and **una pasta** (*ooh*-nah *pahs*-tah) (*a pastry*), which can be **salata** (sah-*lah*-tah) (*savory*), **semplice** (*sehm*-plee-cheh) (*plain*) or filled with **marmellata** (mahr-mehl-*lah*-tah) (*jam*), **crema** (*kreh*-mah) (*custard*), or **cioccolato** (chohk-koh-*lah*-toh) (*chocolate*).

Talkin' the Talk

The man behind the counter in a coffee bar in Italy is called **il barista** (eel bah-*rees*-tah) (the barman).

Barista:	**Buongiorno!** bwohn-*johr*-noh Good morning!
Sig. Zampieri:	**Buongiorno! Un caffè e una pasta alla crema per favore.** bwohn-*johr*-noh oohn kahf-*feh* eh *ooh*-nah *pahs*-tah ahl-lah *kreh*-mah pehr fah-*voh*-reh Good morning! One espresso and a custard pastry please.
Barista:	**Qualcos'altro?** qwahl-kohs-*ahl*-troh Anything else?

Sig. Zampieri:	**Una spremuta d'arancia, per favore.**
	ooh-nah spreh-*mooh*-tah dah-*rahn*-chah pehr fah-*voh*-reh
	One fresh-squeezed orange juice, please.
Barista:	**Ecco la spremuta. Prego.**
	ehk-koh lah spreh-*mooh*-tah *preh*-goh
	Here's the juice. Here you go.

Eating Lunch

Italians do **il pranzo** (eel *prahn*-zoh) lunch differently from many other countries. The traditional courses are:

✔ **antipasto** (ahn-tee-*pahs*-toh) (*appetizer*): Usually served hot and cold, **antipasti** vary from region to region.

✔ **primo piatto** (*pree*-moh *pyaht*-toh) (*first course*): Although this comes after the antipasto, it is still called a first course): The **primo** consists of all kinds of **pasta** (*pahs*-tah) (*pasta*), **risotto** (ree-*zoht*-toh) (*risotto*), (or **minestra** (mee-*nehs*-trah) (*soup*).

✔ **il secondo** (eel seh-*kohn*-doh) (*the second course*): This generally consists of **carne** (*kahr*-neh) (*meat*) or **pesce** (*peh*-sheh) (*fish*), prepared in a wide variety of ways.

✔ **contorni** (kohn-*tohr*-nee) (*side dishes*): Vegetables may be ordered separately.

✔ **il dolce** (eel *dohl*-cheh) (the dessert): Last, but certainly not least, dessert may be **un dolce** (oohn *dohl*-cheh) (a sweet), **frutta fresca** (*froot*-tah *frehs*-kah) (fresh fruit), or **una macedonia** (*ooh*-nah mah-cheh-*doh*-nee-ah) (fruit salad).

Figure 7-1 shows a typical Italian lunch menu.

The verb **prendere** (*prehn*-deh-reh) (literally: to take, but here, to have) is the verb to use when talking about food and drinks.

Conjugation	*Pronunciation*
io prendo	*ee*-oh *prehn*-doh
tu prendi	tooh *prehn*-dee
lui/lei prende	*looh*-ee/ley *prehn*-deh
noi prendiamo	noi prehn-dee-*ah*-moh
voi prendete	voi prehn-*deh*-teh
loro prendono	*loh*-roh *prehn*-doh-noh

Figure 7-1:
A typical
Italian lunch
menu, from
antipasti to
il dolce.

Pasta usually means durum wheat made with flour and water. The different types include: **spaghetti** (spah-*geht*-tee) (*spaghetti*), **bucatini** (booh-kah-*tee*-nee) (*thick, tube-like spaghetti*), **penne** (*pehn*-neh) (*short, cylinder-shaped pasta shaped to a point at each end*), **fusilli** (fooh-*zeel*-lee) (*spiral-shaped pasta*), **rigatoni** (ree-gah-*toh*-nee) (*short, cylinder-shaped, and grooved pasta*), and so on.

On the other hand, **pasta fresca** (*pahs*-tah *frehs*-kah) (*fresh pasta*) means **pasta all'uovo** (*pahs*-tah ahl-*lwoh*-voh) (*egg noodles*), also called **pasta fatta in casa** (*pahs*-tah *faht*-tah een *kah*-sah) (*home made pasta*). These are **tagliatelle** (tah-lyah-*tehl*-leh) (*flat noodles*), **fettuccine** (feht-toohch-*chee*-neh) (*narrow, flat noodles*), and **tonnarelli** (tohn-nah-*rehl*-lee) (*tubular noodles*), to mention just a few.

Incidentally, when you have a bite of pasta, you should make sure that it is **al dente** (ahl *dehn*-teh) (Literally: *to the tooth*. It means that the pasta is a little hard so that you really need to use your teeth!)

The many meanings of "prego"

Prego (*preh*-goh) has several meanings. When you say it in response to grazie (*grah*-tsee-eh) (*thank you*), it means "you're welcome." But clerks and servers also use it to ask you what you would like or if they can help you. You often hear prego when you enter a public office or shop. You also use prego when you give something to someone. In this case, the word is translated as "here you are." Prego is also a very formal answer when you ask for permission. Following are a few examples of how prego is used:

✔ Grazie. (*grah*-tsee-eh) (*Thank you.*)

   Prego. (*preh*-goh) (*You're welcome.*)

✔ Prego? (*preh*-goh) (*Can I help you?*)

   Posso entrare? (*pohs*-soh ehn-*trah*-reh) (*May I come in?*)

   Prego. (*preh*-goh) (*Please.*)

✔ Prego, signore. (*preh*-goh see-*nyoh*-reh) (*Here you are, sir.*)

   Grazie. (*grah*-tsee-eh) (*Thank you.*)

The following conjugation shows you the polite form of the verb **volere** (voh-*leh*-reh) (*to want*). You have another verb for when you're being polite: "to like." Italian, however, uses a conditional to express politeness.

Conjugation	*Pronunciation*
io vorrei	*ee*-oh vohr-*rey*
tu vorresti	too vohr-*rehs*-tee
lui/lei vorrebbe	*looh*-ee/ley vohr-*rehb*-beh
noi vorremmo	noi vohr-*rehm*-moh
voi vorreste	voi vohr-*rehs*-teh
loro vorrebbero	*loh*-roh vohr-*rehb*-beh-roh

Enjoying Dinner

Italians often have **la cena** (lah *cheh*-nah) (*supper*) at home, but they also eat out. In this chapter, you are also introduced to the different types of eateries available to you. Supper time varies throughout the peninsula; for example, restaurants in Venice stop serving dinner earlier than those in Rome, where you can go as late as 9 or 10 p.m.

Talkin' the Talk

A group of friends gather at a local pizzeria for dinner. Their exchanges are quite informal. (Track 14)

Sandra: **Che cosa prendiamo?**
            keh *koh*-zah prehn-dee-*ah*-moh
            What should we have?

Laura: **Non lo so! Guardiamo il menù.**
            nohn loh soh gwahr-dee-*ah*-moh eel meh-*nooh*
            I don't know! Let's look at the menu.

Silvio: **Avete fame?**
            ah-veh-teh *fah*-meh
            Are you hungry?

Laura: **Ho fame; prendo una pizza margherita.**
            oh *fah*-meh *prehn*-doh *ooh*-nah *peet*-tsah
            mahr-gehr-*ee*-tah
            I'm hungry; I'm getting a pizza margherita.

Sandra: **Io non tanto.**
            ee-oh nohn *tahn*-toh
            I'm not so hungry.

Silvio: **Allora cosa prendi Sandra?**
            ahl-*loh*-rah *koh*-zah *prehn*-dee *sahn*-drah
            So what are you going to have, Sandra?

Sandra: **Vorrei qualcosa di leggero.**
            vohr-*rey* kwahl-*koh*-zah dee lehj-*jeh*-roh
            I'd like something light.

            Un'insalatona.
            oohn-een-sah-*lah*-toh-nah
            A big salad.

Silvio: **Poco originale . . .**
            pohk-koh oh-ree-jee-*nah*-leh
            Kind of boring . . .

Most Italian pizzerias have a wide range of pizzas. They are individual servings. You can also get pasta and salads there, and afterwards a dessert.

You have certainly heard of Italian **gelato** (jeh-*lah*-toh) (*ice cream*). Go for the **gelato artigianale** (jeh-*lah*-tee ahr-tee-jah-*nah*-lee) (*homemade ice cream* — made in a **gelateria** (jeh-lah-teh-*ree*-ah). You can have it in a **cono** (*koh*-noh) (*cone*) or a **coppetta** (kohp-*peht*-tah) (*cup*). You also have to decide on the **gusto** (*goohs*-toh) (*flavor*) and size, which usually goes according to euros or according to **palline** (pahl-*lee*-neh) (*scoops*).

Talkin' the Talk

 Laura and Silvio stop for some ice cream. (Track 15)

Server:	**Prego?** *preh*-goh What would you like?
Laura:	**Due coni, per favore.** *dooh*-eh *koh*-nee pehr fah-*voh*-reh Two ice cream cones, please.
Server:	**Da quanto?** dah *kwahn*-toh What size?
Silvio:	**Uno da due euro, e l'altro da 1 euro e 50.** *oohn*-oh dah *dooh*-eh *eh*-ooh-roh eh *lahl*-troh dah oohn *eh*-ooh-roh eh cheen-*qwahn*-tah One two-euro size and one for 1½ euros.
Server:	**Che gusti?** keh *goohs*-tee Which flavors?
Silvio:	**Fragola e limone.** *frah*-goh-lah eh lee-*moh*-neh Strawberry and lemon.
Server:	**Prego. E Lei?** *preh*-goh eh ley Here you are. And you?
Laura:	**Crema, cioccolato, cocco, e noce.** *kreh*-mah chohk-koh-*lah*-toh *kohk*-koh eh *noh*-cheh Custard, chocolate, coconut, and walnut.

Silvio:	**3 euro e 50?**
	treh *eh*-ooh-roh eh cheen-*qwahn*-tah
	Three and a half euros?
Server:	**Sì, grazie. Ecco lo scontrino.**
	See, *grats*-ee-eh *ehk*-koh loh *skohn*-tree-noh
	Yes, thanks. Here's the receipt.

In a **gelateria**, you can also find **frullati** (froohl-*lah*-tee) (*mixed fruit juice*), **frappé** (frahp-*peh*) (which can be a *fruit milk shake* or a *frozen fruit shake*), and **lo yogurt** (*frozen yogurt*).

Shopping for Food

Many people do their marketing in a **supermercato** (*sooh*-pehr-mehr-*kah*-toh) (*supermarket*) even if there are other places to get it. But most Italian cities have specialty shops, starting with the **alimentari** (ah-lee-mehn-*tah*-ree), where you can get many items . . . everything from **latte** (*laht*-teh) (*milk*) to toilet paper (*kahr*-tah ee-*jeh*-nee-kah) **carta igienica**. These shops, with their specific selection of goods, provide the personal attention often lacking in supermarkets.

Al macellaio (ahl mah-chehl-lahy-oh) (at the butcher's)

From the butcher shop you might select items like the following:

- **agnello** (ah-*nyehl*-loh) (*lamb*)
- **coniglio** (koh-*nee*-lyoh) (*rabbit*)
- **maiale** (mah-*yah*-leh) (*pork*)
- **manzo** (*mahn*-zoh) (*beef*)
- **pollo** (*pohl*-loh) (*chicken*)
- **vitello** (vee-*tehl*-loh) (*veal*)
- **bistecca** (bees-*tehk*-kah) (*steak*)

Pesce (fish) (peh-sheh)

Not all restaurants serve fresh fish. To be sure, the better restaurants offer fresh (not frozen) fish, and this is usually listed as a special of the day. Getting fresh fish certainly depends on the region, such as if you're close to the sea or not. If you are in doubt about the fish a restaurant offers, it's better to ask someone local for a recommendation. Better safe than sorry!

> **Dove si può mangiare il pesce fresco?** (*doh*-veh see pwoh mahn-*jah*-reh eel *peh*-sheh *frehs*-koh) (*Where can we eat fresh fish?*)

Some common types of fish, depending on the region, include:

- ✔ **acciughe fresche** (ahch-*chooh*-geh *frehs*-keh) (*fresh anchovies*)
- ✔ **calamari** (kah-lah-*mah*-ree) (*squid*)
- ✔ **seppia** (*sehp*-pee-ah) (*cuttlefish*)
- ✔ **branzino** (brahn-*zee*-noh) (*sea bass*)
- ✔ **orata** (*oh*-rah-tah) (*sea bream*)
- ✔ **merluzzo** (mehr-*loot*-tsoh) (*cod*)
- ✔ **polpo/polipo** (*pohl*-poh poh-*lee*-poh) (*octopus*)
- ✔ **pesce spada** (*peh*-sheh *spah*-dah) (*swordfish*)
- ✔ **sogliola** (soh-*lyoh*-lah) (*sole*)
- ✔ **spigola** (*spee*-goh-lah) (*snapper*)
- ✔ **tonno fresco** (*tohn*-noh *frehs*-koh) (*fresh tuna*)
- ✔ **frutti di mare** (*frooht*-tee dee *mah*-reh) (*shell fish*)
- ✔ **cozze** (*koht*-tseh) (*mussels*)
- ✔ **vongole** (*vohn*-goh-leh) (*clams*)
- ✔ **gamberetti** (gahm-beh-*reht*-tee) (*small shrimp*)
- ✔ **gamberi** (*gahm*-beh-ree) (*prawns*)

Common simple preparations are **al forno** (ahl-*for*-noh) (*baked*), **alla griglia** (*ahl*-lah *greel*-yah) (*grilled*), and **in padella** (een pah-*dehl*-lah) (*in the skillet*).

At the panetteria (breadshop)

In a **panetteria** (pah-neht-teh-*ree*-ah) (*breadshop*), you can try all sorts of different kinds of **pane** (*pah*-neh) (*bread*), as well as some oven-baked **dolci** (*dohl*-chee) (*sweets*).

In some Italian breadshops, you can also find **pizza al taglio** (*peet*-tsah ahl *tah*-lyoh) (*slices of pizza*) and **focaccia** (foh-*ka*-chah), and pay according to weight.

Talkin' the Talk

Sig.ra Belli:	**Ha del pane biologico?** ah dehl *pah*-neh bee-oh-*loh*-jee-koh Do you have any organic bread?
Baker:	**Ho dei panini, o questo tipo Matera, tutti cotti nel forno a legna.** oh dey pah-*nee*-nee oh *kwehs*-toh *tee*-poh mah-*teh*-rah *tooht*-tee *kot*-tee nehl *fohr*-noh ah *lehn*-yah I have these rolls or this Matera-style one all baked in our wood-burning oven.
Aig.ra Belli	**Mi dà quello rustico per favore.** mee dah *kwehl*-loh *rooh*-stee-koh peh fah-*voh*-reh I'll take that hard-crust one please.
	Quant'è? kwahn-*teh* How much is it?
Baker:	**3 euro e 50 centesimi.** treh *eh*-ooh-roh eh cheen-*qwahn*-tah chehn-*teh*-zee-mee Three euros and 50 cents.
Sig.ra Belli	**Grazie e arrivederla.** *grats*-ee-eh eh ahr-ree-veh-*dehr*-lah *Thank you, and good-bye.*

Baker:	**Desidera?**
to another	deh-*zee*-deh-rah
customer:	What would you like?

Paolo:	**Un pezzo di pizza al pomodoro.**
	oohn *peht*-tsoh dee *peet*-tsah ahl poh-moh-*doh*-roh
	A piece of pizza with tomatoes.

Baker:	**Così va bene?**
	koh-*zee* vah *beh*-neh
	Is this okay?

Paolo	**Un po' più grande, per favore.**
	oohn poh pyooh *grahn*-deh pehr fah-*voh*-reh
	A little bigger please.

Baker	**Così?**
	koh-*zee*
	Like this?

Items are priced according to weight, usually by **chilo** (*kee*-loh) (*kilo*). You know that when you hear **un etto** (oohn *eht*-toh), it means 100 grams. **Mezz'etto** (mehdz-*tseht*-toh) is 50 grams, because **mezzo** (*mehdz*-tsoh) means "half." Likewise, a **mezzo chilo** (*mehdz*-tsoh *kee*-loh) is half a kilo. Meat, fish, fruits, cheese, cold cuts and vegetables are sold by weight.

Table 7-1 lists common fruits and vegetables that you might find at an open-air farmer's market.

Table 7-1	**Fruits and Vegetables**	
Italian/Plural	*Pronunciation*	*Translation*
albicocca/albicocche [f]	ahl-bee-*kohk*-kah/-keh	*apricot/s*
ananas [m]	*ah*-nah-nahs	*pineapple*
arancia/arance [f]	ah-*rahn*-chah/-cheh	*orange/s*
asparago/i [m]	ah-*spah*-rah-goh/-jee	*asparagus*
banana/e [f]	bah-*nah*-nah/-neh	*banana/s*
broccoli [m]	*brohk*-koh-lee	*broccoli*
carota/e [f]	kah-*roh*-tah/-teh	*carrot/s*

(continued)

Table 7-1 *(continued)*

Italian/Plural	Pronunciation	Translation
cavolo/i [m]	*kah*-voh-loh/-lee	cabbage/s
ciliegia/e [f]	chee-*lyeh*-jah/-jeh	cherry/cherries
cocomero/i [m]	koh-*koh*-meh-roh/-ree	watermelon/s
fico/fichi [m]	*fee*-koh/-kee	fig/s
fragola/e [f]	*frah*-goh-lah/-leh	strawberry/strawberries
fungo/funghi [m]	*foohn*-goh/-gee	mushroom/s
limone/i [m]	lee-*moh*-neh/-nee	lemon/s
mela/e [f]	*meh*-lah/-leh	apple/s
melanzana/e [f]	meh-lahn-*zah*-nah/-neh	eggplant/s
melone/i [m]	meh-*loh*-neh/-nee	melon/s
peperone/i [m]	peh-peh-*roh*-neh/-nee	pepper/s
pera/e [f]	*peh*-rah/-reh	pear/s
pesca/pesche [f]	*pehs*-kah/-keh	peach/es
pomodoro/i [m]	poh-moh-*doh*-roh/-ree	tomato/es
pompelmo/i [m]	pohm-*pehl*-moh/-mee	grapefruit/s
prugna/e [f]	*prooh*-nyah/-nyeh	plum/s
spinaci [m]	spee-*nah*-chee	spinach
uva [f]	*ooh*-vah	grapes
zucchino/i [f/m]	dzoohk-*kee*-noh/-nee	zucchini

CULTURAL WISDOM

The typical Italian market

You may recognize typical Italian markets from a vacation or maybe from watching a film. Some of them seem to be made exclusively for tourists, but Italians themselves use them. You may think that haggling and bargaining are common at Italian markets, but this is not true. You can certainly try it with a leather jacket at the market in a big city like Florence, but it's better to leave it alone when buying food items.

Fun & Games

We talk a lot about food in this chapter. To reward ourselves at the end, we allow ourselves a really good fruit shake. Fill in the Italian for the following various fruits. See Appendix D for the answer key. Have fun!

1. pineapple _ _ _ _ _ _

2. cherry _ _ _ _ _ _ _ _

3. grape _ _ _

4. pear _ _ _ _

5. watermelon _ _ _ _ _ _ _ _ _

6. strawberry _ _ _ _ _ _ _

Chapter 8

Shopping, Italian Style

In This Chapter

▶ Shopping at department stores and boutiques

▶ Getting the right size

▶ Finding colors, materials, and accessories to suit you

▶ Trying on shoes

Italy is famous throughout the world for its fashion, **la moda** (lah *moh*-dah), as well as for its **stilisti** (stee-*lees*-tee) (*designers*) — such as **Armani** (ahr-*mah*-nee) and **Valentino** (vah-lehn-*tee*-noh). You might suddenly feel inspired to shop, and what better place to shop than in Italy! In Italian, a famous brand is called **la griffe** (lah greef) (a French word) or **la firma** (lah *feer*-mah) that means literally "the signature." So to say that a good is "signed" (designed) by a famous stylist we say that it is **griffato** (greef-*fah*-toh) or **firmato** (feer-*mah*-toh) — "signed."

Clothing Yourself

Shopping can be an informative and fun way to learn about a culture because of the ways that colors and fabrics differ. For example, you can always tell what color is in fashion and how careful Italians are about wearing ironed clothes just by walking down a city street. In Italy, you can explore lots of boutiques and designer shops, as well as numerous department stores.

Deciding between department stores and boutiques

North Americans have access to huge **centri commerciali** (*chehn*-tree kohm-*mehr*-chah-lee) (*shopping malls*), where you really can find everything. In Italy, people shop in **grandi magazzini** (*grahn*-dee mah-gaht-*dzee*-nee) (*department stores*), which are tiny compared to American ones. The biggest Italian department stores are **Coin** (koh-*ehn*), **Upim** (*ooh*-peem), and **Rinascente** (ree-nah-*shehn*-teh). All three carry a variety of items; however, many Italians prefer to shop in smaller, privately owned stores where service is key (and where there is little to no browsing and self-service).

Incidentally, what's shopping in Italian? They say **fare la spesa** (*fah*-reh la *speh*-zah) when you buy food, and **fare spese** and **fare lo shopping** (*fah*-reh loh *shohp*-peeng) for everything else. Good news is that you only have to conjugate the verb **fare**. (See Chapter 2 and Appendix A for this verb conjugated).

In some places, you will notice some elementary signs — like the one over the door reading **uscita di sicurezza** (ooh-*shee*-tah dee see-kooh-*reht*-tsah) (*emergency exit*) — can be very useful. Some of these are:

- ✔ **entrata** (ehn-*trah*-tah) (*entrance*)
- ✔ **uscita** (ooh-*shee*-tah) (*exit*)
- ✔ **spingere** (*speen*-jeh-reh) (*to push*)
- ✔ **tirare** (tee-*rah*-reh) (*to pull*)
- ✔ **orario di apertura** (oh-*rah*-ree-oh dee ah-pehr-*tooh*-rah) (*business hours*)
- ✔ **aperto** (ah-*pehr*-toh) (*open*)
- ✔ **chiuso** (*kyooh*-zoh) (*closed*)
- ✔ **la scala mobile** (lah *skah*-lah *moh*-bee-leh) (*escalator*)
- ✔ **l'ascensore** (lah-shehn-*soh*-reh) (*elevator*)
- ✔ **la cassa** (lah *kahs*-sah) (*cash register*)

Italian stores offer a great variety of products and still maintain an air of typical Italian style. Prices are clearly labeled in euros. Often, during **saldi** (*sahl*-dee) and **svendite** (*zvehn*-dee-teh) (*sales*), the **il prezzo** (eel *preht*-tsoh) (*price*) on the label is already reduced, but you may find tags reading **saldi alla cassa** (*sahl*-dee ahl-lah *kahs*-sah) (*reduction at the cash register*).

Following are some signs pointing to the various **reparti** (reh-*pahr*-tee) (*departments*) or individual boutiques.

- ✔ **abbigliamento da donna/ da uomo** (ahb-bee-lyah-*mehn*-toh dah *dohn*-nah/*woh*-moh) (*women's/men's wear*)
- ✔ **intimo donna** (*een*-tee-moh *dohn*-nah) (*ladies' intimate apparel*)
- ✔ **intimo uomo** (*een*-tee-moh *woh*-moh) (*men's intimate apparel*)
- ✔ **accessori** (ahch-chehs-*soh*-ree) (*accessories*)
- ✔ **profumeria** (proh-fooh-meh-*ree*-ah) (*perfumery*; here you can buy shampoo, barrettes, creams, makeup, and other related items).
- ✔ **casalinghi** (kah-sah-*leen*-gee) (*housewares*)
- ✔ **biancheria per la casa** (byahn-keh-*ree*-ah pehr lah *kah*-sah) (*household linens and towels*)

Talkin' the Talk

Here, a clerk is kept busy giving directions for various departments.

Sig.ra Verdi: **Sto cercando l'abbigliamento da bambino.**
stoh chehr-*kahn*-doh lahb-bee-lyah-*mehn*-toh
dah bahm-*bee*-noh
I'm looking for children's wear.

Clerk: **Al secondo piano.**
ahl seh-*kohn*-doh *pyah*-noh
On the second floor.

Sig. Marchi: **Dove devo andare per ritirare un paio di pantaloni?**
doh-veh *deh*-voh ahn-*dah*-reh *pehr* ree-tee-*rah*-reh
oohn *pah*-yoh dee pahn-tah-*loh*-nee
Where should I go to pick up a pair of trousers?

Clerk: **Deve rivolgersi al commesso del reparto uomo.**
deh-veh ree-*vohl*-jehr-see ahl kohm-*mehs*-soh dehl
reh-*pahr*-toh *woh*-moh
You need to see the clerk in the men's department.

Anna: **Dove sono i camerini, per favore?**
doh-veh *soh*-noh ee kah-meh-*ree*-nee pehr
fah-*voh*-reh
Where are the fitting rooms, please?

Clerk: **Vede l'uscita di sicurezza? I camerini sono sulla sinistra.**
veh-deh looh-*shee*-tah dee see-kooh-*reht*-tsah ee
kah-meh-*ree*-nee *soh*-noh soohl-lah see-*nees*-trah
Do you see the emergency exit there? The fitting rooms are to the left.

Avere bisogno di (ah-*veh*-reh bee-*zoh*-nyoh dee) (*to need*) is a frequent expression in Italian. You use it in any kind of store. See Chapter 2 and Appendix A for the common verb **avere** (*to have*). The form that you use as a speaker goes like this:

Ho bisogno di . . . (oh bee-*zoh*-nyoh dee) (*I need . . .*)

When you're in a store and have a question or need some advice, you turn to **la commessa** [f] (lah kohm-*mehs*-sah) or **il commesso** [m] (eel kohm-*mehs*-soh) (*the sales clerk*) and say, **Mi può aiutare, per favore** (mee pwoh ah-yooh-tah-reh pehr fah-*voh*-reh) (*Can you help me, please?*) Of course, if you're just looking and a salesperson asks, **"Desidera?"** (deh-*zee*-deh-rah) (*Can I be of help? Can I help you?*), you can answer, **"Posso dare un'occhiata?"** (*pohs*-soh *dah*-reh oohn-ohk-*kyah*-tah) (*Is it all right if I just look?*)

Words to Know

vestiti [m]	vehs-tee-tee	clothes
abito [m]	ah-bee-toh	suit
camicetta [f]	kah-mee-cheht-tah	blouse
camicia [f]	kah-mee-chah	shirt
cappotto [m]	kahp-poht-toh	coat
completo [m]	kohm-pleht-oh	outfit
costume da bagno [m]	kohs-tooh-meh dah bahn-yoh	bathing suit
giacca [f]	jahk-kah	jacket; sports jacket
gonna [f]	gohn-nah	skirt
impermeabile [m]	eem-pehr-meh-ah-bee-leh	raincoat
jeans [m]	jeenz	jeans
maglia [f]	mah-lyah	sweater
maglietta [f];	mahl-yeht-tah	T-shirt
pantaloni [m]	pahn-tah-loh-nee	pants
tailleur [m]	tah-lyehr	skirt or pants and jacket
vestito [m]	vehs-tee-toh	dress
piccolo	pee-koh-loh	small
grande	grahn-deh	large

Sizing up Italian sizes

You know the problem: Whenever you go to another country, and this is particularly true in Europe, the sizes — called **taglie** (*tah*-lyeh) or **misure** (mee-*zooh*-reh) in Italy — change and you never know which one corresponds to yours. Table 8-1 helps you with this problem by giving you the most common sizes.

Table 8-1	Clothing Sizes	
Italian Size	*American Size*	*Canadian Size*
Women's dress sizes		
40	4	6
42	6	8
44	8	10
46	10	12
48	12	14
Men's suit sizes		
48	38	40
50	40	42
52	42	44
54	44	46
56	46	48

In Italy you won't have any difficulties with sizes like S, M, L, and XL because they are used the same way: S for small, M for medium, L for large, and XL for extra large. Beware, though, that an Italian L seems to correspond to a North American S.

Talkin' the Talk

Giovanna has found the skirt she's been looking for. She asks the saleswoman if she can try it on. (Track 16)

Giovanna: **Posso provare questa gonna?**
pohs-soh proh-*vah*-reh *kwehs*-tah gohn-*nah*
May I try on this skirt?

Saleswoman: **Certo. Che taglia porta?**
chehr-toh keh *tah*-lyah *pohr*-tah
Sure. What size do you wear?

Giovanna:	**La quarantadue.** lah kwah-*rahn*-tah-*dooh*-eh Forty-two.
Saleswoman:	**Forse è un po' piccola.** *fohr*-seh eh oohn poh *peek*-koh-lah Perhaps it's a little bit too small.
Giovanna:	**Me la provo.** meh lah *proh*-voh I'll try it on.

Giovanna returns from the dressing room.

Saleswoman:	**Va bene?** vah *beh*-neh Does it fit?
Giovanna:	**È troppo stretta. Ha una taglia più grande?** eh *trohp*-poh *streht*-tah ah *ooh*-nah *tah*-lyah pyooh *grahn*-deh It's too tight. Do you have it in a larger size?
Saleswoman:	**Nella sua taglia solo blu.** *nehl*-lah *sooh*-ah *tah*-lyah *soh*-loh blooh In your size, only in blue.

Talking definitely and indefinitely

When you're shopping for something, even if you're looking for something as specific as a blue skirt, you don't say, "I'm looking for the blue skirt." Instead, you say that you're looking for a blue skirt, where the a is an indefinite article showing that you don't have a specific object in mind.

You use exactly the same construction in Italian: I'm looking for a blue skirt becomes "**Sto cercando una gonna blu.**" (stoh cher-*kahn*-doh *ooh*-nah *gohn*-nah blooh), and **una** here is your indefinite article: the indefinite articles correspond to the English a and an. In Italian the article has to match the gender of the word: Feminine words, which usually end with -a, use **una** and **un'** and masculine words (which usually end with **o**) use **un** or **uno**.

Coloring your words

Of course, knowing some **colori** (koh-*loh*-ree) (*colors*) is important. We want to make life a little easier for you, so we put the most common colors in Table 8-2. Some colors agree in number and gender, some agree only in number, and some are invariable! The following table is organized accordingly (with the first set agreeing in number and gender).

Table 8-2	Colors	
Italian	*Pronunciation*	*Translation*
Color adjectives that agree in number and gender (o/a/i/e/i)		
rosso	*rohs*-soh	*red*
giallo	*jahl*-loh	*yellow*
azzurro	ahd-*dzoohr*-roh	*sky blue*
bianco	*byahn*-koh	*white*
grigio	*gree*-joh	*gray*
nero	*neh*-roh	*black*
Color adjectives that agree only in number (e/i)		
verde	*vehr*-deh	*green*
Color adjectives that never change, invariable!		
marrone	mahr-*roh*-neh	*brown*
rosa	*roh*-zah	*pink*
beige	*beh*-jeh	*beige*
blu	blooh	*blue*
arancione	ah-rahn-*choh*-neh	*orange*
viola	vee-*oh*-lah	*purple*

Talkin' the Talk

Matteo is looking for a new suit for the summer.

Salesman: **La posso aiutare?**
lah *pohs*-soh ah-yooh-*tah*-reh
May I help you?

Matteo: **Sì. Cerco una giacca sportiva blu . . .**
see *chehr*-koh *ooh*-nah *jak*-kah spohr-*tee*-vah blooh
Yes. I'm looking for a casual blue jacket . . .

. . . con i pantaloni bianchi di lino
kohn ee pahn-tah-*loh*-nee *biahn*-kee dee *lee*-noh
. . . and also some white linen pants.

Salesman: **Benissimo. Ecco . . . Provi questi**
behn-*ees*-see-moh *ehk*-koh *proh*-vee *kwehs*-tee
Very well. Here you are . . . try these on.

Matteo returns with a smile on his face.

Salesman: **Va bene?**
vah *beh*-neh
Okay?

Matteo: **Sì, mi vanno bene. Li prendo.**
see mee *vahn*-noh *beh*-neh lee *prehn*-doh
Yes, they fit me well. I'll take them.

Words to Know

camoscio [m]	kah-*moh*-shoh	suede
cotone [m]	koh-*toh*-neh	cotton
fodera [f]	*foh*-deh-rah	lining
lana [f]	*lah*-nah	wool
lino [m]	*lee*-noh	linen
pelle [f]	*pehl*-leh	leather
seta [f]	*seh*-tah	silk
velluto [m]	vehl-*looh*-toh	velvet
viscosa [f]	vees-*koh*-zah	rayon

Accessorizing

Of course, you want to complement your outfit with beautiful **accessori** (ahch-chehs-*soh*-ree) (*accessories*) to give it that final touch. We list some of them to give you an impression of the variety:

- ✔ **berretto** (behr-*reht*-toh) (*cap*)
- ✔ **borsa** (*bohr*-sah) (*bag*)
- ✔ **calze** (kahl-*tseh*) (*stockings*)
- ✔ **cappello** (kahp-*pehl*-loh) (*hat*)
- ✔ **cintura** (cheen-*tooh*-rah) (*belt*)
- ✔ **collant** (kohl-lahn) (*tights/pantyhose*)
- ✔ **cravatta** (krah-*vaht*-tah) (*tie*)
- ✔ **guanti** (*gwahn*-tee) (*gloves*)
- ✔ **ombrello** (ohm-*brehl*-loh) (*umbrella*)
- ✔ **sciarpa** (*shahr*-pah) (*scarf*)

If you want to go shopping and ask for one of these accessories, you could do it like this:

Talkin' the Talk

Giovanni wants to buy a scarf for his wife. He asks the sales clerk for help.

Giovanni:	**Vorrei una sciarpa rossa.** vohr-*rey ooh*-nah *shahr*-pah *rohs*-sah I'd like a red scarf.
Sales clerk:	**Ne abbiamo una bellissima, di cachemire.** neh ahb-bee-*ah*-moh *ooh*-nah behl-*lees*-see-mah dee *kahsh*-meer We have a very beautiful cashmere one.
	È in saldo. eh een *sahl*-doh It's on sale.
Giovanni:	**Sono scontati questi guanti viola?** *soh*-noh *skohn*-tah-tee *kwehs*-tee *gwahn*-tee vee-*oh*-lah Are these purple gloves on sale?

Sales clerk: **Sì.**
                see
                Yes.

Stepping out in style

Oh yes, this is important stuff. You know that Italy is the leader in the shoe industry. You won't believe what good taste Italians have in **scarpe** (*skahr*-peh) (*shoes*). You may just find the shoes of your dreams, whether they be a regular **paio di scarpe** (*pah*-yoh dee *skahr*-peh) (*pair of shoes*), **pantofole** (pahn-*toh*-foh-leh) (*slippers*), **sandali** (*sahn*-dah-lee) (*sandals*), or **stivali** (stee-*vah*-lee) (*boots*).

When you try on footwear, some words you may need to use are:

   ✔ **stretta/e/o/i** (*streht*-tah/teh/toh/tee) (*tight*)

   ✔ **larga/ghe/go/ghi** (*lahr*-gah/geh/goh/gee) (*loose*)

   ✔ **corta/e/o/i** (*kohr*-tah/the/ teh/toh/tee) (*short*)

   ✔ **lunga/ghe/go/ghi** (*loohn*-gah/ge goh/gee) (*long*)

You may notice that Italian uses **numero** (*nooh*-meh-roh) (*number*) to talk about shoes, but **taglia** (*tah*-lyah) or **misura** (mee-*sooh*-rah) (*size*) to talk about clothes.

Table 8-3 shows women's shoe sizes and their conversions.

Table 8-3	Women's Shoe Sizes	
US and Canada	*European*	*United Kingdom*
5	35	2.5
5.5	35.5	3
6	36	3.5
6.5	36.5	4
7	37	4.5
7.5	37.5	5
8	38	5.5
8.5	38.5	6
9	39	6.5
9.5	39.5	7
10	40	7.5
10.5	40.5	8

Talkin' the Talk

If you have seen the pair of shoes of your dreams **in vetrina** (een veh-*tree*-nah) (*in the shop window*) and you'd like to try them on, you can follow Michela's example: (Track 17)

Michela: **Posso provare le scarpe esposte in vetrina?**
pohs-soh proh-*vah*-reh leh *skahr*-peh ehs-*pohs*-teh een veh-*tree*-nah
May I try on a pair of shoes in the window?

Saleswoman: **Quali sono?**
kwah-lee *soh*-noh
Which ones?

Michela: **Quelle blu, a destra.**
kwehl-leh blooh ah *dehs*-trah
Those blue ones there, on the right.

Saleswoman: **Che numero porta?**
keh *nooh*-meh-roh *pohr*-tah
Which size do you wear?

Michela: **Trentasette.**
trehn-tah-*seht*-teh
Thirty-seven.

Saleswoman: **Ecco qua. Un trentasette . . . sono strette?**
ehk-koh kwah oohn trehn-tah-*seht*-teh *soh*-noh *streht*-teh
Here we are. A 37 . . . Are they tight?

Michela: **No. Sono comodissime.**
noh *soh*-noh koh-moh-*dees*-see-meh
No. They are very comfortable.

Michela: **Quanto vengono?**
kwahn-toh *vehn*-goh-noh
How much do they cost?

Saleswoman: **Novanta euro.**
noh-*vahn*-tah *eh*-ooh-roh
Ninety euros.

Fun & Games

I give you a lot of information and vocabulary about clothes shopping in this chapter. See how many articles of clothing you can identify on the following couple. See Appendix D for the answer key.

Chapter 9

Having Fun Out on the Town

In This Chapter

▶ Having fun in Italy

▶ Enjoying movies, art, theater, and other forms of entertainment

▶ Giving and receiving invitations

Doing the town is always fun. In general, Italians are sociable people who enjoy having a good time. You see them having espressos together **al bar** (ahl bahr) (*in the bar*) or drinks at night **in piazza** (een *pyaht*-tsah) (*on the public square*). Most Italians love to go out in the evening, crowding the streets until late at night.

Italy is a popular vacation destination, and Italian cities have a great variety of cultural offerings, from the numerous local fairs and **sagre** (*sah*-greh) (*town celebrations relating to harvest, wild boar, or saints, for example*) to open-air festivals and music events to city-wide celebrations. The variety is endless, and fun is guaranteed. The festivals relating to saints are for the **santo patrono** (*sahn*-toh pah-*troh*-noh) (*patron saint*). The **sagre** are to celebrate agricultural products. These two things are different.

In this chapter, I give you a lot of information you need to take in cultural attractions and socialize.

Acquiring Culture

No matter where you live or where you travel, most major cities have a weekly **pubblicazione** (poohb-blee-kah-*tsyoh*-neh) (*publication*) listing information about upcoming events. These publications include dates, descriptions, and time schedules for theaters, exhibitions, festivals, films, and so on. They also provide tips for shopping and restaurants.

In smaller towns without weekly magazines, you may see events announced on posters. You can also find information in the local newspapers.

Of course, newspapers aren't your only source of information about things to do and see. Asking the following questions can get you answers you want.

- **Cosa c'è da fare di sera?** (*koh*-zah cheh dah *fah*-reh dee *seh*-rah) (*Are there any events in the evenings?*)

- **Può suggerirmi qualcosa?** (pwoh soohj-jeh-*reer*-mee kwahl-*koh*-zah) (*Can you recommend something to me?*)

- **C'è un concerto stasera?** (cheh oohn kohn-*chehr*-toh stah-*seh*-rah) (*Is there a concert tonight?*)

- **Ci sono ancora posti?** (chee *soh*-noh ahn-*koh*-rah *pohs*-tee) (*Are there any seats left?*)

- **Dove si comprano i biglietti?** (*doh*-veh see *kohm*-prah-noh ee bee-*lyeht*-tee) (*Where can we get tickets?*)

- **Quanto vengono i biglietti?** (*kwahn*-toh *vehn*-goh-noh ee bee-*lyeht*-tee) (*How much are the tickets?*)

- **A che ora comincia lo spettacolo?** (ah keh *oh*-rah koh-*meen*-chah loh speht-*tahk*-koh-loh) (*What time does the show begin?*)

- **Non c'è niente di più economico?** (nohn cheh nee-*ehn*-teh dee *pyooh* eh-koh-*noh*-mee-koh) (*Isn't there anything cheaper?*)

Talkin' the Talk

Arturo works at a theater. He is bombarded with questions from patrons before the show.

Sig. Paoli:	**Quando comincia lo spettacolo?**
	kwahn-doh koh-*meen*-chah loh speht-*tah*-koh-loh
	When does the show start?
Arturo:	**Alle sette e mezza.**
	ahl-leh *seht*-teh eh *mehdz*-dzah
	At half past seven.
Erika:	**A che ora finisce lo spettacolo?**
	ah keh *oh*-rah fee-*nee*-sheh loh speht-*tah*-koh-loh
	What time is the show going to end?
Arturo:	**Verso le dieci.**
	vehr-soh leh *dyeh*-chee
	About ten p.m.
Erika:	**C'è un intervallo?**
	cheh oohn een-tehr-*vahl*-loh
	Is there an intermission?

Arturo: **Sì, tra il secondo e il terzo atto.**
see trah eel seh-*kohn*-doh eh eel *tehr*-tsoh *aht*-toh
Yes, between the second and third acts.

Words to Know

a che ora?	ah keh <u>oh</u>-rah	what time?
quando?	<u>kwahn</u>-doh	when?
dove?	<u>doh</u>-veh	where?
divertente	dee-vehr-<u>tehn</u>-teh	fun
biglietto [m]	bee-<u>lyeht</u>-toh	ticket
spettacolo [m]	speht-<u>tah</u>-koh-loh	show
cominciare	koh-meen-<u>chah</u>-reh	to start
finire	fee-<u>nee</u>-reh	to end

Italian films

It's well known that Italy produces a great number of films, and there are many Italian directors who are famous throughout the world: Fellini, Rossellini, Bertolucci, De Sica, and Nanni Moretti, to name a few. Some of their works are considered classics of Italian culture, and I highly recommend them to you. Other contemporary directors to look for include Giuseppe Tornatore, Gabriele Salvatores, Francesca Archibugi, and Emanuele Crialese.

La dolce vita and *La strada* are among Fellini's masterpieces. The dramatic and moving *Roma, città aperta* (*Open City*) is one of Rossellini's most significant movies. To complete the image of the Italian cinema between 1945 and 1957, you need to include De Sica's *Ladri di biciclette* (*The Bicycle Thief*). Bertolucci belongs to a subsequent period and is known for his *Il conformista* (*The Conformist*) whereas Moretti's *Caro diario* and *La stanza del figlio* made big contributions to disseminating Italian culture abroad in the 1990s.

Then we have Roberto Benigni, who not only directed one of the most successful "foreign" films of modern times but won an Academy Award for acting in *La vita è bella* — *Life is Beautiful*.

Going to the movies

Going **al cinema** (ahl *chee*-neh-mah) (*to the movies*) is a popular activity almost everywhere. In Italy, American films usually are **doppiati** (dohp-*pyah*-tee) (*dubbed*) into Italian. On the other hand, why not go to an original Italian film? Doing so provides you with a good opportunity to polish your Italian.

Some special questions for the movies include:

- ✔ **Andiamo al cinema?** (ahn-*dyah*-moh ahl *chee*-neh-mah) (*Shall we go to the movies?*)

- ✔ **Cosa danno?** (*koh*-zah *dahn*-noh) (*What's playing?*)

- ✔ **Dove lo danno?** (*doh*-veh loh *dahn*-noh) (*Where is [the movie] being shown?*)

- ✔ **È in lingua** (versione) **originale?** (eh in *leen*-gwah [vehr-see-*ohn*-neh] oh-ree-jee-*nah*-leh) (*Is the film in the original language?*)

- ✔ **Dov'è il cinema Trianon?** (doh-*veh* eel *chee*-neh-mah *tree*-ah-nohn) (*Where is the Trianon cinema?*)

  Often saying the name of the movie theater is sufficient, for example, **Dov'è il Trianon?** (doh-*veh* eel *tree*-ah-nohn) (*Where is the Trianon?*)

Talkin' the Talk

Ugo and Bianca are two Fellini fans. Ugo wants to go to the movies and asks his girlfriend Bianca if she feels like going with him. (Track 18)

Ugo:	**Andiamo al cinema?** ahn-*dyah*-moh ahl *chee*-neh-mah Shall we go to the movies?
Bianca:	**Che film vuoi vedere?** keh feelm vwoi veh-*deh*-reh Which movie would you like to see?
Ugo:	**La dolce vita, naturalmente.** lah *dohl*-cheh *vee*-tah *nah*-tooh-rahl-*mehn*-teh La dolce vita, of course.
Bianca:	**Oh, l'ho visto solo tre volte!** oh loh *vees*-toh *soh*-loh treh *vohl*-teh Oh, I've only seen it three times!
	Dove lo danno? *doh*-veh loh *dahn*-noh Where is it being shown?

Ugo: **Al Tiziano, qui vicino.**
ahl tee-tsee-*ah*-noh kwee vee-*chee*-noh
At the Tiziano, nearby.

Bianca: **A che ora comincia?**
ah keh *oh*-rah koh-*meen*-chah
What time does it start?

Ugo: **Esattamente fra cinque minuti!**
eh-zaht-tah-*mehn*-teh frah *cheen*-kweh
mee-*nooh*-tee
In exactly five minutes!

Bianca: **Cosa aspettiamo?**
koh-zah ahs-peht-*tyah*-moh
What are we waiting for?

Italian movie theaters used to be rather small, showing only one movie at a time. Now virtually all large Italian cities have big **multisala** (moohl-tee-*sah*-lah) (*multiplex*) cinemas, with many screens.

Talkin' the Talk

Films are an interesting topic of conversation. Here is a typical dialogue between two friends, Chiara and Alberto.

Chiara: **Hai visto l'ultimo film di Salvatores?**
ahy *vees*-toh *loohl*-tee-moh feelm dee
sahl-vah-*toh*-rez
Have you seen the new Salvatores film?

Alberto: **Ancora no, e tu?**
ahn-*koh*-rah noh eh tooh
Not yet, and you?

Chiara: **Sì, ieri sera.**
see *yeh*-ree *seh*-rah
Yes, last night.

Alberto: **Com'è?**
koh-*meh*
How is it?

Chiara: **L'attore principale è bravissimo!**
laht-*toh*-reh preen-chee-*pah*-leh eh
brah-*vees*-see-moh
The lead actor is really good!

Alberto:	**Ma dai! Lo dici perché è bello!**
	mah dahy loh *dee*-chee pehr-*keh* eh *behl*-loh
	Come on! You say that because he's good looking!

Chiara:	**E allora? E il film è così divertente!**
	eh ahl-*loh*-rah eh eel feelm eh koh-*zee*
	dee-vehr-*tehn*-teh
	So what? And the movie is so amusing!

Alberto:	**L'ultimo film di Salvatores era così serio.**
	loohl-tee-moh feelm dee sahl-vah-*toh*-rez *eh*-rah
	koh-*zee seh*-ree-oh
	Salvatores' last film was so serious.

Words to Know

Chi è il regista?	kee eh eel reh-<u>jees</u>-tah	Who is the director?
Chi sono gli attori?	kee <u>soh</u>-noh lyee aht-<u>toh</u>-ree	Who's starring?
attore [m]	aht-<u>toh</u>-reh	actor
regista [f/m]	reh-<u>jees</u>-tah	director
trama [f]	<u>trah</u>-mah	plot
scena [f]	<u>sheh</u>-nah	scene

Going to the theater

The language of the theater and the cinema is very similar. Of course, when you attend a play, opera, or symphony performance, there is a variety of seats. For example, you can sit in the **platea** (plah-*teh*-ah) (*orchestra*) **i palchi** (*pahl*-kee) (*box seats*) or **il loggione** (eel lohj-*joh*-neh) (*the gallery*), which used to be called **la piccionaia** (lah peech-choh-*nah*-yah) (Literally: *the pigeonhouse*) because it is high up.

Talkin' the Talk

In the following dialogue, Eugenio wants to know whether seats are available for a certain performance of a play he wants to see. He's speaking on the phone with the person at the theater box office.

Ticket Agent:	**Pronto?** *prohn*-toh Hello?
Eugenio:	**Buongiorno. È il Teatro Valle?** bwohn-*johr*-noh eh eel teh-*ah*-tro *vahl*-leh Good morning. Is this the Valle Theater?
Ticket Agent:	**Sì. Mi dica.** see mee *dee*-kah Yes. Can I help you? (Literally: Tell me.)
Eugenio:	**Vorrei prenotare dei posti.** vohr-*rey* preh-noh-*tah*-reh dey *pohs*-tee I'd like to reserve some seats.
Ticket Agent:	**Per quale spettacolo?** pehr *kwah*-leh speht-*tah*-koh-loh For which performance?
Eugenio:	Aspettando Godot, **domani sera.** ahs-peht-*tahn*-doh goh-*doh* doh-*mah*-nee *seh*-rah *Waiting for Godot*, tomorrow evening.
Ticket Agent:	**Mi dispiace: È tutto esaurito.** mee dees-*pyah*-cheh eh *tooht*-toh eh-zou-*ree*-toh I'm sorry: It's sold out.
Eugenio:	**Ci sono repliche?** chee *soh*-noh *reh*-plee-keh Are there other performances?
Ticket Agent:	**L'ultima è dopodomani.** *loohl*-tee-mah eh *doh*-poh-doh-*mah*-nee The last one is the day after tomorrow.

Did you notice that the title of the play, *Waiting for Godot*, has no preposition in Italian? In English, you wait for someone, but Italians say "waiting somebody" — **aspettare qualcuno** (ahs-peht-*tah*-reh kwahl-*kooh*-noh). You may also hear **ti aspetto** (tee ahs-*peht*-toh) (*I'm waiting for you*).

Talkin' the Talk

Eugenio asks his friends about changing the date they see the play and then calls the box office again.

Voice:	**Pronto?** *prohn*-toh Hello?
Eugenio:	**Ho telefonato due minuti fa.** oh teh-leh-foh-*nah*-toh *dooh*-eh mee-*nooh*-tee fah I called two minutes ago.
Voice:	**Sì, mi dica!** See mee *dee*-kah Yes, how can I help you?
Eugenio:	**Sì, vorrei prenotare tre posti per dopodomani** see vohr-*rey* preh-noh-*tah*-reh treh *pohs*-tee pehr *doh*-poh-doh-*mah*-nee Yes, I'd like to reserve three seats for day after tomorrow.
Voice:	**Che posti desidera?** keh *pohs*-tee deh-*zee*-deh-rah Which seats would you like?
Eugenio:	**Non troppo cari.** nohn *trohp*-poh *kah*-ree Not too expensive.
Voice:	**La platea costa trentadue Euro.** lah plah-*teh*-ah *kohs*-tah trehn-tah-*dooh*-eh *eh*-ooh-roh The orchestra is thirty-two euros.

Eugenio:	**Ci sono tre posti centrali?**
	chee *soh*-noh treh *pohs*-tee chehn-*trah*-lee
	Are there three middle seats?
Voice:	**Un momento . . . sì, tre posti nella quindicesima fila.**
	oohn moh-*mehn*-toh see tre *pohs*-tee *nehl*-lah
	kween-dee-*cheh*-zee-mah *fee*-lah
	Just a moment . . . yes, three seats in row 15.
	Paga con Bancomat o con carta di credito?
	pah-gah kohn *bahn*-koh-maht oh kohn *kahr*-tah
	dee *kreh*-dee-toh
	Will you pay with an debit card or a credit card?
Eugenio:	**Bancomat, per favore.**
	bahn-koh-maht pehr fah-*voh*-reh
	Debit card, thank you.

If you come to Italy, you can catch an opera by Verdi, Puccini, or Rossini in wonderful theaters such as Milan's **La Scala** (lah *skah*-lah), Naples's **San Carlo** (sahn *kahr*-loh), and the theaters of Florence and Palermo. In the summer months, try to check out theater festivals (which include a wide variety of repertoires and venues citywide), like the famous Ravenna Festival. You can also see outdoor operas in Verona, at the old Roman **Arena** (ah-*reh*-nah). Following are some phrases concerning performances:

- ✔ **la danza classica/moderna/contemporanea** (lah *dahn*-zah *klahs*-see-kah/moh-*dehr*-nah/kohn-tehm-poh-*rah*-neh-ah) (*classical/modern/contemporary dance*)

- ✔ **lo spettacolo** (loh speht-*tah*-koh-loh) (*the show; the performance*)

- ✔ **la prova generale pubblica** (lah *proh*-vah jeh-neh-*rah*-leh *poohb*-blee-kah) (*public dress rehearsal*)

- ✔ **la replica** (lah *reh*-plee-kah) (*repeat performance*)

- ✔ **il matinée** (eel mah-tee-*neh*) (*matinee*)

- ✔ **lo spettacolo pomeridiano** (loh speht-*tah*-koh-loh poh-meh-ree-*dyah*-noh) (*afternoon performance*)

Some theaters don't accept telephone reservations; you can only "reserve at the box office" — **prenotazione al botteghino** (preh-noh-tah-*tsyoh*-neh ahl boht-teh-*gee*-noh). You can pay for the tickets and either pick them up immediately or before the performance begins.

Going to a museum

Here are some of the most frequented museums with the richest collections: the **Uffizi** (oohf-*fee*-tsee) Gallery in Florence; **La Galleria Borghese** (lah gahl-leh-*ree*-ah bohr-*geh*-seh) and the **Musei Vaticani** (mooh-*zeh*-ee vah-tee-*kah*-nee) in Rome; the **Peggy Guggenheim Collection** in Venice; and **Il Museo della Scienza e della Tecnica** (eel mooh-*zeh*-oh dehl-lah *shehn*-zah eh *dehl*-lah *tehk*-nee-kah) in Milan. Every two years there is also the **Biennale di Venezia** (bee-ehn-*nah*-leh dee veh-*nets*-ee-ah) where you can view the work of many well-known and emerging contemporary international artists.

Talkin' the Talk

Take a look at this dialogue between two friends who are about to go **al museo** (ahl mooh-*zeh*-oh) (*to the museum*).

Luisa:	**Ciao, Flavia, dove vai?** chou *flah*-vee-ah *doh*-veh vahy Hello, Flavia, where are you going?
Flavia:	**Ciao! Alla mostra di Caravaggio.** chou *ahl*-lah *mohs*-trah dee kah-rah-*vaj*-joh Hello! To the Caravaggio exhibit.
Luisa:	**Ma dai: ci vado anch'io!** mah dahy chee *vah*-doh ahn-*kee*-oh You don't say! I'm going there too!
Flavia:	**Allora andiamo insieme!** ahl-*loh*-rah ahn-*dyah*-moh een-*syeh*-meh In that case, let's go together!
Luisa:	**Certo! Viene anche Janet.** *chehr*-toh *vyeh*-neh *ahn*-keh jah-*neht* Sure! Janet is coming also.
Flavia:	**La conosco?** lah koh-*nohs*-koh Do I know her?
Luisa:	**Sì, la mia amica americana.** see lah *mee*-ah ah-*mee*-kah ah-meh-ree-*kah*-nah Yes, my American friend.

Flavia:	**Dove avete appuntamento?**
	doh-veh ah-*veh*-teh ahp-poohn-tah-*mehn*-toh
	Where are you meeting?
Luisa:	**Davanti al museo.**
	dah-*vahn*-tee ahl mooh-*zeh*-oh
	In front of the museum.

Going to a local festival

In this chapter's introduction I refer to the many local **sagre** (*sah*-greh) (*fairs*) and festivals you can find in Italy especially during the spring, summer, and fall. The themes of these fairs vary, ranging from the ones that are political in origin such as **La festa dell 'Unità** (lah *fehs*-tah dee-looh-nee-*tah*) (*a left-leaning newspaper*) to the ones that are nature-related: **La sagra del cinghiale** (lah *sah*-grah dehl cheen-*gyah*-leh) (*the wild-boar festival*) and **La sagra del pesce azzurro** (lah *sah*-grah dehl *peh*-sheh adz-*zooh*-roh) (*the Blue Fish Fair*) are two that come to mind. Do drop in if you find one because these are often the perfect venues for experiencing local culture and homemade food.

Talkin' the Talk

Paola tries to convince Martino to visit the cathedral.

Paola:	**Lo sai che oggi c'è la Sagra dell'uva a Bertinoro?**
	loh sahy keh *oj*-jee cheh lah *sah*-grah dehl-*looh*-vah ah behr-teen-*oh*-roh
	Did you know that today there is the grape festival in Bertinoro?
Martino:	**Divertente! O facciamoci un salto!**
	dee-vehr-*tehn*-teh oh fahch-*chah*-moh-chee oohn *sahl*-toh
	What fun! Oh, Let's stop by!
Paola:	**Partiamo subito?**
	pahr-*tyah*-moh *sooh*-bee-toh
	Shall we leave right away?
Martino:	**Sì, perché no?**
	see pehr-*keh* noh
	Yes, why not?

Paola: **In quel paese fanno anche degli ottimi cappelletti!**
in kwehl pah-eh-zeh fahn-noh dehl-yee oht-tee-mee kahp-pehl-leht-tee
They make great cappelletti in that town.

Martino: **Ottimo, così ci fermiamo a cena.**
oht-tee-moh koh-zee chee fehr-mee-ah-moh ah cheh-nah
Great! This way we can stay for supper.

Going to a concert

If you're interested in music, you will certainly be able to hear some in Italy, from the **Umbria** (*oohm-bree-ah*) **Jazz Festival** to the **Festival dei due mondi** (*fehs-tee-vahl dey dooh-eh mohn-dee*) in Spoleto to your favorite Italian **cantautore** (*kahn-tou-toh-reh*) (*singer–songwriter*).

Italy is full of old and beautiful churches and cathedrals where **musicisti** (*mooh-zee-chees-tee*) (*musicians*) often present classical music concerts. You can also hear concerts in other places — sometimes in the center of a city in a piazza.

Talkin' the Talk

La signora and il signor Tiberi are reading the morning paper. Suddenly, la signora Tiberi cries out:

Sig.ra Tiberi: **Guarda qui!**
gwahr-dah kwee
Look here!

Sig. Tiberi: **Che c'è?**
keh cheh
What's up?

Sig.ra Tiberi: **Martedì c'è Pollini a Roma!**
mahr-teh-dee cheh pohl-lee-nee ah roh-mah
Pollini is in Rome on Tuesday!

Sig. Tiberi: **Tiene un concerto?**
tyeh-neh oohn kohn-chehr-toh
Is he going to give a concert?

Sig.ra Tiberi: **Sì, al Conservatorio.**
see ahl kohn-sehr-vah-*toh*-ree-oh
Yes, at the Conservatory.

Sig. Tiberi: **Sarà tutto esaurito?**
sah-*rah tooht*-toh eh-zou-*ree*-toh
Will it already be sold out?

Sig.ra Tiberi: **Forse no!**
fohr-seh noh
Maybe not!

Sig. Tiberi: **Vai al botteghino?**
vahy ahl boht-teh-*gee*-noh
Are you going to the box office?

Sig.ra Tiberi: **Prima telefono.**
pree-mah teh-*leh*-foh-noh
I'm going to call first.

Maurizio Pollini is an internationally famous Italian pianist. We do hope that signor and signora Tiberi find two tickets for this event. **Buona fortuna!** (*bwoh*-nah fohr-*tooh*-nah) (*Good luck!*)

Words to Know

musica [f]	mooh-zee-kah	music
concerto [m]	kohn-chehr-toh	concert
esaurito	eh-zou-ree-toh	sold out
piano(forte) [m]	pee-ah-noh(fohr-teh)	piano
museo [m]	mooh-zeh-oh	museum
insieme	een-syeh-meh	together

Maybe you know a musician or someone who plays an instrument in his or her leisure time. You are probably curious about some things, such as:

- ✔ **Che strumento suoni?** (keh strooh-*mehn*-toh *swoh*-nee) (*Which instrument do you play?*)

  Suono il violino. (*swoh*-noh eel vee-oh-*lee*-noh) (*I play the violin.*)

- ✔ **Dove suonate stasera?** (*doh*-veh swoh-*nah*-teh stah-*seh*-rah) (*Where are you playing tonight?*)

  Suoniamo al Blu Notte. (swoh-*nyah*-moh ahl blooh *noht*-teh) (*We play/ We're playing at the Blu Notte.*)

- ✔ **Chi suona in famiglia?** (kee *swoh*-nah in fah-*mee*-lyah) (*Who in the family plays?*)

  Suonano tutti. (*swoh*-nah-noh *tooht*-tee) (*All of them play.*)

Inviting Fun

Getting or giving **un invito** (oohn een-*vee*-toh) (*an invitation*) is always a pleasurable experience. A party (**una festa**) (*ooh*-nah *fehs*-tah) is a good opportunity to meet new people. In Italian, the verb **invitare** (een-vee-*tah*-reh) frequently means to treat someone to something. For example, if someone says "**Posso invitarti a teatro?**" (*pohs*-soh een-vee-*tahr*-tee ah teh-*ah*-troh) (*May I invite you to the theater?*), it means that the person is going to make the arrangements and pay for you.

The following expressions are other ways to suggest an activity:

- ✔ **Che ne pensa di andare a Roma?** (formal) (keh neh *pehn*-sah dee ahn-*dah*-reh ah *roh*-mah) (*What do you think of going to Rome?*)

- ✔ **Che ne dici di uscire stasera?** (informal) (keh neh *dee*-chee dee ooh-*shee*-reh stah-*seh*-rah) (*What do you say about going out tonight?*)

- ✔ **Andiamo in piscina!** (ahn-*dyah*-moh in pee-*shee*-nah) (*Let's go to the swimming pool!*)

- ✔ **Mangiamo una pizza!** (mahn-*jah*-moh *ooh*-nah *peet*-tsah) (*Let's eat a pizza!*)

- ✔ **Perché non andiamo a teatro?** (pehr-*keh* nohn ahn-*dyah*-moh ah teh-*ah*-troh) (*Why don't we go to the theater?*)

You can see that suggesting an activity in Italian is not so different from the way you do it in English. You can ask **Perché non . . .** (pehr-*keh* nohn) (*Why don't we . . .*) or **Che ne pensi . . .** (keh neh *pehn*-see) (*What do you think about . . .*).

The word **perché** is special. I use it in this chapter to ask the question "why." However, it can also mean "because." A dialogue can go like this:

Perché non mangi? (pehr-*keh* nohn *mahn*-jee) (*Why aren't you eating?*)

Perché non ho fame. (pehr-*keh* nohn oh *fah*-meh) (*Because I'm not hungry.*)

Talkin' the Talk

Guido has a new job. He's very happy and wants to share his happiness with a couple of friends. He decides to **dare una festa** (*dah*-reh *ooh*-nah *fehs*-tah) (*have a party*) and tells his friend Caterina about it.

Guido:	**Ho deciso!** oh deh-*chee*-zoh I've decided!
Caterina:	**Cosa?** *koh*-zah What?
Guido:	**Faccio una festa!** *fahch*-choh *ooh*-nah *fehs*-tah I'm giving a party!
Caterina:	**Perchè? Quando?** pehr-*keh kwahn*-doh Why? When?
Guido:	**Per il mio nuovo lavoro. Sabato sera.** pehr il *mee*-oh *nwoh*-voh lah-*voh*-roh *sah*-bah-toh *seh*-rah For my new job. Saturday night.
Caterina:	**Una festa con musica, ballo, birra??** *ooh*-nah *fehs*-tah kohn *mooh*-zee-kah *bahl*-loh *beer*-rah A party with music, dancing, and beer?
Guido:	**Certo. Mi aiuti?** *chehr*-toh mee ah-*yooh*-tee Certainly. Will you help me?
Caterina:	**Come no!** *koh*-meh noh Of course!

Nowadays, you can issue and receive invitations any number of ways. You can receive an invitation by phone, by fax, via e-mail, or you may be asked by your **ospite** (*ohs*-pee-teh) (*host*) face to face.

Talkin' the Talk

Guido will have a party at his house next Saturday. He calls Sara to invite her. (Track 19)

Sara:	**Ciao Guido, come va?**
	chou *gwee*-doh *koh*-meh vah
	Hi Guido, how are you?
Guido:	**Molto bene! Sei libera sabato sera?**
	mohl-toh *beh*-neh sey *lee*-beh-rah *sah*-bah-toh *seh*-rah
	Very well. Are you free Saturday night?
Sara:	**È un invito?**
	eh oohn een-*vee*-toh
	Is this an invitation?
Guido:	**Sì, alla mia festa.**
	see *ahl*-lah *mee*-ah *fehs*-tah
	Yes, to my party.
Sara:	**Fantastico! A che ora?**
	fahn-*tahs*-tee-koh ah keh *oh*-rah
	Great! What time?
Guido:	**Verso le nove.**
	vehr-soh leh *noh*-veh
	About nine.
Sara:	**Cosa posso portare? Il gelato va bene?**
	koh-zah *pohs*-soh pohr-*tahr*-eh eel jeh-*lah*-toh vah *beh*-neh
	What can I bring? Is ice cream okay?
Guido:	**Ottimo. Quello piace a tutti.**
	oht-tee-moh *qwehl*-loh *pyah*-cheh ah *tooht*-tee
	Great. Everyone likes ice cream.
Sara:	**Allora, d'accordo. Grazie!**
	ahl-*loh*-rah dahk-*kohr*-doh *grah*-tsee-eh
	Okay then. Thanks!

Figure 9-1 shows the fax Guido sent to friends he couldn't reach by phone.

Figure 9-1:
A casual
invitation,
suitable for
faxing.

Talkin' the Talk

Both Franco and Emma have received Guido's invitation. They are now talking about whether or not they will go to the party.

Franco: **Vieni alla festa di Guido?**
vyeh-nee *ahl*-lah *fehs*-tah dee *gwee*-doh
Are you going to Guido's party?

Emma: **No, mi annoio alle feste.**
noh mee ahn-*noi*-oh *ahl*-leh *fehs*-teh
No, I get bored at parties.

Franco: **Ti annoi?**
tee ahn-*noi*
You get bored?

Emma: **Sì, non ballo e non bevo.**
see nohn *bahl*-loh eh nohn *beh*-voh
Yes, I don't dance and don't drink.

Non mi diverto
nohn mee dee-*vehr*-toh
I don't have fun.

Franco: **Ma chiacchieri!**
mah *kyahk*-kyeh-ree
But you do chat!

Emma: **Sì, ma senza musica di sottofondo.**
see mah *sehn*-zah *mooh*-zee-kah dee
soht-toh-*fohn*-doh
Yes, but without background music.

Figure 9-2 is an example of a formal invitation to an opening of an exhibition by artist Elisa Catalini.

LA SIGNORIA VOSTRA È INVITATA
ALL'INAUGRAZZIONE DELLA MOSTRA:
LAH SEE-NYOH-REE-AH VOHS-TRA EH EEN-VEE-TAH-TAH
AHL-LEEN-OU-GOOH-RAH-TSYOH-NEH DEHL-LAH MOH-STRA
YOU ARE INVITED TO THE OPENING OF THE EXHIBITION:

"RICORDI DI UNA VITA"
REE-KOHR-DEE DEE OOH-NAH VEE-TAH
"MEMORIES OF LIFE"

DIPINTI A OLIO E SCULTURE DI
DEE PEEN-TEE AH OH-LYOH EH SKOOL-TOOH-REH DEE
OIL PAINTINGS AND SCULPTURES BY

ELISA CATALINI
VENERDI 28 MARZO ALLE 19.30
VEH-NEHR-DEE VEHNT-OHT-TOH MAHR-TSOH AHL-LEH
DEE-CHAHN-NOH-VEH EH TREHN-TAH
FRIDAY, MARCH 28 AT 7:30 PM

GALLERIA ARTE & ARTE
GAH-LEH-REE-AH AHR-TEH EH AHR-TEH
GALLERY ARTE & ARTE

VIA GABRIELLE SISTI 18
PIACENZA
L'ARTISTA SARÀ PRESENTE.
LAHR-TEES-TAH SAH-RAH PREH-ZEHN-TEH
THE ARTIST WILL BE PRESENT.

Figure 9-2:
The classic
formal,
engraved
invitation.

Words to Know

invito [m]	een-_vee_-toh	invitation
festa [f]	_fehs_-tah	party
suonare	swoh-_nah_-reh	to play (a musical instrument)
perché	pehr-_keh_	why; because
bere	_beh_-reh	to drink
ballare	bahl-_lah_-reh	to dance

Fun & Games

Now it's your turn to invite an Italian friend to your party. Use the following words to fill in the blanks in this invitation. See Appendix D for answer key.

aspetto, dove, festa, invitato, ora, perche, sabato, verso

C'è una (1) _____ **e tu sei** (2) _____. (There's a party and you're invited.)

Quando? (3) _____ **24 luglio** (When? Saturday, July 24.)

A che (4) _____? (5) _____ **le 9.** (What time? About 9 o'clock.)

(6) _____? **A casa mia.** (Where? At my place.)

(7) _____? **Per festeggiare insieme!** (Why? To celebrate together!)

Ti (8) _____. (I'll be waiting for you.)

Buon divertimento! (Have a nice time!)

Chapter 10

Taking Care of Business and Telecommunicating

In This Chapter
▶ Phoning and texting
▶ Making reservations and appointments over the phone
▶ Getting through to the person you want and leaving messages
▶ Using the past tense

In this chapter you encounter expressions and phrases that relate to telephones and telecommunication — for example, how to behave when someone calls you and how to leave a message. In addition, I show you some samples of common phone dialogues.

Phoning Made Simple

Pronto! (*prohn*-toh) (*Hello!*) is the first thing you hear when you talk to an Italian on the phone. In most languages, you answer the phone with the same word you use for saying hello in person, but in Italian, you use **pronto** to say hello only on the phone.

You can answer the phone and say **"Pronto. Chi parla?"** (*prohn*-toh kee *pahr*-lah) (*Hello, who's speaking?*)

And a typical response might be **"Pronto! Sono Sabrina. C'è Stefano?"** (*prohn*-toh *soh*-noh sah-*bree*-nah cheh *steh*-fah-noh). (*Hello! This is Sabrina. Is Stefano there?*)

You can also say, **"Sono Susanna. Posso parlare con Michele per favore?"** (*soh*-noh sooh-*sahn*-nah *pohs*-soh pahr-*lah*-reh kohn mee-*keh*-leh pehr fah-*voh*-reh) (*This is Susan. May I please speak with Michael?*)

Connecting via cellphones, texts, and Skype

Italians love their **cellulari** (*chehl*-looh-*lah*-ree) (*cellphones*), there's no doubt about that. They were one of the first cultures to embrace full force the **telefonino** (teh-leh-foh-*nee*-noh) (*little phone*) back in the eighties, when they adopted this useful accessory as a fashion.

Cellphones

When you're in Italy you need to have your own cell phone because public phones are hard to find and hotel phones are very expensive to use. If you take your phone with you from, say, the United States, make certain that it will work in Italy and that calls won't cost you a mint. Of course, you can buy a phone when you get there. If you buy one, phone time can be purchased two ways at the local **tabaccaio** (tah-bahk-*kahy*-oh) (*tobacconist*). You can either purchase **una scheda telefonica** (*ooh*-nah *skeh*-dah teh-leh-*foh*-nee-kah) (*phone card*), or you can ask the salesperson to charge your phone for you by putting on a specific number of minutes or euros. You can do the same thing at any branch of the phone store where you bought your cell phone.

Text messaging

Because Italians tend to text more frequently than make phone calls these days (because it is so much cheaper and also trendy), you should know how to say a couple of important things, such as "**messaggino**" (mehs-sahj-*jee*-noh) or "**sms**" (ehs-seh-*ehm*-meh-ehs-seh) (*text message*), and "**mandami un messaggino**" (*mahn*-dah-mee oohn mehs-sahj-*jee*-noh) (*"Text me."* Literally: *"Send me a text message."*)

Using the Internet to connect

All cities have their share of Internet stations, where you can pay a per-minute fee to use the Internet. All you have to ask is "**Posso usare l'Internet**?" (*pohs*-soh ooh-*zah*-reh *leen*-tehr-neht) (*May I use the Internet?*) whereupon you will be asked for **un documento** (oohn dohk-ooh-*mehn*-toh) (*identification*) and assigned to a computer station. There, you can Skype or e-mail to your heart's content.

Here are a couple more useful phone phrases:

- ✔ **Avete un telefono?** (ah-*veh*-teh oohn teh-*leh*-foh-noh) (*Is there/Do you have a [public] telephone?*)

- ✔ **Avete schede telefoniche?** (ah-*veh*-teh *skeh*-deh teh-leh-*foh*-nee-keh) (*Do you sell phone cards?*)

✔ **Ha un recapito telefonico?** (ah oohn reh-*kah*-pee-toh teh-leh-*foh*-nee-koh) (*Do you have a contact phone number?*) (You might hear this when you go to change money at the bank.)

✔ **Qual è il suo/tuo numero di telefono?** (kwahl eh eel *sooh*-oh *nooh*-meh-roh dee teh-*leh*-foh-noh) (*What is your phone number?*)

Talkin' the Talk

 Giorgio is back in Naples again and decides to give an old friend of his a call. (Track 20)

Simona:	**Pronto!**
	prohn-toh
	Hello!
Giorgio:	**Pronto, Simona?**
	prohn-toh see-*moh*-nah
	Hello, Simona?
Simona:	**Sì, chi parla?**
	see kee *pahr*-lah
	Yes, who's speaking?
Giorgio:	**Sono Giorgio.**
	soh-noh *johr*-joh
	It's Giorgio.
Simona:	**Che bella sorpresa!**
	keh *behl*-lah sohr-*preh*-zah
	What a nice surprise!
	Sei di nuovo a Napoli?
	sey dee *nwoh*-voh ah *nah*-poh-lee
	Are you in Naples again?
Giorgio:	**Sì, sono arrivato stamattina.**
	see *soh*-noh ahr-ree-*vah*-toh stah-maht-*tee*-nah
	Yes, I arrived this morning.
Simona:	**Ci vediamo stasera?**
	chee veh-*dyah*-moh stah-*seh*-rah
	Are we going to meet tonight?
Giorgio:	**Ti chiamo per questo!**
	tee *kyah*-moh pehr *kwehs*-toh
	That's why I'm calling!

In Italy, when you don't know a **numero di telefono** (*nooh*-meh-roh dee teh-*leh*-foh-noh) (*phone number*), look it up in the **elenco telefonico** (eh-*lehn*-koh teh-leh-*foh*-nee-koh) (*phone book*). If it's a business number you can also look in the **pagine gialle** (*pah*-jee-neh *jahl*-leh) (*yellow pages*).

Calling for business or pleasure

Whether you want to find out what time a show starts, make a dental appointment, or just chat with a friend, the easiest way to accomplish any of these tasks is usually to pick up the telephone. This section takes you through the nuts and bolts of talking on the telephone.

Talkin' the Talk

The following is a formal dialogue between two **signori** (see-*nyoh*-ree) (*gentlemen*) who have met only once.

Sig. Palladino:	**Pronto?** *prohn*-toh Hello?
Sig. Nieddu:	**Pronto, il signor Palladino?** *prohn*-toh eel see-*nyohr* pahl-lah-*dee*-noh Hello, Mr. Palladino?
Sig. Palladino:	**Sì. Con chi parlo?** see kohn kee *pahr*-loh Yes. Who am I speaking to?
Sig. Nieddu:	**Sono Carlo Nieddu.** *soh*-noh *kahr*-loh nee-*ehd*-dooh This is Carlo Nieddu.
Sig. Nieddu:	**Si ricorda di me?** see ree-*kohr*-dah dee meh Do you remember me?
Sig. Palladino:	**No, mi dispiace.** noh mee dees-*pyah*-cheh I don't, I'm sorry.
Sig. Nieddu:	**Il cugino di Enza.** eel kooh-*jee*-noh dee *ehn*-zah Enza's cousin.

Sig. Palladino: **Ma certo, mi scusi tanto!**
mah *chehr*-toh mee *skooh*-zee *tahn*-toh
Why, of course! Excuse me!

Sometimes you call just to chat on the phone — **fare due chiacchiere al telefono** (*fah*-reh *dooh*-eh *kyahk*-kyeh-reh ahl teh-*leh*-foh-noh). But the person on the other end of the line may not be prepared for a lengthy chat.

When you are really busy and don't even have one second to speak, you may need the following phrases. The first is informal, and the second is one you might use at work.

Ti posso richiamare più tardi? (tee *pohs*-soh ree-kyah-*mah*-reh pyooh *tahr*-dee) (*Can I call you back later?*)

or

La posso richiamare fra mezz'ora? (lah *pohs*-soh ree-kyah-*mah*-reh frah mehd-*dzoh*-rah) (*Can I call you back in half an hour?*)

Talkin' the Talk

On other occasions your call may be quite welcome, as is Monica's:

Monica: **Ciao, mamma, ti disturbo?**
chou *mahm*-mah tee dees-*toohr*-boh
Hello, Mom. Am I disturbing you?

Lucia: **No, assolutamente.**
noh ahs-soh-looh-tah-*mehn*-teh
Not at all.

Monica: **Volevo sentire cosa fate per Pasqua.**
voh-*leh*-voh sehn-*tee*-reh *koh*-sah *fah*-teh pehr *pahs*-qwah
I wanted to hear what you were doing for Easter.

Lucia: **Andiamo tutti dalla nonna.**
ahn-*dyah*-moh *tooht*-tee *dahl*-lah *nohn*-nah
We're all going to Grandma's.

Monica: **Ottimo! Buon'idea.**
oht-tee-moh bwohn-ee-*dee*-ah
Great! Good idea!

Words to Know

cellulare	chehl-looh-<u>lah</u>-reh	cellular phone
telefonino [m] telefonica [f]	teh-leh-foh-<u>nee</u>-noh/ teh-leh-<u>foh</u>-nee-kah	telephone
telefono pubblico [m]	teh-<u>leh</u>-foh-noh <u>poohb</u>-blee-koh	public phone
scheda telefonica	<u>skeh</u>-dah teh-leh-foh-<u>nee</u>-kah	phone card
messaggino	mehs-sahj-<u>jee</u>-noh	text message

Making Arrangements over the Phone

Making an appointment, reserving a table at a restaurant, ordering tickets for a concert are all activities you usually do by phone. In this section I introduce you to the Italian way to handle these matters. (Track 21)

Talkin' the Talk

Mrs. Elmi calls her doctor's office to make an appointment. She is speaking with the doctor's nurse. (Track 21)

Sig.ra Elmi: **Buongiorno, sono la signora Elmi. Vorrei prendere un appuntamento.**
bwohn-*johr*-noh *soh*-noh lah see-*nyoh*-rah *ehl*-mee vohr-*rey prehn*-deh-reh oohn ahp-poon-tah-*mehn*-toh
Good morning, this is Ms. Elmi. I'd like to make an appointment.

Nurse: **È urgente?**
eh oohr-*jehn*-teh
Is it urgent?

Sig.ra Elmi: **Purtroppo sì.**
poohr-*trohp*-poh see
Unfortunately, it is.

Nurse: **Va bene alle quattro e mezza?**
vah *beh*-neh *ahl*-leh *kwaht*-troh eh *mehd*-dzah
Today at four-thirty?

Sig.ra Elmi: **Va benissimo, grazie.**
vah beh-*nees*-see-moh *grah*-tsee-eh
That's great, thank you.

Nurse: **Prego. Ci vediamo più tardi.**
preh-goh chee veh-*dyah*-moh *pyooh tahr*-dee
You're welcome. See you later.

The expression **a domani** (ah doh-*mah*-nee) (*see you tomorrow*) is a bit different in Italian, in that it doesn't have a verb. In English, the verb "to see" indicates that you will see the other person tomorrow. Italian is more concise; you say **a domani** — literally, "until tomorrow."

Asking for People and Getting the Message

This section offers useful terminology about asking to speak to people and leaving messages. You know how often the person you want isn't available, so you need to be comfortable getting a message across.

You're familiar with the situation: You're waiting for a call, but the telephone doesn't ring. Then, you have to go out. When you get back, you want to know whether anyone called for you. You can ask that question several ways:

✔ **Ha chiamato qualcuno per me?** (ah kyah-*mah*-toh kwahl-*kooh*-noh pehr meh) (*Has anybody called for me?*)

✔ **Mi ha chiamato qualcuno?** (mee ah kyah-*mah*-toh kwahl-*kooh*-noh) (*Did anybody call me?*)

✔ **Mi ha cercato nessuno?** (mee ah chehr-*kah*-toh nehs-*sooh*-noh) (*Has anybody looked for me?*)

Talkin' the Talk

Leo wants to give Camilla a call, but she's not home. Therefore, he leaves a message for her.

Leo:	**Buongiorno, sono Leo.** bwohn-*johr*-noh *soh*-noh *leh*-oh Good morning, this is Leo.
Voice:	**Ciao Leo.** chou *leh*-oh Hello, Leo.
Leo:	**C'è Camilla?** cheh kah-*meel*-lah Is Camilla in?
Voice:	**No, è appena uscita.** noh eh ahp-*peh*-nah ooh-*shee*-tah No, she's just gone out.
Leo:	**Quando la trovo?** *kwahn*-doh lah *troh*-voh When can I reach her?
Voice:	**Verso le nove.** *vehr*-soh leh *noh*-veh Around nine.
Leo:	**Le posso lasciare un messaggio?** leh *pohs*-soh lah-*shah*-reh oohn mehs-*sahj*-joh Can I leave her a message?
Voice:	**Come no, dimmi.** *koh*-meh noh *deem*-mee Of course, tell me.

As you can see, there are different ways for asking for people as well as for saying that they're not in and asking if you can leave a message. The informal dialogue above gives you one way of saying these things, and the dialogue that follows recasts the situation into a formal exchange.

Talkin' the Talk

 Mr. Marchi calls Mr. Trevi's office to talk about an upcoming meeting. Mr. Trevi's secretary picks up the phone. (Track 22)

Secretary:	**Pronto?**
	prohn-toh
	Hello?
Sig. Marchi:	**Buongiorno, sono Ennio Marchi.**
	bwohn-*johr*-noh *soh*-noh *ehn*-nee-oh *mahr*-kee
	Good morning, this is Ennio Marchi.
Secretary:	**Buongiorno, dica.**
	bwohn-*johr*-noh *dee*-kah
	Good morning, can I help you?
Sig. Marchi:	**Potrei parlare con il signor Trevi?**
	poh-*trey* pahr-*lah*-reh kohn eel see-*nyoh*-reh *treh*-vee
	Can I speak to Mr. Trevi?
Secretary:	**Mi dispiace, è in riunione.**
	mee dees-*pyah*-cheh eh een ree-oohn-*yoh*-neh
	I'm sorry, he's in a meeting.
Sig. Marchi:	**Potrei lasciargli un messaggio?**
	poh-*trey* lah-*shahr*-lyee oohn mehs-*sahj*-joh
	May I leave him a message?
Secretary:	**Certo. Prego.**
	chehr-toh *preh*-goh
	Of course. Go on . . .

Sometimes you don't understand the name of the person you're talking to and you have to ask for the spelling. If someone needs you to spell your name, you may hear either of the following questions:

- **Come si scrive?** (*koh*-meh-see *skree*-veh) (*How do you write it?*)

- **Può fare lo spelling?** (pwoh *fah*-reh loh spelling) (*Can you spell it?*)

Don't worry too much about this; as long as you know the basic Italian alphabet in Chapter 1, you'll be able to spell your name and town to anyone!

Words to Know

pronto	prohn-toh	hello
chiacchierare	kyahk-kyeh-rah-reh	to chat
Attenda in linea!	aht-tehn-dah een lee-neh-ah	Please hold!
chiamare	kyah-mah-reh	to call
chiamata [f]	kyah-mah-tah	call
informazione [f]	een-fohr-mah-tsyoh-neh	information
sorpresa [f]	sohr-preh-zah	surprise

What Did You Do Last Weekend? — Talking about the Past

Not all phone calls have to do with leaving messages, of course. One age-old reason for a phone conversation is so friends can catch up on each other's lives. Imagine you had such a great time at the beach last weekend that you can't wait to call and tell your best friend all about it. But to be able to communicate what you did, who you saw, and where you went, you first need to understand the Italian equivalent of the present perfect and simple past.

When you speak about something that happened in the past — for example, I have spoken — you mostly use the **passato prossimo** (pahs-*sah*-toh *prohs*-see-moh) in Italian, which corresponds to both the English present perfect and the simple past (*I spoke*).

The **passato prossimo** is a compound tense: It consists of more than one word, as in "I have heard." Take a look at how it works in these examples:

✔ **Ho ascoltato un CD.** (oh ahs-kohl-*tah*-toh oohn chee-*dee*) (*I have listened/ listened to a CD.*)

✔ **Sono andata alla spiaggia.** (*soh*-noh ahn-*dah*-tah *ahl*-lah *spyahj*-jah) (*I went to the beach.*)

The structure of the **passato prossimo** is similar to the present perfect. It is composed of the present tense of either the verb **avere** (ah-*veh*-reh) (*to have*) or **essere** (ehs-ser-reh) (*to be*) plus the past participle of the verb that describes what happened. In the preceding examples, **ascoltato** (ahs-kohl-*tah*-toh) (*listened*) is the past participle of **ascoltare** (ahs-kohl-*tah*-reh) (*to listen*), and **andata** (ahn-*dah*-tah) (*spoken*) is the past participle of **andare** (ahn-*dah*-reh) (*to go*).

In sum: helping verb **essere** or **avere** + past participle of verb (generally ending in **–ato, –uto, –ito** (*ah*-toh, *ooh*-toh *ee*-toh). To form past participles, you take the infinitive of the verb, keep the stem, and add the ending.

Lei (ley) is the formal way of saying "you." Use **lei** to address someone you don't know well, or to whom you want to be polite.

So how do you know when to use **essere** or **avere** as your helping verb in the **passato prossimo**? Transitive verbs take **avere** and intransitive verbs take **essere**. Usage will be your guide, but basically all verbs like: to come, to go, to go in, to go out, to stay, to return, to be born and to die take **essere**.

Let's start with transitive verbs, as shown in Table 10-1:

Table 10-1	Passato Prossimo with Avere
Avere +Past Participle	*Translation*
ho chiamato (oh kyah-*mah-toh*)	*I called/have called/I did call*
hai chiamato (ahy kyah-*mah-toh*)	*you called/have called/you did call*
ha chiamato (ah kyah-*mah-toh*)	*he/she called/ has called*
abbiamo chiamato (ahb-*byah*-moh kyah-*mah-toh*)	*we called /have called*
avete chiamato (ah-*veh*-teh kyah-*mah-toh*)	*you (pl.) called/have called*
hanno chiamato (*ahn*-noh kyah-*mah-toh*)	*they called/have called*

Some past participles are irregular and will come at the end of this section: They follow no rule, and simply have to be memorized. See Appendix A for more examples.

Table 10-2 provides you with some common regular past participles and also some very common irregular past participles of verbs that are conjugated with avere.

Table 10-2	Past Participles Using "Avere" — To Have
Infinitive	**Past Participle**
ascoltare (ahs-kohl-*tah*-reh) (*to listen*)	**ascoltato** (ahs-kohl-*tah*-toh) (*listened*)
comprare (kohm-*prah*-reh) (*to buy*)	**comprato** (kohm-*prah*-toh) (*bought*)
telefonare (teh-leh-foh-*nah*-reh) (*to phone*)	**telefonato** (teh-leh-foh-*nah*-toh) (*called*)
conoscere (koh-*noh*-sheh-reh) (*to meet, the first time*)	**conosciuto** (koh-noh-*shooh*-toh) (*met*)
ricevere (ree-*cheh*-veh-reh) (*to receive*)	**ricevuto** (ree-cheh-*vooh*-toh) (*received*)
partire (pahr-*tee*-reh) (*to leave/depart*)	**partito** (pahr-*tee*-toh) (*left/departed*)
dire (*dee*-reh) (*to say*)	**detto** (*deht*-toh) (*said*)
fare (*fah*-reh) (*to do*)	**fatto** (*faht*-toh) (*done*)
leggere (*lehj*-jeh-reh) (*to read*)	**letto** (*leht*-toh) (*read*)
scrivere (*skree*-veh-reh) (*to write*)	**scritto** (*skreet*-toh) (*written*)
vedere (veh-*deh*-reh) (*to see*)	**visto** (*vees*-toh) (*seen*)

Asking about last weekend is always a reason to call your friend to hear what he or she did.

Talkin' the Talk

Rosa calls her best friend Tiziana to catch up on her weekend.

Rosa: **Che cosa hai fatto questo fine settimana?**
keh *koh*-zah ahy *faht*-toh *kwehs*-toh *fee*-neh seht-tee-*mah*-nah
What did you do last weekend?

Tiziana: **Ho conosciuto un uomo meraviglioso!**
oh koh-noh-*shooh*-toh oohn *woh*-moh meh-rah-vee-*lyoh*-zoh
I met a wonderful man!

Rosa: **Racconta tutto!**
rahk-*kohn*-tah *tooht*-toh
Tell me everything!

Tiziana: **Sabato sono andata al mare.**
sah-bah-toh *soh*-noh ahn-*dah*-tah ahl *mah*-reh
Saturday I went to the beach.

Rosa: **Da sola?**
dah *soh*-lah
Alone?

Tiziana: **Sì, e lì ho incontrato Enrico.**
see eh lee oh een-kohn-*trah*-toh ehn-*ree*-koh
Yes, and I met Enrico there.

Rosa: **Per caso?**
pehr *kah*-zoh
By chance?

Tiziana: **No, me l'ha presentato Davide.**
noh meh lah preh-zehn-*tah*-toh *dah*-vee-deh
No, David introduced me to him.

Now take a look at some intransitive verbs that take **essere** as their helping verb.

When the **passato prossimo** is compounded with the present tense of **essere** (to be), the past participle ends according to the subject: feminine singular -**a**, masculine singular -**o**, feminine plural -**e**, or masculine plural -**i**. Note the endings of the past participles in Table 10-3.

Table 10-3	**Passato Prossimo with Essere**	
Essere + Past participle		*Translation*
io sono uscita/o	(*ee*-oh *soh*-noh ooh-*shee*-tah/oh)	*I went out.*
tu sei uscita/o	(tooh sey ooh-*shee*-tah/oh)	*You went out.*
lei/lui è uscita/o	(ley *looh*-ee eh ooh-*shee*-tah/oh)	*He/she went out.*
noi siamo uscite/i	(noi see-*ah*-moh ooh-*shee*-teh/ee)	*We went out.*
voi siete uscite/i	(voi see-*eh*-teh ooh-*shee*-teh/ee)	*You went out.*
loro sono uscite/i	(*loh*-roh *soh*-noh ooh-*shee*-teh/ee)	*They went out.*

Do familiarize yourself well with the intransitive verbs in Table 10-4 that are always conjugated with **essere**, not only in the present perfect tense, but in any other compound tense in Italian.

Table 10-4	Past Participles Using "Essere" — To Be	
Infinitive	**Past Participle**	**Translation**
andare (ahn-*dah*-reh) (*to go*)	**andata/-o/-e/-i** (ahn-*dah*-tah/toh/teh/tee)	*gone*
arrivare (ahr-ree-*vah*-reh) (*to arrive*)	**arrivata/-o/-e/-i** (ahr-ree-*vah*-tah/toh/teh/tee)	*arrived*
entrare (ehn-*trah*-reh) *(to enter)*	**entrata/-o/-e/-i** (ehn-*trah*-tah/toh/teh/tee)	*entered*
partire (pahr-*tee*-reh) (*to leave*)	**partita/-o/-e/-i** (pahr-*tee*-tah/toh/teh/tee)	*left*
venire (veh-*nee*-reh) (*to come*)	**venuta/-o/-e/-i** (veh-*nooh*-tah/toh/teh/tee)	*came*
tornare (tohr-*nah*-reh) (*to return*)	**tornata/-o/-e/-i** (tohr-*nah*-tah/toh/teh/tee)	*returned*

Discussing Your Job

The world is getting smaller, and business contact with people in other countries is getting more common. Whether by phone, fax, or e-mail, it's becoming more and more important to know how to communicate to business colleagues around the world. If you happen to have business contacts with Italian companies, knowing some basic Italian business vocabulary may be useful.

Italian has at least four words for "company" — **la compagnia** (lah kohm-pah-*nyee*-ah), **la ditta** (lah *deet*-tah) (which also means *the firm*), **l'azienda** (lah-*dzehn*-dah) and **la società** (lah soh-cheh-*tah*). These words are virtually interchangeable.

L'ufficio (loohf-*fee*-choh) is Italian for "office." The following sentences give you a taste of the phrases you hear in **uffici** (oohf-*fee*-chee) (*offices*) everywhere:

✔ **La mia scrivania è troppo piccola.** (lah *mee*-ah skree-vah-*nee*-ah eh *trohp*-poh *peek*-koh-lah) (*My desk is too small.*)

✔ **È una grande società?** (eh *ooh*-nah *grahn*-deh soh-cheh-*tah*) (*Is it a big company?*)

✔ **Lavora per una piccola agenzia.** (lah-*voh*-rah pehr *ooh*-nah *peek*-koh-lah ah-jehn-*tsee*-ah) (*He works for a small agency.*)

✔ **Amo il mio lavoro.** (*ah*-moh eel *mee*-oh lah-*voh*-roh) (*I like my job.*)

The human element

Even if you are **libero professionista** (*lee*-beh-roh proh-fehs-see-oh-*nees*-tah) (*self-employed*), chances are that your **lavoro** (lah-*voh*-roh) (*job*) puts you in contact with other people. All those people have titles and names, as the following short exchanges show:

✔ **Il mio capo è una donna.** (eel *mee*-oh *kah*-poh eh *ooh*-nah *dohn*-nah) (*My boss is a woman.*)

✔ **Hai un'assistente personale?** (*ahy* ooh-nahs-sees-*tehn*-teh pehr-soh-*nah*-leh) (*Do you have a personal assistant?*)

No, il nostro team ha un segretario. (noh eel *nohs*-troh team ah oohn seh-greh-*tah*-ree-oh) (*No, our team has a secretary.*)

✔ **Dov'è il direttore?** (doh-*veh* eel dee-reht-*toh*-reh) (*Where is the director?*)

Nel suo ufficio. (nehl *sooh*-oh oohf-*fee*-choh) (*In her office.*)

Office equipment

Even the smallest offices today utilize a wide variety of equipment. Many of these "technology" words are the same in Italian as they are in English: computer, fax, and e-mail are used and pronounced as they are in English, and the Italian for "photocopy" and "photocopier" are fairly intuitive — **fotocopia** (foh-toh-*koh*-pee-ah) and **fotocopiatrice** (foh-toh-koh-pee-ah-*tree*-cheh), respectively.

The following sentences can help you develop your Italian office vocabulary to a respectable level.

✔ **Posso usare la stampante, per favore?** (*pohs*-soh ooh-*zah*-reh lah stahm-*pahn*-teh pehr fah-*voh*-reh) (*May I use the printer, please?*)

✔ **Il lavoro non va bene.** (eel lah-*voh*-roh nohn vah *beh*-neh) (*Work isn't going well.*)

✔ **Il fax è arrivato.** (eel *fahks* eh ahr-ree-*vah*-toh) (*The fax arrived.*)

✔ **Quando ha spedito l'e-mail?** (*kwahn*-doh ah speh-*dee*-toh lee-*mail*) (*When did you send the e-mail?*)

Talkin' the Talk

Mr. Miller, an American businessman, has been trying unsuccess-
fully to send his Italian associate, il signor Tosi, some important
information.

Mr. Miller: **Ha ricevuto la mia raccomandata?**
ah ree-cheh-*vooh*-toh lah *mee*-ah
rahk-koh-mahn-*dah*-tah
Have you received the express letter I sent?

Sig. Tosi: **No, oggi non è arrivato niente.**
noh *ohj*-jee nohn eh ahr-ree-*vah*-toh nee-*ehn*-teh
No, nothing has arrived yet today.

Mr. Miller: **Le mando subito un fax.**
leh *mahn*-doh *sooh*-bee-toh oohn fahks
I'll send you a fax immediately.

Sig. Tosi: **Purtroppo è rotto.**
poohr-*trohp*-poh eh *roht*-toh
Unfortunately, it's broken

Mr. Miller: **Le invio un'e-mail allora.**
leh een-*vee*-oh oohn e-*mail* ahl-*loh*-rah
I'll send you an e-mail then.

Sig. Tosi: **Va bene. E può mandarmi il documento?**
vah *beh*-neh eh pwoh mahn-*dahr*-mee eel
doh-kooh-*mehn*-toh
Yes. And can you send me the document?

Mr. Miller: **Certo, glielo mando come allegato, ma avrò bisogno
di più tempo.**
chehr-toh *lyee*-loh *mahn*-doh *koh*-meh ahl-leh-*gah*-
toh mah ah-*vroh* bee-*zoh*-nyoh dee pyooh *tehm*-poh
Of course, I'll send it as an attachment, but I'll need a
bit more time.

Sig. Tosi: **Va benissimo. Oggi lavoro fino a tardi.**
vah beh-*nees*-see-moh *ohj*-jee lah-*voh*-roh *fee*-noh
ah *tahr*-dee
That's great. I'm working late today.

Words to Know

messaggio [m]	mehs-_sahj_-joh	message
lavoro [m]	lah-_voh_-roh	work
È rotto.	eh _roht_-toh	It's broken.
macchina [f]	_mahk_-kee-nah	machine
tempo [m]	_tehm_-poh	time
tardi	_tahr_-dee	late

In Italy, want ads often request information on an applicant's personality. Also, job advertisements do not usually contain mailing addresses. Instead, ads list fax or e-mail addresses. You send your **domanda d'assunzione** (doh-_mahn_-dah dahs-soohn-_tsyoh_-neh) (*job application*) and/or your curriculum vitae or resume via fax or e-mail.

Words to Know

colloquio [m]	kohl-_loh_-kwee-oh	interview
assistente [f/m]	ahs-sees-_tehn_-teh	assistant
annuncio [m]	ahn-_noohn_-choh	advertisement
responsabile	reh-spohn-_sah_-bee-leh	responsible
affidabile	ahf-fee-_dah_-bee-leh	dependable

Fun & Games

You're Mario's guest, but he's gone out for a moment. The telephone rings and you have to answer it. Fill the gaps in this incomplete phone conversation. See Appendix D for answer key.

You: (1) _____! (Hello!)

Caller: Ciao, sono Chiara. Con chi (2) _____? (Hello, I'm Chiara. With whom am I speaking?)

You: Sono un (3) _____ di Mario. (I'm a friend of Mario's.)

Caller: (4) _____ Mario? (Is Mario in?)

You: No, è (5) _____ uscito. (No, he's just gone out.)

Caller: Gli posso (6) _____? (Can I leave him a message?)

You: Certo (7) _____. (Of course. Please.)

Mario returns and asks:

Mario: Ha (8) _____ qualcuno per me? (Has anybody called for me?)

Chapter 11

Recreation and the Outdoors

In This Chapter

▶ Discovering the great outdoors through animals and plants

▶ Enjoying yourself with reflexive verbs and **piacere**

▶ Exploring sports and other hobbies

*I*n this chapter, we talk about the fun stuff — playing sports, pastimes, and generally enjoying yourself. Plus, we throw in a section about reflexive verbs so that you can talk correctly about enjoying yourself.

Maybe you use your **fine settimana** (*fee*-neh *seht*-tee-*mah*-nah) (*weekends*) as a chance to play sports like **calcio** (*kahl*-choh) (*soccer*), **tennis** (*tehn*-nees) (*tennis*), or **pallavolo** (*pahl*-lah-*voh*-loh) (*volleyball*). Or perhaps you park yourself in front of the TV to watch **pallacanestro** (*pahl*-lah-kah-*nehs*-troh) (*basketball*). In any case, being able to talk sports and other recreational activities is a plus in any language.

Taking a Tour

Whether you're in a city or rural area, you can usually find fun and interesting sights to see. You can take a car trip, or leave the driving to someone else and sign up for an organized bus tour to take you to special places. Bus tours are, for the most part, organized in great detail and the price generally includes the cost of the hotel, lunch, dinner, and the services of a tour guide.

A guided tour may be the most efficient, cost-effective, and informative way to check out the attractions of an unfamiliar city. You can use the following questions to help find out more about **una gita organizzata** (*ooh*-nah *jee*-tah ohr-gah-nee-*dzah*-tah) (*an organized tour*). Notice that Italian has two, basically interchangeable ways to say "go on a tour": **fare una gita** (*fah*-reh *ooh*-nah *jee*-tah) and **fare un'escursione** (*fah*-reh oohn ehs-koohr-*syoh*-neh).

✔ **Ci sono gite organizzate?** (chee *soh*-noh *jee*-teh ohr-gah-nee-*dzah*-teh) (*Are there any organized tours?*)

✔ **Che cosa c'è da vedere?** (keh *koh*-zah cheh dah veh-*deh*-reh) (*What sights are included?*)

✔ **Quanto costa la gita?** (*kwahn*-toh *kohs*-tah lah *jee*-tah) (*How much does the tour cost?*)

✔ **C'è una guida inglese?** (cheh *ooh*-nah *gwee*-dah een-*gleh*-zeh) (*Is there an English-speaking guide?*)

✔ **Dove si comprano i biglietti?** (*doh*-veh see *kohm*-prah-noh ee bee-*lyeht*-tee) (*Where do you buy tickets?*)

Notice in the following sentences that the Italians have appropriated a few English words — picnic and jog.

✔ **Mi piace camminare nel verde.** (mee *pyah*-cheh kahm-mee-*nah*-reh nehl *vehr*-deh) (*I like to walk in nature.*)

✔ **Facciamo un picnic sul prato?** (fahch-*chah*-moh oohn peek-*neek* soohl *prah*-toh) (*Should we have a picnic on the lawn?*)

✔ **Ti piace l'osservazione degli uccelli?** (tee *pyah*-cheh lohs-sehr-vah-*tsyoh*-neh *dehl*-yee ooch-*chehl*-lee) (*Do you like bird-watching?*)

✔ **Faccio jogging nel parco.** (*fahch*-choh *johg*-geeng nehl *pahr*-koh) (*I go jogging in the park.*)

Maybe you like to go up into the mountains to be close to nature. Even when **ti godi** (tee *goh*-dee) (*you enjoy*) Mother Nature on your own, however, you may want to know some vocabulary to express the wonders you see, such as "**Che bel panorama!**" (keh behl pah-noh-*rah*-mah) (*What a great view!*) Here we go!

✔ **l'albero** (*lahl*-beh-roh) (*tree*)

✔ **il bosco** (eel *bohs*-koh) (*woods*)

✔ **il fiore** (eel *fyoh*-reh) (*flower*)

✔ **la pianta** (lah *pyahn*-tah) (*plant*)

✔ **il pino** (eel *pee*-noh) (*pine*)

✔ **il prato** (eel *prah*-toh) (*meadow; lawn*)

✔ **la quercia** (lah *kwehr*-chah) (*oak*)

✔ **il tramonto** (trah-*mohn*-toh) (*sunset*)

✔ **il panorama** (pah-noh-*rah*-mah) (*view*)

Words to Know

campagna [f]	kahm-<u>pah</u>-nyah	countryside
fiume [m]	<u>fyooh</u>-meh	river
lago [m]	<u>lah</u>-goh	lake
mare [m]	<u>mah</u>-reh	sea
montagna [f]	mohn-<u>tah</u>-nyah	mountain

Talkin' the Talk

Animals are always an interesting topic, and knowing the names of some of them in another language can be helpful. Here's a dialogue about animals:

Carla: **Ti piacciono gli animali?**
tee *pyach*-choh-noh lyee ah-nee-*mah*-lee
Do you like animals?

Alessandra: **Sì, ho una piccola fattoria.**
see oh *ooh*-nah *peek*-koh-lah faht-toh-*ree*-ah
Yes, I have a small farm.

Carla: **Davvero?**
dahv-*veh*-roh
Really?

Alessandra: **Ho un cane, due gatti e un maialino.**
oh oohn *kah*-neh *dooh*-eh *gaht*-tee eh oohn mah-yah-*lee*-noh
I have a dog, two cats, and a small pig.

Carla: **Ti piacciono i cavalli?**
tee *pyahch*-choh-noh ee kah-*vahl*-lee
Do you like horses?

Alessandra: **No, preferisco le mucche.**
noh preh-feh-*rees*-koh leh *moohk*-keh
No, I prefer cows.

Words to Know

cane [m]	kah-neh	dog
cavallo [m]	kah-vahl-loh	horse
capra [f]	kah-prah	goat
gallo [m]	gahl-loh	rooster
gatto [m]	gaht-toh	cat
gallina [f]	gahl-lee-nah	chicken
maiale [m]	mahy-ah-leh	pig
mucca [f]	moohk-kah	cow
uccello [m]	oohch-chehl-loh	bird
lupo [m]	looh-poh	wolf
pecora [f]	peh-koh-rah	sheep
tacchino [m]	tahk-kee-noh	turkey

Speaking Reflexively

When you say "to enjoy yourself," you use a reflexive verb. That is, you turn the action back to yourself. The same applies in Italian. But not all Italian reflexive verbs are reflexive in English, and vice versa. Some verbs, such as **riposarsi** (ree-poh-*zahr*-see) (*to rest oneself*) and **svegliarsi** (zveh-*lyahr*-see) (*to wake oneself*), are not reflexive in English, although they are in Italian.

In Italian, you can tell whether a verb is reflexive by looking at the infinitive form. If the last syllable of the infinitive is **-si** (*see*), which translates as "oneself," then the verb is reflexive. When you conjugate a reflexive verb, you must change the last syllable from **-si** to something else. The following conjugation of **divertirsi** (dee-vehr-*teer*-see) (*to enjoy oneself, to have a good time*) demonstrates the conjugation of the verb. After you have removed the **–si** at the end of a reflexive verb, you conjugate it just like any other **–are, –ere, and –ire** verb. The only difference is that you add the reflexive pronoun, which refers to the person concerned (the subject). Notice how **divertirsi** becomes a regular present tense **–ire** verb, with the exception that you then need the reflexive pronouns.

Conjugation	Pronunciation	Translation
mi diverto	mee dee-*vehr*-toh	*I have fun.*
ti diverti	tee dee-*vehr*-tee	*You're having fun.*
si diverte	see dee-*vehr*-teh	*He/she is enjoying him/herself.*
ci divertiamo	chee dee-vehr-*tyah*-moh	*We have fun.*
vi divertite	vee dee-vehr-*tee*-teh	*You're enjoying yourself.*
si divertono	see dee-*vehr*-toh-noh	*They have fun.*

Here are some more examples:

- ✔ **divertirsi: Mi diverto molto a cantare.** (mee dee-*vehr*-toh *mohl*-toh ah kahn-*tah*-reh) (*I really enjoy myself singing.*)

- ✔ **annoiarsi** (ahn-noi-*ahr*-see) (to be bored): **Vi annoiate in campagna?** (vee ahn-noi-*ah*-teh een kahm-*pah*-nyah) (*Do you get bored in the country?*)

✔ **svegliarsi** (zvehl-*yahr*-see) (to wake up) **A che ora ti svegli?** (ah keh oh-rah tee *zveh*-lyee) (*What time do you wake up?*)

✔ **mettersi** (*meht*-tehr-see) (to put on/to wear) **Mi metto la giacca nera.** (mee *meht*-toh lah *jahk*-kah *neh*-rah) (*I'm going to wear my black jacket.*)

✔ **lavarsi** (lah-*vahr*-see) **Ti sei lavata i denti?** (tee sey lah-*vah*-tah ee *dehn*-tee) (*Did you brush your teeth?*)

Talkin' the Talk

Maria Pia and Mauro are discussing what they enjoy doing on their weekends. (Track 23)

Maria Pia: **Cosa fai durante i fine settimana?**
koh-sah fahy dooh-*rahn*-teh ee *fee*-neh
seht-tee-*mah*-nah
How do you spend your weekends?

Mauro: **Faccio sport, leggo, incontro amici.**
fahch-choh sport *lehg*-goh een-*kohn*-troh
ah-*mee*-chee
I play sports, I read, I meet friends.

Ti piace leggere?
tee *pyah*-cheh *lehj*-jeh-reh
Do you like to read?

Maria Pia: **È la mia passione!**
eh lah *mee*-ah pahs-*syoh*-neh
It's my passion!

Che cosa leggi?
keh *koh*-zah *lehj*-jee
What do you read?

Mauro: **Soprattutto letteratura contemporanea.**
soh-praht-*tooht*-toh leht-teh-rah-*tooh*-rah
kohn-tehm-poh-*rah*-neh-ah
Mostly contemporary literature.

Playing Sports

Playing and talking about sports is a favored pastime of people the world over. And whether you travel to Italy, or just want to invite your Italian neighbor to play tennis, knowing sports terms is always helpful.

Some sports you do in Italian. Therefore, you pair those words with **fare** (*fah*-reh) (*to do; to practice*). With other sports, however, you must use **giocare** (joh-*kah*-reh) (*to play*) or **andare** (ahn-*dah*-reh) (*to go*). Then there are sports that use the verb that describes the sport itself, like **pattinare** (paht-tee-*nah*-reh) (*to skate*). Table 11-1 lists most sports and the verbs you use with them.

Table 11-1	Sports Verbs	
Italian	*Pronunciation*	*Translation*
*fare	*fah*-reh	*to do; to practice*
atletica leggera	aht-leh-*tee*-kah lehj-*jeh*-rah	*track*
canotaggio	kahn-oh-*taj*-joh	*crew/rowing*
ciclismo	chee-*klees*-moh	*cycling*
danza	*dahn*-zah	*dance*
equitazione	eh-kwee-tah-*tsyoh*-neh	*riding*
ginnastica artistica	gin-*nahs*-tee-kah ahr-*tees*-tee-kah	*gymnastics*
jogging	*johg*-geeng	*jogging*
lotta	*loht*-tah	*wrestling*
nuoto	*nwoh*-toh	*swimming*
palestra	pah-*lehs*-trah	*going to the gym*
scherma	*skehr*-mah	*fencing*
lo sci	loh shee	*skiing*
lo sci nautico	loh shee *nou*-tee-koh	*water skiing*
sollevamento pesi	sohl-leh-vah-*mehn*-toh *peh*-zee	*weight lifting*
lo sno/snowboarding	*fah*-reh loh snoh/snoh-*borh*-ding	*snowboarding*
giocare a	joh-*kah*-reh ah	*to play*
calcio	*kahl*-choh	*soccer*
pallacanestro	*pahl*-lah-kah-*nehs*-troh	*basketball*
pallavolo	*pahl*-lah-*voh*-loh	*volleyball*
ping pong	peeng-pohng	*ping-pong*
tennis	*tehn*-nees	*tennis*
golf	gohlf	*golf*
*andare	ahn-*dah*-reh	*to go*
a cavallo	ah kah-*vahl*-loh	*to ride*
in bicicletta	een bee-chee-*kleht*-tah	*to cycle*

The following conjugations are for these three important sports verbs: **fare**, **andare**, and **giocare**.

Conjugation	Pronunciation
io faccio	*ee*-oh *fahch*-choh
tu fai	tooh fahy
lui/lei fa	*looh*-ee/ley fah
noi facciamo	noi fahch-*chah*-moh
voi fate	voi *fah*-teh
loro fanno	*loh*-roh *fahn*-noh
io vado	*ee*-oh *vah*-doh
tu vai	tooh vahy
lui/lei va	*looh*-ee/ley vah
noi andiamo	noi ahn-*dyah*-moh
voi andate	voi ahn-*dah*-teh
loro vanno	*loh*-roh *vahn*-noh
io gioco	*ee*-oh *joh*-koh
tu giochi	tooh *joh*-kee
lui/lei gioca	*looh*-ee/ley *joh*-kah
noi giochiamo	noi joh-*kyah*-moh
voi giocate	voi joh-*kah*-teh
loro giocano	*loh*-roh *joh*-kah-noh

Italians love to follow sports on TV, ranked more or less by their popularity:

calcio (*kahl*-choh) (*soccer*)

Formula 1 (*fohr*-mooh-lah *ooh*-noh) (*Formula One car racing*)

ciclismo (chee-*klees*-moh) (*cycling*)

moto GP (*moh*-toh gee-pee) (*motorcycle racing*)

pugilato (pooh-jee-*lah*-toh) (*boxing*)

lo sci alpino (loh shee ahl-*pee*-noh) (*downhill ski racing*)

Le ragazze (leh rah-*gaht*-tse) (*girls*) don't play **calcio** in Italy the way they do in other countries, but they do play **pallavolo**. Many **ragazzi** (rah-*gaht*-tsee) (*boys*) play **calcio**, and men play **calcetto** (kahl-*cheht*-toh), also called **calcio a cinque** (*kahl*-choh ah *cheen*-kweh), which is five-against-five soccer, often played indoors on a smaller field.

Then there is **bocce** (*bohch*-cheh) (*lawn bowling*). Many towns offer small **bocce** courts where older men usually play.

Talkin' the Talk

Giulia and Stefano have just met at the university and found out that they live in the same neighborhood. On the way to the bus stop Stefano strikes up a conversation about his favorite topic, sports. (Track 24)

Stefano: **Che sport pratichi?**
keh sport *prah*-tee-kee
What sports do you play?

Giulia: **Faccio nuoto e vado a cavallo.**
fahch-choh *nwoh*-toh eh *vah*-doh ah kah-*vahl*-loh
I swim and ride.

Stefano: **Equitazione?**
eh-kwee-tah-*tsyoh*-neh
Riding?

Giulia: **È il mio sport preferito!**
eh eel *mee*-oh sport preh-feh-*ree*-toh
It's my favorite sport!

Giochi a tennis?
joh-kee ah *tehn*-nees
Do you play tennis?

Stefano: **No, faccio palestra.**
noh *fahch*-choh pah-*lehs*-trah
No, I go to the gym.

Giulia: **Body building?**
boh-dee *beeld*-eeng
Body building?

Stefano:	**Uso le machine come il tapis roulant* in inverno e corro in pineta in estate.**
	ooh-zoh leh *mahk*-kee-neh *koh*-meh eel tah-pee-rooh-*lahn* een een-*vehr*-noh eh *kohr*-roh een pee-*neh*-tah een ehs-*tah*-teh
	Oh no — I use the machines like the treadmill in the winter and I run in the pine forest in the summer.

*Italians use the French word **tapis roulant** for treadmill.

Talking about Hobbies and Interests

You can certainly do a lot of other things in your leisure time besides wear yourself out playing sports. Here you learn about a variety of them in Italian.

Some typical questions (and varied responses) to ask about **il tempo libero** (eel *tehm*-poh *lee*-behr-oh) (*free time*) include:

✔ **Che cosa ti piace fare nel tempo libero?**

keh *koh*-zah tee *pyah*-che *fah*-reh nehl *tehm*-poh *lee*-beh-roh

What do you like to do in your free time?

Mi piace cucinare e fare l'uncinetto.

mee *pyah*-cheh kooh-chee-*nah*-reh eh *fah*-reh loohn-chee-*neht*-toh

I look to cook and crochet.

✔ **Qual è il tuo passatempo preferito?**

kwahl eh eel *tooh*-oh pahs-sah-*tehm*-poh preh-feh-*ree*-toh

What is your favorite pastime?

Il mio passatempo preferito è . . . /i miei passatempi preferiti sono . . .

eel *mee*-oh pahs-sah-*tehm*-poh preh-feh-*ree*-toh eh/ee myey pahs-sah-*tehm*-pee preh-feh-*ree*-tee *soh*-noh

My favorite pastime is . . . /My favorite pastimes are . . .

You might want to start your sentence with the possessive adjective in the preceding sentence if you're writing to someone rather than speaking.

> **. . . fare i giochi da tavolo e giocare a scacchi.**
>
> *fah*-reh ee *joh*-kee dah *tah*-voh-loh eh joh-*kahr*-reh ah *skahk*-kee
>
> *playing board games or chess.*
>
> **. . . stare con gli amici.**
>
> *stah*-reh kohn lyee ah-*mee*-chee
>
> *. . . hanging out with friends.*
>
> ✔ **Quali sport fai?**
>
> *kwah*-lee spohrt fahy
>
> *What sports do you play?*
>
> **Faccio lo sci./Gioco a tennis.**
>
> *fahch*-cho loh shee/*joh*-koh ah *tehn*-nees
>
> *I ski/I play tennis.*

Liking things

You spend your free time doing recreational things that you like. And when you say you like something, use the verb **piacere** (pyah-*cheh*-reh). This verb is a bit weird in that you usually use it only in the third person singular or the third person plural of any verb tense.

Third person singular: if what you like is singular or an infinitive.

–Mi piace correre.	mee *pyach*-eh *kohr*-reh-reh	*I like to run.*
–Mi piace il mare.	mee *pyach*-eh eel *mah*-reh	*I like the sea.*

Third person plural: if what you like is plural.

Mi piacciono gli sport invernali.	mee *pyach*-choh-noh lyee spohrt een-vehr-*nah*-lee	*I like winter sports.*

Only your pronouns change, which are indirect object pronouns and literally mean "such and such a thing is pleasing to 'me'." These are **mi, ti, gli, le, ci, vi, loro** (mee, tee, lyee, leh, chee, vee, *loh*-roh) (*me, you, him, her, us, you, them*). You don't use personal pronouns (**io, tu, lui, lei** etc.) with the verb **piacere**.

Talkin' the Talk

Have a look at what Serena and Nicoletta are talking about. Nicoletta apparently prefers peaceful and calm activities, whereas Serena likes to participate in sports that make her sweat.

Serena: **Cosa fai questo fine settimana?**
koh-zah fahy *kwehs*-toh *fee*-neh-seht-tee-*mah*-nah
What are you going to do this weekend?

Nicoletta: **Vado in campagna.**
vah-doh een kahm-*pah*-nyah
I'm going to the countryside.

Serena: **È un'idea fantastica!**
eh ooh-nee-*deh*-ah fahn-*tahs*-tee-kah
That's a great idea!

Nicoletta: **Ho una casetta vicino al lago.**
oh *ooh*-nah kah-*zeht*-tah vee-*chee*-noh ahl *lah*-goh
I have a small house close to the lake.

Serena: **Ideale per riposarsi.**
ee-deh-*ah*-leh pehr ree-poh-*zahr*-see
Ideal for relaxing.

Nicoletta: **Sì, leggo, scrivo, passeggio lungo il lago.**
see *lehg*-goh *skree*-voh pahs-*sehj*-joh *loohn*-goh eel *lah*-goh
Yes, I read, I write, I take walks around the lake.

Serena: **Non fai sport?**
nohn fahy sport
Don't you play any sports?

Nicoletta: **Vado in bicicletta.**
vah-doh een bee-chee-*kleht*-tah
I bicycle.

Obviously, participating in sports isn't the only hobby you can have. Some hobbies are more sedentary, like reading, sewing, or playing musical instruments.

Talkin' the Talk

 Ernesto and Tommaso are discovering that not all sports are physical. (Track 25)

Ernesto:	**Non ti annoi mai?**
	nohn tee ahn-*noi* mahy
	Don't you ever get bored?

Tommaso:	**No, ho molti interessi.**
	noh oh *mohl*-tee een-teh-*rehs*-see
	No, I have many interests.

Ernesto:	**Per esempio?**
	pehr eh-*zehm*-pee-oh
	For example?

Tommaso:	**Amo leggere e andare al cinema.**
	ah-moh *lehj*-jeh-reh eh ahn-*dah*-reh ahl *chee*-neh-mah
	I love to to read and go to the movies.

Ernesto:	**Non fai sport?**
	nohn fahy sport
	Don't you play any sports?

Tommaso:	**Faccio yoga e meditazione.**
	fach-choh *yoh*-gah eh mehd-ee-tah-*tsyoh*-neh
	I do yoga and meditate.

Many people love music, whether they like to **ascoltare la musica** (ahs-kohl-*tah*-reh lah *mooh*-zee-kah) (*listen to music*) or **suonare uno strumento** (swoh-*nah*-reh *ooh*-noh strooh-*mehn*-toh). Of course, there are all kinds of music, from **classica** (*klahs*-see-kah) (*classical*) to **jazz** (jats) to **rock** (rohk).

Talkin' the Talk

Emilia and Isabel are two classmates getting to know each other a little better.

Emilia:	**Mi piace molto ascoltare la musica. E tu?** mee *pyah*-cheh *mohl*-toh ahs-kohl-*tah*-reh lah *mooh*-zee-kah eh tooh I like to listen to music a lot. And you?
Isabel:	**Ho molta musica sul mio i-Pod.** oh *mohl*-tah *mooh*-zee-kah soohl *mee*-oh ahy-pohd I have a lot of music on my iPod.
Emilia:	**Tu suoni uno strumento?** tooh *swoh*-nee *ooh*-noh strooh-*mehn*-toh Do you play an instrument?
Isabel:	**Suono il violoncello e il pianoforte.** *swoh*-noh eel vee-oh-lohn-*chehl*-loh eh eel pee-*ah*-noh-*fohr*-teh I play the cello and the piano.
Emilia:	**Sei brava?** sey *brah*-vah Are you good?
Isabel:	**Si, mi piace molto suonare. E tu?** see mee *pyah*-cheh *mohl*-toh swoh-*nah*-reh eh tooh I guess so. I really like to play music. And you?
Emilia:	**Suono il flauto, ma preferisco cantare nel coro.** *swoh*-noh eel *flou*-toh mah preh-feh-*rees*-koh kahn-*tah*-reh nehl *koh*-roh I play the flute, but I prefer to sing in the chorus.

Words to Know

ascoltare	ahs-kohl-<u>tah</u>-reh	to listen to
batteria	baht-teh-<u>ree</u>-ah	drums
chitarra	kee-<u>tahr</u>-rah	guitar
clarinetto	klah-reen-<u>eht</u>-toh	clarinet
flauto	<u>flou</u>-toh	flute
giocare	joh-<u>kah</u>-reh	to play a sport, cards, game
pianoforte	pee-<u>ah</u>-noh-<u>fohr</u>-teh	piano
sassofono	sahs-<u>soh</u>-foh-noh	saxophone
suonare	swoh-<u>nah</u>-reh	to play an instrument
tromba	<u>trohm</u>-bah	trumpet
violoncello	vee-oh-lohn-<u>chehl</u>-loh	cello
violino	vee-oh-<u>lee</u>-noh	violin
voce	<u>voh</u>-cheh	voice

Fun & Games

Now it's time for you to have some fun! In the following box, try to find the names of some plants and animals I introduced in this chapter. I provide the English, but you have to find the Italian.

Find the Italian for these words: horse, flower, bird, cat, wolf, oak, pine, cow, sheep, tree. See Appendix D for answer key.

Word Seek

A	J	A	R	O	C	E	P	O	S
U	I	V	S	W	S	O	P	A	B
A	H	C	E	M	L	U	Y	O	A
C	I	K	R	L	L	U	V	G	D
C	G	B	A	E	F	O	L	E	D
U	N	V	M	Z	U	I	N	S	D
M	A	R	X	J	C	Q	O	I	Y
C	G	A	T	T	O	E	I	R	P
A	L	B	E	R	O	P	S	T	E
F	R	H	O	L	L	E	C	C	U

Part III
Italian on the Go

The 5th Wave   By Rich Tennant

"So far you've called a rickshaw, a unicyclist, and a Zamboni. I really wish you'd learn the Italian word for taxicab."

In this part . . .

These chapters help you appreciate the adventure of travel. Here, you'll get help with every aspect of your trip — from getting a visa to making hotel reservations, and from changing U.S. dollars into euros to getting around on public transportation. I also include a chapter on handling those unexpected emergency situations. So **Buon viaggio!** (bwohn *vyahj*-joh) (*Have a nice trip!*)

Chapter 12

Planning a Trip

. . . .

In This Chapter

▶ Making travel plans

▶ Coming and going: **arrivare** and **partire**

▶ Taking a tour

▶ Going to the beach

▶ Looking forward to your trip: The simple future

. . . .

*E*verybody likes to get away from the daily grind and check out new environments and activities during their free time. Tourists and Italians alike flock to **la spiaggia** (lah *spyahj-j*ah) (*to the beach*), head **in montagna** (een mohn-*tah*-nyah) (*to the mountains*), or **in campagna** (een kahm-*pahn*-yah) (*to the countryside*). Some Italians take long trips outside of Italy. Whatever you do, **buon viaggio!** (bwohn *vyahj*-joh) (*have a nice trip!*) or **buone vacanze!** (*bwoh*-neh vah-*kahn*-zeh) (*have a nice vacation!*)

Deciding When and Where to Go

Deciding when to take a trip can be just as important as choosing your destination. You probably don't want to visit Washington, D.C. in August when the weather can be unbearably hot and humid. Italy also has many cities that really heat up in the summer. In fact, many Italians living in those cities escape for most of August to cooler places, such as the beaches of Sardegna or the cool Dolomites. On the other hand, summer months are also **l'alta stagione** *(lahl-tah stah-joh-neh) (high season)* for tourists.

Talkin' the Talk

Enzo is talking to Cristina about their vacation for the summer. He has it all figured out already, but Cristina is skeptical. (Track 26)

Enzo:
Quest'anno andiamo in montagna!
kwehs-tahn-noh ahn-dyah-moh een mohn-tah-nyah
This year we're going to the mountains!

Cristina:
Stai scherzando?
stahy skehr-tsahn-doh
Are you kidding?

Enzo:
È rilassante: boschi, aria fresca . . .
eh ree-lahs-sahn-teh bohs-kee ah-ree-ah frehs-kah
It's relaxing: woods, fresh air. . . .

Cristina:
È noioso! E non si può nuotare!
eh noi-oh-zoh eh nohn see pwoh nwoh-tah-reh
It's boring. And you can't swim!

Enzo:
Ci sono le piscine, i laghi, e i fiumi!
chee soh-noh leh pee-shee-neh ee lah-gee eh ee fyooh-mee
There are swimming pools, lakes, and rivers!

Cristina:
Ma dai, pensa al mare, al sole. . . .
mah dahy pehn-sah ahl mah-reh ahl soh-leh
Come on, think of the sea, the sun. . . .

Enzo:
Facciamo passeggiate, visitiamo i rifugi, mangiamo quel buon cibo di montagna.
fach-chah-moh pahs-sehj-jaht-teh vee-zee-tyah-moh ee ree-fooh-jee mahn-jah-moh qwel bwohn chee-boh dee mohn-tahn-yah
We can go hiking, visit some rifugi, and eat that good mountain food.

Cristina:
Oh no. Io rimango a casa!
oh noh ee-oh ree-mahn-goh ah kah-sah
Oh no. I'll stay home!

The Alps and Dolomites offer marvelous terrain for hiking and skiing. A **rifugio** (ree-fooh-joh) is a rustic mountain retreat that people hike or ski to, for the most part. You can enjoy a warm home-cooked meal there, and even spend the night in some.

Taking a Tour

Whether you're in a city or rural area, you can usually find fun and interesting sights to see. Bus tours are for the most part organized in great detail and the price generally includes the cost of the bus, lunch, dinner, and the services of a tour guide. A guided tour, or day-trip, **una gita organizzata** (*ooh*-nah *jee*-tah ohr-gah-nee-*dzah*-tah) (an organized tour), may be the most efficient, cost-effective, and informative way to check out nearby attractions.

✔ **Ci sono gite organizzate?** (chee *soh*-noh *jee*-teh ohr-gah-need-*dzah*-teh) (Are there any organized tours?)

✔ **Quanto costa la gita?** (*kwahn*-toh *kohs*-tah lah *jee*-tah) (How much does the tour cost?)

✔ **C'è una guida che parla inglese?** (cheh *ooh*-nah *gwee*-dah keh *pahr*-lah een-*gleh*-zeh) (Is there an English-speaking guide?)

✔ **Dove si comprano i biglietti?** (*doh*-veh see *kohm*-prah-noh ee bee-*lyeht*-tee) (Where do you buy tickets?)

Talkin' the Talk

Lucia and Renzo are in a tour office, talking to a tour agent and deciding which trip to go on the next day.

Lucia: **C'è una bella gita sul lago di Como domani.**
cheh *ooh*-nah *behl*-lah *gee*-tah soohl *lah*-goh dee *koh*-moh doh-*mah*-nee
There's a nice trip to Lake Como tomorrow.

Renzo: **Vuoi andare, vero?**
vwoi ahn-*dah*-reh *veh*-roh
You want to go, don't you?

Lucia: **Sarebbe carino. E tu?**
sah-*rehb*-beh kah-*ree*-noh eh tooh
It would be nice. What about you?

Renzo: **Non amo le gite in autobus.**
nohn *ah*-moh leh *gee*-teh een *ou*-toh-boohs
I don't like bus trips.

Lucia: **Ma è una gita a piedi!**
mah eh *ooh*-nah *jee*-tah ah *pyeh*-dee
But it's a walking tour!

Renzo:	**Ottimo! A che ora inizia la gita?**
	*oht-*tee-moh. ah keh *oh-*rah ee-*nee-tsyah* lah *jee-*tah
	Great! What time does the trip start?

Agent:	**Alle sette e trenta.**
	*ahl-*leh *seht-*teh eh *trehn-*tah
	At seven-thirty a.m.

Renzo:	**Quanto dura?**
	*kwahn-*toh *dooh-*rah
	How long is it going to last?

Agent:	**Circa cinque ore.**
	*cheer-*kah *cheen-*kweh *oh-*reh
	About five hours.

Words to Know

campagna [f]	kahm-pah-nyah	countryside
gita [f]	jee-tah	tour
fiume [m]	fyooh-meh	river
guida [f]	gwee-dah	guide
lago [m]	lah-goh	lake
mare [f]	mah-reh	sea
montagna [f]	mohn-tah-nyah	mountain

Booking a Trip/Traveling to Foreign Lands

You never know — you just might want to book a trip to another country while you're in Italy. When you're ready to book your flight or hotel, you may want to consider using **un'agenzia viaggi** (ooh-nah-jehn-*tsee*-ah vee-*ahj*-jee) (*a travel agency*). There you can get plane tickets, hotel reservations, or complete tour packages.

As you walk by the travel agency, undoubtedly your eye will be drawn to special all-inclusive package deals to Malta, Tunisia, and the Canary Islands, to name a few.

INCREDIBILI OFFERTE!! Gran Canaria, La Palma. Euro 616 a persona. Comprende: volo + hotel + tasse e commissioni. Colazione a buffet.

een-creh-*dee*-bee-lee ohf-*fehr*-teh. grahn kah-*nah*-ree-ah lah *pahl*-mah. sehy-*chehn*-toh *eh*-ooh-roh ah pehr-*soh*-nah. kohm-*prehn*-deh *voh*-loh oh-*tehl* *tahs*-seh eh kom-mees-*syoh*-neh. koh-lah-*tsyoh*-neh ah booh-*fey*

Incredible deals! Gran Canaria. La Palma. 616 euros per person. Includes flight, hotel, departure fees, and buffet breakfast.

Talkin' the Talk

Alessandro has just seen this sign for the Canary Islands. He is talking to Giorgio the travel agent.

Giorgio: **Buongiorno, mi dica.**
bwohn-*johr*-noh mee *dee*-kah
Good morning, can I help you? (Literally: Tell me.)

Alessandro: **Vorrei fare un viaggio alle Isole Canarie.**
vohr-*rey fah*-reh oohn vee-*ahj*-joh *ahl*-leh ee-zoh-leh kah-*nah*-ree-eh
I'd like to take a trip to the Canary Islands.

Giorgio: **Dove, esattamente?**
doh-veh eh-zaht-tah-*mehn*-teh
Where exactly?

Alessandro: **Tenerife o La Palma.**
the-neh-*ree*-feh oh lah *pahl*-ma
Tenerife or La Palma.

Giorgio: **Un viaggio organizzato?**
oohn *vyahj*-joh ohr-gah-nee-*dzah*-toh
An organized trip?

Alessandro: **No, vorrei soltanto prenotare il volo.**
noh vohr-*rey* sohl-*tahn*-toh preh-noh-*tah*-reh eel
voh-loh
No, I'd like to book just the flight.

Giorgio: **E per gli spostamenti interni?**
eh pehr lyee *spoh*-stah-*mehn*-tee een-*tehr*-nee
And what about moving around between islands?

Alessandro: **No, mi sposterò in autobus e traghetto.**
noh, mee spohs-tehr-*oh* een *ou*-toh-boohs eh
trah-*geht*-toh
No, I'll get around by bus and ferry.

Giorgio: **Quando vuole partire?**
kwahn-doh *vwoh*-leh pahr-*tee*-reh
When do you want to leave?

Alessandro: **La prima settimana di febbraio.**
lah *pree*-mah seht-tee-*mah*-nah dee fehb-*brahy*-oh
The first week of February.

Giorgio: **E il ritorno?**
eh eel ree-*tohr*-noh
And return?

Alessandro: **La terza settimana di febbraio.**
lah tehr-tsah seht-tee-*mah*-nah dee fehb-*brahy*-oh
The third week of Ferbruary.

Visas and passports

All you need is a passport (**un passaporto**) (oohn pahs-sah-*pohr*-toh) to visit Italy if you're going for less than six months. If you go for longer, you will need **un visto** (oohn *vees*-toh) (a visa).

If you fly to Italy, the main airports are **Malpensa** (mahl-*pehn*-sah) in Milan, and **Leonardo da Vinci** (leh-oh-*nahr*-doh dah *veen*-chee) in Rome, but you can also fly into Venice, Bologna, Palermo, and Naples, other popular (and less hectic) airports.

Several years ago, a new vacation concept became popular in Italy: **l'agriturismo** (lah-gree-tooh-*reez*-moh) (*the farm holiday*). During these types of vacations, people travel to the country or the mountains where they stay in farmhouses. These accommodations range from Spartan to luxurious and romantic; most are good options for families. Guests can help out on the farm, ride horses, and swim at some **agriturismi**. This type of lodging also enables you to eat the traditional food of the region, and you're miles away from formal, impersonal hotels.

Another popular type of lodging is the bed and breakfast, which you can find throughout the countryside as well in big cities like Rome and Milan.

You can easily find an abundance of both on the Web as you're doing your research for your trip.

Words to Know

rimanere	ree-mah-<u>neh</u>-reh	to stay
in treno	een <u>treh</u>-noh	by train
viaggiare	vee-ahj-<u>jah</u>-reh	to travel
viaggio organizzato [m]	vyahj-joh ohr-gah-nee-<u>dzah</u>-toh	organized trip
volo [m]	<u>voh</u>-loh	flight
traghetto [m]	trah-<u>geht</u>-toh	ferry

Arriving and Leaving: The Verbs "Arrivare" and "Partire"

To help you understand the verbs **arrivare** (ahr-ree-*vah*-reh) (*to arrive*) and **partire** (pahr-*tee*-reh) (*to leave*), we use them in some simple sentences in the following list. As you can see, when you use these verbs in connection with a specific place (city) **arrivare** is always followed by the preposition **a** (ah) (*at/to/in*), and when you arrive in a country you use the preposition **in** (een) (*in*). **Partire** is always followed by the preposition **da** (dah) (*from*) when leaving from a place; when leaving for a place it is followed by the preposition **per** (pehr) (*for*).

- ✔ **Luca parte da Torino alle cinque.** (*looh*-kah *pahr*-teh dah toh-*ree*-noh *ahl*-leh *cheen*-kweh) (*Luca leaves from Turin at 5 o'clock.*)

- ✔ **Arrivo a Taormina nel pomeriggio.** (ahr-*ree*-voh ah tah-ohr-*mee*-nah nehl poh-meh-*reej*-joh) (*I'm arriving in Taormina in the afternoon.*) The verbs **partire** (pahr-*tee*-reh) (*to leave*) and **arrivare** (ahr-ree-*vah*-reh) (*to arrive*) are conjugated like other regular _ARE, and _IRE verbs, which you can check out in Chapter 2 or in Appendix A.

Talkin' the Talk

Filippo and Marzia are spending some time together before Filippo has to catch a plane. (Track 27)

Marzia:	**A che ora parte l'aereo?** ah keh *oh*-rah *pahr*-teh lah-*eh*-reh-oh What time does the plane leave?
Filippo:	**Alle nove di mattina.** *ahl*-leh *noh*-veh dee maht-*tee*-nah At nine a.m.
Marzia:	**A che ora arrivi a Los Angeles?** ah keh *oh*-rah ahr-*ree*-vee ah lohs *ahn*-jeh-lehs What time will you arrive in Los Angeles?
Filippo:	**Alle undici di notte.** *ahl*-leh *oohn*-dee-chee dee *noht*-teh At eleven p.m.

Going to the Beach and Spa

Italy has 7,600 kilometers of coastline, so it is no surprise that Italians and tourists alike flock to Italy's famous beaches, which can be both sandy (**sabbiose**, sahb-bee-*yoh*-sey) or rocky (**scoglio** *skoh*-lyoh), each with its decided advantages (and clientele). Most beaches have that most wonderful of Italian institutions called **il bagno** (eel *bahn*-yoh). This is not a bathroom or a bath, but a combination bar/beach club/restaurant, where you can show up and rent an **ombrellone** (ohm-brehl-*loh*-neh) (*beach umbrella*) and **un lettino** (oohn leht-*tee*-noh) (*a lounge chair*) for the day, week, or month. Here you and the children can also play **beach volley** (*beach volleyball*) or **racchettone** (rahk-eht-*toh*-neh) (*beach tennis*), or rent a **pedalò** (peh-dah-*loh*) (*paddle boat*).

Italy also has many wonderful naturally heated thermal springs, spas or **terme** (*tehr*-meh). Some of these are quite well-equipped, and for whose services you pay (like Chianciano, Montecatini, and Fiuggi). Other **terme** can be accessed for free in places like Vulcano, Ischia, and Calabria.

Using the Simple Future Tense

Sometimes you need a verb form that indicates that something will happen in the near future. In Italian, this tense is called **futuro semplice** (foh-*tooh*-roh *sehm*-plee-cheh) (simple future). However, you can also use the present tense when referring to a point in the future. The following sentences use the simple future tense:

- ✔ **Andrò in Italia.** (ahn-*droh* een ee-*tah*-lee-ah) (*I will go to Italy.*)

- ✔ **Quando arriverai a Palermo?** (*kwahn*-doh ahr-ree-veh-*rahy* ah pah-*lehr*-moh) (*When will you arrive in Palermo?*)

- ✔ **Non torneremo troppo tardi.** (nohn tohr-neh-*reh*-moh *trohp*-poh *tahr*-dee) (*We won't be back too late.*)

To form the simple future of regular verbs, take the whole infinitive, cut off the final **e**, and add the same set of endings (**ò, ai, à, emo, ete, anno**). For _are verbs you need to change the -**a** in the infinitive to an -**e**. Note the stem change in Table 12-1.

Sending letters and postcards

So if you're one of those people who still like to send **cartoline** (kahr-toh-*lee*-neh) (*postcards*) and **lettere** (*leht*-teh-reh) (*letters*) while traveling, you're going to need to find an **ufficio postale** (oohf-*fee*-choh pohs-*tah*-leh) (*post office*) or **tabaccaio** (tah-bahk-*kahy*-oh)

(*tobacconist*) where you can purchase stamps, **francobolli** (frahn-koh-*bohl*-lee) and **buste** (*boohs*-teh) (*envelopes*). You can also find stamps and envelopes in a **cartoleria** (kahr-toh-leh-*ree*-ah) (*stationery shop*).

Table 12-1		Simple Future		
Parlare = **PARLER-**	**Prendere=** **PRENDER**	**Partire=** **PARTIR**	**Finire=** **FINIR**	**Translation**
parlerò	prenderò	partirò	finirò	(*I will talk, have, leave, finish*)
parlerai	prenderai	partirai	finirai	(*you will talk, have, leave, finish*)
parlerà	prenderà	partirà	finirà	(*he/she/you will talk, have, leave, finish*)
parleremo	prenderemo	partiremo	finiremo	(*we will speak, have, leave, finish*)
parlerete	prenderete	partirete	finirete	(*you will speak, have, leave, finish*)
perleranno	prenderanno	partiranno	finiranno	(*they will speak, have, leave, finish*)

Fun & Games

Fill in the missing words with one of three possible answers under each sentence. See Appendix D for the answer key.

1. **Quest'anno andiamo in _____.** (This year we're going to the mountains.)

   a. albergo

   b. montagna

   c. aereo

2. **Il volo parte _____ Palermo alle tre.** (The flight leaves from Palermo at three o'clock.)

   a. da

   b. su

   c. a

3. **Passo le vacanze in _____.** (I spend my vacation in the country.)

   a. mare

   b. campagna

   c. montagna

4. **Dov'è la mia _____?** (Where is my suitcase?)

   a. stanza

   b. piscina

   c. valigia

5. **È un _____ organizzato.** (It's an organized trip.)

   a. viaggio

   b. treno

   c. volo

Chapter 13
Money, Money, Money

In This Chapter

▶ Banking transactions

▶ Trading currencies

▶ Charging purchases

▶ Knowing various currencies

*O*n the one hand, you can never have enough of it; on the other hand, money can cause trouble. This is particularly true for situations abroad or when you're dealing with foreign money in general. This chapter doesn't cover only currency — you know how tiresome converting foreign currencies can be — but all the terms you need to know about money.

Going to the Bank

Dealing with banks isn't always fun, but sometimes you can't avoid them. You aren't often in the position of being able to cash a big check; you may have other, more painful, transactions to perform. In this section, we give you some banking terms that can help you manage a dialogue in a bank.

You may need to go to the bank for several reasons. For example, you may want to **cambiare valuta** (kahm-bee-*ah*-reh *vah*-looh-tah) (*to change money*), **prelevare contanti** (preh-leh-*vah*-reh cohn-*tahn*-tee) (*to withdraw money*), **versare soldi sul tuo conto** (vehr-*sah*-reh *sohl*-dee soohl *tooh*-oh *kohn*-toh) (*to deposit money into your account*). Other reasons could be **aprire un conto** (ah-*pree*-reh oohn *kohn*-toh) (*to open an account*), or **riscuotere un assegno** (rees-*kwoh*-teh-reh oohn ahs-*seh*-nyoh) (*to cash a check*).

Other phrases you may find helpful include:

✔ **Mi dispiace, il suo conto è scoperto.** (mee dees-*pyah*-cheh eel *sooh*-oh *kohn*-toh eh skoh-*pehr*-toh) (*I'm sorry, your account is overdrawn.*)

✔ **Può girare l'assegno per favore?** (*pwoh* jee-*rah*-re lahs-*seh*-nyoh pehr fah-*voh*-reh) (*Could you endorse the check, please?*)

✔ **Quant'è il tasso d'interesse?** (kwant-*eh* eel *tahs*-soh deen-teh-*rehs*-seh) (*What is the interest rate?*)

✔ **Vorrei cambiare dei traveler's checks.** (vohr-*ray* kahn-bee-*ah*-reh dehy traveler's checks) (*I'd like to change some traveler's checks.*)

When you are in the lucky situation of having money left, you may like to invest it. Here is some of the present tense conjugation for **investire** (een-vehs-*tee*-reh) (*to invest*), which is conjugated like any other regular **–IRE** verb without the "isc" (see Chapter 2).

Conjugation	Pronunciation	Translation
io investo	*ee*-oh een-*vehs*-toh	*I invest*
tu investi	tooh een-*vehs*-tee	*you invest*
lui/lei investe	*looh*-ee/ley een-*vehs*-teh	*he/she invests*

To make life easier for you and to help you avoid standing in front of closed doors, we give you the hours of Italian banks: Banks are open Monday through Friday, generally from 8:30 a.m. to 1:30 p.m; then they reopen from 2:30 to 4 p.m. These are general guidelines; the hours differ from city to city.

Talkin' the Talk

Il signor Blasio asks for a statement of his account. He talks to un'impiegata (ooh-neem-pyeh-*gah*-tah) (a female employee).

Sig. Blasio: **Vorrei riscuotere un assegno.**
vohr-*rey* rees-*kwoh*-teh-reh oohn ahs-*seh*-nyoh
I'd like to cash a check.

Clerk: **Un documento, per favore. Firmi questa ricevuta, per favore.**
oohn doh-kooh-*mehn*-toh pehr fah-*voh*-reh. *feer*-mee *kwehs*-tah ree-cheh-*vooh*-tah pehr fah-*voh*-reh
Some ID please. Please sign this receipt.

Sig. Blasio: **Vorrei anche il mio estratto conto.**
vohr-rey *ahn*-keh eel *mee*-oh ehs-*traht*-toh *kohn*-toh
I'd like to get my bank statement too.

Clerk: **Il suo numero di conto?**
eel *sooh*-oh *nooh*-meh-roh dee *kohn*-toh
Your account number?

Sig. Blasio:	**Sette zero cinque nove.**
	seht-teh *dzeh*-roh *cheen*-kweh *noh*-veh
	Seven zero five nine.

Clerk:	**Grazie. Attenda un momento. . .**
	grah-tsee-eh aht-*tehn*-dah oohn moh-*mehn*-toh
	Thank you. Wait one moment. . .

	Ecco a lei!
	ehk-koh ah ley
	Here you are!

Sig. Blasio:	**Grazie mille, arrivederci!**
	grah-tsee-eh *meel*-leh ahr-ree-veh-*dehr*-chee
	Thanks so much, good-bye!

Words to Know

conto [m] corrente	kohn-toh kohr-rehn-teh	checking account
estratto conto [m]	ehs-traht-toh kohn-toh	bank statement
tasso d'interesse	tahs-soh deen-teh-rehs-seh	interest rate
libretto [m] degli assegni	lee-breht-toh deh-lyee ahs-seh-nyee	checkbook
carta di credito	kahr-tah dee kreh-dee-toh	credit card
ricevuta [f]	ree-cheh-vooh-tah	receipt
girare	jee-rah-reh	to endorse
riscuotere	rees-kwoh-teh-reh	to cash

Changing Money

You're more likely to need to change money when you're abroad. If you're in Italy and want to change some dollars into euros (*eh*-ooh-roh), you would go either to a **banca** (*bahn*-kah) (*to the bank*) or to an **ufficio di cambio** (oohf-*fee*-choh dee *kahm*-bee-oh) (*exchange office*), or more common still, an ATM machine. Some places definitely offer better exchange rates, so shop around if you have time.

Because Italy is highly frequented by tourists from all over the world, the clerks in exchange offices have experience with people speaking English. Still, you just might want to complete a transaction in an exchange office in Italian.

Talkin' the Talk

Liza Campbell, an American tourist, needs to change some dollars for euros. She goes to a bank and talks to the teller. (Track 28)

Ms. Campbell: **Buongiorno, vorrei cambiare alcuni dollari in euro.**
bwohn-*johr*-noh vohr-*rey* kahm-bee-*ah*-reh ahl-*kooh*-nee *dohl*-lah-ree een *eh*-ooh-roh
Hello, I'd like to change some dollars into euros.

Teller: **Benissimo. Quanti dollari?**
beh-*nees*-see-moh *kwahn*-tee *dohl*-lah-ree
Very well. How many dollars?

Ms. Campbell: **Duecento. Quant'è il cambio?**
dooh-eh-*chehn*-toh *kwahn*-teh eel *kahm*-bee-oh
Two hundred. What's the exchange?

Teller: **Oggi un euro costa un dollaro e venti più cinque euro di commissione**
oj-jee oohn *eh*-ooh-roh *kohs*-tah oohn *dohl*-lah-roh eh *vehn*-tee pyooh *cheen*-kweh *eh*-oohr-oh dee kohm-mees-*syoh*-neh
Today the euro costs a dollar and twenty cents plus five euros for the service charge.

Ms. Campbell: **Va bene.**
vah *beh*-neh
Okay.

Teller:	**Mi serve un documento.**
	mee *sehr*-veh oohn dok-ooh-*mehn*-toh
	I need some ID.
Ms. Campbell:	**Ecco.**
	ehk-koh
	Here.
Teller:	**Sono 175 Euro meno i 5 Euro di commmissione.**
	soh-noh *chehn*-toh seht-*tahn*-tah *cheen*-kweh *eh*-ooh-roh *meh*-noh ee *cheen*-kweh *eh*-ooh roh dee kom-mee-*syoh*-neh
	It comes to 175 euros less the 5 euro exchange fee.
Ms. Campbell:	**Grazie mille!**
	grah-tsee-eh *meel*-leh
	Thanks a million!

Nowadays, changing money is not the most efficient way to get the local currency. In Italy, as in most Western countries, you can find a **bancomat** (*bahn-koh-maht*) (*ATM*) almost anywhere. Also, depending on where you shop and eat, you can pay directly with a **carta di credito** (*kahr*-tah dee *kreh*-dee-toh) (*credit card*). The following phrases can help you find the cash you need (or at least the cash machine):

- **Dov'è il bancomat più vicino?** (doh-*veh* eel *bahn*-koh-maht pyooh vee-*chee*-noh) (*Where is the nearest ATM?*)

- **Posso pagare con la carta di credito?** (*pohs*-soh pah-*gah*-reh kohn lah *kahr*-tah dee *kreh*-dee-toh) (*May I pay with my credit card?*)

- **Mi scusi, potrebbe cambiarmi una banconota da 100 euro?** (mee *skooh*-zee poh-*trehb*-beh kahm-bee-*ahr*-mee *ooh*-nah bahn-koh-*noh*-tah da *chehn*-toh *eh*-ooh-roh) (*Excuse me, would you be able to change a 100 euro bill?*)

- **Mi dispiace, non accettiamo carte di credito.** (mee dees-*pyah*-cheh nohn ahch-cheht-*tyah*-moh *kahr*-teh dee *kreh*-dee-toh) (*I'm sorry, we don't accept credit cards.*)

- **Mi dispiace, non ho spiccioli.** (mee dees-*pyah*-cheh nohn oh *speech*-choh-lee) (*I'm sorry, I haven't any small change.*)

Words to Know

in contanti	een kohn-_tahn_-tee	in cash
riscuotere	rees-_kwoh_-teh-reh	to cash
accettare	ahch-cheht-_tah_-reh	to accept
bancomat [m]	_bahn_-koh-maht	ATM
cambiare	kahm-bee-_ah_-reh	to change
spiccioli [m]	_speech_-choh-lee	small change

Using Credit Cards

In Canada and the United States you could take care of almost all your financial needs without ever handling cash. You can pay for almost everything with your debit or credit card. You can even use your credit card to get cash at ATMs and in some banks. This is the same in Italy, although cash is still the customary form of payment in many parts of Italy.

Talkin' the Talk

Ms. Johnson wants to withdraw some euros with her credit card but discovers that the ATM is out of order. She enters the bank and asks the cashier what's up.

Ms. Johnson: **Scusi, il bancomat non funziona.**
skooh-zee eel _bahn_-koh-maht nohn
foohn-_tsyoh_-nah
Excuse me, the ATM isn't working.

Cashier: **Lo so, signora, mi dispiace!**
loh soh see-_nyoh_-rah mee dees-_pyah_-cheh
I know, madam, I'm sorry!

Ms. Johnson:	**Ma ho bisogno di contanti.**
	mah oh bee-*zoh*-nyoh dee kohn-*tahn*-tee
	But I need cash.

Cashier:	**Può prelevarli qui alla cassa.**
	pwoh preh-leh-*vahr*-lee kwee *ahl*-lah *kahs*-sah
	You can withdraw it here at the counter.

Ms. Johnson:	**D'accordo, grazie.**
	dak-*kohr-doh grahts*-ee-eh
	OK, thanks.

Normally, things go easily and you don't have any problems using credit cards. But you may be asked to show your identification for security purposes. The following phrases can help you be prepared for this situation:

- ✔ **Potrei vedere un documento per favore?** (poh-*trey* veh-*deh*-reh oohn dohk-ooh-*mehn*-toh pehr fah-*voh*-reh) (*May I please see your identification?*)

- ✔ **Potrebbe darmi il suo passaporto, per favore?** (poh-*trehb*-beh *dahr*-mee eel *sooh*-oh pahs-sah-*pohr*-toh pehr fah-*voh*-reh) (*Would you please give me your passport?*)

- ✔ **Il suo indirizzo?** (eel *sooh*-oh een-dee-*reet*-tsoh) (*What is your address?*)

You may have to wait to exchange money. The following sentence says all you need to know about this rather formal verb: **attendere** (aht-*tehn*-deh-reh) (*to wait*).

Attenda, per favore	(aht-*tehn*-dah pehr fah-*voh*-reh)	(*Please wait.*)

Talkin' the Talk

While Ms. Johnson explores her options with the cashier, another person enters the bank and starts to complain:

Signora Gradi:	**Il bancomat ha mangiato la mia carta.**
	eel *bahn*-koh-maht ah mahn-*jah*-toh lah *mee*-ah kahr-tah
	The cash machine has eaten my card.

Teller:	**Ha digitato il numero giusto?**
	ah dee-jee-*tah*-toh eel *nooh*-eh-roh *joohs*-toh
	Did you enter the right number?

Signora Gradi: **Certo! Che domanda!**
chehr-toh keh doh-*mahn*-dah
Of course! What a question!

Teller: **Mi scusi, a volte capita.**
mee *skooh*-zee ah *vohl*-teh *kah*-pee-tah
Excuse me, but it can happen.

Signora Gradi: **Cosa posso fare?**
koh-sah *pohs*-soh *fah*-reh
What can I do?

Teller: **Attenda un momento . . .**
aht-*tehn*-dah oohn moh-*mehn*-toh
Wait a moment . . .

Words to Know

Certo!	chehr-toh	Of course!
il bancomat [m]	eel bahn-koh-maht	the ATM
digitare	dee-gee-tah-reh	to enter
prelevare	preh-leh-vah-reh	to withdraw
funzionare	foohn-tsyoh-nah-reh	to work; to function
contanti [m]	kohn-tahn-tee	cash
Che domanda!	keh doh-mahn-dah	What a question!

Looking at Various Currencies

Along with many other European countries, the Italian monetary unit is the
euro (*eh*-ooh-roh). There are 1 euro coins and 2 euro coins, and then larger
bills (5, 10, 20, 50, 100, and so on). The plural form is **euro** (*eh*-ooh-roh), and
the abbreviation is €. (That's right, the singular and the plural forms are

exactly the same). Smaller denominations are in **centesimi** (chehn-*teh*-zee-mee) (*cents*), and are coins. (You can check out Chapter 4 for numbers.)

Talkin' the Talk

Patrizia is planning her vacation to Croatia. She is planning on taking the **aliscafo** (ah-leeh-*skah*-foh) (high-speed ferry) from Ancona tomorrow. She talks to her friend, Milena, about exchanging her money.

Patrizia:	**Sai qual'è il cambio euro in kuna croata?** sayh kwah-*leh* eel *kahm*-bee-oh *eh*-ooh-roh een *kooh*-nah *kroh*-ah-tah Do you know the exchange rate for euros to Croatian kuna?
Milena:	**Non ne ho idea!** nohn neh oh ee-*deh*-ah I have no idea!
Patrizia:	**Domani parto per Zara per un mese. . .** doh-*mah*-nee *pahr*-toh pehr *dsah*-rah perh oohn *meh*-zeh Tomorrow I'm leaving for Zara for a month.
Milena:	**. . . e non hai ancora cambiato!** eh nohn ahy ahn-*koh*-rah kahm-bee-*ah*-toh . . . and you haven't changed your money yet!
Patrizia:	**Posso farlo al porto.** *pohs*-soh *fahr*-loh ahl *pohr*-toh I can do it at the port.
Milena:	**Ma no, è più caro!** mah noh eh pyooh *kah*-roh No, that's more expensive!
Patrizia:	**Mi accompagni in banca?** mee ahk-kohm-*pah*-nyee een *bahn*-kah Will you come with me to the bank?

The **euro** is legal tender in 17 of the 27 countries that belong to the European Union (EU). So, if you travel among EU countries after you have euros in your possession, you don't have to change money in every country you visit. Since 2002, the Italian **lira** has disappeared, and the euro is the only valid currency in Italy.

Table 13-1 shows the currencies of various countries.

Table 13-1		Currencies	
Italian	*Pronunciation*	*English single/ plural*	*Where used*
dollaro/dollari	*dohl*-lah-roh/ *dohl*-lah-ree	*dollar/dollars*	Canada; United States
lira/e sterlina/e	*lee*-rah/eh stehr-*lee*-nah/neh	*pound/pounds*	Ireland; United Kingdom
peseta/pesetas	peh-*seh*-tah/ peh-*seh*-tahs	*pesetas/pesetas*	Mexico

Talkin' the Talk

Cristina is at the bank. **Allo sportello** (*ahl*-loh spohr-*tehl*-loh) (at the counter), she sees that her high school buddy Paolo is now the bank teller.

Patrizia:	**Ciao Paolo. Vorrei cambiare cinquecento euro in sterline.**
	chou *pah*-oh-loh vohr-*rey* kahm-bee-*ah*-reh *cheen*-kweh-*chehn*-toh *eh*-oohr-roh een stehr-*lee*-neh
	Hi Paolo. I'd like to change 500 euros into British pounds.
Teller:	**Vai in Inghilterra?**
	vahy een een-geehl-*tehr*-rah
	Are you going to England?
Patrizia:	**Sì.**
	see
	Yes.

Teller: **Sai che puoi usare il bancomat ed è anche più sicuro?**
sahy keh pwoi ooh-*zah*-reh eel *bahn*-koh-maht ehd
eh *ahn*-keh pyooh see-*kooh*-roh
Do you know that you can use the ATM machine and
that it's even safer?

Patrizia: **Hai ragione, allora cambio solo duecento euro.**
ahy rah-*joh*-neh ahl-*loh*-rah *kahm*-bee-oh *soh*-loh
dooh-eh-*chehn*-toh *eh*-ooh-roh
You're right: I'm just going to change 200 euros.

Teller: **Ecco le tue sterline, fai buon viaggio!**
ehk-koh leh *tooh*-eh stehr-*lee*-neh fahy bwon
vyahj-joh
Here are your pounds, have a good trip!

Words to Know

prendere	prehn-deh-reh	to take
viaggio [m]	vyahj-joh	trip
aeroporto [m]	ah-eh-roh-pohr-toh	airport
cambiare	kahm-bee-ah-reh	to exchange
domani	doh-mah-nee	tomorrow

Fun & Games

Here's a little game for you. First define each word from this chapter, and then find them in the word search puzzle. See Appendix D for the answer key.

```
C A R T A D I C R E D I T O D D
S O K S Z N B O Y D O Y Y D O
E R R Y P A Z G E C L S A M C
T R J U N O G P S D L P N F U
A X A C E B R P Q Z A K U L M
M G A I A M I T Q S R X K J E
O L W A B C T O E Y O R J I N
C H L N C M E N I L R E T S T
N C K I E B A I N V L N L H O
A J O A S S A C K R A O Z P H
B L T R I C E V U T A A S E K
I E H T W N L C N X M K Q G V
Q J A U Y C V Q Q A G M N A Q
Q L N Q E K C Y P D F Q L V W
Z Q X X B E J M W F Y Y A L N
```

Banca _____

Bancomat _____

Cambiare _____

Carta di credito _____

Contanti _____

Documento _____

Dollaro _____

Euro _____

Kuna _____

Ricevuta _____

Spiccioli _____

Sportello _____

Sterline _____

Chapter 14

Getting Around: Planes, Trains, Taxis, and Buses

. . . .

In This Chapter

▶ Traveling by airplane

▶ Declaring your goods to customs

▶ Losing your luggage

▶ Renting a car

▶ Using public transportation

▶ Understanding maps and schedules

▶ Arriving early, late, or on time

. . . .

*W*hether you're visiting Italy or you just need to explain to an Italian-speaking friend how to get across town, transportation vocabulary really comes in handy. This chapter helps you make your way through the airport and also helps you secure transportation to get where you're going once you're on the ground, either by taxi, bus, car, or train. Further, I show you what to do at customs, how to find missing luggage, and how to rent a car. Andiamo (ahn-*dyah*-moh) — let's go!

Getting through the Airport

You're lucky, because it's very likely that you can get by with English when you're at an Italian airport. Both Italian and English are usually spoken there. But you just may be in a situation where the person next to you in an airport only knows Italian. Just in case, I want to provide you with some useful navigational material. Besides, you'll probably want a chance to practice the language in which you will be immersed once you step outside the airport.

Checking in

The moment you finally get rid of your luggage is called check-in — in Italian **accettazione** (ahch-cheht-tah-*tsyoh*-neh). Actually, people often use "check-in" in Italian, too. You also pick up your boarding pass at the check-in counter, so speaking is usually inevitable. The following dialogue contains some of the sentences people commonly exchange.

Talkin' the Talk

Ms. Adami is checking in. She shows her ticket and passport to the agent and leaves her suitcases at the counter.

Agent: **Il suo biglietto, per favore.**
eel *sooh*-oh bee-*lyeht*-toh pehr fah-*voh*-reh
Your ticket, please.

Sig.ra Adami: **Ecco.**
ehk-koh
Here it is.

Agent: **Passaporto?**
pahs-sah-*pohr*-toh
Passport?

Sig.ra Adami: **Prego.**
preh-goh
Here you are.

Agent: **Quanti bagagli ha?**
kwahn-tee bah-*gah*-lyee ah
How many suitcases do you have?

Sig.ra Adami: **Due valigie e un bagalio a mano.**
dooh-eh vah-*lee*-jeh eh oohn bah-*gah*-lyoh ah *mah*-noh
Two suitcases and one piece of carry-on luggage.

Agent: **Qual è la sua destinazione?**
qwahl eh lah *sooh*-ah deh-stee-nahts-*yoh*-neh
What is your destination?

Sig.ra Adami:	**New York.**
	nooh yohrk
	New York.

Agent:	**Ha fatto Lei le proprie valige?**
	ah *faht*-toh ley leh *proh*-pree-eh vah-*lee*-jeh
	Did you pack you own bags?

Sig.ra Adami:	**Sí.**
	see
	Yes.

Agent:	**Le ha sempre avute sotto mano da quando le ha chiuse?**
	leh ah *sehm*-preh ah-*vooh*-teh *soht*-toh *mah*-noh dah *qwahn*-doh leh ah *kyooh*-zeh
	Have they been with you the whole time since you closed them?

Sig. ra Adami:	**Sí; posso avere un posto vicino al finestrino, per favore?**
	see *pohs*-soh ah-*veh*-reh oohn *pohs*-toh vee-*chee*-noh ahl fee-nehs-*tree*-noh pehr fah-*voh*-reh
	Yes (they have); may I please have a window seat?

Agent:	**Un attimo. Ora controllo: si, glielo do. Ecco la sua carta d'imbarco.**
	oohn *aht*-tee-moh *oh*-rah kohn-*trohl*-loh see *lyeh*-lo doh *ehk*-koh lah *sooh*-ah *kahr*-tah deem-*bahr*-koh
	One second, I'm going to check now. Yes, I can. Here is your boarding pass.

	L'imbarco è alle nove e quindici, uscita tre. Prosegua al controllo di sicurezza.
	leem-*bahr*-koh eh *ahl*-leh *noh*-veh eh *kween*-dee-chee ooh-*shee*-tah treh proh-*seh*-gwah ahl kohn-*trohl*-loh dee see-koohr-*ehts*-tsah
	Boarding is at 9:15, gate 3. You can move on to security now.

Words to Know

imbarco [m]	eem-*bahr*-koh	boarding
valigia [f]	vah-*lee*-jah	suitcase
uscita [f]	ooh-*shee*-tah	gate
bagaglio a mano [m]	bah-*gah*-lyoh ah *mah*-noh	carry-on luggage
passaporto [m]	pahs-sah-*pohr*-toh	passport
bagaglio [m]	bah-*gah*-lyoh	baggage

Dealing with excess baggage

Sometimes you take so many things with you, and your suitcases are so heavy, that the airline charges an extra fee to transport your luggage. The truth is that you really can't say much; you simply have to pay.

- ✔ **Questa valigia eccede il limite.** (*qwehs*-tah vah-*lee*-jah ehch-*cheh*-deh eel *lee*-mee-teh) (*This bag is over the weight limit.*)

- ✔ **Ha un eccesso di bagaglio.** (ah oohn ehch-*ches*-soh dee bah-*gah*-lyoh) (*You have excess luggage.*)

- ✔ **Deve pagare un supplemento.** (*deh*-veh pah-*gah*-reh oohn soohp-pleh-*mehn*-toh) (*You have to pay a surcharge.*)

- ✔ **Questo bagaglio a mano eccede le misure.** (*kwehs*-toh bah-*gah*-lyoh ah *mah*-noh ehch-*che*-deh leh mee-*zooh*-reh) (*This carry-on bag exceeds the size limit.*)

Before you go to the airport, always find out the weight limit of your bags and how much an extra suitcase will cost. This way you can buy an extra suitcase if necessary and avoid having to throw out precious items at check-in.

Waiting to board the plane

Before boarding, you may encounter unforeseen situations, such as delays. If you do, you'll probably want to ask some questions. Read the following dialogue for an example of what you can say when you're dealing with a delay.

Talkin' the Talk

Mr. Campo is in the boarding area. He asks the agent if his flight is on time. Always be prepared for cryptic answers.

Sig. Campo: **Il volo è in orario?**
eel *voh*-loh eh een oh-*rah*-ree-oh
Is the flight on time?

Agent: **No, è in ritardo.**
noh eh een ree-*tahr*-doh
No, there has been a delay.

Sig. Campo: **Di quanto?**
dee *kwahn*-toh
How much?

Agent: **Non si sa.**
nohn see sah
No one knows.

Words to Know

supplemento [m]	soohp-pleh-mehn-toh	supplement
circa	cheer-kah	about
in ritardo	een ree-tahr-doh	late; delayed
volo [m]	voh-loh	flight
in orario	een oh-rah-ree-oh	on time

Coping after landing

After you exit a plane in Italy, you are immediately hit by voices speaking a foreign language. You have to take care of necessities, such as finding a bathroom, changing money, looking for the baggage claim area, and securing a luggage cart and a taxi. The following dialogues give you an idea of how these situations may play out.

Talkin' the Talk

Mrs. Johnson just arrived at the airport in Milan. First, she wants to withdraw money to pay for a taxi and to hold her over for the first few days. She asks a porter where she can do so.

Mrs. Johnson:	**Mi scusi?** mee *skooh*-zee Excuse me?
Porter:	**Prego!** *preh*-goh Yes, how can I help you?
Mrs. Johnson:	**Dov'è un bancomat?** doh-*veh* oohn *bahn*-koh-maht Where is an ATM?
Porter:	**In fondo al corridoio vicino all'ufficio cambio, signora.** een *fohn*-doh ahl coh-ree-*doi*-oh vee-*chee*-noh ahl-loohf-*feech*-oh *kahm*-bee-oh see-*nyoh*-rah At the end of the corridor near the money exchange office, Ma'am?
Mrs. Johnson:	**C'è anche una banca?** cheh *ahn*-keh *ooh*-nah *bahn*-kah Is there also a bank?

Passerby:	**No, c'è soltanto uno sportello di cambio.** noh cheh sohl-*tahn*-toh *ooh*-noh spohr-*tehl*-loh dee *kahm*-bee-oh No, there is only a window to change money.
Mrs. Johnson:	**Benissimo. Grazie mille.** beh-*nees*-see-moh. *grah*-tsee-eh *meel*-leh Thank you very much.

Mrs. Johnson withdraws some money and then needs to pick up her luggage. She asks a woman passing by where she can find a luggage cart.

Mrs. Johnson:	**Scusi, dove sono i carrelli?** *skooh*-zee *doh*-veh *soh*-noh ee kahr-*rehl*-lee Excuse me. Where are the luggage carts?
Woman:	**Al ritiro bagagli.** ahl ree-*tee*-roh bah-*gah*-lyee At the baggage claim.
Mrs. Johnson:	**Servono monete?** *sehr*-voh-noh moh-*neh*-teh Do I need coins/change?
Woman:	**Sì, da un Euro.** see dah oohn *eh*-ooh-roh Yes, 1 euro.

Visitors from countries in the European Union need only **la carta d'identità** (lah *kahr*-tah dee-dehn-tee-*tah*) (*the identity card*) to enter Italy. Nationals of all other countries need a valid **passaporto** (pahs-sah-*pohr*-toh) (*passport*), and sometimes also a visa. Usually, at **controllo passaporti** (kohn-*trohl*-loh pahs-sah-*pohr*-tee) (*passport control*), you don't exchange many words, and the ones you do exchange are usually routine. The following section gives you a typical dialogue at passport control.

Words to Know

arrivo [m]	ahr-<u>ree</u>-voh	arrival
partenza [f]	pahr-<u>tehn</u>-zah	departure
vacanza [f]	vah-<u>kahn</u>-zah	vacation
consegna bagagli [f]	kohn-<u>seh</u>-nyah bah-<u>gah</u>-lyee	baggage claim
cambio [m]	<u>kahm</u>-bee-oh	money exchange
destinazione [f]	dehs-tee-nah-<u>zyoh</u>-neh	destination
entrata [f]	ehn-<u>trah</u>-tah	entrance

Going through Customs

You can't get into a foreign country without going through customs. When you have something to declare, you do so **alla dogana** (ahl-lah doh-gah-nah) (*at customs*). These examples should relieve you of any possible worries. Generally, you can just walk through the line that says "**Niente da dichiarare,**" (nee-ehn-teh dah dee-kyah-rah-reh) (*nothing to declare*) and no one one will say anything to you, but sometimes you may be stopped.

Niente da dichiarare? (nee-ehn-teh dah dee-kyah-rah-reh) (*Anything to declare?*)

No, niente. (noh nee-ehn-teh) (*No, nothing.*)

Per favore, apra questa valigia. (pehr fah-voh-reh ah-prah kwehs-tah vah-lee-jah) (*Please, open this suitcase.*)

È nuovo il computer? (eh nwoh-voh eel kohm-pu-tehr) (*Is this computer new?*)

Sì, ma è per uso personale. (see mah eh pehr ooh-zoh pehr-soh-nah-leh) (*Yes, but it's for personal use.*)

Per questo deve pagare il dazio. (pehr kwehs-toh deh-veh pah-gah-reh eel dah-tsee-oh) (*You have to pay duty on this.*)

When you pass through customs, you may have to declare any goods that you purchased, if over a certain dollar/euro amount.

Ho questo/queste cosa/cose da dichiarare. (oh kw*ehs*-toh/kw*ehs*-teh *koh*-zah/*koh*-zeh dah dee-kyah-*rah*-reh) (*I have to declare this/these things.*)

Losing Luggage

Losing luggage is always a possibility when flying to Italy, especially if you're changing planes, but don't despair: 80 percent of misplaced luggage turns up within 24 hours, and the other 20 percent within three days (usually). The airline will deliver your bags to your hotel or apartment, or you can go back to the airport for them if you need them sooner.

What follows is a typical dialogue.

Talkin' the Talk

Giancarlo, Teresa, and Emilia have just arrived at the Bologna airport via Amsterdam, but their bags are not on the baggage claim belt.

Giancarlo: **Ci sono altre valige dal volo da Amsterdam?**
chee *soh*-noh *ahl*-treh vah-*lee*-jeh dahl *voh*-loh dah *ahm*-stehr-dahm
Are there other bags from the Amsterdam flight?

Facchino (Porter): **Non ce ne sono altre.**
nohn cheh neh *soh*-noh *ahl*-treh
No, there are no more.

Giancarlo: **Le nostre mancano.**
leh *nohs*-treh *mahn*-kah-noh.
Ours are missing.

Cosa dobbiamo fare?
koh-sah dohb-*byah*-moh *fah*-reh
What should we do?

Facchino: **Si rivolga allo sportello Bagagli Smarriti.**
see ree-*vohl*-gah *ahl*-loh spohr-*tehl*-loh bah-*gah*-lyee zmahr-*ree*-tee
Go to the the Missing Baggage window.

(At the Missing Baggage window.)

Impiegato (Employee): **Dica pure.**
dee-kah *pooh*-reh
How can I help you?

Giancarlo: **Non sono arrivati i nostri bagagli da Amsterdam.**
nohn *soh*-noh ahr-ree-*vah*-tee ee *noh*-stree bah-*gah*-lyee dah *ahm*-stehr-dahm
Our bags from Amsterdam didn't arrive.

Impiegato: **Avete le ricevute dei bagagli?**
ah-*veh*-teh leh ree-cheh-*vooh*-teh dey bah-gah-lyee
Do you have the baggage receipts?

Giancarlo: **Eccole qui.**
ehk-koh-leh qwee
Here they are.

Impiegato: **Bisogna riempire questo modulo con il vostro recapito, numero di telefono, e descrizione dei bagagli.**
bee-*zoh*-nyah ree-ehm-*pee*-reh *qwehs*-toh *moh*-dooh-loh kohn eel *vohs*-troh reh-*kahp*-ee-toh *nooh*-mehr-oh dee teh-*leh*-foh-noh eh deh-skree-*zyoh*-neh dey bah-*gah*-lyee
You need to fill out this form with your address, phone number and description of the bags.

Noi vi telefoneremo appena arriveranno.
noi vee teh-leh-fohn-eh-*reh*-moh ahp-*peh*-nah ahr-ree-veh-*rahn*-noh
We'll call you as soon as they arrive.

Words to Know

dogana [f]	doh-<u>gah</u>-nah	customs
dichiarare	dee-kyah-<u>rah</u>-reh	to declare
niente	nee-<u>ehn</u>-teh	nothing
pagare	pah-<u>gah</u>-reh	to pay
uso personale	<u>ooh</u>-zoh pehr-soh-<u>nah</u>-leh	personal use
modulo	<u>moh</u>-dooh-loh	form
ricevute	ree-cheh-<u>vooh</u>-teh	receipts

Renting a Car

Italy is a beautiful country, and if you visit, you may want to consider taking driving tours of the cities and the countryside. If you don't have a car, renting one to visit various places is a good idea, but don't forget that Italian traffic is not very relaxed. Italians don't stay in their own lanes on highways, and finding a place to park can tax your patience — especially in town centers, some of which don't even allow cars. Even medium-sized cars often cannot get through narrow streets and make turns where cars are allowed. I don't want to scare you, though; just enjoy the adventure!

To drive a car or motorcycle in Italy, you must be at least 18 years old. Furthermore, you need a valid **patente** (pah-*tehn*-teh) (*driver's license*). Finding a car to rent is easy at all airports.

Whether you rent a car by phone, online, or directly from a rental service, the process is the same: Just tell the rental company what kind of car you want and under what conditions you want to rent it. Research your options before getting to Italy if possible. This way, you will have a car waiting for you upon your arrival. The following dialogue represents a typical conversation on this topic.

Talkin' the Talk

Mr. Brown is staying in Italy for two weeks and wants to rent a car to visit different cities. He goes to the rental service booth at the airport and talks to **l'impiegato** (leem-pyeh-*gah*-toh) (*the employee*).

Mr. Brown: **Vorrei noleggiare una macchina.**
vohr-*rey* noh-lehj-*jah*-reh *ooh*-nah *mahk*-kee-nah
I would like to rent a car.

Agent: **Che tipo?**
keh *tee*-poh
What kind?

Mr. Brown: **Di media cilindrata col cambio automatico.**
dee *meh*-dee-ah chee-leen-*drah*-tah kohl *kahm*-bee-oh ou-toh-*mah*-tee-koh
A mid-size with an automatic transmission.

Agent: **Per quanto tempo?**
pehr *kwahn*-toh *tehm*-poh
For how long?

Mr. Brown: **Una settimana.**
ooh-nah seht-tee-*mah*-nah
One week.

Quanto è per la settimana?
kwahn-toh eh pehr lah seht-tee-*mah*-nah
What does it cost for a week?

Agent: **C'è una tariffa speciale: 18 Euro al giorno.**
cheh *ooh*-nah tah-*reef*-fah speh-*chah*-leh deech-*oht*-toh eh-oohr-oh ahl *johr*-noh
There is a special rate; 18 Euros per day.

Mr. Brown:	**L'assicurazione è inclusa?**
	lahs-see-kooh-rah-*tsyoh*-neh eh een-*klooh*-zah
	Is insurance included?
Agent:	**Sì, con la polizza casco.**
	see kohn lah *poh*-leets-tsah *kahs*-koh
	Yes, a comprehensive policy.

Other words and expressions that you may need when renting a car or getting fuel at a gas station include the following:

- **l'aria condizionata** (*lah*-ree-ah kohn-dee-tsee-oh-*nah*-tah) (*air conditioning*)

- **il cabriolet** (eel *kah*-bree-oh-leh) (*convertible*)

- **fare benzina** (*fah*-reh behn-*dzee*-nah) (*to put in gas*)

- **Faccia il pieno.** (*fahch*-chah eel *pyeh*-noh) (*Fill it up.*)

- **la benzina verde** (lah behn-*dzee*-nah *vehr*-deh) (*unleaded fuel*)

- **la benzina super** (lah behn-*dzee*-nah *sooh*-pehr) (*premium fuel*)

- **Controlli l'olio.** (kohn-*trohl*-lee *loh*-lyoh) (*Check the oil.*)

A car with an automatic transmission will cost you significantly more because these are rare in Italy, where everyone drives a car with a manual shift.

Navigating Public Transportation

If you'd rather not drive yourself, you can get around quite comfortably using public transportation, such as taxis, trains, and buses. The following sections tell you how to do so in Italian.

Calling a taxi

The process of hailing a taxi is the same in Italy as it is in the United States — you even use the same word: **Taxi** (*tah*-ksee) has entered the Italian language. The only challenge for you is that you have to communicate in Italian. Here are some phrases to help you on your way:

- **Può chiamarmi un taxi?** (pwoh kyah-*mahr*-mee oohn *tah*-ksee)
  (*Can you call me a taxi?*)

✔ **Vorrei un taxi, per favore.** (vohr-*rey* oohn *tah*-ksee pehr fah-*voh*-reh) (*I'd like a taxi, please.*)

In case you are asked **per quando?** (pehr *kwahn*-doh) (*for when?*), you need to be prepared with an answer. Following are some common ones:

✔ **subito** (*sooh*-bee-toh) (*right now*)

✔ **fra un'ora** (frah oohn-*oh*-rah) (*in one hour*)

✔ **alle due del pomeriggio** (*ahl*-leh *dooh*-eh dehl poh-meh-*reej*-joh) (*at 2:00 p.m.*)

✔ **domani mattina alle 5 e mezzo** (doh-*mah*-nee maht-*tee*-nah *ahl*-leh *cheen*-qweh eh *medz*-zoh) (*tomorrow morning at 5:00 a.m.*)

After you seat yourself in a taxi, the driver will ask where to take you. Here are some potential destinations:

✔ **Alla stazione, per favore.** (*ahl*-lah stah-*tsyoh*-neh pehr fah-*voh*-reh) (*To the station, please.*)

✔ **All'areoporto.** (*ahl*-lah-reh-oh-*pohr*-toh) (*To the airport.*)

✔ **In via Veneto.** (een *vee*-ah *veh*-neh-toh) (*To via Veneto.*)

✔ **A questo indirizzo: via Leopardi, numero 3.** (ah *kwehs*-toh een-dee-*ree*-tsoh *vee*-ah leh-oh-*pahr*-dee *nooh*-meh-roh treh) (*To this address: via Leopardi, number 3.*)

Finally, you have to pay. Simply ask the driver **Quant'è?** (kwahn-*teh*) (*How much is it?*) For more information about money, see Chapter 13.

Moving by train

You can buy a train ticket **alla stazione** (*ahl*-lah stah-*tsyoh*-neh) (*at the station*) or at **un'agenzia di viaggi** (ooh-nah-jehn-*tsee*-ah dee vee-*ahj*-jee) (*a travel agency*). If you want to take a **treno rapido** (*treh*-noh *rah*-pee-doh) (*express train*) that stops only in the main stations, you pay a **supplemento** (soohp-pleh-*mehn*-toh) (*surcharge*). You can travel first class or second class. On some trains it's a good idea to reserve your seat; on others a reservation is absolutely required. The faster trains in Italy are called **Inter City (IC)** — or **Euro City (EC)**, if their final destination is outside Italy. **The Euro Star** and the different kinds of **Freccia** are even faster options (the **Frecciarossa** and **Frecciaargento** being the fastest at 250 + kilometers per hour).

Keep in mind that in Italy you have to validate your ticket before entering **il binario** (eel bee-*nah*-ree-oh) (*the platform; the track*). Therefore, the train station positions validation boxes in front of the platforms.

You can find out all about trains by checking out the Italian national rail website www.trenitalia.com. This will tell you about duration, price, and even let you purchase your ticket ahead of time.

Talkin' the Talk

 Bianca is at the train station in Rome. She goes to an information counter (**ufficio informazioni**) (oohf-*feech*-oh een-fohr-mats-*yoh*-neh) to ask about a connection to Perugia. (Track 29)

Bianca: **Ci sono treni diretti per Perugia?**
chee *soh*-noh *treh*-nee dee-*reht*-tee pehr
peh-*rooh*-jah
Are there direct trains to Perugia?

Agent: **No, deve prendere un treno per Terni.**
noh *deh*-veh *prehn*-deh-reh oohn *treh*-noh pehr
tehr-nee
No, you have to take a train to Terni.

Bianca: **E poi devo cambiare?**
eh poi *deh*-voh kahm-*byah*-reh
And then do I have to change [trains]?

Agent: **Sì, prende un locale per Perugia.**
see *prehn*-deh oohn loh-*kah*-leh pehr peh-*rooh*-jah
Yes, you take a local (slow) train for Perugia.

Bianca: **A che ora parte il prossimo treno?**
ah keh *oh*-rah *pahr*-teh eel *prohs*-see-moh *treh*-noh
What time does the next train leave?

Agent: **Alle diciotto e arriva a Terni alle diciannove.**
ahl-leh dee-*choht*-toh eh ahr-*ree*-vah ah *tehr*-nee
ahl-leh dee-chahn-*noh*-veh
At 18 hours (6 p.m.). It arrives in Terni at 19 hours
(7 p.m.).

Bianca: **E per Perugia?**
eh pehr peh-*rooh*-jah
And to Perugia?

Agent: **C'è subito la coincidenza.**
cheh *sooh*-bee-toh lah koh-een-chee-*dehn*-zah
There is an immediate connection.

After exploring your options, you have to make a decision and buy a ticket. In the following dialogue, Bianca does just that.

Talkin' the Talk

 Bianca goes to the ticket counter and buys her ticket. (Track 30)

Bianca:	**Un biglietto per Perugia, per favore.**
	oohn bee-*lyeht*-toh pehr peh-*rooh*-jah pehr fah-*voh*-reh
	One ticket to Perugia, please.
Agent:	**Andata e ritorno?**
	ahn-*dah*-tah eh ree-*tohr*-noh
	Round trip?
Bianca:	**Solo andata. Quanto viene?**
	soh-loh ahn-*dah*-tah *kwahn*-toh *vyeh*-neh
	One-way. How much does it cost?
Agent:	**In prima classe 30 euro.**
	een *pree*-mah *klahs*-seh *trehn*-tah eh-ooo-roh
	First class [costs] 30 euros.
Bianca:	**E in seconda?**
	eh een seh-*kohn*-dah
	And second [class]?
Agent:	**Diciotto.**
	deech-*oht*-toh
	18.
Bianca:	**Seconda classe, per favore.**
	seh-*kohn*-dah *klahs*-seh pehr fah-*voh*-reh
	Second class, please.
	Da che binario parte?
	dah keh bee-*nah*-ree-oh *pahr*-teh
	From which track does it leave?
Agent:	**Binario tre.**
	bee-*nah*-ree-oh treh
	Track 3.

Words to Know

binario [m]	bee-<u>nah</u>-ree-oh	platform; track
biglietto [m]	bee-<u>lyeht</u>-toh	ticket
andata [f]	ahn-<u>dah</u>-tah	one way
ritorno [m]	ree-<u>tohr</u>-noh	return trip
supplemento [m]	soohp-pleh-<u>mehn</u>-toh	surcharge

Going by bus or tram

To get from point A to point B without a car, you most likely walk or take the bus or tram or subway in bigger cities. We provide the appropriate Italian vocabulary for such situations in this section.

Some Italian cities have streetcars, or trams, and most have buses. Incidentally, in Italian they spell it **il tram** and pronounce it *eel trahm*. The Italian word for bus is **l'autobus** (*lou*-toh-boohs) — and the little buses are called **il pulmino** (eel poohl-*mee*-noh). Big buses that take you from one city to another are called **il pullman** (eel *poohl*-mahn) or **la corriera** (lah kohr-ree-*eh*-rah).

You can buy bus or tram tickets in Italian bars, **dal giornalaio** (dahl johr-nah-*lah*-yoh) (*at newspaper stands*), or **dal tabaccaio** (dahl tah-bahk-*kahy*-oh) (*tobacco shop*). The latter are little shops where you can purchase cigarettes, stamps, newspapers, and so on. You can find them on virtually every street corner in Italy; they're recognizable by either a black-and-white sign or a blue-and-white sign with a big T on it.

Talkin' the Talk

Gerardo wants to get to the train station. He's standing at a bus stop but is a little unsure about which bus to take. He asks a man who is also waiting.

Gerardo:	**Mi scusi.**
	mee *skooh*-zee
	Excuse me.

Man:	**Prego?**
	preh-goh
	Yes?

Gerardo:	**Quest'autobus va alla stazione?**
	kwehs-*tou*-toh-boohs vah *ahl*-lah stah-*tsyoh*-neh
	Does this bus go to the station?

Man:	**Sì.**
	see
	Yes.

Gerardo:	**Dove si comprano i biglietti?**
	doh-veh see *kohm*-prah-noh ee bee-*lyeht*-tee
	Where can I buy tickets?

Man:	**In questo bar.**
	een *kwehs*-toh bahr
	In this bar.

You probably aim to take the most convenient and fastest means of transport. To know which one this is, you have to know what's what and your way about. If you don't, hopefully you can find a nice person to help you.

Talkin' the Talk

Tom, a Canadian tourist, wants to visit the cathedral downtown. He asks about the bus, but a woman advises him to take the subway because it takes less time. (There are subways in Milan, Rome, Catania, and Naples.) (Track 31)

Tom:	**Scusi, quale autobus va al Duomo?**
	skooh-zee *kwah*-leh *ou*-toh-boos vah ahl *dwoh*-moh
	Excuse me, which bus goes to the Cathedral?

Woman:	**Perché non prende la metropolitana?**
	pehr-*keh* nohn *prehn*-deh lah
	meh-troh-poh-lee-*tah*-nah
	Why don't you take the subway?

Tom:	**È meglio?**
	eh *meh*-lyoh
	Is it better?

Woman:	**Sì, ci mette cinque minuti!**
	see chee *meht*-teh *cheen*-kweh mee-*nooh*-tee
	Yes, it takes five minutes!

Tom:	**Dov'è la fermata della metropolitana?**
	doh-*veh* lah fehr-*mah*-tah *dehl*-lah
	meh-troh-poh-lee-*tah*-nah
	Where is the subway station?

Woman:	**Dietro l'angolo.**
	dee-*eh*-troh *lahn*-goh-loh
	Around the corner.

On the subway, Tom asks a student where he should get off: Note that he uses the **tu** informal form now.

Tom:	**Scusa, sai qual è la fermata per il Duomo?**
	skooh-zah sahy kwahl eh lah fehr-*mah*-tah pehr eel
	dwoh-moh
	Excuse me, do you know which is the stop for the
	Cathedral?

Student:	**La prossima fermata.**
	lah *pros*-see-mah fehr-*mah*-tah
	The next stop.

Tom:	**Grazie!**
	grah-tsee-eh
	Thanks!

Student:	**Prego.**
	preh-goh
	You're welcome.

Reading maps and schedules

You don't need to know much about reading maps except for the little bit of vocabulary written on them. Reading a schedule can be more difficult for travelers because the schedules are usually written only in Italian. You frequently find the following words on schedules:

➧ **l'orario** (loh-*rah*-ree-oh) (*the timetable*)

➧ **partenze** (pahr-*tehn*-tseh) (*departures*)

➧ **arrivi** (ahr-*ree*-vee) (*arrivals*)

➧ **giorni feriali** (*johr*-nee feh-ree-*ah*-lee) (*weekdays*)

➧ **giorni festivi** (*johr*-nee fehs-*tee*-vee) (*Sundays and holidays*)

➧ **il binario** (eel bee-*nah*-ree-oh) (*the track; the platform*)

The schedule shown in Figure 14-1 shows you train names, length of trip, and the difference in prices between first and second class.

DEPARTURE STATION: BOLOGNA (TUTTE LE STAZIONI)	ARRIVAL STATION: ROMA (TUTTE LE STAZIONI)			DATE: 19/1/2011	

DEPARTURE	ARRIVAL	LENGTH OF JOURNEY	TRAIN NO.	TRAIN CATEGORY	1ST CLASS*	2ND CLASS*	SELECT
10:53 BOLOGNA	13:13 ROMA TE	02:20	9413 FRECCIARGENTO	🚄	80,00€	58,00€	●
10:23 BOLOGNA	12:45 ROMA TE	02:22	9519 FRECCIAROSSA	🚄	80,00€	58,00€	●
10:38 BOLOGNA	12:55 ROMA TE	02:17	9415 FRECCIARGENTO	🚄	80,00€	58,00€	●
11:18 BOLOGNA	15:24 ROMA TE	04:06	589	IC	52,00€	38,50€	●
13:00 BOLOGNA	15:22 ROMA TE	02:22	9521 FRECCIAROSSA	🚄	80,00€	58,00€	●

Figure 14-1:
Typical Italian train schedule.

CULTURAL WISDOM

Keep in mind that Europeans don't write a.m. or p.m.; they count the hours from 0.00 to 24.00, otherwise known as military time. Therefore, 1.00 is the hour after midnight, whereas 1:00 p.m. is 13.00.

Being Early or Late

You don't always arrive on time, and you may have to communicate that you'll be late or early, or apologize to someone for being delayed. The following list contains important terms that you can use to do so:

- ✔ **essere in anticipo** (*ehs*-seh-reh een ahn-*tee*-chee-poh) (*to be early*)

    Probabilmente sarò in anticipo. (proh-bah-beel-*mehn*-teh sah-*roh* een ahn *tee*-chee-poh) (*[I'll] probably be early.*)

- ✔ **essere puntuale** (*ehs*-seh-reh poohn-tooh-*ah*-leh) (*to be on time*)

    L'autobus non è mai puntuale. (*lou*-toh-boohs nohn eh mahy poohn-tooh-*ah*-leh) (*The bus is never on time.*)

- ✔ **essere in ritardo** (ehs-seh-*reh* een ree-*tahr*-doh) (*to be late*)

- ✔ **L'aereo è in ritardo.** (lah-*eh*-reh-oh eh een ree-*tahr*-doh) (*The plane is late.*)

These examples use the preceding phrases in sentences:

- ✔ **Mi scusi, sono arrivata in ritardo.** (mee *skooh*-zee *soh*-noh ahr-ree-*vah*-tah een ree-*tahr*-doh) (*I'm sorry, I arrived late.*)

- ✔ **Meno male che sei puntuale.** (*meh*-noh *mah*-leh keh sey poohn-tooh-*ah*-leh) (*It's a good thing you're on time.*)

When talking about lateness, you probably can't avoid the verb **aspettare** (ahs-peht-*tah*-reh) (to wait). Following are a few examples of this verb:

- ✔ **Aspetto l'autobus da un'ora.** (ahs-*peht*-toh *lou*-toh-boohs dah ooh-*noh*-rah) (*I've been waiting for the bus for an hour.*)

- ✔ **Aspetta anche lei il ventitré?** (ahs-*peht*-tah *ahn*-keh ley eel *vehn*-tee-*treh*) (*Are you also waiting for the number 23 bus?*)

- ✔ **Aspetto mia madre.** (ahs-*peht*-toh *mee*-ah *mah*-dreh) (*I'm waiting for my mother.*)

Note that the verb **aspettare** takes no preposition, as the English to wait (for) does.

*Fun & Games

What a mess! This schedule is really jumbled. The Italian words for **train, bus stop, train station, track, ticket, one way, return trip,** and **surcharge** are hidden in the following puzzle. If you want to get to your train on time, you have to solve it. Hurry up!! See Appendix D for the answer key.

Word Seek

B	S	M	T	A	T	A	M	R	E	F	O
I	T	U	D	H	G	L	T	X	L	N	C
N	S	Y	P	V	X	L	A	B	E	D	G
A	P	J	Y	P	B	E	I	R	S	H	D
R	K	D	A	J	L	G	T	X	F	X	V
I	V	D	U	Y	L	E	M	R	C	D	Q
O	I	D	Y	I	K	A	M	G	G	D	R
R	Z	J	E	L	X	S	T	E	E	L	K
B	C	T	C	P	M	D	Q	A	N	C	I
B	T	H	P	R	S	P	U	F	D	T	K
O	R	I	T	O	R	N	O	S	O	N	O
S	T	A	Z	I	O	N	E	Z	A	G	A

Chapter 15

Finding a Place to Stay

. . . .

In This Chapter

▶ Reserving a place

▶ Arriving at your hotel

▶ Using possessive pronouns and adjectives

. . . .

To really get to know Italians and the Italian language, and to enjoy the Italian lifestyle, you need to travel to Italy. If you're not lucky enough to have Italian friends who can offer you a place to stay, you have to find a hotel, of which there are many creative varieties. This chapter shows you how to make yourself understood when you ask for a room or check into a hotel. Plus, we give you a crash course on possessive pronouns and adjectives and the imperative (or command) verb tense.

Choosing a Place to Stay

Do some research about the different places you can stay while you're in Italy, and try to find those with an authentic flair to them. There is a broad range of places to suit everyone. There are conventional three-to-five-star **alberghi** (ahl-*behr*-gee) (*hotels*) and **villaggi turistici** (veel-*laj*-jee tooh-*rees*-tee-chee) (*resorts in hot spots like Sardegna that offer either* **mezza pensione** [*medz*-ah pehn-*syoh*-neh] [*breakfast plus one other meal*]) or **pensione completa** (pehn-*syoh*-neh kohm-*pleh*-tah) (*breakfast, lunch, and dinner included in the price*) options. Then there are smaller, more personal lodgings, which include family-run **bed and breakfasts** (pronounced just the same as in English, but with the rolled r), and **pensioni** (pehn-*syoh*-nee) (*small hotels or part of someone's house where breakfast is usually served*) to mountain **rifugi** (ree-*fooh*-jee) (*mountain huts that range from spartan to spa quality*), and the increasingly popular **agriturismo** (ah-gree-tooh-*reez*-moh) (*farm stay*). And don't forget all of those former monasteries and convents!

Reserving a Room

When you reserve a room in a hotel, you use the same terms as you do **prenotare/fare una prenotazione** (preh-noh-*tah*-reh/fah-reh *ooh*-nah preh-noh-tats-*yoh*-neh) (*to make a reservation*) in a restaurant. Use either of the synonyms **la camera** (lah *kah*-meh-rah) or **la stanza** (lah *stahn*-zah) (*the room*). Italian hotel terms may be different than those you're used to, so I want to spend some time telling you how to ask for what you want in Italian.

La camera singola (lah *kah*-meh-rah *seen*-goh-lah) is a room with one twin bed. **La camera doppia** (lah *kah*-meh-rah *dohp*-pee-ah) is a room with two twin beds, whereas **la camera matrimoniale** (lah *kah*-meh-rah *mah*-tree-moh-nee-*ah*-leh) has one big bed for two persons.

In Italy, people commonly refer to rooms simply as **una doppia**, **una matrimoniale**, and **una singola**. Everyone understands that you're talking about hotel rooms. Breakfast is generally included in most hotels, but ask just to be certain. We're sure we don't have to tell you that making reservations in advance is important. This is particularly true for the **alta stagione** (*ahl*-tah stah-*joh*-neh) (*peak season*) — in Italy it's the summer months.

When you're making reservations or staying at a hotel, you may have a few questions about the room and the amenities. You'll probably encounter and use some of these common Italian sentences and phrases (You can hear common Italian when planning a trip on Track 33 on the CD.):

- ✔ **La stanza è con bagno?** (lah *stahn*-zah eh kohn *bah*-nyoh) (*Does the room have a bathroom?*) (Even fabulous five-star hotels have some single rooms without bathrooms still, but ask this question only when you're in a nice hotel if you're asking for an inexpensive single.)

- ✔ **Posso avere una stanza con doccia?** (*pohs*-soh ah-*veh*-reh *ooh*-nah *stahn*-zah kohn *dohch*-chah) (*May I have a room with a shower?*)

- ✔ **Non avete stanze con la vasca?** (nohn ah-*veh*-teh *stahn*-zeh kohn lah *vahs*-kah) (*Don't you have rooms with bathtubs?*)

- ✔ **Avete una doppia al primo piano?** (ah-*veh*-teh *ooh*-nah *dohp*-pee-ah ahl *pree*-moh *pyah*-noh) (*Do you have a double room on the first floor?* Note that this would be the second floor for Americans: Chapter 5 goes into the different floors.)

- ✔ **È una stanza tranquillissima e dà sul giardino.** (eh *ooh*-nah *stahn*-zah trahn-kweel-*lees*-see-mah eh dah soohl jahr-*dee*-noh) (*The room is very quiet and looks out onto the garden.*)

- ✔ **La doppia viene duecento Euro a notte.** (lah *dohp*-pee-ah *vyeh*-neh dooh-eh-*chehn*-toh ee-ooh-roh ah *noht*-teh) (*A double room costs 200 euros lire per night.*)

✔ **La colazione è compresa?** (lah koh-lah-*tsyoh*-neh eh kohm-*preh*-zah)
(*Is breakfast included?*)

✔ **Può darmi una camera con aria condizionata?** (pwoh *dahr*-mee *ooh*-nah
kah-meh-rah kohn *ah*-ree-ah kohn-dee-tsee-oh-*nah*-tah) (*Can you give me
a room with air conditioning?*)

✔ **Dove sono i suoi bagagli?** (*doh*-veh *soh*-noh ee swoi bah-*gah*-lyee)
(*Where is your baggage?*)

✔ **Può far portare le mie valige in camera, per favore?** (pwoh fahr pohr-
tah-reh leh *mee*-eh vah-*lee*-jeh *een kah*-meh-rah pehr fah-*voh*-reh)
(*Would you please have my bags brought to my room?*)

Talkin' the Talk

Donatella is making reservations for five people. The receptionist
says that only two double rooms are left, so Donatella has to
figure out how to accommodate all five people.

Donatella: **Buonasera.**
             bwoh-nah-*seh*-rah
             Good evening.

Receptionist: **Buonasera, prego.**
             bwoh-nah-seh-*rah preh*-goh
             Good evening, can I help you?

Donatella: **Avete stanze libere?**
             ah-*veh*-teh *stahn*-zeh *lee*-beh-reh
             Do you have any vacant rooms?

Receptionist: **Non ha la prenotazione?**
             nohn ah lah preh-noh-tah-*tsyoh*-neh
             You don't have a reservation?

Donatella: **Eh, no . . .**
             eh noh
             No . . .

Receptionist: **Abbiamo soltanto due doppie.**
             ahb-*byah*-moh sohl-*tahn*-toh *dooh*-eh *dohp*-pee-eh
             We have just two double rooms.

Donatella: **Non c'è una stanza con tre letti?**
             nohn cheh *ooh*-nah *stahn*-zah kohn treh *leht*-tee
             Isn't there a room with three beds?

Receptionist: **Possiamo aggiungere un letto.**
pohs-see-*ah*-moh ahj-*joohn*-jeh-reh oohn *leht*-toh
We can add a bed.

Donatella: **Benissimo, grazie.**
beh-*nees*-see-moh *grah*-tsee-eh
Very well, thank you.

Words to Know

aria condizionata [f]	<u>ah</u>-ree-ah kohn-dee-<u>tsee</u>-oh-nah-tah	airconditioning
camera [f] stanza [f]	kah-meh-rah <u>stahn</u>-zah	room
camera singola [f]	kah-meh-rah <u>seen</u>-goh-lah	single room
camera doppia [f]	kah-meh-rah <u>dohp</u>-pee-ah	room with two twin beds
camera matrimoniale [f]	kah-meh-rah mah-tree-moh-nee-ah-leh	room with a double bed
colazione [f]	koh-lah-<u>tsyoh</u>-neh	breakfast
culla [f]	<u>koohl</u>-lah	crib
letto supplementare [m]	<u>leht</u>-toh soohp-pleh-mehn-tah-reh	extra bed
servizio in camera [m]	sehr-<u>vee</u>-tsee-oh een <u>kah</u>-meh-rah	room service
mezza pensione	<u>medz</u>-ah pehn-<u>syoh</u>-neh	half board
pensione completa	pehn-<u>syoh</u>-neh kohm-<u>pleh</u>-tah	full board
servizio sveglia [m]	sehr-<u>vee</u>-tsee-oh <u>sveh</u>-lyah	wake-up call

Checking In

Registering at an Italian hotel isn't as difficult as you might imagine. But do expect the person at the front desk to ask for **un documento** (oohn dohk-ooh-*mehn*-toh), such as a passport. They might even want to hang on to it for a few hours, but don't worry, you'll get it back!

After you're in your room, you may find that you forgot to bring something you need, or discover that you need something in addition to all you brought. Many rooms come with items like **una cassaforte** (*ooh*-nah kahs-sah-*fohr*-teh) (*a safe*) for your valuables, and **un frigorifero** (oohn free-goh-*ree*-feh-roh) (*a refrigerator*), but you may need help in figuring out how they work. You might also need a **fon** (fohn) (*blow dryer*). In these instances, you can ask the receptionist, the doorman, or the maid for what you need. The following phrases can help you ask for the things you need. Don't forget to say **scusi** (*skooh*-zee) (*excuse me*) and **per favore** (pehr-fah-*voh*-reh) (*please*)!

- ✔ **Non trovo l'asciugacapelli/il fon.** (nohn *troh*-voh lah-*shooh*-gah-kah-*pehl*-lee/il fohn) (*I can't find the hair dryer.*)

- ✔ **Manca la carta igenica.** *mahn*-kah lah *kahr*-tah ee-*jeh*-nee-kah) (*There is no toilet paper.*)

- ✔ **È ancora aperto il bar?** (eh ahn-*koh*-rah ah-*pehr*-toh eel bahr) (*Is the bar still open?*)

- ✔ **Vorrei un'altra coperta per favore.** (vohr-*rey* oohn-*ahl*-trah koh-*pehr*-tah pehr fah-*voh*-reh) (*I'd like one more blanket please.*)

- ✔ **Dov'è la farmacia più vicina?** (doh-*veh* lah fahr-mah-*chee*-ah pyooh vee-*chee*-nah) (*Where is the closest pharmacy?*)

- ✔ **Vorrei la sveglia domattina.** (vohr-*ray* lah *sveh*-lyah doh-maht-*tee*-nah) (*I'd like to get an early wake-up call tomorrow morning.*)

- ✔ **C'è un telefono nella mia stanza?** (cheh oohn teh-*leh*-foh-noh *nehl*-lah mee-ah *stahn*-zah) (*Is there a telephone in my room?*)

If you want another something, notice that you write the feminine form **un'altra** (oohn-*ahl*-trah) differently than the masculine **un altro** (oohn *ahl*-troh). Feminine words require an apostrophe; masculine words don't. This is also valid for all other words that begin with a vowel.

The following list contains more words you may find useful during a hotel stay:

- **fazzolettino di carta** (faht-tsoh-leht-*tee*-noh dee *kahr*-tah) (*tissue*)
- **lettino** (leht-*tee*-noh) (*cot*)
- **negozio di regali** (neh-*goh*-tsee-oh dee reh-*gah*-lee) (*gift shop*)
- **parrucchiere** (pahr-roohk-*kyeh*-reh) (*hairdresser*)
- **portacenere** (pohr-tah-*cheh*-neh-reh) (*ashtray*)
- **piscina** (pee-*shee*-nah) (*swimming pool*)

Talkin' the Talk

Mr. Baricco arrives at the hotel where he made reservations two weeks ago. He walks up to the receptionist. (Track 32)

Sig. Baricco: **Buonasera, ho una stanza prenotata.**
bwoh-nah-*seh*-rah oh *ooh*-nah *stahn*-zah preh-noh-*tah*-tah
Good evening, I have a reservation.

Receptionist: **Il suo nome, prego?**
eel *sooh*-oh *noh*-meh *preh*-goh
Your name, please?

Sig. Baricco: **Baricco.**
bah-*reek*-koh
Barrico.

Receptionist: **Sì, una singola per due notti.**
see *ooh*-nah *seen*-goh-lah pehr *dooh*-eh *noht*-tee
Yes, a single (room) for two nights.

Può riempire la scheda, per favore?
pwoh ree-ehm-*pee*-reh lah *skeh*-dah pehr fah-*voh*-reh
Could you fill out the form, please?

Sig. Baricco: **Certo. Vuole un documento?**
chehr-toh *vwoh*-leh oohn doh-kooh-*mehn*-toh
Sure. Do you want identification?

Receptionist: **Sì, grazie . . . Bene . . . la sua chiave la stanza numero quarantadue al quarto piano.**
see *grah*-tsee-eh *beh*-neh lah *sooh*-ah *kyah*-veh lah *stahn*-zah *nooh*-meh-roh kwah-*rahn*-tah-*dooh*-eh ahl *kwahr*-toh *pyah*-noh
Yes, thanks . . . Here is your key to room number forty-two, fourth floor.

Sig. Baricco: **Grazie. A che ora è la colazione?**
grah-tsee-eh ah keh *oh*-rah eh lah koh-lah-*tsyoh*-neh
Thank you. What time is breakfast?

Receptionist: **Dalle sette alle nove.**
dahl-leh *seht*-teh *ahl*-leh *noh*-veh
From seven till nine.

Sig. Baricco: **Grazie. Buonanotte.**
grah-tsee-eh *bwoh*-nah-*noht*-teh
Thank you. Good-night.

Receptionist: **Buonanotte.**
bwoh-nah-*noht*-teh
Good-night.

Words to Know

avete	ah-<u>veh</u>-teh	do you (plural) have
dov'è	doh-<u>veh</u>	where is
dove sono	<u>doh</u>-veh <u>soh</u>-noh	where are
Può ripetere per favore?	pwoh ree-<u>peh</u>-teh-reh pehr fah-<u>voh</u>-reh	Could you repeat that please?
saldare il conto	sahl-<u>dah</u>-reh eel <u>kohn</u>-toh	to check out
indirizzo [m]	een-dee-<u>reet</u>-tsoh	address

Table 15-1 shows the singular and plural form of several hotel-related words with their proper articles. For more on forming singular and plural articles and nouns, see Chapter 2.

Table 15-1	Making Plurals	
Singular Plural	*Pronunciation*	*Translation*
la cameriera, le cameriere	lah kah-meh-*ryeh*-rah leh kah-meh-*ryeh*-reh	*chambermaid chambermaids, waitress, waitresses*
il bagno, i bagni	eel *bah*-nyoh ee *bah*-nyee	*bathroom, bathrooms*
la chiave, le chiavi	lah *kyah*-veh leh *kyah*-vee	*key, keys*
il cameriere, i camerieri	eel kah-meh-*ryeh*-reh ee kah-meh-*ryeh*-ree	*waiter, waiters*
lo specchio, gli specchi	loh *spehk*-kyoh lyee *spehk*-kyee	*mirror, mirrors*
l'albergo, gli alberghi	lahl-*behr*-goh lyee ahl-*behr*-gee	*hotel, hotels*
la stanza, le stanze	lah *stahn*-zah leh *stahn*-zeh	*room, rooms*
la camera, le camere	lah *kah*-meh-rah leh *kah*-meh-reh	*room, rooms*
la persona, le persone	lah pehr-*soh*-nah leh pehr-*soh*-neh	*person, persons*
il letto, i letti	eel *leht*-toh ee *leht*-tee	*bed, beds*
la notte, le notti	lah *noht*-teh leh *noht*-tee	*night, nights*
l'entrata, le entrate	lehn-*trah*-tah leh 'ehn-*trah*-teh	*entrance, entrances*

Personalizing pronouns

As you know, a pronoun is a word you use in a place of a noun: When you say "I go," you substitute your name with I. I is the personal or subject pronoun. Sometimes you use a pronoun that not only takes the place of a noun but also indicates to whom it belongs. For example, when you say "My bag is red and yours is black," the possessive pronoun "yours" represents bag and indicates to whom the bag belongs.

This or these: Demonstrative adjectives and pronouns

In English, you use the pronouns *this* and *these* (called demonstrative pronouns) to specify what you're talking about. *This* is singular, and *these* is plural. In Italian, however, which word you use depends on both number and gender because there are masculine and feminine nouns. The demonstrative adjective **questo** (*kwehs*-toh) has four forms which agree with the noun that follows (or that it's substituting, in which case it becomes a pronoun): **questo**, **questa**, **questi**, **queste** (*kwehs*-toh, *kwehs*-tah, *kwehs*-tee, *kwehs*-teh). Consider these examples:

- ✔ **Questa è la sua valigia?** (*kwehs*-tah eh lah *sooh*-ah vah-*lee*-jah) (*Is this your suitcase?*)

- ✔ **No, le mie sono queste.** (noh leh *mee*-eh *soh*-noh *kwehs*-teh) (*No, these are mine.*)

In the preceding examples, you see the feminine version of singular and plural (**questa** and **queste**, respectively). The following shows the masculine version of singular and plural (**questo** and **questi**):

- ✔ **Signore, questo messaggio è per lei.** (see-*nyoh*-reh *kwehs*-toh mehs-*sahj*-joh eh pehr ley) (*Sir, this message is for you.*)

- ✔ **Questi spaghetti sono ottimi!** (*kwehs*-tee spah-*geht*-tee *soh*-noh *oht*-tee-mee) (*This spaghetti is great! A literal translation: "these spaghetti are great!" You get the point.*)

Yours, mine, and ours: Possessive pronouns

Possessive pronouns (such as my, your, his) indicate possession of something (the noun). In Italian, these words vary according to the gender of the item they refer to. The possessive pronoun must agree in number and gender with the possessed thing or person. Unlike in English, in Italian you almost always put the definite article in front of the possessive determiner. The following table shows the singular and plural definite articles for each gender (but you'll see that you only need four of these to form possessive adjectives and pronouns):

Gender	Number	Article
Feminine	Singular	la/l'
Feminine	Plural	le
Masculine	Singular	il/l'/lo
Masculine	Plural	i/gli

When you want to show that something belongs to you and that something is a feminine noun, the possessive **mia** ends in **a** — such as **la mia valigia** (lah *mee*-ah vah-*lee*-jah) (*my suitcase*). When you refer to a masculine word, the possessive ends in **o**, as in **il mio letto** (eel *mee*-oh *leht*-toh) (*my bed*).

So, these pronouns get their form from the possessor — **il mio** (eel *mee*-oh) (*mine*), **il tuo** (eel *tooh*-oh) (*yours*), and so on — but their number and gender from the thing possessed. For example, in **è la mia chiave** (eh lah *mee*-ah *kyah*-veh) (*it's my key*), **la chiave** is singular and feminine and is, therefore, replaced by the possessive pronoun **mia**. Table 15-2 lists possessive pronouns and their articles.

Table 15-2		Possessive Pronouns			
Possessive Pronoun	**Singular Masculine**	**Singular Feminine**	**Plural Masculine**	**Plural Feminine**	**Pronunciation**
my/mine	**il mio**	**la mia**	**i miei**	**le mie**	eel *mee*-oh/lah *mee*-ah/ee myei/ leh *mee*-eh
your/yours	**il tuo**	**la tua**	**i tuoi**	**le tue**	eel *tooh*-oh/lah *tooh*-ah/ee twoi/ leh *tooh*-eh
yours (formal)	**il suo**	**la sua**	**i suoi**	**le sue**	eel *sooh*-oh/lah *sooh*-ah/ee swoi/ le *sooh*-eh
his/her/ hers	**il suo**	**la sua**	**i suoi**	**le sue**	eel *sooh*-oh/lah *sooh*-ah/ee swoi/ le *sooh*-eh
our/ours	**il nostro**	**la nostra**	**i nostri**	**le nostre**	eel *nohs*-troh/ lah *nohs*-trah/ ee *nohs*-tree/leh *nohs*-treh
your/yours (formal and informal)	**il vostro**	**la vostra**	**i vostri**	**le vostre**	eel *vohs*-troh/ lah *vohs*-trah/ ee *vohs*-tree/leh *vohs*-treh
their/theirs	**il loro**	**la loro**	**i loro**	**le loro**	eel/lah/ee/leh *loh*-roh

Following are some practical examples using possessive adjectives and pronouns:

- ✔ **È grande la vostra stanza?** (eh *grahn*-deh lah *vohs*-trah *stahn*-zah)
  (*Is your room big?*) (plural)

- ✔ **Dov'è il tuo albergo?** (doh-*veh* eel *tooh*-oh ahl-*behr*-goh) (*Where is your hotel?*)

- ✔ **Ecco i vostri documenti.** (*ehk*-koh ee *vohs*-tree doh-kooh-*mehn*-tee)
  (*Here are your documents.*) (plural)

- ✔ **Questa è la sua chiave.** (*kwehs*-tah eh lah *sooh*-ah *kyah*-veh) (*This is your [formal] key.*) and also (*This is his/her key.*)

- ✔ **La mia camera è molto tranquilla.** (lah *mee*-ah *kah*-meh-rah eh *mohl*-toh trahn-*kweel*-lah) (*My room is very quiet.*)

- ✔ **Anche la nostra. E la tua?** (*ahn*-keh lah *nohs*-trah eh lah *tooh*-ah)
  (*Ours, too. And yours [singular]?*)

Talkin' the Talk

You frequently use possessive pronouns and adjectives, so you need to know how to use them. The following dialogue takes place between members of a family who are trying to sort out who has whose luggage.

Mamma:	**Dove sono i vostri bagagli?**
	doh-veh *soh*-noh ee *vohs*-treh bah-*gahl*-yee
	Where are your [plural] bags?
Michela:	**Il mio è questo.**
	eel *mee*-oh eh *kwehs*-toh
	Mine is this one.
Mamma:	**E il tuo, Carla?**
	eh eel *tooh*-oh *kahr*-lah
	And yours, Carla?
Carla:	**Lo porta Giulio.**
	loh *pohr*-tah *jooh*-lee-oh
	Giulio is carrying it.

Mamma:	**No, Giulio porta il suo.**
	noh *jooh*-lee-oh *pohr*-tah eel *sooh*-oh
	No, Giulio is carrying his.

Carla:	**Giulio, hai il mio bagaglio?**
	jooh-lee-oh ahy eel *mee*-oh bah-*gahl*-yoh
	Giulio, do you have my bag?

Giulio:	**No, questi sono i miei!**
	noh *kwehs*-tee *soh*-noh ee myei
	No, these are mine!

Carla:	**Sei sicuro?**
	say see-*kooh*-roh
	Are you sure?

Giulio:	**Com'è la tua valigia?**
	koh-*meh* lah *tooh*-ah vah-*lee*-jah
	What does your suitcase look like?

Carla:	**È rossa.**
	eh *rohs*-sah
	It's red.

Words to Know

bagaglio [m]	bah-<u>gah</u>-lyoh	baggage
camieriera [f]	kah-meh-<u>ryeh</u>-rah	chambermaid, waitress
garage [m]	gah-<u>rahj</u>	car park, garage
messaggio [m]	mehs-<u>sahj</u>-joh	message
portiere [m]	pohr-<u>tyeh</u>-reh	doorman
valigia [f]	vah-<u>lee</u>-jah	suitcase

Bending Others to Your Will: Imperatives

When your boss says **Venga nel mio ufficio!** (*vehn*-gah nehl *mee*-oh oohf-*fee*-choh) (*Come in my office!*) or you say to your children **Mettete in ordine le vostre camere!** (meht-*teh*-teh een *ohr*-dee-neh leh *vohs*-treh *kah*-meh-reh) (*Clean up your rooms!*), you use an imperative — a request, a demand, or an invitation for someone to do something. Four forms of imperatives exist:

- **Singular informal:** You speak (and command) informally to a person you know — for example, a friend or a family member.

  In Italian, if a verb ends in -are, as in **mandare** (mahn-*dah*-reh) (*to send*), the informal imperative form ends in -a, as in **Manda!** (*mahn*-dah) (*Send!*). If a verb ends in -ere or -ire, as in **prendere** (*prehn*-deh-reh) (*to take*) and **finire** (fee-*nee*-reh) (*to finish*), the informal imperative ends in -i, as in **Prendi!** (*prehn*-dee) (*Take!*) and **Finisci!** (fee-*nee*-shee) (*Finish!*).

- **Singular formal:** You formally command a person you don't know well. The command form is different when you speak to a person formally. If the verb ends in -are, as in **mandare**, the formal imperative form ends in -i, as in **Mandi!** (*mahn*-dee) (*Send!*). If the verb ends in -ere or -ire, as in **prendere**, **aprire**, and **finire**, the formal imperative ends in -a, as in **Prenda!** (*prehn*-dah) (*Take!*), **Apra!** (*Open!*), and **Finisca!** (fee-*nees*-kah) (*Finish!*). As you can see, you simply switch the informal and formal endings.

- **Plural:** You command/speak to more than one person.

  You use the plural imperative form for two or more people, even if you would address the separate individuals formally. Verbs that end in -are, like **mandare**, have the plural imperative ending -ate, as in **Mandate!** (mahn-*dah*-teh) (*Send!*). Verbs that end in -ere change their endings to -ete, as in **Prendete!** (*prehn*-deh-teh) (*Take!*). Verbs that end in -ire change their endings to -ite, as in **Finite!** (fee-*nee*-teh) (*Finish!*)

- **Plural, including yourself:** You include yourself by saying, for example, "Let's go!"

  Good news! All verbs, including our examples **mandare**, **prendere**, **aprire**, and **finire**, change their endings to the imperative ending -iamo — namely, **Mandiamo!** (mahn-dee-*ah*-moh . . . (*Let's send!*), **Prendiamo!** (prehn-dee-*ah*-moh) (*Let's take/have . . . !*), **Apriamo!** (ah-pree-*ah*-moh) (*Let's open . . . !*) and **Finiamo!** (fee-*nyah*-moh) (*Let's finish!*). That's pretty easy, isn't it?

In case you're still struggling to grasp this scheme, Table 15-3 gives a quick overview.

Table 15-3	Imperative Verb Endings		
Form	**-are Verb Ending**	**-ere Verb Ending**	**-ire Verb Ending**
Informal singular	-a	-i	-i
Formal singular	-i	-a	-a
Plural	-ate	-ete	-ite
We form	-iamo	-iamo	-iamo

We can't let you get away without looking at some common exceptions to the preceding rules. Table 15-4 shows some of these exceptions. They are exceptions to the regular pattern.

Table 15-4	Exceptional Imperatives	
Informal Singular	**Formal Singular**	**Translation**
Abbi pazienza! (*ahb*-bee pah-tsee-*ehn*-tsah)	**Abbia pazienza!** (*ahb*-bee-ah pah-tsee-*ehn*-tsah)	*Be patient!* (Literally, have patience)
Da'! (dah)	**Dia!** (*dee*-ah)	*Give!*
Di' qualcosa! (dee kwahl-*koh*-zah)	**Dica qualcosa!** (*dee*-kah kwahl-*koh*-zah)	*Say something!*
Fa' qualcosa! (fah kwahl-*koh*-zah)	**Faccia qualcosa!** (*fahch*-chah kwahl-*koh*-zah)	*Do something!*
Sii buono! (see *bwoh*-noh)	**Sia buono!** (*see*-ah *bwoh*-noh)	*Be good!*
Sta' fermo! (stah *fehr*-moh)	**Stia fermo!** (*stee*-ah *fehr*-moh)	*Be still!*
Stai tranquillo! (stai trahn-*kweel*-loh)	**Stia tranquillo** (*stee*-ah trahn-*kweel*-loh)	*Be calm! Don't worry!*
Va via! (vah *vee*-ah)	**Vada via!** (*vah*-dah *vee*-ah)	*Go away!*
Vieni qua! (*vyeh*-nee kwah)	**Venga qua!** (*vehn*-gah kwah)	*Come here!*

We haven't even gotten to the negative commands (and if you want more on commands see *Italian Verbs For Dummies*), but here are two phrases you may hear in Italy:

Non ti preoccupare! (nohn tee preh-ohk-kooh-*pah*-reh) (*Don't worry!*) (informal)

Non si preoccupi! (nohn see preh-*ohk*-kooh-pee) (*Don't worry!*) (formal)

Fun & Games

Unscramble the following words below and then match them with their definitions in the following column. See Appendix D for the answer key.

gorblea	bed
oinpnsee	luggage
rcaaem	suitcases
asznat	room
glevia	bathroom
aneoepozirtn	room
tnloaireimma	small hotel
culla	crib
cniapsi	pool
aehicv	key
ttelo	room with a large bed for two
ricmeeaer	reservation
bgoan	waiter
ggbalaoi	

Chapter 16

Handling Emergencies

. . . .

In This Chapter

▶ Asking for help

▶ Talking to doctors

▶ Visiting the dentist

▶ Dealing with car troubles

▶ Alerting the police to an emergency

▶ Protecting your legal rights

. . . .

Asking for help is never fun, because you only need help when you're in a jam. For the purposes of this chapter, think about what unfortunate things could happen to you and in what difficulties you may find yourself. Some of these situations are minor, and others are much more serious. We give you the language tools you need to communicate your woes to the people who can help.

Here is a general sampling of asking-for-help sentences. The first two are important for real emergencies:

▶ **Aiuto!** (ah-*yooh*-toh) (*Help!*)

▶ **Aiutami!** (ah-*yooh*-tah-mee) (*Help me!*) (Informal)

▶ **Mi aiuti, per favore.** (mee ah-*yooh*-tee pehr fah-*voh*-reh) (*Help me, please.*) (Formal)

▶ **Chiamate la polizia!** (kyah-*mah*-teh lah poh-lee-*tsee*-ah) (*Call the police!*)

▶ **Ho bisogno di un medico.** (oh bee-*zoh*-nyoh dee oohn *meh*-dee-koh) (*I need a doctor.*)

▶ **Dov'è il pronto soccorso?** (doh-*veh* eel *prohn*-toh sohk-kohr-*soh*) (*Where's the emergency room?*)

▶ **Chiamate un'ambulanza!** (kyah-*mah*-teh ooh-nahm-booh-*lahn*-tsah) (*Call an ambulance!*)

As you may have noticed, you conjugate sentences directed at a group of people in the plural **voi** form (**chiamate**). In an emergency situation, you can use this with anyone who may be listening to you.

In some situations, you must ask for a competent authority who speaks English. Do so by saying:

- ✔ **Mi scusi, parla inglese?** (mee *skooh*-zee *pahr*-lah een-*gleh*-zeh) (*Excuse me, do you speak English?*)

- ✔ **C'è un medico che parli inglese?** (cheh oohn *meh*-dee-koh keh *pahr*-lee een-*gleh*-zeh) (*Is there a doctor who speaks English?*)

- ✔ **Dove posso trovare un avvocato che parli inglese?** (*doh*-veh *pohs*-soh troh-*vah*-reh oohn ahv-voh-*kah*-toh keh *pahr*-lee een-*gleh*-zeh) (*Where can I find a lawyer who speaks English?*)

If you can't find a professional who speaks English, you may be able to find **un interprete** (oohn een-*tehr*-preh-teh) (*an interpreter*) to help you.

Talking to Doctors

When you're in **l'ospedale** (lohs-peh-*dah*-leh) (*the hospital*) or at **il medico** (eel *meh*-dee-koh) (*the doctor*), you must explain where you hurt or what the problem is. This task isn't always easy, because pointing to a spot may not be sufficient. But don't worry, we won't leave you in the lurch. This section shows you, among other things, how to refer to your body parts in Italian (in Table 16-1) and what to say in a medical emergency.

Table 16-1	Basic Body Parts	
Italian	*Pronunciation*	*Translation*
il braccio	eel *brahch*-choh	the arm
il collo	eel *kohl*-loh	the neck
la gamba	lah *gahm*-bah	the leg
la mano	lah *mah*-noh	the hand
l'occhio	*lohk*-kyoh	the eye
la pancia	lah *pahn*-chah	the belly
il petto	eel *peht*-toh	the chest
il piede	eel *pyeh*-deh	the foot
lo stomaco	loh *stoh*-mah-koh	the stomach
la testa	lah *tehs*-tah	the head

Describing what ails you

The following phrases indicate how to say something hurts. There are two ways to say this: The first takes the construction **fare male** (*fah*-reh *mah*-leh) (*to hurt*). Use **fa** (fah) for body parts in the singular that hurt.

> **Mi fa male la gamba.** (mee fah *mah*-leh lah *gahm*-bah). (*My leg hurts.*)

> **Mi fa male lo stomaco.** (mee fah *mah*-leh loh *stoh*-mah-koh) (*My stomach hurts.*)

> **Mi fa male tutto il corpo.** (mee fah *mah*-leh *tooht*-toh eel *kohr*-poh) (*My whole body aches.*)

Use **fanno** (*fahn*-noh) for things in the plural that hurt.

> **Mi fanno male gli occhi.** (mee *fahn*-noh *mah*-leh lyee *ohk*-kee) (*My eyes hurt.*)

The other way to say something hurts is **avere mal di** (ah-*veh*-reh mahl dee), but you need to conjugate the verb **avere** (ah-*veh*-reh) (*to have*), depending on who has the pain. Here are some examples:

> **Ho mal di schiena.** (oh mahl dee *skyeh*-nah) (*I have a backache.*)

> **Ho mal di testa.** (oh mahl dee *tehs*-tah) (*I have a headache.*)

> **Mia figlia ha mal di denti.** (*mee*-ah *feel*-yah ah mahl dee *dehn*-tee) (*My daughter has a toothache.*)

There are still other ways to describe what ails you and explain your symptoms.

> ✔ **Mi sono rotto/rotta una gamba.** (mee *soh*-noh *roht*-toh/*rot*-tah *ooh*-nah *gahm*-bah) (*I broke my leg.*) (Use the feminine participle if you are a woman.)

> ✔ **Ho la gola arrossata.** (oh lah *goh*-lah ahr-rohs-*sah*-tah) (*I have a sore throat.*)

> ✔ **Ho la pelle irritata.** (oh lah *pehl*-leh eer-ee-*tah*-tah) (*My skin is irritated.*)

> ✔ **Mi sono storto/storta il piede/la caviglia.** (mee *soh*-noh *stohr*-toh/*stohr*-tah eel *pyeh*-deh/lah cah-*veel*-yah) (*I sprained my foot/ankle.*)

> ✔ **Ho disturbi al cuore.** (oh dees-*toohr*-bee ahl *kwoh*-reh) (*I have heart problems.*)

> ✔ **Mi bruciano gli occhi.** (mee *brooh*-chah-noh lyee *ohk*-kee) (*My eyes burn.*)

> ✔ **Mi sono slogata la spalla.** (mee *soh*-noh zloh-*gah*-tah lah *spahl*-lah) (*I've dislocated my shoulder.*)

> ✔ **Mi sono fatta/o male alla mano.** (mee *soh*-noh *faht*-tah/toh *mah*-leh *ahl*-lah *mah*-noh). (*I've hurt my hand.*)

> ✔ **Sono caduta/o.** (*soh*-noh cah-*dooh*-tah/toh) (*I fell.*)
>
> ✔ **Mia figlia ha questa brutta orticaria.** (*mee*-ah *feel*-yah ah *qwehs*-tah *brooht*-tah ohr-tee-*kahr*-ee-ah) (*My daughter has this terrible rash.*)
>
> ✔ **Mio figlio ha la febbre a 40.** (*mee*-oh *fee*-lyoh ah lah *fehb*-breh ah qwah-*rahn*-tah) (*My son's temperature is 40 degrees.*)

When you want to indicate the left or right body part, you must know that body part's gender. For a masculine part, you say **destro** (*dehs*-troh) (right) and **sinistro** (see-*nees*-troh) (left), whereas for a feminine part you change the ending: **destra** (*dehs*-trah) and **sinistra** (see-*nees*-trah).

Another little hurdle is the plural form. Where body parts are concerned, a lot of irregular plurals exist. Table 16-2 shows you some of the most frequent irregular plural forms.

Table 16-2	Body Parts Plurals	
Singular (Pronunciation)	**Plural (Pronunciation)**	**Translation**
il braccio (eel *brahch*-choh)	**le braccia** (leh *brahch*-chah)	arm(s)
il dito (eel *dee*-toh)	**le dita** (leh *dee*-tah)	finger(s)
il dito del piede (eel *dee*-toh dehl *pyeh*-deh)	**le dita del piede** (le *dee*-tah dehl *pyeh*-deh)	toe(s)
il labbro (eel *lahb*-broh)	**le labbra** (leh *lahb*-brah)	lip(s)
il ginocchio (eel jee-*nohk*-kyoh)	**le ginocchia** (leh jee-*nohk*-kyah)	knee(s)
la mano (lah *mah*-noh)	**le mani** (leh *mah*-nee)	hand(s)
l'orecchio (loh-*rehk*-kyoh)	**le orecchie** (leh oh-*rehk*-kyeh)	ear(s)
l'osso (*lohs*-soh)	**le ossa** (leh *ohs*-sah)	bone(s)

Generally speaking, if you need to tell someone that you're not feeling well, you can always say **mi sento male** (mee *sehn*-toh *mah*-leh) (*I feel sick*), which derives from the verb **sentirsi male** (sehn-*teer*-see *mah*-leh) (*to feel sick*). You could also say **non mi sento bene** (nohn mee *sehn*-toh *beh*-neh) (*I don't feel well*), which comes from **non sentirsi bene** (nohn sehn-*teer*-see *beh*-neh) (*to not feel well*). The following shows you the entire conjugation of this common and typical reflexive verb. For more on reflexive verbs, see Chapters 11 and 17.

Conjugation	Pronunciation	English
mi sento male	mee *sehn*-toh *mah*-leh	*I feel sick.*
ti senti male	tee *sehn*-tee *mah*-leh	*You feel sick.*
si sente male	see *sehn*-teh *mah*-leh	*He/she feels sick.*
ci sentiamo male	chee sehn-tee-*ah*-moh *mah*-leh	*We feel sick.*
vi sentite male	vee sehn-*tee*-teh *mah*-leh	*You feel sick.*
si sentono male	see *sehn*-toh-noh *mah*-leh	*They feel sick.*

You may have noticed that **fa male** is preceded by **mi** (mee) (*me*). This word changes according to the speaker and the person who feels the pain. A doctor may ask you **Cosa le fa male?** (*koh*-zah leh fah *mah*-leh) (*What hurts you?*). **Le** is the indirect object pronoun for the formal "you."

Talkin' the Talk

Gloria goes to the doctor because her leg is swollen. Without further examination, however, the doctor can't determine the problem. (Track 34)

Gloria: **Mi fa molto male questa gamba.**
mee fah *mohl*-toh *mah*-leh *kwehs*-tah *gahm*-bah
This leg hurts very much.

Doctor: **Vedo che è gonfia.**
veh-doh keh eh *gohn*-fee-ah
Yes, I can see it's swollen.

Gloria: **Devo andare all'ospedale?**
deh-voh ahn-*dah*-reh ahl-lohs-peh-*dah*-leh
Do I have to go to the hospital?

Doctor: **Sì, bisogna fare le lastre.**
see bee-*zoh*-nyah *fah*-reh le *lahs*-treh
Yes, you need to have some X-rays.

Words to Know

aiuto [m]	ah-yooh-toh	help
pronto soccorso	prohn-toh sohk-kohr-soh	emergency room
un'ambulanza	oohn ahm-booh-lahn-zah	an ambulance
chiamate	kyah-mah-teh	call
fare male	fah-reh mah-leh	to hurt
ospedale [m]	ohs-peh-dah-leh	hospital
lastre [f/pl]	lahs-treh	X-rays
sinistra/o [f/m]	see-nees-trah/troh	left
gonfia/o [f/m]	gohn-fee-ah/oh	swollen
muscolo [m]	moohs-koh-loh	muscle
tendine [m]	tehn-dee-neh	tendon
mi gira la testa	mee gee-rah lah tehs-tah	I'm dizzy
mi sento svenire	mee-sehn-toh zveh-nee-reh	I'm about to faint
avere mal di	ah-veh-reh mahl dee	to have a _____ache
stomaco	stoh-mah-koh	stomach
febbre	fehb-breh	fever

Understanding professional medical vocabulary

Various professional people — not all of them doctors — can offer you medical help. They include:

- **il medico** (eel *meh*-dee-koh) (*doctor*, both female and male)
- **il dottore** (eel doht-*toh*-reh) (*doctor*, both female and male)

  The female form of this noun, **la dottoressa** (lah doht-toh-*rehs*-sah), is less common.

  You can use either of these words for "doctor."

- **la/lo specialista [f/m]** (lah/loh speh-chah-*lees*-tah) (*specialist*)
- **la/il dentista [f/m]** (lah/eel dehn-*tees*-tah) (*dentist*)
- **il chirurgo [f/m]** (eel kee-*roohr*-goh) (*the surgeon*)
- **l'infermiera** (leen-fehr-*myeh*-rah) (*female nurse*)
- **l'infermiere** (leen-fehr-*myeh*-reh) (*male nurse*)

Here's a question that you may need to ask in a doctor's office, with typical replies:

- **Devo prendere qualcosa?** (*deh*-voh *prehn*-deh-reh kwahl-*koh*-zah) (*Do I have to take anything?*)

  No, si riposi e beva molta acqua. (noh see ree-*poh*-zee eh *beh*-vah *mohl*-tah *ah*-kwah) (*No, rest and drink a lot of water.*)

  Ecco la ricetta. (*ehk*-koh lah ree-*cheht*-tah) (*Here is your prescription.*)

Getting what you need at the pharmacy

If you need **una medicina** (*ooh*-nah meh-dee-*chee*-nah) (*a medicine*) you will probably look for the closest **farmacia** (fahr-mah-*chee*-ah) (*pharmacy*). Usual pharmacy hours are from 8:30 a.m. to 8:00 p.m., generally with a lunch break from 1:00 to 4:00 p.m. But there is always a pharmacy open in case of an emergency! You can find the address and phone number of the open pharmacy (**farmacia di turno**) (fahr-mah-*chee*-ah dee *toohr*-noh) written on all pharmacy doors.

Italy is one of those places where pharmacists still give medical advice: These are true pharmacies without all of the non-drug items for sale like you find in your typical big drug store in the United States, where you can get everything from canned food to beach chairs. Furthermore, you generally don't walk in, browse, and help yourself to even simple things like aspirin. This is the same for many other types of stores in Italy, the **profumeria** (proh-fooh-meh-*ree*-ah) (*toiletries shop*), shoe stores, and small clothing shops in particular. Many items are kept behind the counter. So, if you or a loved one has a slight ailment and it's not an emergency, you can go into the pharmacy for help.

Talkin' the Talk

Anna has just walked into the **farmacia** with her six-year-old daughter, Maria, who was stung by about 100 mosquitoes the night before.

Farmacista:	**Prego. Mi dica.**
	preh-goh mee *dee*-kah
	Hello. How can I help you?
Anna:	**Mia figlia è stata punta dalle zanzare ieri notte.**
	mee-ah *fee*-lyah eh *stah*-tah *poohn*-tah *dahl*-leh dsan-*zah*-reh *yeh*-ree *noht*-teh
	My daughter was stung by some mosquitoes last night.
Farmacista:	**Sì questo lo vedo.**
	see *qwehs*-toh loh *veh*-doh
	Yes, I can see that.
	Le do una pomata contro il prurito.
	leh doh *ooh*-nah *poh*-mah-tah *kohn*-troh eel prooh-*ree*-toh
	I'll give you an anti-itch cream.
Anna:	**Ha un prodotto anti-zanzara per i bambini?**
	ah oohn proh-*doht*-toh *ahn*-tee-dsahn-*zah*-rah pehr ee bahm-*bee*-nee
	Do you have something safe for children to keep the mosquitoes away?

Farmacista:	**Si, ecco uno spray anti-zanzara molto sicuro per i bambini.**
	see *ehk*-koh *ooh*-noh sprahy *ahn*-tee-*dsahn*-zah-rah *mol*-toh see-*kooh*-roh pehr ee bahm-*bee*-nee
	Yes. Here is a mosquito repellant that is very safe for children.

Braving the dentist

Of course, you might just need some emergency dental work while you're in Italy. The first thing to ask the concierge at your hotel, the pharmacist, or the friendly **barista** where you've been having breakfast every morning is "**Scusi, mi può consigliare un dentista di fiducia?**" (*skooh*-zee mee pwoh *kohn*-seel-*yah*-reh oohn dehn-*tees*-tah dee fee-*dooh*-chah) (*Excuse me, would you please recommend a good dentist?*)

Talkin' the Talk

Giancarlo is at the dentist's with a terrible toothache.

Giancarlo:	**Dottore, ho un terribile dolore al molare.**
	doht-*toh*-reh oh oohn tehr-*ree*-bee-leh doh-*loh*-reh ahl moh-*lah*-reh
	Doctor, I have a terrible pain in my molar.

Dentist:	**Vediamo. Purtroppo è infetto.**
	veh-*dyah*-moh poohr-*trohp*-poh eh een-*feht*-toh
	Let's see. Unfortunately, it's infected.

	Non posso fare altro che darle un antibiotico.
	nohn *pohs*-soh *fah*-reh *ahl*-troh keh *dahr*-leh oohn *ahn*-tee-bee-oh-*tee*-koh
	I can't do anything for you but give you an antibiotic.

	Lo prenda due volte al giorno.
	loh *prehn*-dah *dooh*-eh *vohl*-teh ahl *johr*-noh
	Take it twice a day.

Reporting an Accident to the Police

There are other types of emergencies in addition to medical ones. You might have to call the police to report something you've witnessed.

Talkin' the Talk

 Elena has just seen an elderly woman on her bicycle hit by a scooter. She calls the police. (Track 35)

Officer:	**Polizia.**
	poh-lee-*tsee*-ah
	Police.
Elena:	**C'è stato un incidente.**
	cheh *stah*-toh oohn een-chee-*dehn*-teh
	There's been an accident!
Officer:	**Dove?**
	doh-veh
	Where?
Elena:	**Piazza Mattei.**
	pyaht-tsah maht-*tey*
	Piazza Mattei.
Officer:	**Ci sono feriti?**
	chee *soh*-noh fe-*ree*-tee
	Is anyone injured?
Elena:	**C'è una persona ferita incosciente.**
	cheh *ooh*-na pehr-*soh*-nah fehr-*ee*-tah in-koh-*shehn*-teh
	Someone is injured and unconscious.
Officer:	**Mandiamo subito un'ambulanza.**
	mahn-dee-*ah*-moh *sooh*-bee-toh ooh-nahm-booh-*lahn*-tsah
	We'll send an ambulance right away.

 If you are in Italy and you have an emergency, call 113, the Italian national police, who will also send you an ambulance if you need one. This number is valid for all of Italy.

Words to Know

ambulanza [f]	ahm-booh-<u>lahn</u>-tsah	ambulance
Che è successo?	keh eh sooh-<u>chehs</u>-soh	What happened?
emergenza [f]	eh-mehr-<u>jehn</u>-tsah	emergency
incidente [m]	in-chee-<u>dehn</u>-teh	accident
le lenti a contatto	leh <u>lenh</u>-tee ah kohn-<u>taht</u>-toh	contact lenses
soluzione [f]	soh-loohts-<u>yoh</u>-neh	solution
ferito [m]	feh-<u>ree</u>-toh	injured (person)
pomata [f]	poh-<u>mah</u>-tah	cream
ricetta [f]	ree-<u>cheht</u>-tah	prescription

I've Been Robbed! Knowing What to Do and Say When the Police Arrive

We hope you are never the target of a robbery. If you are, however, we want you to be prepared with the important phrases you will need when the police arrive.

✔ **Sono stata/o derubata/o.** (*soh*-noh *stah*-tah/toh deh-rooh-*bah*-tah/toh) (*I've been robbed.*) [f/m]

✔ **C'è stato un furto nel mio appartamento.** (cheh *stah*-toh oohn *foohr*-toh nehl *mee*-oh ahp-pahr-tah-*mehn*-toh) (*There was a burglary in my apartment.*)

✔ **Sono entrati dei ladri in casa nostra.** (*soh*-noh ehn-*trah*-tee dey *lah*-dree een *kah*-sah *nohs*-trah) (*Thieves broke into our house.*)

✔ **Mi hanno rubato la macchina.** (mee *ahn*-noh rooh-*bah*-toh lah *mahk*-kee-nah) (*My car has been stolen.*)

✔ **Mi hanno scippata.** (mee *ahn*-noh sheep-*pah*-tah) (*My handbag was snatched.*)

Talkin' the Talk

A moped driver just stole Anna's **borsa** (*bohr*-sah) (*handbag*). Distraught, she calls 113 for the police to **denunciare** (deh-noohn-*chah*-reh) (*to report*) **il furto** (eel *foohr*-toh) (*the theft*).

Officer:	**Polizia.**
	poh-lee-*tsee*-ah
	Police.

Anna:	**Mi hanno appena scippata!**
	mee *ahn*-noh ahp-*peh*-nah sheep-*pah*-tah
	They just snatched my handbag!

Officer:	**Si calmi e venga in questura.**
	see *kahl*-mee eh *vehn*-gah een kwehs-*tooh*-rah
	Calm down and come to police headquarters.

Anna:	**È stato un uomo in motorino.**
	eh *stah*-toh oohn *woh*-moh een moh-toh-*ree*-noh
	It was a man on a moped.

Officer:	**Ho capito, ma deve venire qui.**
	oh kah-*pee*-toh mah *deh*-veh veh-*nee*-reh kwee
	I got it, but you have to come here.

Anna:	**Dov'è la questura?**
	doh-*veh* lah kwehs-*tooh*-rah
	Where is police headquarters?

Officer:	**Dietro la posta centrale.**
	dee-*eh*-troh lah *pohs*-tah chehn-*trah*-leh
	Behind the main post office.

Anna:	**Vengo subito.**
	vehn-goh *sooh*-bee-toh
	I'm coming at once.

Words to Know

borsa [f]	<u>bohr</u>-sah	handbag
furto [m]	<u>foohr</u>-toh	theft
denunciare	deh-noohn-<u>chah</u>-reh	to report
motorino [m]	moh-toh-<u>ree</u>-noh	moped
questura [f]	kwehs-<u>tooh</u>-rah	police headquarters
scippare	sheep-<u>pah</u>-reh	to snatch a handbag
scippo [m]	<u>sheep</u>-poh	theft of a handbag

When you have to report someone and describe the thief, you must know some essential words, such as hair color, height, and so on. Many of these adjectives will also come in handy when describing other people — friends, family members, classmates — not just thieves! You can form descriptive sentences like this:

La persona era . . . (lah pehr-*soh*-nah *eh*-rah) (*The person was . . .*):

- ✔ **alta** (*ahl*-tah) (*tall*)
- ✔ **bassa** (*bahs*-sah) (*short*)
- ✔ **di media statura** (dee *meh*-dee-ah stah-*tooh*-rah) (*of medium build*)
- ✔ **grassa** (*grahs*-sah) (*fat*)
- ✔ **magra** (*mah*-grah) (*thin*)

Note: The preceding adjectives end in -a because they refer to the noun **la persona**, which is feminine.

I capelli erano . . . (ee kah-*pehl*-lee *eh*-rah-noh) (*The hair was . . .*)

- ✔ **castani** (kahs-*tah*-nee) (*brown*)
- ✔ **biondi** (*byohn*-dee) (*blond*)

✔ **neri** (*neh*-ree) (*black*)

✔ **rossi** (*rohs*-see) (*red*)

✔ **scuri** (*skooh*-ree) (*dark*)

✔ **chiari** (*kyah*-ree) (*fair*)

✔ **lisci** (*lee*-shee) (*straight*)

✔ **ondulati** (ohn-dooh-*lah*-tee) (*wavy*)

✔ **ricci** (*reech*-chee) (*curly*)

✔ **corti** (*kohr*-tee) (*short*)

✔ **lunghi** (*loohn*-gee) (*long*)

Aveva gli occhi . . . (ah-*veh*-vah lyee *ohk*-kee) (*His/Her eyes were . . .*)

✔ **azzurri** (ahdz-*zooh*-ree) (*blue*)

✔ **grigi** (*gree*-jee) (*gray*)

✔ **marroni** (mahr-*roh*-nee) (*brown*)

✔ **neri** (*neh*-ree) (*black; dark*)

✔ **verdi** (*vehr*-dee) (*green*)

Era . . . (*eh*-rah) (*He/she was . . .*)

✔ **calvo** (*kahl*-voh) (*bald*)

✔ **rasato** (rah-*zah*-toh) (*clean-shaven*)

Aveva . . . (ah-*veh*-vah) (*He/She had . . .*)

✔ **la barba** (lah *bahr*-bah) (*a beard*)

✔ **i baffi** (ee *bahf*-fee) (*a moustache*)

✔ **la bocca larga** (lah *bohk*-kah *lahr*-gah) (*a wide mouth*)

✔ **la bocca stretta** (lah *bohk*-kah *streht*-tah) (*thin lips*)

✔ **la bocca carnosa** (lah *bohk*-kah kahr-*noh*-zah) (*a plump mouth*)

✔ **il naso lungo** (eel *nah*-zoh *loohn*-go) (*a long nose*)

✔ **il naso corto** (eel *nah*-zoh *kohr*-toh) (*a short nose*)

Dealing with Car Trouble

You don't have to be involved in a car crash to experience car trouble. Perhaps some sort of mechanical problem makes your car break down. In such cases you need to call an auto mechanic who can help you out of this situation.

Talkin' the Talk

Raffaella's car has broken down. She calls roadside assistance from her cell phone.

Mechanic: **Pronto.**
prohn-toh
Hello.

Raffaella: **Pronto, ho bisogno d'aiuto!**
prohn-toh oh bee-*zoh*-nyoh dah-*yooh*-toh
Hello, I need help!

Mechanic: **Che succede?**
keh soohch-*cheh*-deh
What's wrong?

Raffaella: **Mi si è fermata la macchina.**
mee see eh fehr-*mah*-tah lah *mahk*-kee-nah
My car broke down.

Mechanic: **Dove si trova?**
doh-veh see *troh*-vah
Where are you?

Raffaella: **Sull'autostrada A 1 prima dell'uscita Firenze Nord.**
soohl *au*-to-strah-dah ah *ooh*-noh *pree*-mah dehl-looh-*shee*-tah fee-*rehn*-tseh nohrd
On the highway A 1 before the Florence North exit.

Mechanic: **Bene. Mando un carro attrezzi.**
beh-neh *mahn*-doh oohn *cahr*-roh aht-*treht*-tsee
Okay. I'll send a tow truck.

Raffaella: **Ci vorrà molto?**
chee vohr-*rah mohl*-toh
Will it take a long time?

Mechanic: **Dipende dal traffico. Al massimo mezz'ora.**
dee-*pehn*-deh dahl *trahf*-fee-koh ahl *mahs*-see-moh
medz-*oh*-rah
It depends on the traffic. Half hour at the most.

Raffaella: **Venite il più presto possibile per favore!**
veh-*nee*-teh eel pyooh *prehs*-toh pohs-*see*-bee-leh
pehr fah-*voh*-reh
Come as soon as possible please!

Words to Know

fermare	fehr-<u>mah</u>-reh	to stop
macchina [f]	<u>mahk</u>-kee-nah	car
il più presto possibile	eel pyooh <u>prehs</u>-toh pohs-<u>see</u>-bee-leh	as soon as possible
soccorso stradale [m]	sohk-<u>kohr</u>-soh strah-<u>dah</u>-leh	roadside assistance
corsia di emergenza	kohr-<u>see</u>-ah dee eh-mehr-<u>jehn</u>-za	emergency lane
traffico [m]	<u>trahf</u>-fee-koh	traffic
meccanico [m]	mehk-<u>kah</u>-nee-koh	mechanic
una gomma a terra	<u>ooh</u>-nah <u>gohm</u>-mah ah <u>tehr</u>-rah	a flat tire
carro attrezzi [m]	<u>kahr</u>-roh aht-<u>treht</u>-tsee	tow truck

When You Need a Lawyer: Protecting Your Rights

Many unpleasant moments in life require that you seek the help of an authorized person. Often, this person is a lawyer who can help you in complicated situations. Therefore, knowing how to contact a lawyer is rather important. You can use the following general questions and sentences to request legal help in Italian.

✔ **Mi serve l'aiuto di un avvocato.** (mee *sehr*-veh lah-*yooh*-toh dee oohn ahv-voh-*kah*-toh) (*I need the help of a lawyer.*)

✔ **Ho bisogno di assistenza legale.** (oh bee-*zoh*-nyoh dee ahs-sees-*tehn*-tsah leh-*gah*-leh) (*I need legal assistance.*)

✔ **Vorrei consultare il mio avvocato.** (vohr-*rey* kohn-soohl-*tah*-reh eel *mee*-oh ahv-voh-*kah*-toh) (*I'd like to consult my lawyer.*)

✔ **Chiamate il mio avvocato, per favore.** (kyah-*mah*-teh eel *mee*-oh ahv-voh-*kah*-toh pehr fah-*voh*-reh) (*Call my lawyer, please.*)

After you find a lawyer, you can speak to him or her about your situation. Here are some examples of what you may need to say:

✔ **Sono stato truffato/a.** (*soh*-noh *stah*-toh troohf-*fah*-toh/tah) (*I was cheated.*)

✔ **Voglio denunciare un furto.** (*Voh*-lyoh deh-noohn-*chah*-reh oohn *foohr*-toh) (*I want to report a theft.*)

✔ **Devo stipulare un contratto.** (*deh*-voh stee-pooh-*lah*-reh oohn kohn-*traht*-toh) (*I have to negotiate a contract.*)

✔ **Ho avuto un incidente stradale.** (oh ah-*vooh*-toh oohn een-chee-*dehn*-teh strah-*dah*-leh) (*I've had a traffic accident.*)

✔ **Voglio che mi vengano risarciti i danni.** (*voh*-lyoh keh mee *vehn*-gah-noh ree-sahr-*chee*-tee ee *dahn*-nee) (*I want to be compensated for the damages.*)

✔ **Sono stato/a arrestato/a.** (*soh*-noh *stah*-toh/ah ahr-rehs-*tah*-toh/ah) (*I've been arrested.*)

Words to Know

danno [m]	dahn-noh	damage
denunciare	deh-noohn-chah-reh	to report
denuncia [f]	deh-noohn-chah	report
incidente stradale [m]	een-chee-dehn-teh strah-dah-leh	traffic accident
macchina [f]	mahk-kee-nah	car
targa [f]	tahr-gah	license plate
patente [f]	pah-tehn-teh	license
libretto [m]	lee-breht-toh	registration
assicurazione [f]	ahs-see-kooh-rah-tsee-oh-neh	insurance

Reporting a Lost or Stolen Passport

Imagine you lose your passport, or it gets stolen while you are snoozing on the train. (These things happen!) The conversation that follows will help you get a new one.

Talkin' the Talk

When Diane gets off the train in Florence, she realizes that she no longer has her passport. She goes immediately to the station police.

Diane: **Ho perso il passaporto! Non so cosa fare!**
oh *pehr*-soh eel pahs-sah-*pohr*-toh nohn soh *koh*-zah *fah*-reh
I've lost my passport! I don't know what to do!

Police: **Sa dirmi dove, come, quando?**
sah *deer*-mee *doh*-veh *koh*-meh *kwahn*-doh
Can you tell me where, when, and how?

Diane: **Penso di averlo perso in treno**.
pehn-soh dee ah-*vehr*-loh *pehr*-soh een *treh*-noh
I think I lost it on the train.

Police: **Ora facciamo la denuncia.**
oh-rah fach-*chah*-moh lah deh-*noohn*-chah
We'll file a report now.

Con questa denuncia, deve rivolgersi alla sua ambasciata o consolato.
kohn *kwehs*-tah deh-*noohn*-chah *deh*-veh ree-*vohl*-jehr-see *ahl*-lah *sooh*-ah ahm-bah-*shah*-tah oh kohn-soh-*lah*-toh
You're going to need this report when you go to your Embassy or Consulate to apply for a new one.

Diane: **Grazie.**
grah-tsee-eh
Thank you.

(at the Embassy or Consolate)

Consolate Agent:	**Dica?**
	dee-kah
	How can I help you?
Diane:	(agitated) **Mi serve un nuovo passaporto! Subito!**
	mee *sehr*-veh oohn *nwoh*-voh *pahs*-sah-pohr-toh *sooh*-bee-toh
	I need a new passport. Right away!
Consolate Agent:	**Si calmi. Necessitano due foto tessera. . .**
	see *kahl*-mee. neh-*chehs*-see-tah-noh *dooh*-eh *foh*-toh *tehs*-seh-rah
	Calm down. You're going to need two ID-size photos . . .
	La denuncia della polizia, una copia del passaporto originale. . .
	lah deh-*noohn*-chah *dehl*-lah poh-lee-*tsee*-ah *ooh*-nah *koh*-pee-ah dehl pahs-sah-*pohr*-toh oh-ree-gee-*nah*-leh
	. . . official police report, a copy of your original passport (your hotel should have a copy of this) . . .
	. . . e un altro documento.
	eh oohn *ahl*-troh doh-kooh-*mehn*-toh
	. . . and another form of ID.

Fun & Games

See how many body parts you can remember by labeling as many of them as you can on the following picture. See Appendix D for the answer key.

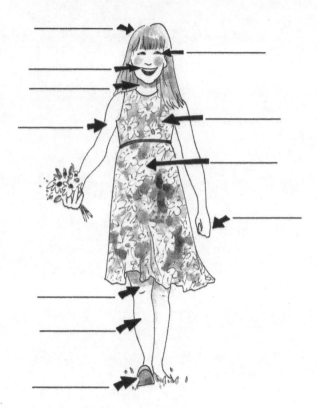

Chapter 17

Small Talk, Wrapping Things Up

In This Chapter

▶ Discovering interrogative pronouns

▶ Asking simple questions

▶ Taking care of basic needs

▶ Talking about yourself and your family

▶ Talking shop

▶ Sending postcards, buying stamps

▶ Speaking reflexively

This chapter wraps things up by presenting you with some of the basic essentials that are smattered throughout the book, but which deserve some space of their own. At this point you probably have figured out how to form questions, but here's that information at your fingertips for quick review and reference. At the end of this chapter, we give you a crash course on reflexive verbs, some of the most common yet unappreciated verbs.

Discovering Interrogative Pronouns

In Italian at least one thing is easier than in English: forming questions. In English, in most cases, you need a form of "to do," "to be," or "to have" to form a question. You also (mostly) have to invert part of your sentence construction. For example, "He goes to the movies" becomes "Does he go to the movies?" In Italian you simply ask **"Lui va al cinema?"** (*looh*-ee vah ahl *chee*-neh-mah) (*Does he go to the movies?*) There is no word for does, just as there is no word for are in the following sentence: **"Vai alla partita?** (vahy *ahl*-lah pahr-*tee*-tah) (*Are you going to the game?*)

In Italian, forming questions is very easy: A question has the same structure as an affirmative statement. You identify a question only by the intonation in your voice and by the use of a question mark in written language. For example:

Luca va a scuola.	**Luca va a scuola?**
looh-kah vah ah *skwoh*-lah	*looh*-kah vah ah *skwoh*-lah
Luca goes to school.	Luca goes to school? or Does Luca go to school?
Mangi la carne.	**Mangi la carne?**
mahn-jee lah *kahr*-neh	*mahn*-jee lah *kahr*-neh
You eat/You're eating meat.	Do you eat/Are you eating (the) meat?

Italian also has interrogative pronouns (when, where, what, and so on) with which you can start questions. Use the following pronouns:

- **Chi?** (kee) (*Who?*)
- **Che?** (keh) (*What?*)
- **Cosa?** (*koh*-sah) (*What?*)
- **Quando?** (*kwahn*-doh) (*When?*)
- **Quanto?** (*kwahn*-toh) (*How much?*)
- **Quanti/e?** (*kwahn*-tee/teh) (*How many?*) (m/f)
- **Quale/i?** (*kwah*-leh/ee) (*Which, what*) sing./pl
- **Dove?** (*doh*-veh) (*Where?*)
- **Perché?** (pehr-*keh*) (*Why?*)
- **Come?** (*koh*-meh) (*How?*)

Che, cosa, and **che cosa** are often used interchangeably.

Some sample questions using these interrogative pronouns include:

- **Chi è?** (kee eh) (*Who is it/this?*)
- **Cosa stai facendo?** (*koh*-sah stahy fah-*chehn*-doh) (*What are you doing?*)
- **Quando arrivi?** (*kwahn*-doh ahr-*ree*-vee) (*When do you arrive?*)
- **Dov'è la stazione?** (doh-*veh* lah stah-*tsyoh*-neh) (*Where is the station?*)
- **Perché non sei venuto?** (pehr-*keh* nohn sehy veh-*nooh*-toh) (*Why didn't you come?*)
- **Come stai?** (*koh*-meh stahy) (*How are you?*)
- **Come si dice "rain" in italiano?** (*koh*-meh see *dee*-cheh . . . in ee-tah-lee-*ah*-noh) (*How do you say "rain" in Italian?*)

Asking simple questions

When you ask a question using an interrogative pronoun, you do not need the interrogative pronoun in the response. For example:

Dov'è la Cappella Sistina? (doh-*veh* lah kahp-*pehl*-lah sees-*tee*-nah) (*Where is the Sistine Chapel?*)

La Cappella Sistina è a Roma. (lah kahp-*pehl*-lah sees-*tee*-nah eh ah *roh*-mah) (*The Sistine Chapel is in Rome.*)

Quante regioni ci sono in Italia? (*kwahn*-teh reh-*joh*-nee chee *soh*-noh in ee-*tah*-lee-ah) (*How many regions are there in Italy?*)

Ci sono 20 regioni. (chee *soh*-noh *vehn*-tee reh-*joh*-nee) (*There are 20 regions.*)

The interrogatives **dove** (*doh*-veh) and **come** (*koh*-meh) can be contracted with the verb **essere** (*ehs*-sehr-reh) (*to be*) in the third person singular. Note that the pronunciation and stress also change. Let's take a look at these interrogatives with third person singular and third person plural verbs.

Dov'è Mario. (doh-*veh mah*-ree-oh) (*Where's Mario?*)

Dove sono i ragazzi? (*doh*-veh *soh*-noh ee rah-*gahts*-tsee) (*Where are the boys?*)

Com'è quel ristorante? (koh-*meh* kwehl rees-toh-*rahn*-teh) (*How is that restaurant? or What's that restaurant like?*)

Come sono gli gnocchi? (*koh*-meh *soh*-noh lyee *nyohk*-kee) (*How are the gnocchi?*)

Use **quale** (*kwah*-leh) in the singular, **quali** (*kwah*-lee) in the plural, but **qual è** (kwahl-*eh*) when combined with the third person singular of **essere**.

Quale (*kwah*-leh): **Quale film vuoi vedere?** (*kwah*-leh feelm vwoi veh-*deh*-reh) (*What/which film do you want to see?*)

Qual è (kwahl-*eh*): **Qual è il mare più profondo in Italia?** (kwahl-*eh* il *mah*-reh pyooh proh-*fohn*-doh in ee-*tah*-lee-ah) (*What is the deepest sea in Italy?*)

Quali amici hai invitato? (*kwahl*-ee ah-*mee*-chee ahy in-vee-*tah*-toh) (*Which friends did you invite?*)

C'è and ci sono

Although seemingly insignificant, you just can't get around in Italian without the essential terms **c'è** (cheh) (*there is*) and **ci sono** (chee *soh*-noh) (*there are*) that are useful both for asking and answering questions. Just remember that both have a "ch" sound!

Cosa c'è nel frigo? (*koh*-zah cheh nehl *free*-goh) (*What's in the fridge?*)

C'è un esame domani? (cheh oohn eh-*zah*-meh doh-*mah*-nee) (*Is there an exam tomorrow?*)

Si, c'è italiano. (see cheh ee-tah-lee-*ah*-noh) (*Yes, there is the Italian one.*)

Ci sono ancora dei ravioli? (chee *soh*-noh ahn-*koh*-rah dehy rah-vee-*oh*-lee) (*Are there any ravioli left?*)

Si, ci sono. (see chee *soh*-noh) (*Yes, there are.*)

Taking care of basic needs

Sometimes you just need to ask for something very basic but necessary. Here are a few phrases that will take you far:

Scusi, dov'è il bagno per favore? (*skooh*-zee doh-*veh* il bah-*nyoh* pehr fah-*voh*-reh) (*Excuse me, where is the bathroom please?*) Some people get fancy and ask for **la toilette** with a Frenchified accent; however, **bagno** gets you where you need to go (no pun intended).

Scusi, dov'è la farmacia più vicina? (*skooh*-zee doh-*veh* lah fahr-mah-*chee*-ah pyooh vee-*chee*-nah) (*Excuse me, where's the nearest pharmacy?*)

Scusi, dov'è una banca? (*skooh*-zee doh-*veh* ooh-nah *bahn*-kah) (*Excuse me, where is a bank?*)

Ho bisogno di/ Mi serve (sing.)/**Mi servono**(pl) (oh bee-*zoh*-nyoh dee/mee sehr-*veh*/mee *sehr*-voh-noh) (*I need*)

    un parucchiere (oohn pah-rooh-*kyeh*-reh) (*a hairdresser*)

    un'estetista (per fare la ceretta) (oohn-esh-teh-*tees*-tah) (pehr *fah*-reh lah chehr-*eht*-tah) (*an esthetician*) (*for waxing*) (No Italian women I know shave with a razor.)

Sto cercando (stoh chehr-*kahn*-doh) (*I'm looking for*)

    il dentifricio (il dehn-tee-*free*-choh) (*toothpaste*)

    la crema solare (lah *kreh*-mah soh-*lah*-reh) (*sun protection lotion*)

i tamponi (ee tahm-*poh*-nee) (*tampons*)

la carta igienica (lah *kar*-tah ee-*jehn*-ee-kah) (*toilet paper*)

qualcosa per le zanzare (qwahl-*koh*-zah pehr leh *dzahn*-zah-reh) (*something for mosquitoes*)

qualcosa per mal di testa (kwah-*koh*-zah pehr mahl dee *tehs*-tah) (*something for a headache*)

Vorrei (vohr-*rey*) (*I'd like*)

Mi può/potrebbe consigliare . . . ? (mee pwoh/poh-*trehb*-beh kohn-seel-*yah*-reh) (*Would you be able to recommend . . . ?*)

Può ripetere lentamente, per favore? (pwoh ree-*peh*-teh-reh lehn-tah-*mehn*-teh pehr fah-*voh*-reh) (*Would you repeat slowly, please?*)

Non capisco. (nohn kah-*pees*-koh) (*I don't understand.*)

Non lo so. (nohn loh soh) (*I don't know.*)

Talkin' the Talk

Massimo and Isa, two colleagues at work, are getting to know each other over a morning cappuccino, and so of course have to use many of the interrogative pronouns that this chapter recapitulates. (Track 36)

Massimo: **Cosa prendi?**
koh-zah *prehn*-dee
What are you having?

Isa: **Un cappuccio e una pasta.**
oohn kahp-poohch-*chee*-noh eh *ooh*-nah *pahs*-tah
A cappuccino and a pastry.

Massimo: **Quando hai cominciato il lavoro qui?**
qwahn-doh ahy koh-meen-*chah*-toh il lah-*voh*-roh kwee
When did you start working here?

Isa: **Due mesi fa.**
dooh-eh *meh*-zee fah
Two months ago.

Massimo:	**Dov'eri prima?**
	dohv-*eh*-ree *pree*-mah
	Where were you before?

Isa:	**Lavoravo per la succursale veneta.**
	lah-voh-*rah*-voh pehr lah soohk-koohr-*sah*-leh
	veh-neh-tah
	I was working for the branch in the Veneto region.

Massimo:	**Come ti trovi?**
	koh-meh tee *troh*-vee
	How do you like it so far?

Isa:	**Mi piace abbastanza.**
	mee *pyach*-cheh ahb-bahs-*tahn*-zah
	I like it well enough.

	E tu, da quanto tempo lavori per la compagnia?
	eh tooh dah *qwahn*-toh *tehm*-poh lah-*voh*-ree pehr
	lah kohm-pahn-ee-ah
	And how long have you been working for the company?

Massimo:	**Da sei anni.**
	dah sey *ahn*-nee
	For six years.

	Da quando mi sono laureato.
	dah *kwahn*-doh mee *soh*-noh lou-reh-*ah*-toh
	Since I graduated.

	Da quale università ti sei laureata?
	dah *qwah*-leh ooh-nee-vehr-see-*tah* tee sey
	lou-reh-*ah*-tah
	What university did you go to?

Isa:	**Dall'Università di Urbino. E tu?**
	dahl-looh-nee-vehr-see-*tah* dee oohr-*bee*-noh eh tooh
	The University of Urbino. And you?

Massimo:	**Bologna.**
	boh-*lohn*-yah
	Bologna.

Isa:	**Vuoi tornare a Bologna?**
	vwoi tohr-*nah*-reh ah boh-*lohn*-yah
	Do you want to go back to Bologna?

Massimo:	**Non lo so.**
	nohn loh soh
	I don't know.

	Si, un giorno vorrei tornarci.
	see oohn *johr*-noh vohr-*rey* tohr-*nahr*-chee
	Yes, some day I'd like to go back there.

Pronto (*prohn*-toh) means more than just "hello" when you pick up the phone. It frequently means "ready," in which case it functions as an adjective and, therefore, changes according to the noun it describes. In other words, when the noun it modifies is masculine, the adjective ends in **-o** — **pronto**. If the noun is feminine, it ends in **-a** — **pronta** (*prohn*-tah). When modifying plural nouns, it ends in **i** (ee) (masculine plural) and **e** (eh) (feminine plural). Consider these examples:

✔ **Ragazzi, siete pronti?** (rah-*gats*-zee see-*eh*-teh *prohn*-tee) (*Guys/kids, are you ready?*)

✔ **La cena è pronta.** (lah *cheh*-nah eh *prohn*-tah) (*Dinner is ready.*)

Another use of **pronto** that you should know is **pronto soccorso** (*prohn*-toh sohk-*kohr*-soh) (*first aid; emergency room*). In this context, **pronto** means "rapid."

Presto (*prehs*-toh), on the other hand, means either early or soon, and as an adverb is invariable (ending always in o): **Siamo arrivati presto.** (see-*ah*-moh ahr-ree-*vah*-tee *prehs*-toh) (*We arrived early.*)

Words to Know

consigliare	kohn-seel-yah-reh	to recommend
pronto	prohn-toh	ready, hello (phone)
presto	prehs-toh	early, soon
non lo so	nohn loh soh	I don't know
da quanto tempo?	dah kwahn-toh tehm-poh	How long?
gemello/a	jeh-mehl-lah	twin (m/f)
ditta	deet-tah	company, firm
come ti trovi	koh-meh tee troh-vee	How do you like . . . ? (used only in certain situations, like a job or new city)
abbastanza	ahb-bahs-tahn-zah	enough
il bagno	il bahn-yoh	bathroom
partita	pahr-tee-tah	game
vorrei	vohr-rey	I would like

Talking About Yourself and Your Family — Possessives Part 2

You already saw how possessive adjectives and pronouns work in Chapter 15, but the story doesn't end there.

There are specific rules for possessive adjectives with family members. For singular family members you *do not* use the article, but plural family members *do* take the article:

Mia sorella (no definite article) (*mee*-ah soh-*rehl*-lah) (*my sister*) — **Le mie sorelle** (with definite article) (leh *mee*-eh soh-*rehl*-leh (*my sisters*)

Table 17-1 shows some other relatives.

Table 17-1		Relatives
Relative	*Pronunciation*	*Definition*
marito	mah-*ree*-toh	husband
moglie	*mohl*-yeh	wife
figlio	*feel*-yoh	son
figlia	*feel*-yah	daughter
figli	*feel*-yee	children
nipote	nee-*poh*-teh	niece, nephew, grand-daughter, grand-son
nipoti	nee-*poh*-tee	nieces, nephews, grand-daughters, grand-sons, grand-children
suocera	*swoh*-cheh-rah	mother-in-law
nuora	*nwoh*-rah	daughter-in-law
genero	*geh*-neh-roh	son-in-law
zia	*dzee*-ah	aunt
zio	*dzee*-oh	uncle
cugina/o/e/i	kooh-*jee*-nah/oh/ee	cousin (f.)/cousin (m)/cousins
nonna/o/i	*nohn*-nah/noh/ee	grand-mother/father/parents
madre	*mah*-dreh	mother
padre	*pah*-dreh	father
genitori	geh-nee-*toh*-ree	parents

Talkin' the Talk

Teresa and Amy are two old friends catching up about their families after not having spoken for about 15 years. Notice they use definite articles in front of plural family relatives, and no article in front of singular family relatives.

Teresa: **Ciao Amy. Sono Teresa.**
chou *ey*-mee *soh*-noh teh-*reh*-sah
Hi Amy. It's Teresa.

Amy: **Da quanto tempo non ti sento!**
dah *kwahn*-toh *tehm*-poh nohn tee *sehn*-toh
What a long time it's been!

Teresa: **Come stai?**
koh-meh stahy
How are you?

Amy: **Sto bene!**
stoh *beh*-neh
I'm well!

Raccontami di te!
rahk-*kohn*-tah-mee dee teh
Tell me about you! (Yourself)

Teresa: **Mi sono sposata undici anni fa.**
mee *soh*-noh spoh-*sah*-tah *oohn*-dee-chee *ahn*-nee fah
I got married 11 years ago.

Ho due figli.
oh *dooh*-eh *feel*-yee
I have two children.

Abito a Ravenna.
ah-bee-toh ah rah-*vehn*-nah
I live in Ravenna.

Amy: **Quanti anni hanno i tuoi figli?**
kwahn-tee *ahn*-nee *ahn*-noh ee twoi *feel*-yee
How old are your children?

Teresa: **Mia figlia Emilia Rosa ha dieci anni.**
Mee-ah *feel*-yah eh-*meel*-yah *roh*-zah ah *dyeh*-chee
ahn-nee
My daughter Emilia Rosa is ten years old.

E mio figlio Pietro ne ha otto.
eh *mee*-oh *feel*-yoh pee-*eh*-troh neh ah *oht*-toh
And my son Pietro is eight.

Come sta la tua famiglia?
koh-meh stah lah *tooh*-ah fah-*meel*-yah
How's your family doing?

Amy: **Mio marito Sandro è sempre in giro per il mondo.**
mee-oh mah-*ree*-toh *sahn*-droh eh *sehm*-preh in
jee-roh pehr il *mohn*-doh
My husband Sandro is always travelling all over
the world.

**Mia figlia Tania adesso ha diciotto anni e frequenta
l'università.**
mee-ah *feel*-yah *tahn*-yah ah-*dehs*-soh ah deech-*oht*-
toh *ahn*-nee eh freh-*kwehn*-tah looh-nee-vehr-see-*tah*
My daughter Tania is 18 years old and goes to college.

E mio figlio Luca ne ha ventidue.
eh *mee*-oh *feel*-yoh *looh*-kah neh ah
vehn-tee-*dooh*-eh
And my son Luca is 22.

Teresa: **Come passano gli anni.**
koh-meh *pahs*-sahn-oh lyee *ahn*-nee
Time really flies.

Amy: **Eh si. Come stanno i tuoi genitori?**
eh see *koh*-meh *stahn*-noh ee twoi jehn-ee-*tohr*-ee
You bet. How are your parents?

Teresa: **Stanno bene grazie.**
stahn-noh *beh*-neh *grah*-tsee-eh
They're well, thanks.

Mio padre è in pensione finalmente.
mee-oh *pah*-dreh eh in pehn-see-*oh*-neh
fee-nahl-*mehn*-teh
My dad finally retired.

E tua sorella? Dove abita?
eh *tooh*-ah soh-*rehl*-lah *doh*-veh *ah*-bee-tah
And your sister? Where does she live?

Amy: **Mia sorella sta benone.**
mee-ah sohr-*ehl*-lah stah beh-*noh*-neh
My sister's doing great.

Fa l'oculista nello studio di mio padre.
fah lohk-ooh-*lees*-tah *nehl*-loh *stooh*-dee-oh dee
mee-oh *pah*-dreh
She's an oculist in my dad's practice.

Abita vicino a me.
ah-bee-tah vee-*chee*-noh ah meh
She lives near me.

Teresa: **Allora, quando possiamo vederci?**
ahl-*loh*-rah *qwahn*-doh pohs-*syah*-moh veh-*dehr*-chee
So, when can we see each other?

Amy: **Molto presto, spero.**
mohl-toh *prehs*-toh *speh*-roh
Very soon, I hope.

Speaking Reflexively

When you say "to enjoy yourself," you use a reflexive verb. That is, you turn the action back to yourself. The same applies in Italian. But not all Italian reflexive verbs are reflexive in English, and vice versa. Some verbs, such as **riposarsi** (ree-poh-*zahr*-see) (*to rest oneself*) and **svegliarsi** (sveh-*lyahr*-see) (*to wake oneself*), are not reflexive in English although they are in Italian.

In Italian, you can tell whether a verb is reflexive by looking at the infinitive form. If the last syllable of the infinitive is -si (*see*), which translates as "oneself," then the verb is reflexive. When you conjugate a reflexive verb, you must remove the last syllable -**si**, and shift that -**si** as a reflexive pronoun to the front of the verb (in most cases). Then, you simply conjugate the verb just like regular -**are**, -**ere**, or -**ire** verbs (from Chapter 2 and Appendix A).

The following conjugation of **vestirsi** (vehs-*teer*-see) (get dressed, to dress oneself) demonstrates that the conjugation of the verb follows the regular pattern. When you chop off the -**si** from the verb **divertirsi** (dee-vehr-*teer*-see) (*to enjoy oneself; to have a good time*), the verb looks like **divertire** and is, therefore, conjugated like **partire** (pahr-*tee*-reh) (*to leave or depart*). The only difference is that you add the reflexive pronoun, which refers to the person concerned (the subject). Repeat those pronouns a few times to yourself like a mantra until they sink in (**mi, ti si, ci vi si**).

Conjugation	Pronunciation	Translation
mi vesto	mee *vehs*-toh	*I'm getting dressed, I get dressed*
ti vesti	tee *vehs*-tee	*You're getting dressed, you get dressed*
si veste	see *vehs*-teh	*He/she is getting dressed, he/she gets dressed*
ci vestiamo	chee vehs-*tyah*-moh	*We're getting dressed, we get dressed*
vi vestite	vee vehs-*tee*-teh	*You're getting dressed, you get dressed*
si vestono	see *vehs*-toh-noh	*They're getting dressed, they get dressed*

Here are some more examples:

- **Mi diverto molto.** (mee dee-*vehr*-toh *mohl*-toh) (*I enjoy myself a lot.*)

- **Vi annoiate in campagna?** (vee ahn-noi-*yah*-teh een kahm-*pah*-nyah) (*Do you get bored in the country?*)

- **A che ora ti svegli?** (ah keh *oh*-rah tee *sveh*-lyee) (*What time do you wake up?*)

Table 17-2 shows a list of some common everyday reflexive verbs.

Table 17-2	Reflexive Verbs	
Verb	*Pronunciation*	*Meaning*
accomodarsi	ahk-koh-moh-*dahr*-see	to make oneself at home, to get comfortable
alzarsi	ahl-*tsahr*-see	to get up
arrabbiarsi	ahr-rahb-bee-*ahr*-see	to be (get) angry
innamorarsi	in-nahm-oh-*rahr*-see	to fall in love
farsi la barba	*fahr*-see lah *bahr*-bah	to shave (for a man)
fermarsi	fehr-*mahr*-see	to stop
laurearsi	lou-reh-*ahr*-see	to graduate from a university
lavarsi	lah-*vahr*-see	to wash (oneself)
mettersi	*meht*-tehr-see	to put on (clothes, contact lenses, glasses)
pettinarsi	peht-teen-*ahr*-see	to comb your hair
sedersi	seh-*dehr*-see	to sit down
svegliarsi	svehl-*yahr*-see	to wake up
trasferirsi	trahs-fehr-*eer*-see	to move form from one city to another
vestirsi	vehs-*teer*-see	to get dressed

Talking shop

Work is such a big part of so many people's lives it's something you might want to be able to talk about when you're in Italy and have just started a conversation with people you've just met.

> So the verb **lavorare** (lah-voh-*rah*-reh) (*to work*) will be useful as will other key terms:

> **Che lavoro fa/fai?** (keh lah-*voh*-roh fah/fahy) (*What work/job do you do?*) (formal/informal)

> **Che mestiere fa/fai?** (keh mehs-*tyeh*-reh fah/fahy) (*What work do you do?*) (formal/informal)

> You can generally answer this question in two ways: Note the verbs, and the use of the definite article in the first example.

> **Faccio il/la dentista.** (*fach*-choh il/lah dehn-*tees*-tah.) (*I'm a dentist.*) (m/f)

> **Sono dentista.** (*soh*-noh dehn-*tees*-tah) (*I'm a dentist.*)

Discussing your job

Italian has at least three words for "company" — **la compagnia** (lah kohm-pah-*nyee*-ah), **la ditta** (lah *deet*-tah) (which also means "the firm"), and **la società** (lah soh-cheh-*tah*). These words are virtually interchangeable.

L'ufficio (loohf-*fee*-choh) is Italian for "office." The following sentences give you a taste of the phrases you hear in **uffici** (oohf-*fee*-chee) (*offices*) everywhere:

- ✔ **È una grande società?** (eh *ooh*-nah *grahn*-deh soh-cheh-*tah*) (*Is it a big company?*)

- ✔ **Non proprio, diciamo media.** (nohn *proh*-pree-oh dee-*chah*-moh *meh*-dee-ah) (*Not really, let's say medium-sized.*)

- ✔ **Lavoro per una piccola agenzia.** (lah-*voh*-roh pehr *ooh*-nah *peek*-koh-lah ah-jehn-*tsee*-ah) (*I work for a small company.*)

- ✔ **Mi piace il mio lavoro.** (mee *pyah*-cheh eel *mee*-oh lah-*voh*-roh) (*I like my job.*)

Table 17-3 shows some of the professions and careers with which you might be familiar.

Table 17-3	Professions/Jobs	
Profession	*Pronunciation*	*Meaning*
agronomo	ah-*groh*-noh-moh	agronomist
archeologo	ahr-keh-*oh*-loh-goh	archeologist
architetto	ahr-kee-*teht*-toh	architect
avvocato	ahv-voh-*kah*-toh	lawyer
bracciante	brach-*chahn*-teh	farm worker
chirurgo	kee-*roohr*-goh	surgeon
commesso	kohm-*mehs*-soh	salesperson
dentista	denhn-*tees*-tah	dentist
falegname	fah-lehn-*yah*-meh	carpenter
giornalista	johr-nah-*lees*-tah	journalist
impiegato	ihm-pyeh-*gah*-toh	clerk (white-collar worker)
ingengnere	in-gehn-*yeh*-reh	engineer
insegnante	in-sehn-*yahn*-teh	teacher (grades 1-8)
meccanico	mehk-*kah*-nee-koh	mechanic
medico	*meh*-dee-koh	doctor
operaio	oh-pehr-*ahy*-oh	factory worker
pasticciere	pahs-teech-*cheh*-reh	baker
psicologo	psee-*koh*-loh-goh	psychologist
professore	proh-fehs-*soh*-reh	professor, teacher (grades 9-university)
segretaria	seh-greh-*tah*-ree-ah	secretary
stilista	stee-*lees*-tah	designer

You might need some of the following words as well when talking about jobs:

Che lavoro vuoi fare da grande? (keh lah-*voh*-roh vwoi *fah*-reh dah *grahn*-deh) (*What work would you like to do when you are older/grow up?*)

Cosa vuoi diventare? (*koh*-zah vwoi dee-vehn-*tah*-reh) (*What do you want to be?*)

fabbrica	*fahb*-bree-kah	*factory*
capo	*kah*-poh	*head, boss*
padrone	pah-*droh*-neh	*boss, owner*
direttore	dee-reht-*toh*-reh	*manager, director*
sciopero	*shoh*-peh-roh	*strike*
stipendio	stee-*pehn*-dee-oh	*salary*

The word **sciopero** (*shoh*-peh-roh) (*strike*) is very important in Italy, where workers go on strike all the time.

Talkin' the Talk

La professoressa Lucia, a high-school teacher, is asking her young second-year Italian students what they want to be when they grow up.

Lucia: **Ermanna, che lavoro vuoi fare da grande?**
ehr-*mahn*-nah keh lah-*voh*-roh vwoi *fah*-reh dah *grahn*-deh
Ermanna, what do you want to be when you grow up?

Ermanna: **Voglio fare la veterinaria.**
vohl-yoh *fah*-reh lah veh-teh-ree-*nahr*-ee-ah
I want to be a veterinarian.

Lucia: **Perché?**
pehr-*keh*
Why?

Ermanna:	**Perché amo gli animali.**
	pehr-*keh ah*-moh lyee ah-nee-*mah*-lee
	Because I love animals.

Lucia:	**Clara, tu cosa vuoi diventare?**
	klah-rah tooh *koh*-zah vwoi dee-vehn-*tah*-reh
	Clara, what do you want to be?

Clara:	**Voglio fare la scrittrice.**
	vohl-yoh *fah*-reh lah skreet-*tree*-cheh
	I want to be a writer.

Lucia:	**So che ti piace scrivere.**
	soh keh tee *pyah*-cheh *skree*-veh-reh
	I know that you like to write.

	Riccardo, e tu?
	reek-*kahr*-doh eh tooh
	And you, Richard?

Riccardo:	**Voglio fare il medico come il mio babbo.**
	vohl-yoh *fah*-reh il *meh*-dee-koh *koh*-meh eel
	mee-oh *bahb*-boh
	I want to be a doctor like my dad.

Lucia:	**Emilia, che lavoro ti interessa?**
	eh-*meel*-yah keh lah-*voh*-roh tee in-teh-*rehs*-sah
	Emilia, what kind of work are you interested in?

Emilia:	**Vorrei fare l'insegnante delle elementari.**
	vohr-*rey fah*-reh lin-sen-*yahn*-teh *dehl*-leh
	eh-leh-mehn-*tah*-ree
	I'd like to be an elementary school teacher.

Lucia:	**Bravi, ragazzi!**
	brah-vee rah-*gats*-tsee
	Good job, children!

There is an exception to the rule about singular family relatives. Whereas most do not take the definite article (**mia madre, e mio padre**) (*mee*-ah *mah*-dreh eh *mee*-oh *pah*-dreh), some shorter terms of endearment do, such as **la mia mamma** (lah *mee*-ah *mahm*-mah) (*my mom*) and **il mio babbo/il mio papà** (eel *mee*-oh *bahb*-boh/eel *mee*-oh pah-*pah*) (*my dad*).

Words to Know

lavoro	lah-_voh_-roh	work, job
insegnante	in-sehn-_yahn_-teh	teacher
babbo	_bahb_-boh	dad, daddy
medico	_meh_-dee-koh	doctor
direttore	dee-reht-_toh_-reh	director, manager
fabbrica	_fahb_-bree-kah	factory
sciopero	_shoh_-peh-roh	strike
stipendio	stee-_pehn_-dee-oh	salary
ti interessa/ mi interessa	tee in-teh-_rehs_-sah/ mee in-teh-_rehs_-sah	you're interested in/ I'm interested in
tasse	_tahs_-seh	taxes, tuition

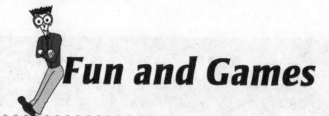

Fun and Games

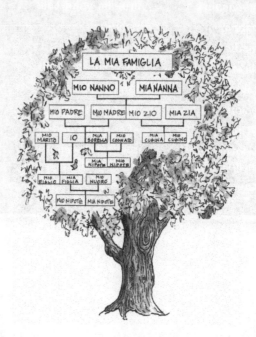

Here are ten fill-in-the-blank questions. Pick words and terms from the family tree to complete each statement. You may need the plural for some of the possessive adjectives and relatives. See Appendix D for the answer key.

1. I miei genitori sono _____ e _____.

2. Il figlio di mia madre è _____.

3. I figli di mio fratello sono _____.

4. La madre della mia mamma è _____.

5. La sorella di mia madre è_____.

6. Il marito di mia sorella è _____.

7. La moglie di mio figlio è _____.

8. La sorella di mio figlio è _____.

9. I figli di mia zia sono _____.

10. La mamma di mio marito è _____.

Part IV
The Part of Tens

"My wife and I are taking the course together. I figure I only have to learn half as much, since she finishes all of my sentences anyway."

In this part . . .

These chapters help you add polish to the basics the rest of the book provides. I give you ten ways to pick up Italian very quickly, from reading Italian food labels to singing along with your favorite Italian song. You also learn ten things to never say in Italian, and ten phrases to use so people will think you're Italian. These chapters might be short, but they're invaluable!

Chapter 18

Ten Ways to Pick Up Italian Quickly

In This Chapter

▶ Enjoying Italian food

▶ Listening to Italian

▶ Going to Italian films

▶ Sharing Italian with other people

▶ Surfing the Web

Of course, you've already chosen one of the quickest ways to learn Italian — you picked up this book! For smaller bites of Italian, nibble on one or all of the suggestions in this chapter. Above all, practice, practice, practice!

Read Italian Food Labels

These days, finding Italian food is easy in most countries. If you buy Italian food, read the original label a couple of times before you throw the package away. Usually, you can find an English translation alongside the Italian. In a few weeks, you won't need to read the English part anymore!

Ask for Food in Italian

If you go to an Italian restaurant or pizzeria, don't be shy! Order your favorite dishes by using their original names and Italian pronunciations. (Don't forget that **bruschetta** is pronounced broohs-*keht*-tah, with the **k** sound, just like **porchetta** (pohr-*keht*-tah)!)

Listen to Italian Songs

You can easily pick up Italian words and pronunciation by listening to Italian music and singing along with **la canzone** (lah kahn-*tsoh*-neh) (*the song*). You have access to scores of Italian singers through the Internet (especially YouTube). You can easily find the lyrics either by Googling them separately, or by modifying your YouTube search by adding the word "karaoke." Put as many songs as you can on your iPod, and listen (and sing) whenever you can!

Read Italian Publications

Trying to read a newspaper in a foreign language can be very frustrating! Don't worry: Experts say that journalistic language is the most difficult to understand. The culture, gossip, crime, and weather articles are undoubtedly the easiest to understand, and many online newspapers also offer small video clips. You can find several Italian newspapers on-line. By the way, Italians call the newspaper **il giornale** (eel johr-*nah*-leh).

Watch Italian Movies

We hope you like movies! Watching a movie in the original language is a pleasant way to pick up words, expressions, and names, and you can even discover something about the country where the story takes place. You can find several Italian movies with English subtitles, from classic **neorealismo** (neh-oh-reh-ah-*leez*-moh) (*neorealism*) to the most recent releases. You can even find old familiar cartoons online, dubbed into Italian. You won't need subtitles for these!

Tune In to Italian Radio and TV Programs

Many countries deliver radio programs (especially the news) in Italian. Find some Italian programs and listen as often as you can. You can at least understand the basics of what the newscaster says because the speakers usually articulate very clearly and slowly, and some of the news is the same as you'd hear in your own national programs, but perhaps with a different perspective. Again, you can pick up words without much effort.

With good Internet access, you can also listen to stations directly from Italy. For several programs on the radio and television, start with these sites:

```
http://www.international.rai.it/

http://italiansinfonia.com/stations.htm
```

Listen to Italian Language Tapes

You can listen to Italian language tapes — or the audio CD that comes with this book — almost any time: when you jog, clean your apartment or house, cook, or whenever you like. And please, don't forget to repeat aloud what you hear.

Share Your Interest

I consider this a valid tip when learning any language: Learning a language with other people is much more pleasant (and easier!) than doing it by yourself. Having company while you broaden your knowledge of Italian is helpful not only because language is primarily a means of communicating with others, but also because fun is a vital element in every learning process. Write an ad and put it in the local library or bookshop to start an Italian conversation or book group — you never know what doors this will open for you!

Surf the Net

Nothing is easier than looking for information on the Internet. To find information about Italy, type **Italia** (ee-*tah*-lee-ah) (*Italy*) or the name of a famous city or monument in Italian, such as **Venezia** (veh-*neh*-tsee-ah) (*Venice*) or **Colosseo** (koh-lohs-*seh*-oh) (*the Colesseum*), to mention just two. Each city and region has its own official website full of all sorts of useful information. The best place to start is www.Google.it, the Italian Google.

Cook!

One of my favorite sites is Italianfoodnet.com. Not only will you find great recipes, but also cooking videos in Italian that you can watch again and again as you cook alongside the chefs. After a while, you'll be confident enough to turn off the subtitles.

Chapter 19

Ten Things Never to Say in Italian

In This Chapter

▶ Using "Ciao" properly

▶ Realizing that literal translations don't always work

▶ Encountering "false friends"

▶ Playing with "to play"

▶ Having hunger

We hope the title to this chapter isn't too dramatic! Remember that you should always approach the learning process as fun. If you don't speak Italian perfectly, you may say something wrong — which might be funny or even embarrassing. Don't worry; messing up is not a tragedy! On the contrary, most people are pleased when non-heritage speakers make any attempt to learn their language, and they allow for mistakes in both speech and behavior. Nevertheless, we want to give you a little advice to help you avoid such situations.

Ciao-ing Down

REMEMBER

Ciao (chou) is a common way to say "hello" and "goodbye" that even people who don't speak Italian know. However, please remember that Italians use it only with persons they address with the informal **tu** (tooh) (*you*) — see Chapter 2 for a discussion of the use of **tu**. Many non-speakers of Italian use the formal **lei** (ley) and still say **ciao**; again, this misstep is not a tragedy, but when you're addressing someone in the formal manner, it's more Italian to say **buongiorno** (bwohn-*johr*-noh) (*good morning*) or **arrivederci** (ahr-ree-veh-*dehr*-chee) (*good-bye*).

Don't Be Literal

A literal translation from English to Italian doesn't work in many cases. Here's a typical example: You may want to ask your Italian friend, "How do you like Los Angeles?" Because you've probably learned a lot, you might translate your question into **"Come ti piace Los Angeles?"** (*koh*-meh tee *pyah*-cheh Los Angeles) knowing that **come** is the translation of "how" and **ti piace** means "do you like." Both are absolutely correct translations, but the whole question doesn't sound Italian. I would ask **"Ti piace Los Angeles?"** (tee *pyah*-cheh Los Angeles) (*Do you like Los Angeles?*).

Five Fickle "False Friends"

We consider some words "false friends." These words sound and look quite similar in two different languages but, unfortunately, don't have the same meaning. One example is the word sympathy. In Italian, **simpatia** (seem-pah-*tee*-ah) is the feeling you have for someone you find nice, funny, and pleasant; it doesn't mean that you feel what the other person feels. **Simpatia's** translation can be "liking." So to say that you find somebody **simpatico** (seem-*pah*-tee-koh) means that you like him or her — the person is nice. Interestingly, English kept the original Greek meaning of the word sympathy, which is "to suffer together."

Another false friend is the word **educazione** (eh-dooh-kah-*tsyoh*-neh). In Italian, it does not mean the level of your schooling, but the way you have grown up — your upbringing. **Educato** (eh-dooh-*kah*-toh) [**educata** (eh-dooh-*kah*-tah) for a female] translates as "well-brought-up" or "polite." A good Italian word for "education" is **istruzione** (ees-trooh-*tsyoh*-neh).

The surprises aren't over. Guess what the Italian word **sensibile** (sehn-*see*-bee-leh) means? The subject of this section tells you already that it doesn't mean "sensible." Instead, it means "sensitive." You can translate the English "sensible" with the adjective **ragionevole** (rah-joh-*neh*-voh-leh).

The adjective **vecchio** (m) (*vehk*-yoh) / **vecchia** (f) (*vehk*-yah) translates as "old," but avoid using it to refer to people. You can use **vecchio** for objects (a car, a book, or whatever), but when referring to a person, say **anziano** (m) (ahn-tsee-*ah*-noh) or **anziana** (f) (ahn-tsee-*ah*-nah). **Anziano** means that the person is not young anymore — but it doesn't sound negative.

Most hotels and inns offer at least breakfast, so you might want to ask for more **marmellata** (mahr-mehl-*lah*-tah) if they have run out. Do not ask for **preservativi** (preh-zehr-vah-*tee*-vee) (*condoms*) or you will be greeted with an incredulous stare.

Food Faux Pas

So if you're trying to blend in and sound like an Italian, don't order a **cappuccino** after, let's say, 11:00 a.m. **Cappuccino** is a breakfast drink.

Do not ask for **parmigiano** cheese for the **pasta** with fish/clams/shrimp that has just been brought to the table. Mixing fish with cheese is tantamount to eating pickles with milk!

And don't be surprised if you don't find spaghetti and meatballs on the menu. More than likely, you won't (and so shouldn't ask for it).

The Problem with "Play"

We'd like to dedicate the last two points of this chapter to the translations of the verb "to play." In English, this verb has different meanings, all of them describing nice activities. The most usual meaning (and the first given in all dictionaries) corresponds to the Italian **giocare** (joh-*kah*-reh): "to have fun" or "to do things to pass the time pleasantly, as children do." But don't use this verb when talking about instruments. Instead, use **suonare** (swoh-*nah*-reh); therefore, the correct sentence is **suono il piano** (*swoh*-noh eel pee-*ah*-noh) (*I play piano*).

Being Careful of "False Friends"

The pitfalls surrounding "false friends" — words that look or sound like words you know but have different meanings — can transfer to idiomatic expressions that can be very funny for a foreigner. Just think of the English expression "It's raining cats and dogs," which is the best example of a funny expression for non-native English speakers. You now must know that you wouldn't say **Sta piovendo gatti e cani** (stah pyoh-*vehn*-doh *gaht*-tee eh *kah*-nee). To express the same sentiment, you say instead **Piove a catinelle** (*pyoh*-veh ah kah-tee-*nehl*-leh) (*It's raining buckets.*).

The same is true for the expression "I'm hungry." In Italian, you "have" hunger; therefore you say **Ho fame** (oh *fah*-meh). You could also say **Sono affamato** (*soh*-noh ahf-fah-*mah*-toh), but this sounds more like "I'm starving," which is much stronger.

Chapter 20

Ten Favorite Italian Expressions

In This Chapter

▶ Expressions you hear all the time

▶ Phrases you can say to sound Italian

Counting how many times a day Italians use some of the following expressions would be an interesting experiment! They are all very typical, and you hear them often in colloquial Italian. So if you remember some of them and use them on the right occasion, you will seem very Italian. Of course, there are, as in any language, always expressions that sound strange coming from the mouth of a foreigner, but the following can be used without hesitation. Exceptions may be **mamma mia** and **uffa**, because they are very spontaneous. But using any or all of the others can make you really sound Italian.

Mamma mia!

Mamma mia! (*mahm*-mah *mee*-ah) Please don't think that all Italians are like children just because you notice how often they call for their mommies! In fact, the literal translation is something like "Oh Mama!" and Italians use the exclamation to express surprise, impatience, happiness, sorrow, and so on — in general, a strong emotion. The figurative translation is something like "My goodness!"

Che bello!

Che bello! (keh *behl*-loh) (*How lovely! How nice! — literally, how beautiful!*) Using this phrase shows that you're enthusiastic about something.

Uffa!

Uffa! (*oohf*-fah) is a very clear way to show that you're annoyed, bored, angry, or simply fed up with a situation. In English, you'd probably express the same by exhaling in exasperation.

Che ne so!/Boh!

When Italians want to say that they have no idea about something, they shrug their shoulders and say **Che ne so!** (keh neh soh) (*How should I know?*) and or **boh!** (boh). We don't need to tell you that both are quite common expressions.

Magari!

Magari! (mah-*gah*-ree) Just one word, but it expresses so much! It indicates a strong wish or hope. It's a good answer, for instance, if somebody asks you if you'd like to win the lottery. A good translation of this word is "If only!" or "I'd love it!"

Ti sta bene!

Ti sta bene! (tee stah *beh*-neh) This is the Italian way to say "Serves you right!" But this can also mean: "It looks good on you!," depending on the context.

Non te la prendere!

If you see that somebody is sad, worried, or upset, you can try to console him or her by saying **Non te la prendere!** (nohn teh lah *prehn*-deh-reh) (*Don't get so upset!*). Sometimes it works.

Che macello!

Figuring out the derivation of this phrase is not difficult. The literal translation of **Che macello!** (keh mah-*chehl*-loh) is "What a slaughterhouse!" Italians usually say this in situations in which an English speaker would say "What a mess!"

Non mi va!

Non mi va! (nohn mee vah) is one of the first phrases Italian children learn. It means that you don't want to do something. The best translation is "I don't feel like it!"

Mi raccomando!

With **Mi raccomando!** (mee rahk-koh-*mahn*-doh), you express a special emphasis in asking for something — like saying "Please, I beg you!" An example is **Telefonami, mi raccomando!** (teh-*leh*-foh-nah-mee mee rahk-koh-*mahn*-doh) ("Don't forget to call me, please!").

Chapter 21

Ten Phrases to Say So That People Think You're Italian

. . . .

In This Chapter

▶ Wishing someone good luck

▶ Shutting your mouth

▶ Being blessed

▶ Contradicting someone emphatically

▶ Telling someone to dream on!

▶ Being unsympathetic

▶ Saying "Stop it!"

▶ Slowing down

▶ Emphasizing a yes

▶ Letting go

. . . .

In Chapter 20, we give you ten typical expressions Italians love and use a lot. Using them can help you sound very Italian. In this chapter, we offer more sophisticated expressions to make you sound even more Italian — these are truly idiomatic expressions. Using these expressions may make an Italian gape in astonishment. Have fun!

In bocca al lupo!

Perhaps you have an Italian friend facing a difficult situation and you want to wish her good luck. The literal translation of **buona fortuna!** (*bwoh*-nah fohr-*tooh*-nah) would work, but we think that this phrase makes you sound really Italian: **in bocca al lupo!** (een *bohk*-kah ahl *looh*-poh). Literally, this means "in the wolf's mouth!" The upcoming difficulty looks like a big wolf, waiting with mouth open wide. Your friend will probably answer **Crepi il lupo!** (*kreh*-pee eel *looh*-poh), which means "May the wolf die!"

Acqua in bocca!

When you want to share a secret with somebody — but want to make sure that he or she won't tell anybody else — say **acqua in bocca!** (*ah*-kwah een *bohk*-kah). This expression means "water in mouth." If your mouth is full of water, you can't speak. Similar idioms in English are "Don't say a word about it!" and "Mum's the word!"

Salute!

Someone sneezes and you say **salute!** (sah-*looh*-teh), which means "health." In fact, it's a way to wish the person to be healthy very soon. "Bless you!" is the English equivalent. You can also use this when making a toast.

Macché!

Italians love to talk, no doubt about it. Nevertheless, situations exist in which they prefer to say just one word. One good example is **macché!** (mahk-*keh*). It's a strong and determined way to say "Of course not" or "Certainly not!"

Neanche per sogno!

Similar to the preceding idiom, **neanche per sogno** (neh-*ahn*-keh pehr *soh*-nyoh) means literally "not even in a dream." It is another way to say "No way!" and is close to the English expression "In your dreams."

Peggio per te!

You don't show much sympathy when saying this phrase, but if you're looking for the Italian equivalent of "Too bad for you!" or "Tough luck!" **peggio per te** (*pehj*-joh pehr teh) is what you need.

Piantala!

This is an informal way to say "Stop it!"or "Cut it out!" The literal translation of **piantala** (*pyahn*-tah-lah) is "Plant it!"

Vacci piano!

"Slow down!" is the translation of the Italian expression **Vacci piano!** (*vahch-chee pyah*-noh). Use it when you feel that somebody is going too fast or being too enthusiastic about something.

Eccome!

This emphatic word sums up the following phrases: "And how!" "You'd better believe it!" "Very!" "And then some." Let's say you ask a friend if someone you might be interested in is married: Your friend responds: "**Eccome!**" (ehk-*koh*-meh).

Lascia perdere!

Let's say something is really bugging your new Italian friend. A quick "**Lascia perdere!**" (*lah*-shah *pehr*-deh-reh) (*Let it go! Forget about it!*) will help put things into a new light. Didn't get the woman you courted? Your son totaled your car but is safe and sound? **Lascia perdere!**

Part V
Appendixes

The 5th Wave   By Rich Tennant

"Here's something. It's a language school that will teach you to speak Italian for $500, or for $200 they'll just give you an accent."

In this part . . .

Here is where the real nuts and bolts are found. Included are verb conjugation tables and an extensive mini-dictionary with both English-to-Italian and Italian-to-English translations. This part also contains the instructions on how to use the CD as well as a list of all the tracks on the CD. Last but not least, you'll find the answer key to all the Fun & Games exercises at the end of the chapters.

Appendix A

Verb Tables

∙∙∙

Italian Verbs

Regular Verbs Ending with *-are*
For example: parlare (to speak);
Past participle: parlato (spoken) (w/avere)

	Present	Past	Future
io (I)	parlo	ho parlato	parlerò
tu (you, inf.)	parli	hai parlato	parlerai
lui/lei (he/she/ you form.)	parla	ha parlato	parlerà
noi (we)	parliamo	abbiamo parlato	parleremo
voi (you)	parlate	avete parlato	parlerete
loro (they/you form. pl.)	parlano	hanno parlato	parleranno

Other common –ARE verbs: **mangiare** (to eat), **studiare** (to study), **imparare** (to learn), **insegnare** (to teach), **suonare** (to play instrument), **giocare** (to play game/sport), **disegnare** (to draw), **cucinare** (to cook), **lavorare** (to work)

Regular Verbs Ending with -ere
For example: vendere (to sell);
Past participle: venduto (sold) (w/avere)

	Present	Past	Future
io (I)	vendo	ho venduto	venderò
tu (you, inf.)	vendi	hai venduto	venderai
lui/lei (he/she/ you form.)	vende	ha venduto	venderà
noi (we)	vendiamo	abbiamo venduto	venderemo
voi (you)	vendete	avete venduto	venderete
loro (they/you form. pl.)	vendono	hanno venduto	venderanno

Other common –ERE verbs: **leggere** (to read), **scrivere** (to write), **mettere** (to put), **prendere** (to take), **vivere** (to live), **vedere** (to see), **chiudere** (to close), **ripetere** (to repeat). Unlike the example, most of these past participles are irregular: **letto, scritto, messo, preso, vissuto, visto/veduto, chiuso.** Only **ripetuto** is regular.

Regular Verbs Ending with -ire *
For example: partire (to leave);
Past participle: partito (left) (w/essere)

	Present	Past	Future
io (I)	parto	sono partito/a	partirò
tu (you, inf.)	parti	sei partito/a	partirai
lui/lei (he/she/ you form.)	parte	è partito/a	partirà
noi (we)	partiamo	siamo partiti/e	partiremo
voi (you)	partite	siete partiti/e	partirete
loro (they/you form. pl.)	partono	sono partiti/e	partiranno

Other common **–IRE** verbs: **aprire** (to open), **dormire** (to sleep), **coprire** (to cover), **sentire** (to hear, feel, taste, touch). Note that **aprire** and **coprire** have irregular past participles (**aperto** and **coperto**)

Note that **–IRE (isc)** verbs come later in this Appendix.

Verb *avere* (to have)
Past Participle: avuto (had) (w/ avere)

	Present	**Past**	**Future**
io (I)	ho	ho avuto	avrò
tu (you, inf.)	hai	hai avuto	avrai
lui/lei (he/she/ you form.)	ha	ha avuto	avrà
noi (we)	abbiamo	abbiamo avuto	avremo
voi (you)	avete	avete avuto	avrete
loro (they/you form. pl.)	hanno	hanno avuto	avranno

Verb *essere* (to be)
Past Participle: stato (been) (w/essere)

	Present	**Past**	**Future**
io (I)	sono	sono stato/a	sarò
tu (you, inf.)	sei	sei stato/a	sarai
lui/lei (he/she/ you form.)	è	è stato/a	sarà
noi (we)	siamo	siamo stati/e	saremo
voi (you)	siete	siete stati/e	sarete
loro (they/you form. pl.)	sono	sono stati/e	saranno

Reflexive Verbs

For example: lavarsi (to wash oneself)

Past Participle: lavato (washed) (essere *ALL reflexive verbs take essere in the past)

	Present	Past	Future
io (I)	mi lavo	mi sono lavato/a	mi laverò
tu (you, inf.)	ti lavi	ti sei lavato/a	ti laverai
lui/lei (he/she/ you form.)	si lava	si è lavato/a	si laverà
noi (we)	ci laviamo	ci siamo lavati/e	ci laveremo
voi (you)	vi lavate	vi siete lavati/e	vi laverete
loro (they/you form. pl.)	si lavano	si sono lavati/e	si laveranno

Other common reflexive verbs include: **alzarsi** (to get up), **divertirsi** (to have fun), **sentirsi** (to feel), **innamorarsi** (to fall in love), **mettersi** (to put [something] on), **addormentarsi** (to fall asleep), **permettersi** (to afford)

Irregular Italian Verbs

		Present	Future	Past Participle
andare	io	vado	andrò	
	tu	vai	andrai	
to go	lui/lei	va	andrà	andato/a/i/e
	noi	andiamo	andremo	(w/essere)
	voi	andate	andrete	
	loro	vanno	andranno	

		Present	Future	Past Participle
	Io	bevo	berrò	
bere	*tu*	bevi	berrai	
to drink	*lui/lei*	beve	berrà	bevuto (w/avere)
	noi	beviamo	berremo	
	voi	bevete	berrete	
	loro	bevono	berranno	

		Present	Future	Past Participle
	io	do	darò	
dare	*tu*	dai	darai	
to give	*lui/lei*	dà	darà	dato (w/avere)
	noi	diamo	daremo	
	voi	date	darete	
	loro	danno	daranno	

		Present	Future	Past Participle
	io	dico	dirò	
dire	*tu*	dici	dirai	
to say;	*lui/lei*	dice	dirà	detto (w/avere)
to tell	*noi*	diciamo	diremo	
	voi	dite	direte	
	loro	dicono	diranno	

		Present	Future	Past Participle
dovere to have to; ought to; must	io	devo	dovrò	
	tu	devi	dovrai	
	lui/lei	deve	dovrà	dovuto
	noi	dobbiamo	dovremo	(w/avere, usually)
	voi	dovete	dovrete	
	loro	devono	dovranno	

		Present	Future	Past Participle
fare to do; to make	io	faccio	farò	
	tu	fai	farai	
	lui/lei	fa	farà	fatto
	noi	facciamo	faremo	(w/avere)
	voi	fate	farete	
	loro	fanno	faranno	

		Present	Future	Past Participle
morire to die	io	muoio	morirò	
	tu	muori	morirai	
	lui/lei	muore	morirà	morto/a/i/e
	noi	moriamo	moriremo	(w/essere)
	voi	morite	morirete	
	loro	muoiono	moriranno	

		Present	Future	Past Participle
piacere to like	mi/ti/le/ci/ gli/loro	piace	piacerà	piaciuto/a/i/e (w/essere)
	loro	piacciono	piaceranno	

The verb **piacere** takes indirect object pronouns and you usually only need the third person singular and plural of this verb.

		Present	Future	Past Participle
porre	io	pongo	porrò	
to put	tu	poni	porrai	
	lui/lei	pone	porrà	posto
	noi	poniamo	porremo	(w/avere)
	voi	ponete	porrete	
	loro	pongono	porranno	

Other verbs conjugated like **porre** include: **opporsi** (to oppose) e **imporre** (to impose), and **proporre** (to propose or suggest)

		Present	Future	Past Participle
potere	io	posso	potrò	
can;	tu	puoi	potrai	
to able to	lui/lei	può	potrà	potuto
	noi	possiamo	potremo	(w/avere)
	voi	potete	potrete	
	loro	possono	potranno	

		Present	Future	Past Participle
rimanere	io	rimango	rimarrò	
to stay;	tu	rimani	rimarrai	
to remain	lui/lei	rimane	rimarrà	rimasto/a/i/e
	noi	rimaniamo	rimarremo	(w/essere)
	voi	rimanete	rimarrete	
	loro	rimangono	rimarranno	

	Present	Future	Past Participle
io	salgo	salirò	
tu	sali	salirai	
salire lui/lei	sale	salirà	salito/a/i/e
to go up noi	saliamo	saliremo	(w/essere)
voi	salite	salirete	
loro	salgono	saliranno	

	Present	Future	Past Participle
io	so	saprò	
tu	sai	saprai	
sapere lui/lei	sa	saprà	saputo
to know noi	sappiamo	sapremo	(w/avere)
voi	sapete	saprete	
loro	sanno	sapranno	

	Present	Future	Past Participle
io	scelgo	sceglierò	
tu	scegli	sceglierai	
scegliere lui/lei	sceglie	sceglierà	scelto
to choose noi	scegliamo	sceglieremo	(w/avere)
voi	scegliete	sceglierete	
loro	scelgono	sceglieranno	

		Present	Future	Past Participle
sedersi	*io*	mi siedo		
to sit	*tu*	ti siedi		
	lui/lei	si siede		seduto
	noi	ci sediamo		(w/essere)
	voi	vi sedete		
	loro	si siedono		

		Present	Future	Past Participle
	io	sto	starò	
stare	*tu*	stai	starai	
to stay;	*lui/lei*	sta	starà	stato/a/i/e
to be	*noi*	stiamo	staremo	(w/essere)
	voi	state	starete	
	loro	stanno	staranno	

		Present	Future	Past Participle
	io	taccio	tacerò	
tacere	*tu*	taci	tacerai	
to be silent	*lui/lei*	tace	tacerà	taciuto
	noi	taciamo	taceremo	(w/avere)
	voi	tacete	tacerete	
	loro	tacciono	taceranno	

		Present	**Future**	**Past Participle**
tenere	io	tengo	terrò	
to hold	tu	tieni	terrai	
	lui/lei	tiene	terrà	tenuto
	noi	teniamo	terremo	(w/avere)
	voi	tenete	terrete	
	loro	tengono	terranno	

		Present	**Future**	**Past Participle**
togliere	io	tolgo	toglierò	
to take away	tu	togli	toglierai	
	lui/lei	toglie	toglierà	tolto
	noi	togliamo	toglieremo	(w/avere)
	voi	togliete	toglierete	
	loro	tolgono	toglieranno	

		Present	**Future**	**Past Participle**
uscire	io	esco	uscirò	
to go out	tu	esci	uscirai	
	lui/lei	esce	uscirà	uscito/a/i/e
	noi	usciamo	usciremo	(w/essere)
	voi	uscite	uscirete	
	loro	escono	usciranno	

		Present	Future	Past Participle
	io	vengo	verrò	
venire	*tu*	vieni	verrai	
to come	*lui/lei*	viene	verrà	venuto/a/i/e
	noi	veniamo	verremo	(w/essere)
	voi	venite	verrete	
	loro	vengono	verranno	

		Present	Future	Past Participle
	io	voglio	vorrò	
volere	*tu*	vuoi	vorrai	
to want	*lui/lei*	vuole	vorrà	voluto
	noi	vogliamo	vorremo	(w/avere)
	voi	volete	vorrete	
	loro	vogliono	vorranno	

Italian –IRE Verbs with a Special Pattern (-isc-)

		Present	Future	Past Participle
	io	capisco	capirò	
capire	*tu*	capisci	capirai	
to understand	*lui/lei*	capisce	capirà	capito
	noi	capiamo	capiremo	(w/avere)
	voi	capite	capirete	
	loro	capiscono	capiranno	

		Present	**Future**	**Past Participle**
finire	*io*	finisco	finirò	
to finish	*tu*	finisci	finirai	
	lui/lei	finisce	finirà	finito
	noi	finiamo	finiremo	(w/avere)
	voi	finite	finirete	
	loro	finiscono	finiranno	

		Present	**Future**	**Past Participle**
preferire	*io*	preferisco	preferirò	
to prefer	*tu*	preferisci	preferirai	
	lui/lei	preferisce	preferirà	preferito
	noi	preferiamo	preferiremo	(w/avere)
	voi	preferite	preferirete	
	loro	preferiscono	preferiranno	

Other common –ISC verbs include: **pulire** (to clean), **interferire** (to interfere), and **costruire** (to build)

Common Irregular Past Participles

	Past Participle	Definition
cuocere (to cook)	cotto	*cooked*
decidere (to decide)	deciso	*decided*
leggere (to read)	letto	*read*
mettere (to put)	messo	*put*
morire (to die)	morto	*died*
nascere (to be born)	nato	*born*
perdere (to lose)	perso, perduto	*lost*
prendere (to take, to have)	preso	*took, had, taken*
rispondere (to reply/respond)	risposto	*replied/responded/answered*
scogliere (to melt)	sciolto	*melted*
scrivere (to write)	scritto	*wrote, written*
vedere (to see)	visto, veduto	*saw, seen*
vivere (to live)	vissuto	*lived*

For more on Italian verbs and also practice exercises, see *Italian Verbs For Dummies* (John Wiley & Sons, Inc.).

Italian-English Mini Dictionary

A

a destra/ah *dehs*-trah/(on the) right

a domani/ah doh-*mah*-nee/see you tomorrow

a dopo/ah *doh*-poh/see you later

a sinistra/ah see-*nees*-trah/(on the) left

abitare/ah-bee-*tah*-reh/to live

abito/m/*ah*-bee-toh/suit

acqua/f/*ah*-kwah/water

aereo/m/ah-*eh*-reh-oh/airplane

aeroporto/m/ah-eh-roh-*pohr*-toh/airport

affittare (v.)/ahf-feet-*tah*-reh/to rent

agosto/ah-*gohs*-toh/August

albergo/m/ahl-*behr*-goh/hotel

amare (v.)/ah-*mah*-reh/to love

americana/f/**americano**/m (v.)/ ah-meh-ree-*kah*-nah/ah-meh-ree-*kah*-noh/American

amica/f/**amico**/m/ ah-*mee*-kah/ah-*mee*-koh/friend

amore/m/ah-*moh*-reh/love

anche/*ahn*-keh/also

andare (v.)/ahn-*dah*-reh/to go

andata/f/ahn-*dah*-tah/one-way (ticket)

andata/f/**e ritorno**/m/ahn-*dah*-tah eh ree-*tohr*-noh/round trip

anno/m/*ahn*-noh/year

antipasti/m/ahn-tee-*pahs*-tee/appetizers

anziana/f/**anziano**/m/ahn-tsee-*ah*-nah/ ahn-tsee-*ah*-noh/old (for persons)

appartamento/m/ahp-pahr-tah-*mehn*-toh/apartment

aprile/ah-*pree*-leh/April

architetto/m/ahr-kee-*teht*-toh/architect

arrivare/ahr-ree-*vah*-reh/to arrive

arrivederci/ahr-ree-veh-*dehr*-chee/ see you; good-bye

assegno/m/ahs-*seh*-nyoh/check

autobus/m/*ou*-toh-boohs/bus

automobile/f/*ou*-toh-*moh*-bee-leh/car

avere (v.)/ah-*veh*-reh/to have

avvocato/m/ahv-voh-*kah*-toh/lawyer

B

bambina/f/**bambino**/m/bahm-*bee*-nah/ bahm-*bee*-noh/child

banca/f/*bahn*-kah/bank

bella/f/**bello**/m/*behl*-lah/*behl*-loh/ beautiful

bene/*beh*-neh/well, good (adverb)

bere (v.)/*beh*-reh/to drink

bianca/f/**bianco**/m/*byahn*-kah/*byahn*-koh/white

bicchiere/m/beek-*kyeh*-reh/glass

bicicletta/f/bee-chee-*kleht*-tah/bicycle

biglietto/m/bee-*lyeht*-toh/ticket

birra/f/*beer*-rah/beer

blu/f/m/blooh/blue

borsa/f/*bohr*-sah/bag, hand-bag

bottiglia/f/boht-*tee*-lyah/bottle

braccio/m/*brahch*-choh/arm

buona/f/**buono**/m/*bwoh*-nah/
bwoh-noh/good

buonanotte/*bwoh*-nah-*noht*-teh/
good-night

buonasera/*bwoh*-nah-*seh*-rah/
good evening

buongiorno/bwohn-*johr*-noh/
good morning; good day

C

c'è/cheh/there is

caffè/m/kahf-*feh*/coffee

calcio/m/*kahl*-choh/soccer

calda/f/**caldo**/m/*kahl*-dah/*kahl*-doh/
warm; hot

cambiare/kahm-bee-*ah*-reh/to change

cameriera/f/**cameriere**/m/kah-meh-*ryeh*-
rah/kah-meh-*ryeh*-reh/waitress/waiter

camicia/f/kah-*mee*-chah/shirt

campagna/f/kahm-*pah*-nyah/country
(countryside)

canadese/f/m/kah-nah-*deh*-zeh/Canadian

cane/m/*kah*-neh/dog

capelli/m.pl./kah-*pehl*-lee/hair

cappello/m/kahp-*pehl*-loh/hat

cappotto/m/kahp-*poht*-toh/coat

cara/f/**caro**/m/*kah*-rah/*kah*-roh/
dear; expensive

carina/f/**carino**/m/kah-*ree*-nah/
kah-*ree*-noh/nice

carta di credito/f/*kahr*-tah dee
kreh-dee-toh/credit card

casa/f/*kah*-zah/house; home

cassa/f/*kahs*-sah/cash register

cavallo/m/kah-*vahl*-loh/horse

cena/f/*cheh*-nah/dinner

cento/*chehn*-toh/hundred

chi/kee/who

chiara/f/**chiaro**/m/*kyah*-rah/*kyah*-roh/
light-colored (clear)

ci sono/chee *soh*-noh/there are

ciao/chou/hello; good-bye

cinema/m/*chee*-neh-mah/cinema

cinquanta/cheen-*kwahn*-tah/fifty

cinque/*cheen*-kweh/five

cioccolata/f/choh-koh-*lah*-tah/chocolate

città/f/cheet-*tah*/city, town

codice postale/m/*koh*-dee-cheh
pohs-*tah*-leh/zip code

colazione/f/koh-lah-*tsyoh*-neh/breakfast

collo/m/*kohl*-loh/neck

colore/m/koh-*loh*-reh/color

come/*koh*-meh/how

commessa/f/**commesso**/m/kohm-*mehs*-
sah/kohm-*mehs*-soh/sales clerk

comprare (v.)/kohm-*prah*-reh/to buy

costume da bagno/m/kohs-*tooh*-meh dah
bah-nyoh/bathing suit

cravatta/f/krah-*vaht*-tah/tie

crema/f/*kreh*-mah/custard

D

d'accordo/dahk-*kohr*-doh/all right; okay

dai!/dahy/come on!

dare (v.)/*dah*-reh/to give

dentista/f/m/dehn-*tees*-tah/dentist

dicembre/dee-*chehm*-breh/December

diciannove/dee-chahn-*noh*-veh/nineteen

diciassette/dee-chahs-*seht*-teh/seventeen

diciotto/dee-*choht*-toh/eighteen

dieci/*dyeh*-chee/ten

dire (v.)/*dee*-reh/to say

dito/m/*dee*-toh/finger

dodici/*doh*-dee-chee/twelve

dolce/f/m/*dohl*-cheh/sweet

domani/doh-*mah*-nee/tomorrow

donna/f/*dohn*-nah/woman

dormire (v.)/dohr-*mee*-reh/to sleep

dottore/m/doht-*toh*-reh/doctor

dove/*doh*-veh/where

dovere (v.)/doh-*veh*-reh/to have to, must

due/*dooh*-eh/two

E

emergenza/f/eh-mehr-*jehn*-tsah/
   emergency

entrata/f/ehn-*trah*-tah/entrance

entrare/ehn-*trah*-reh/to enter

essere (v.)/*ehs*-seh-reh/to be

est/m/ehst/east

F

faccia/f/*fahch*-chah/face

facile (adj)/*fah*-chee-leh/easy

fame/f/*fah*-meh/hunger

fare (v.)/*fah*-reh/to do

febbraio/fehb-*brah*-yoh/February

felice (adj.)/feh-*lee*-cheh/happy

festa/f/*fehs*-tah/party, holiday

figlia/f/*fee*-lyah/daughter

figlio/m/*fee*-lyoh/son

fine/f/*fee*-neh/end

finestra/f/fee-*nehs*-trah/window

finire/fee-*nee*-reh/to finish

fiore/m/*fyoh*-reh/flower

formaggio/m/fohr-*mahj*-joh/cheese

fragola/f/*frah*-goh-lah/strawberry

fratello/m/frah-*tehl*-loh/brother

fredda/f/**freddo**/m/*frehd*-dah/
   frehd-doh/cold

frutta/f/*frooht*-tah/fruit

G

gatto/m/*gaht*-toh/cat

gelato/m/jeh-*lah*-toh/ice cream

gennaio/jehn-*nah*-yoh/January

gente/f/*jehn*-teh/people

ghiaccio/m/*gyahch*-choh/ice

giacca/f/*jahk*-kah/jacket; blazer

gialla/f/**giallo**/m/*jahl*-lah/*jahl*-loh/yellow

giardino/m/jahr-*dee*-noh/garden

ginocchio/m/jee-*nohk*-kyoh/knee

giocare (v.)/joh-*kah*-reh/to play

gioco/m/*joh*-koh/game

giornale/m/johr-*nah*-leh/newspaper

giorno/m/*johr*-noh/day

giovane/f/m/*joh*-vah-neh/young

giugno/*jooh*-nyoh/June

gonna/f/*gohn*-nah/skirt

grande/f/m/*grahn*-deh/big; tall; large

grande magazzino/m/*grahn*-deh mah-
   gaht-*tsee*-noh/department store

grazie/*grah*-tsee-eh/thank you

grigia/f/**grigio**/m/gree-jah/*gree*-joh/gray

I

ieri/*yeh*-ree/yesterday

impermeabile/m/eem-pehr-meh-*ah*-
   bee-leh/raincoat

impiegata/f/**impiegato**/m/eem-pyeh-*gah*-tah/eem-pyeh-*gah*-toh/employee

in ritardo/een ree-*tahr*-doh/late

indirizzo/m/een-dee-*reet*-tsoh/address

infermiera/f/een-fehr-*myeh*-rah/nurse

ingegnere/m/een-jeh-*nyeh*-reh/engineer

insalata/f/een-sah-*lah*-tah/salad

invito/m/een-*vee*-toh/invitation

io/*ee*-oh/I

italiana/f/**italiano**/m/ee-tah-lee-*ah*-nah/ee-tah-lee-*ah*-noh/Italian

J

jeans/m/jeenz/jeans

L

lago/m/*lah*-goh/lake

lana/f/*lah*-nah/wool

larga/f/**largo**/m/*lahr*-gah/*lahr*-goh/wide

latte/m/*laht*-teh/milk

lavoro/m/lah-*voh*-roh/work

lei/ley/she; formal you

libro/m/*lee*-broh/book

loro/*loh*-roh/they

luglio/*looh*-lyoh/July

lui/*looh*-ee/he

M

ma/mah/but

macchina/f/*mahk*-kee-nah/car

madre/f/*mah*-dreh/mother

maggio/*mahj*-joh/May

mai/mahy/never

malata/f/**malato**/m/mah-*lah*-tah/mah-*lah*-toh/ill

mamma/f/*mahm*-mah/mom

mangiare (v.)/mahn-*jah*-reh/to eat

mano/f/*mah*-noh/hand

mare/m/*mah*-reh/sea

marito/m/mah-*ree*-toh/husband

marrone (adj.)/mahr-*roh*-neh/brown

marzo/*mahr*-tsoh/March

me/meh/me

medicina/f/meh-dee-*chee*-nah/medicine

medico/m/*meh*-dee-koh/physician

mercato/m/mehr-*kah*-toh/market

mese/m/*meh*-zeh/month

metropolitana/f/meh-troh-poh-lee-*tah*-nah/subway

mettersi/*meht*-tehr-see/to wear

mia/f/**mio**/m/*mee*-ah/*mee*-oh/my

mille/*meel*-leh/thousand

moglie/f/*moh*-lyeh/wife

montagna/f/mohn-*tah*-nyah/mountain

N

naso/m/*nah*-zoh/nose

nebbia/f/*nehb*-byah/fog

negozio/m/neh-*goh*-tsee-oh/shop

nera/f/ **nero**/m/*neh*-rah/*neh*-roh/black

neve/f/*neh*-veh/snow

noi/noi/we

noiosa/f/**noioso**/m/noi-*oh*-zah/noi-*oh*-zoh/boring

nome/m/*noh*-meh/name

nord/m/nohrd/north

nove/*noh*-veh/nine

novembre/noh-*vehm*-breh/November

numero/m/*nooh*-meh-roh/number

nuoto/m/*nwoh*-toh/swimming

O

occhio/m/*ohk*-kyoh/eye
orecchio/m/oh-*rehk*-kyoh/ear
ospedale/m/ohs-peh-*dah*-leh/hospital
otto/*oht*-toh/eight
ottobre/oht-*toh*-breh/October
ovest/m/*oh*-vehst/west

P

padre/m/*pah*-dreh/father
pagare/pah-*gah*-reh/to pay
pane/m/*pah*-neh/bread
panna/f/ *pahn*-nah/cream
pantaloni/m.pl./pahn-tah-*loh*-nee/pants
parlare (v.)/pahr-*lah*-reh/to talk
partire (v.)/pahr-*tee*-reh/to leave
passaporto/m/pahs-sah-*pohr*-toh/
  passport
pasticceria/f/pahs-teech-cheh-*ree*-ah/
  pastry shop
per favore/pehr fah-*voh*-reh/please
perché/pehr-*keh*/why; because
pesce/m/*peh*-sheh/fish
piacere (v.)/pyah-*cheh*-reh/nice to
  meet you; to like; pleasure
piazza/f/*pyaht*-tsah/square
piccola/f/**piccolo**/m/ *peek*-koh-lah/
  peek-koh-loh/small; short
pioggia/f/*pyohj*-jah/rain
piove/*pyoh*-veh/it's raining
polizia/f/poh-lee-*tsee*-ah/police
potere/poh-*teh*-reh/can; may
pranzo/m/*prahn*-zoh/lunch
preferire (v.)/preh-feh-*ree*-reh/to prefer
prego/*preh*-goh/you're welcome

prendere/*prehn*-deh-reh/to take; to order,
  such as in a bar or restaurant
presentare/preh-zehn-*tah*-reh/to
  introduce

Q

qualcosa/kwahl-*koh*-zah/something
quale/*kwah*-leh/which
quando/*kwahn*-doh/when
quanti/*kwahn*-tee/how many
quanto/m/*kwahn*-toh/how much
quattro/m/*kwaht*-troh/four
quattordici/m/kwaht-*tohr*-dee-chee/
  fourteen
qui/kwee/here
quindici/*kween*-dee-chee/fifteen

R

ragazza/f/rah-*gaht*-tsah/girl
ragazzo/m/rah-*gaht*-tsoh/boy
ridere (v.)/*ree*-deh-reh/to laugh
riso/m/*ree*-zoh/rice, laughter
rossa/f/**rosso**/m/*rohs*-sah/*rohs*-soh/red

S

saldi/m.pl./*sahl*-dee/sales
sale/m/*sah*-leh/salt
scarpa/f/*skahr*-pah/shoe
scura/f/**scuro**/m/*skooh*-rah/
  skooh-roh/dark
sedici/*seh*-dee-chee/sixteen
segretaria/f/**segretario**/m/seh-greh-*tah*-
  ree-ah/seh-greh-*tah*-ree-oh/secretary
sei/sey/six

sempre/*sehm*-preh/always
sete/f/*seh*-teh/thirst
sette/*seht*-teh/seven
settembre/seht-*tehm*-breh/September
settimana/f/seht-tee-*mah*-nah/week
signora/f/see-*nyoh*-rah/Mrs.; Ms.; woman
signore/m/see-*nyoh*-reh/Mr.; a gentleman
soldi/m.pl./*sohl*-dee/money
sole/m/*soh*-leh/sun
solo/*soh*-loh/only, just
sorella/f/soh-*rehl*-lah/sister
spalla/f/*spahl*-lah/shoulder
stanca/f/stanco/m/*stahn*-kah/
   stahn-koh/tired
stazione/f/stah-*tsyoh*-neh/station
strada/f/*strah*-dah/street; road
stretta/f/stretto/m/*streht*-tah/*streht*-toh/
   tight; narrow
sud/soohd/south
supermercato/m/*sooh*-pehr-mehr-
   kah-toh/supermarket

T

tazza/f/*taht*-tsah/cup
teatro/m/teh-*ah*-troh/theater
telefono/m/teh-*leh*-foh-noh/phone
tempo/m/*tehm*-poh/time; weather
tre/treh/three
tredici/*treh*-dee-chee/thirteen
treno/m/*treh*-noh/train
troppo/*trohp*-poh/too much
tu/tooh/you
tutti/*tooht*-tee/everybody
tutto/*tooht*-toh/everything

U

ufficio/m/oohf-*fee*-choh/office
uno/*ooh*-noh/one
uscita/f/ooh-*shee*-tah/exit
uomo/*woh*-moh/man

V

vacanza/f/vah-*kahn*-tsah/vacation
valigia/f/vah-*lee*-jah/suitcase
vedere/veh-*deh*-reh/to see
vendere/*vehn*-deh-reh/to sell
venire/veh-*nee*-reh/to come
venti/*vehn*-tee/twenty
verde/f/m/*vehr*-deh/green
verdura/f/vehr-*dooh*-rah/vegetables
vestito/m/vehs-*tee*-toh/dress
via/f/*vee*-ah/street
viaggiare/vee-ahj-*jah*-reh/to travel
viaggio/m/*vyahj*-joh/travel
viale/m/vee-*ah*-leh/avenue
vino/m/*vee*-noh/wine
voi/*voi*/you
volere/voh-*leh*-reh/to want

Z

zero/*dzeh*-roh/zero
zia/f/*dzee*-ah/ant
zio/m/*dzee*-oh/uncle
zucchero/m/*dzoohk*-keh-roh/sugar

English-Italian Mini Dictionary

A

address/**indirizzo**/m/een-dee-*reet*-tsoh

airplane/**aereo**/m/ah-*eh*-reh-oh

airport/**aeroporto**/m/ah-eh-roh-*pohr*-toh

all right; okay/**d'accordo**/dahk-*kohr*-doh

also/**anche**/*ahn*-keh

always/**sempre**/*sehm*-preh

American/**americana**/f/**americano**/m/ah-meh-ree-*kah*-nah/ah-meh-ree-*kah*-noh

aunt **zia**/f/*dzee*-ah

apartment/**appartamento**/m/ahp-pahr-tah-*mehn*-toh

appetizers/**antipasti**/m/ahn-tee-*pahs*-tee

April/**aprile**/ah-*pree*-leh

architect/**architetto**/m/ahr-kee-*teht*-toh

arm/**braccio**/m/*brahch*-choh

arrive (v.)/**arrivare**/ahr-ree-*vah*-reh

August/**agosto**/ah-*gohs*-toh

avenue/**viale**/m/vee-*ah*-leh

B

bad/**cattivo**/m/**cattiva**/f/kaht-*tee*-voh/kaht-*tee*-vah

bag/**borsa**/f/*bohr*-sah

bakery/**pasticceria**/f/pahs-teech-cheh-*ree*-ah

bank/**banca**/f/*bahn*-kah

bathing suit/**costume da bagno**/m/kohs-*tooh*-meh dah *bah*-nyoh

be (v.)/**essere**/*ehs*-seh-reh

beach/**spiaggia**/f/*spyahj*-jah

beautiful/**bella**/f/**bello**/m/*behl*-lah/*behl*-loh

because/**perché**/pehr-*keh*

beer/**birra**/f/*beer*-rah

bicycle/**bicicletta**/f/bee-chee-*kleht*-tah

big; tall; large/**grande**/f/m/*grahn*-deh

black/**nera**/f/**nero**/m/*neh*-rah/neh-roh

blue/**blu**/f/m/blooh

book/**libro**/m/*lee*-broh

boring/**noiosa**/f/**noioso**/m/noi-*oh*-zah/noi-*oh*-zoh

bottle/**bottiglia**/f/boht-*tee*-lyah

boy/**ragazzo**/m/rah-*gaht*-tsoh

bread/**pane**/m/*pah*-neh

breakfast/**colazione**/f/koh-lah-*tsyoh*-neh

brother/**fratello**/m/frah-*tehl*-loh

brown/**marrone**/f/m/mahr-*roh*-neh

bus/**autobus**/m/*ou*-toh-boohs

but/**ma**/mah

buy (v.)/**comprare**/kohm-*prah*-reh

C

can, may (v.)/**potere**/poh-*teh*-reh

Canadian/**canadese**/f/m/kah-nah-*deh*-zeh

car/**automobile**/f/ou-toh-*moh*-bee-leh

car/**macchina**/*mahk*-kee-nah

cash register/f/**cassa**/*kahs*-sah

cat/**gatto**/m/*gaht*-toh

change (v.)/**cambiare**/kahm-bee-*ah*-reh

check/**assegno**/m/ahs-*seh*-nyoh

cheese/**formaggio**/m/fohr-*mahj*-joh

child (female)/**bambina**/f/bahm-*bee*-nah

child (male)/**bambino**/m/bahm-*bee*-noh

chocolate/**cioccolata**/f/choh-koh-*lah*-tah

cinema/**cinema**/m/*chee*-neh-mah

city; town/**città**/f/cheet-*tah*

coat/**cappotto**/m/kahp-*poht*-toh

coffee/**caffè**/m/*kahf*-feh

cold/**fredda**/f/**freddo**/m/*frehd*-dah/
    frehd-doh

color/**colore**/m/koh-*loh*-reh

come on/**dai**/dahy

come (v.)/**venire**/veh-*nee*-reh

country/**campagna**/f/kahm-*pah*-nyah

cream/**panna**/f/*pahn*-nah

credit card/**carta di credito**/f/*kahr*-tah
    dee *kreh*-dee-toh

cup/**tazza**/f/*taht*-tsah

custard/**crema**/f/*kreh*-mah

D

dark/**scura**/f/**scuro**/m/*skooh*-rah/
    skooh-roh

daughter/**figlia**/f/*fee*-lyah

day/**giorno**/m/*johr*-noh

dear/**cara**/f/**caro**/m/*kah*-rah/*kah*-roh

December/**dicembre**/dee-*chehm*-breh

dentist/**dentista**/f/m/dehn-*tees*-tah

department store/**grande magazzino**/m/
    grahn-deh mah-gaht-*tsee*-noh

dessert (sweet)/**dolce**/m/ *dohl*-cheh

dinner/**cena**/f/*cheh*-nah

doctor/**dottore**/m/doht-*toh*-reh

dog/**cane**/m/*kah*-neh

dress/**vestito**/m/vehs-*tee*-toh

drink (v.)/**bere**/*beh*-reh

E

ear/**orecchio**/m/oh-*rehk*-kyoh

east/**est**/m/ehst

easy/**facile**/f/m/*fah*-chee-leh

eat (v.)/**mangiare**/mahn-*jah*-reh

eight/**otto**/*oht*-toh

eighteen/**diciotto**/dee-*choht*-toh

eleven/**undici**/*oohn*-dee-chee

emergency/**emergenza**/f/
    eh-mehr-*jehn*-tsah

employee/**impiegata**/f/**impiegato**/m/
    eem-pyeh-*gah*-tah/eem-pyeh-*gah*-toh

end/**fine**/f/*fee*-neh

engineer/**ingegnere**/m/een-jeh-*nyeh*-reh

enter (v.)/**entrare**/ehn-*trah*-reh

entrance/**entrata**/f/ehn-*trah*-tah

everybody/**tutti**/*tooht*-tee

everything/**tutto**/*tooht*-toh

exit/**uscita**/f/ooh-*shee*-tah

expensive/**cara**/f/**caro**/m/*kah*-rah/*kah*-roh

eye/**occhio**/m/*ohk*-kyoh

F

face/**faccia**/f/*fahch*-chah

father/**padre**/m/*pah*-dreh

February/**febbraio**/fehb-*brah*-yoh

fifteen/**quindici**/*kween*-dee-chee

fifty/**cinquanta**/cheen-*kwahn*-tah

finger/**dito**/m/*dee*-toh

finish (v.)/**finire**/fee-*nee*-reh

fish/**pesce**/m/*peh*-sheh

five/**cinque**/*cheen*-kweh

flower/**fiore**/m/*fyoh*-reh

fog/**nebbia**/f/*nehb*-byah
four/**quattro**/*kwaht*-troh
fourteen/**quattordici**/kwaht-*tohr*-dee-chee
friend/**amica**/f/**amico**/m/ah-*mee*-kah/
   ah-*mee*-koh
fruit/**frutta**/f/*frooht*-tah

G

garden/**giardino**/m/jahr-*dee*-noh
girl/**ragazza**/f/rah-*gaht*-tsah
give (v.)/**dare**/*dah*-reh
glass/**bicchiere**/m/beek-*kyeh*-reh
go/**andare**/ahn-*dah*-reh
good/**buona**/f/**buono**/m/*bwoh*-nah/
   bwoh-noh
good-bye/**ciao**/chou
good evening/**buonasera**/
   bwoh-nah-*seh*-rah
good morning; good day/**buongiorno**/
   bwohn-*johr*-noh
good-night/**buonanotte**/
   bwoh-nah-*noht*-teh
green/**verde**/f/m/*vehr*-deh
gray/**grigia**/f/**grigio**/m/*gree*-jah/*gree*-joh

H

hair/**capelli**/m/kah-*pehl*-lee (plural)
hand/**mano**/f/*mah*-noh
happy/**felice**/feh-*lee*-cheh
hat/**cappello**/m/kahp-*pehl*-loh
have (v.)/**avere**/ah-*veh*-reh
have, take (bar, restaurant) (v.)/
   prendere/ *prehn*-deh-reh
have to (v.)/**dovere**/doh-*veh*-reh
he/**lui**/*looh*-ee
hello/**ciao**/chou
help/**aiuto**/ah-*yooh*-toh

here/**qui**/kwee
horse/**cavallo**/m/kah-*vahl*-loh
hospital/**ospedale**/m/ohs-peh-*dah*-leh
hot/**calda**/f/**caldo**/m/*kahl*-dah/*kahl*-doh
hotel/**albergo**/m/ahl-*behr*-goh
house; home/**casa**/f/*kah*-sah
how/**come**/*koh*-meh
how many/**quanti**/*kwahn*-tee
how much/**quanto**/*kwahn*-toh
hundred/**cento**/*chehn*-toh
hunger/**fame**/f/*fah*-meh
husband/**marito**/m/mah-*ree*-toh

I

I/**io**/*ee*-oh
ice/**ghiaccio**/m/*gyahch*-choh
ice cream/**gelato**/m/jeh-*lah*-toh
ill/**malata**/f/**malato**/m/mah-*lah*-tah/
   mah-*lah*-toh
introduce (v.)/**presentare**/
   preh-zehn-*tah*-reh
invitation/**invito**/m/een-*vee*-toh
Italian/**italiana**/f/**italiano**/m/ee-tah-lee-
   ah-nah/ee-tah-lee-*ah*-noh

J

jacket; blazer/f/**giacca**/*jahk*-kah
January/**gennaio**/jehn-*nah*-yoh
jeans/**jeans**/m/jeenz
July/**luglio**/*looh*-lyoh
June/**giugno**/*jooh*-nyoh

K

knee/**ginocchio**/m/jee-*nohk*-kyoh
knife/**coltello**/m/kohl-*tehl*-loh

L

lake/**lago**/m/*lah*-goh

large/**larga**/f/**largo**/m/*lahr*-gah/*lahr*-goh

late/**in ritardo**/een ree-*tahr*-doh

laugh (v.)/**ridere**/*ree*-deh-reh

lawyer/**avvocato**/m/ahv-voh-*kah*-toh

leave (v.)/**partire**/pahr-*tee*-reh

(on the) left/**a sinistra**/ah see-*nees*-trah

light-colored/**chiara**/f/**chiaro**/m/*kyah*-rah/ *kyah*-roh

live (v.)/**abitare**/ah-bee-*tah*-reh

love (v.)/**amare**/ah-*mah*-reh

love/**amore**/m/ah-*moh*-reh

lunch/**pranzo**/m/*prahn*-tsoh

M

man/**uomo**/*woh*-moh

March/**marzo**/*mahr*-tsoh

market/**mercato**/m/mehr-*kah*-toh

May/**maggio**/*mahj*-joh

me/**me**/meh

meat/**carne**/f/*kahr*-neh

medicine/**medicina**/f/meh-dee-*chee*-nah

milk/**latte**/m/*laht*-teh

mom/**mamma**/f/*mahm*-mah

money/**soldi**/m/*sohl*-dee

month/**mese**/m/*meh*-zeh

mother/**madre**/f/*mah*-dreh

mountain/**montagna**/f/mohn-*tah*-nyah

Mr./**signore**/m/see-*nyoh*-reh

Mrs./**signora**/f/see-*nyoh*-rah

my/**mia**/f/**mio**/m/*mee*-ah/*mee*-oh

N

name/**nome**/m/*noh*-meh

neck/**collo**/m/*kohl*-loh

never/**mai**/mahy

newspaper/**giornale**/m/johr-*nah*-leh

nice/**carina**/f/**carino**/m/kah-*ree*-nah/ kah-*ree*-noh

nice to meet you/**piacere**/pyah-*cheh*-reh

nine/**nove**/*noh*-veh

nineteen/**diciannove**/dee-chahn-*noh*-veh

north/**nord**/m/nohrd

nose/**naso**/m/*nah*-zoh

November/**novembre**/noh-*vehm*-breh

number/**numero**/m/nooh-*meh*-roh

nurse/**infermiera**/f/een-fehr-*myeh*-rah

O

October/**ottobre**/oht-*toh*-breh

office/**ufficio**/m/oohf-*fee*-choh

old (for persons)/**anziana**/f/**anziano**/m/ ahn-tsee-*ah*-nah/ahn-tsee-*ah*-noh

one/**uno**/*ooh*-noh

one-way (ticket)/**andata**/f/ahn-*dah*-tah

only; just/**solo**/*soh*-loh

P

party; holiday/**festa**/f/*fehs*-tah

passport/**passaporto**/m/ *pahs*-sah-*pohr*-toh

pay (v.)/**pagare**/pah-*gah*-reh

people/**gente**/f/*jehn*-teh

phone/**telefono**/m/teh-*leh*-foh-noh

physician/**medico**/m/*meh*-dee-koh

play (v.)/**giocare**/joh-*kah*-reh

play/**gioco**/m/*joh*-koh

please/**per favore**/pehr fah-*voh*-reh

police/**polizia**/f/poh-lee-*tsee*-ah

prefer (v.)/**preferire**/preh-feh-*ree*-reh

R

rain/**pioggia**/f/*pyohj*-jah

raincoat/**impermeabile**/m/
eem-pehr-meh-*ah*-bee-leh

red/**rossa**/f/**rosso**/m/*rohs*-sah/*rohs*-soh

rent (v.)/**affittare**/ahf-feet-*tah*-reh

(on the) right/**a destra**/ah *dehs*-trah

rice/**riso**/m/*ree*-zoh

round trip/**andata**/f/**e ritorno**/m/
ahn-*dah*-tah eh ree-*tohr*-noh

S

salad/**insalata**/f/een-sah-*lah*-tah

sales/**saldi**/m.pl./*sahl*-dee

sales clerk/**commessa**/f/**commesso**/m/
kohm-*mehs*-sah/kohm-*mehs*-soh

salt/**sale**/m/*sah*-leh

say (v.)/**dire**/*dee*-reh

sea/**mare**/m/*mah*-reh

secretary/**segretaria**/f/**segretario**/m/seh-
greh-*tah*-ree-ah/seh-greh-*tah*-ree-oh

see (v.)/**vedere**/veh-*deh*-reh

see you; good-bye/**arrivederci**/
ahr-ree-veh-*dehr*-chee

see you later/**a dopo**/ah *doh*-poh

see you tomorrow/**a domani**/ah
doh-*mah*-nee

sell (v.)/**vendere**/vehn-*deh*-reh

September/**settembre**/seht-*tehm*-breh

seven/**sette**/*seht*-teh

seventeen/**diciassette**/dee-chahs-*seht*-teh

she/**lei**/ley

shirt/**camicia**/f/kah-*mee*-chah

shoe/**scarpa**/f/*skahr*-pah

shop/**negozio**/m/neh-*goh*-tsee-oh

shoulder/**spalla**/f/*spahl*-lah

sister/**sorella**/f/soh-*rehl*-lah

six/**sei**/sey

sixteen/**sedici**/*seh*-dee-chee

skirt/**gonna**/f/*gohn*-nah

sleep (v.)/**dormire**/dohr-*mee*-reh

small; short/**piccola**/f/**piccolo**/m/
peek-koh-lah/*peek*-koh-loh

snow/**neve**/f/*neh*-veh

soccer/**calcio**/m/*kahl*-choh

something/**qualcosa**/kwahl-*koh*-zah

son/**figlio**/m/*fee*-lyoh

south/**sud**/m/soohd

square/**piazza**/f/*pyaht*-tsah

station/**stazione**/f/stah-tsee-*oh*-neh

strawberry/**fragola**/f/*frah*-goh-lah

street; road/**strada**/f/*strah*-dah or via/
f/*vee*-ah

subway/**metropolitana**/f/
meh-troh-poh-lee-*tah*-nah

sugar/**zucchero**/m/*dzook*-keh-roh

suit/**abito**/m/*ah*-bee-toh

suitcase/**valigia**/f/vah-*lee*-jah

sun/**sole**/m/*soh*-leh

supermarket/**supermercato**/m/
sooh-pehr-mehr-*kah*-toh

sweet/**dolce**/f/m/*dohl*-cheh

swimming/**nuoto**/m/*nwoh*-toh

T

take (v.)/**prendere**/*prehn*-deh-reh

talk (v.)/**parlare**/pahr-*lah*-reh

tax/**dazio**/m/*dah*-tsee-oh

telephone/**telefono**/m/teh-*leh*-foh-noh

ten/**dieci**/*dyeh*-chee

thank you/**grazie**/*grah*-tsee-eh

theater/**teatro**/m/teh-*ah*-troh

there are/**ci sono**/chee *soh*-noh

there is/**c'è**/cheh

they/**loro**/*loh*-roh

thirst/**sete**/f/*seh*-teh

thirteen/**tredici**/*treh*-dee-chee

thousand/**mille**/*meel*-leh

three/**tre**/treh

ticket/**biglietto**/m/bee-*lyeht*-toh

tie/**cravatta**/f/krah-*vaht*-tah

tight; narrow/**stretta**/f/**stretto**/m/*streht*-tah/*streht*-toh

time; weather/**tempo**/m/*tehm*-poh

tired/**stanca**/f/**stanco**/m/*stahn*-kah/*stahn*-koh

today/**oggi**/*ohj*-jee

tomorrow/**domani**/doh-*mah*-nee

too much/**troppo**/*trohp*-poh

train/**treno**/m/*treh*-noh

travel (v.)/**viaggiare**/vee-ahj-*jah*-reh

travel/**viaggio**/m/vee-*ahj*-joh

trousers/**pantaloni**/m/pahn-tah-*loh*-nee

twelve/**dodici**/*doh*-dee-chee

twenty/**venti**/*vehn*-tee

two/**due**/*dooh*-eh

U

uncle/**zio**/m/*dzee*-oh

V

vacation/**vacanza**/f/vah-*kahn*-tsah

vegetables/**verdura**/f/vehr-*dooh*-rah

W

waitress/waiter/**cameriera**/f/**cameriere**/m/kah-meh-*ryeh*-rah/kah-meh-*ryeh*-reh

wallet/**portafoglio**/pohr-tah-*foh*-lyoh

want (v.)/**volere**/voh-*leh*-reh

warm/**calda**/f/**caldo**/m/*kahl*-dah/*kahl*-doh

water/**acqua**/f/*ah*-kwah

we/**noi**/noi

wear (v.)/**mettersi**/*meht*-tehr-see

week/**settimana**/f/seht-tee-*mah*-nah

well (adverb)/**bene**/*beh*-neh

west/**ovest**/m/*oh*-vehst

what/**cosa**/*koh*-sah

when/**quando**/*kwahn*-doh

where/**dove**/*doh*-veh

which/**quale**/f/m/*kwah*-leh

white/**bianca**/f/**bianco**/m/*byahn*-kah/*byahn*-koh

who/**chi**/kee

why/**perché**/pehr-*keh*

wife/**moglie**/f/*moh*-lyeh

window/**finestra**/f/fee-*nehs*-trah

wine/**vino**/m/*vee*-noh

woman/**donna**/f/*dohn*-nah

wool/**lana**/f/*lah*-nah

work/**lavoro**/m/lah-*voh*-roh

Y

year/**anno**/m/*ahn*-noh

yellow/**gialla**/f/**giallo**/m/*jahl*-lah/*jahl*-loh

yesterday/**ieri**/*yeh*-ree

you (formal)/**Lei**/ley

you (plural, informal/formal)/**voi**/voi

you (singular, informal)/**tu**/tooh

you're welcome/**prego**/*preh*-goh

young/**giovane**/f/m/*joh*-vah-neh

Z

zero/**zero**/*dzeh*-roh

zip code/**codice postale**/m/*koh*-dee-cheh pohs-*tah*-leh

Appendix C

About the CD

Track Listing

Following is a list of the tracks that appear on this book's audio CD, which you can find inside the back cover. Note that this is an audio-only CD — just pop it into your stereo (or whatever you use to listing to regular music CDs).

Track 1: Introduction and pronunciation guide (Chapter 1)

Track 2: Common phrases (Chapter 1)

Track 3: Asking directions (Chapter 2)

Track 4: Making informal small talk (Chapter 2)

Track 5: Having a formal conversation (Chapter 3)

Track 6: Talking with friends (Chapter 3)

Track 7: Talking about the weather (Chapter 4)

Track 8: Days of the week (Chapter 4)

Track 9: Months of the year (Chapter 4)

Track 10: Following a recipe (Chapter 5)

Track 11: Finding a place to meet (Chapter 6)

Track 12: Getting back to the train station (Chapter 6)

Track 13: Making dinner reservations (Chapter 7)

Track 14: Let's Eat! (Si mangia!) (Chapter 7)

Track 15: Enjoying some after-dinner ice cream (Chapter 7)

Track 16: Shopping for clothes (Chapter 8)

Track 17: Shopping for shoes (Chapter 8)

Track 18: Going to the movies (Chapter 9)

Track 19: Inviting friends to a party (Chapter 9)

Track 20: Talking on the phone to a friend (Chapter 10)

Track 21: Making a doctor's appointment (Chapter 10)

Track 22: Leaving a message (Chapter 10)

Track 23: Talking about the weekend (Chapter 11)

Track 24: Talking about sports (Chapter 11)

Track 25: Discussing free-time activities (Chapter 11)

Track 26: Planning a vacation (Chapter 12)

Track 27: Talking about a plane schedule (Chapter 12)

Track 28: Changing dollars to euros (Chapter 13)

Track 29: Making train connections (Chapter 14)

Track 30: Purchasing train tickets (Chapter 14)

Track 31: Taking the subway (Chapter 14)

Track 32: Checking in to a hotel (Chapter 15)

Track 33: Common Italian when planning a trip (Chapter 15)

Track 34: Visiting a doctor (Chapter 16)

Track 35: Reporting an accident to the police (Chapter 16)

Track 36: Using interrogative pronouns (Chapter 17)

Customer Care

If you have trouble with the CD, please call Wiley Product Technical Support at 877-762-2974. Outside the United States, call 317-572-3993. You can also contact Wiley Product Technical Support at support.wiley.com. Wiley Publishing will provide technical support only for installation and other general quality control items.

To place additional orders or to request information about other Wiley products, please call 877-762-2974.

Appendix D

Answer Keys

The following are the answers to the Fun & Games activities.

Chapter 2: Jumping Into the Basics of Italian

albergo			facile					
amica			fame					
avere			fare					
bici			italiano					
caldo			partire					
capire			pausa					
dire			ragazza					
dove			rosso					
dovere			sete					
esame			volere					
essere			zio					

Chapter 3: Buongiorno! Salutations!

come sta   conoscerla

e lei   il piacere

le presento

Chapter 4: Getting Your Numbers and Time Straight

Chapter 5: Casa dolce casa (Home Sweet Home)

1. il bagno (the bathroom)

2. la camera da letto (the bedroom)

3. il letto (the bed)

4. il soggiorno (the living room)

5. il divano (the couch)

6. i fornelli (the stove-top)

7. la cucina (the kitchen)

8. la tavola (the table)

Chapter 6: Where Is the Colosseum? Asking Directions

1. Via della Vigna Nuova
2. Ponte Santa Trinità and Ponte Vecchio
3. Arno
4. Palazzo Vecchio
5. Piazza Duomo and Piazza San Giovanni
6. Lungarno
7. Piazza della Repubblica

Chapter 7: Food Glorious Food – and Don't Forget the Drink

1. ananas
2. ciliegia
3. uva
4. pera
5. cocomero
6. fragola

Chapter 8: Shopping, Italian Style

1. cappello
2. camicia
3. cravatta
4. completo
5. pantaloni
6. scarpe
7. gonna
8. camicetta

Chapter 9: Having Fun Out on the Town

1. festa
2. invitato
3. sabato
4. ora
5. verso
6. dove

7. perchè

8. aspetto

Chapter 10: Taking Care of Business and Telecommunicating

1. pronto

2. parlo

3. amico

4. C'è

5. appena

6. lasciare un messaggio

7. prego

8. chiamato

Chapter 11: Recreation and the Outdoors

cavallo, fiore, uccello, gatto, lupo, quercia, pino, mucca, pecora, albero

Chapter 12: Planning a Trip

1. b

2. a

3. b

4. c

5. a

Chapter 13: Money, Money, Money

Banca	Dollaro
Bancomat	Euro
Cambiare	Kuna
Cartadicredito	Ricevuta
Cassa	Spiccioli
Contanti	Sportello
Documento	Sterline

Bank	identification	small change
ATM	dollar	door
to change	euro	counter
credit card	Croatian currency	British pound
cash	receipt	

Chapter 14: Getting Around: Planes, Trains, Taxis, and Buses

```
B S M T A T A M R E F O
I T U D H G L T X L N C
N S Y P V X L A B E D G
A P J Y P B E I R S H D
R K D A J L G T X F X V
I V D U Y L E M R C D Q
O I D Y I K A M G G D R
R Z J E L X S T E E L K
B C T C P M D Q A N C I
B T H P R S P U F D T K
O R I T O R N O S O N O
S T A Z I O N E Z A G A
```

treno, fermata, stazione, binario, biglietto, andata, ritorno, supplemento

Chapter 15: Finding a Place to Stay

valige, cameriere, culla, camera, matrimoniale, letto, piscine, stanza, albergo, prenotazione, pensione, chiave, bagaglio, bagno

Chapter 16: Handling Emergencies

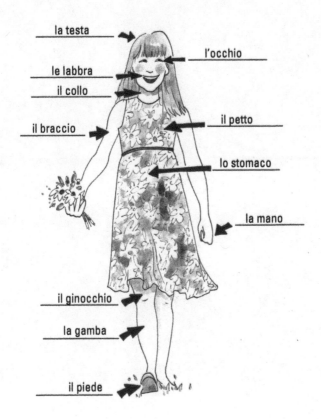

Chapter 17: Small Talk, Wrapping Things Up

1. mia madre e mio padre

2. mio fratello

3. i miei nipoti

4. mia nonna

5. mia zia

6. mio cognato

7. mia nuora

8. mia figlia

9. i miei cugini

10. mia suocera

Index

• *Symbols and Numerics* •

24-hour clock, 71

• *A* •

a che ora (what time), 171
a che piano è (what floor is it on), 86
a destra (on the right), 106, 117
a domani (see you tomorrow), 46, 179
a dopo (see you later), 46
a presto (see you soon), 46
a proposito (by the way), 80
a sinistra (on the left), 106, 117
abbastanza (enough), 300
abbigliamento da donna/da uomo
    (women's/men's wear), 140
abito (suit), 142
accanto (next to), 95
accessori (accessories), 147
accessorizing clothes, 147
accettare (to accept), 226
accettazione (check-in), 234
accidenti (wow, darn it), 12
accidents, reporting to police, 280–281
acciughe fresche (fresh anchovies), 133
accommodations
    checking in, 259–262
    choosing, 255
    Fun & Games, 269
    imperatives, 267–268
    pronouns, 262–266
    reserving rooms, 256–258
    Talkin' the Talk, 255, 257–258, 260–261,
        265–266
acqua frizzante (sparkling water), 121
acqua gassata/gasata (sparkling
    water), 121

acqua in bocca (water in mouth), 328
acqua liscia/naturale (still water), 121
acqua minerale (mineral water), 121
addormentarsi (to fall asleep), 336
adjectives
    demonstrative, 263
    possessive, 300–304
    relationship with gender, 25–26
aeroporto (airport), 11, 117, 231
affidabile (dependable), 189
affittare (to rent), 88
agenzia di viaggi (travel agency),
    213, 246
agenzia immobiliare (real estate
    agency), 87
agnello (lamb), 132
agriturismo (farm stay), 215, 255
airports
    checking in, 234–236
    excess baggage, 236
    after landing, 238–239
    waiting to board, 237
aiutami (help me), 271
aiuto (help), 271, 276
al bar (in the bar), 120, 126
al forno (baked), 133
al macellaio (at the butcher's), 132
albergho/i (hotel/hotels), 40, 255
albero (tree), 14, 192
alla dogana (at customs), 240
alla griglia (grilled), 133
alla stazione (at the station), 246
all'angolo (at the corner), 106
all'incrocio (at the intersection), 106
alphabet, 13
alta (tall), 283
alta stagione (high/peak season),
    209, 256
alzarsi (to get up), 336

ambulanza (ambulance), 276, 281

amica/amiche (girl-friend/s), 26

amico/i (male friends or mixed gender friends), 26

ammobiliata (furnished), 87

amore (love), 10

anch'lo (I also, me too), 40

andare (to go), 32, 33, 109, 183, 197, 198, 336

andata (one way), 249

andate (go), 110

andiamo (let's go), 12

angolo cottura (cooking area), 88

anni (years), 80

annoiarsi (to be bored), 195

annuncio (advertisement), 87, 189

Answer Key for Fun & Games, 361–367

antipasto (appetizers), 127

aperitivo (before-dinner drink), 122

aperto (open), 140

apparecchiare (to set the table), 97

appartamento (apartment), 87

appliances, 95

apra (open), 267

apriamo (let's open), 267

aprire (to open), 29, 267, 335

aprire un conto (to open an account), 221

arancione (orange), 145

Arena, 159

aria condizionata (air conditioning), 87, 245, 258

armadio (armoire), 94

arrivare (to arrive), 216

arrivederci (good bye), 44, 319

arrivo/i (arrival/arrivals), 240, 252

articles

  definite, 24–25, 144

  indefinite, 23–24, 144

ascensore (elevator), 88, 140

ascoltare (to listen), 183, 205

ascoltare la musica (listen to music), 203

asiugamano/gli, asciumagmani (towel/s), 94

asking simple questions, 295

aspettare (to wait), 253

aspiravpolvere (vacuum cleaner), 95

assicurazione (insurance), 288

assistente (assistant), 189

attenda in linea (please hold), 182

attenzione (attention), 11

attore (actor), 156

attraversa/attraversi/attraversate/ attraversino (cross), 110

auto (car), 15

autobus (bus), 113, 249

autunno (autumn, fall), 73

avanti (come in), 10

avere (to have)

  about, 30, 273

  idiomatic uses of, 32–35

  passato prossimo with, 183

  past participles using, 184

avere bisogno di (to need), 141

avere mal di (to have a __ache), 276

avete (do you (plural) have), 261

azienda (company), 186

azzurri (blue), 284

azzurro (sky blue), 145

• B •

babbo (dad, daddy), 311

baffi (moustache), 284

bagaglio (baggage, carry-on luggage), 236, 266

bagno (bathroom), 88, 94, 300

balcone (balcony), 88

ballare (to dance), 170

bambino/a (child), 10

banca (bank), 224

bancomat (ATM), 225, 226, 228

barba (beard), 284

barista (bar-person), 120

bassa (short), 283
batteria (drums), 205
beach, 217
bed and breakfasts (bed and
  breakfasts), 255
beige (beige), 145
bello (beautiful), 19
bene (well), 15
benzina super (premium fuel), 245
benzina verde (unleaded fuel), 245
bere (to drink), 14, 170, 337
berretto (cap), 147
biancheria per la casa (household
  linens and towels), 140
bianco (white), 145
bicchiere/i (glass/glasses), 97
bidet (bidèt), 94
Biennale di Venezia, 160
biglietto (ticket), 153, 249
bilocali (two-room apartments), 87
bimbo (little boy), 14
binario (platform, track), 246, 249, 252
biondi (blond), 283
birra (beer), 123
bistecca (steak), 132
blu (blue), 145
boarding planes, 237
bocca carnosa (plump mouth), 284
bocca larga (wide mouth), 284
bocca stretta (thin lips), 284
bocce (lawn bowling), 199
body language, 46
boh (How should I know), 324
booking trips, 213–215
borsa (bag, handbag), 147, 283
bosco (woods), 192
bottiglia (bottle), 123
boutiques, 139–142
branzino (sea bass), 133
bravo/a (bravo), 10
breakfast, 126–127
bucatini (thick, tube-like spaghetti), 128

buona giornata (have a good day), 44
buona serata (have a good evening), 44
buon viaggio (have a nice trip), 209
buona fortuna (good luck), 163
buonanotte (good-night), 44
buonasera (good afternoon,
  good evening), 44
buone vacanze (have a nice
  vacation), 209
buongiorno (hello, good morning),
  43, 44, 319
buono (good), 26
buses, 249–251
business and telecommuting
  asking for people, 179–182
  discussing your job, 186–189
  Fun & Games, 190
  getting messages, 179–182
  making arrangements over phones,
    178–179
  past tense, 182–186
  phones, 173–178
  Talkin' the Talk, 175, 176–177, 178–179,
    180, 181, 184–185, 188
buste (envelopes), 218

• C •

cabriolet (convertible), 245
caffè (coffee), 19, 120, 126
calamari (squid), 133
calcio (soccer), 191, 198
calendar, 68–72
calle (narrow Venetian street), 107
calvo (bald), 284
calze (stockings), 147
cambiare (to change/exchange), 226, 231
cambiare valuta (to change money), 221
cambio (money exchange), 240
camera (room), 101, 256, 258
camera da letto (bedroom), 88, 94

camera doppia (room with two twin beds), 258

camera matrimoniale (room with a double bed), 258

camera singola (single room), 258

camere da letto (bedrooms), 87

cameriera (chambermaid, waitress), 266, 262

cameriere (waiter), 120, 125, 262

camicetta (blouse), 142

camicia (shirt), 142

camoscio (suede), 146

campagna (countryside), 87, 193, 209, 212

cane (dog), 194

cantautore (singer-songwriter), 162

cantina (cellar), 88

canzone (song), 316

capello (hair), 18

capire (to understand), 29, 30, 343

capo (head, boss), 309

cappello (hat), 18, 147

cappotto (coat), 142

capra (goat), 194

car rentals, 243–245

car trouble, 285–286

carne (meat), 127

caro (expensive), 90

Caro diario (film), 153

carro attrezzi (tow truck), 286

carta di credito (credit card), 223, 225

carta d'identità (identity card), 239

carta igienica (toilet paper), 132, 297

carta/scheda (phone card), 178

cartoline (postcards), 218

casa (house), 12, 14, 16, 26

casalinghi (housewares), 140

casco (helmet), 40

cassa (cash register), 140

cassaforte (safe), 259

castani (brown), 283

cattivo (bad), 26

cavallo (horse), 194

CD track listing, 359–360

c'è (there is), 296

cè l'ascensore (There is an elevator), 90

cellphones, 174, 178

cellulari (cellphones), 174, 178

cena (dinner), 16, 119, 129

centesimi (cents), 229

centimetro (centimeter), 78

centri commerciali (shopping malls), 139

centro (downtown, city center), 109

certo (certainty, of course), 16, 228

changing money, 224–226

che (what), 294

che bello (how beautiful), 323

che c'è (what's up), 12

che domanda (what a question), 228

che è successo (what happened), 281

che macello (what a mess), 325

che ne so (how should I know), 324

che ora è (what time is it), 70

che ore sono (what time is it), 70

checking in
to accommodations, 259–262
for flights, 234–236

chi (who), 294

chi è il regista (who is the director), 156

chi sono gli attori (who's starring), 156

chiacchierare (to chat), 182

chiamare (to call), 182

chiamarsi (to call oneself), 47

chiamata/e (call), 182, 276

chiari (fair), 284

chiave (key), 16

chiesa (church), 16, 18, 117

chilogrammo (kilogram), 78

chilo/i (kilo/s), 78, 80, 135

chilometro (kilometer), 78

chirugo (surgeon), 277

chitarra (guitar), 205

chiudere (to close), 334

chiuso (closed), 140
ci sono (there are), 296
ci vediamo (see you), 46
ciao (hello, goodbye), 10, 16, 40, 44, 319
cibo (food), 16
ciclismo (cycling), 198
cinema (cinema), 14, 117, 154
cinema, going to, 154–156
cinquanta centesimi (50 cents), 78
cintura (belt), 147
cioccolata (chocolate), 16, 126
cioccolata calda (hot cocoa), 121
circa (about), 237
città (city), 19
ciuccio (baby's pacifier), 16
clarinetto (clarinet), 205
classica (classical), 203
cleaning, 99–100
cognates, 11
colazione (breakfast), 258
collant (tights/pantyhose), 147
colloquio (interview), 189
color, 145
colori (colors), 145
Colosseo (Colosseum), 318
colpa (guilt), 16
coltello/i (knife/knives), 97
come (how), 294
come, scusi/a (I beg your pardon), 112
come al solito (as usual), 77
come ti trovi (how do you like), 300
cominciare (to start), 153
commessa/commesso (sales clerk), 141
communicazione (communication), 11
comò (dresser), 94
comodino (nightstand), 94
compagnia (company), 186, 307
compleanno (birthday), 80
completo (outfit), 142
concert, going to, 162–164
concerto (concert), 163
condominio (condominum building), 87

coniglio (rabbit), 132
cono (cone), 131
consegna bagagli (baggage claim), 240
consigliare (to recommend), 300
consonants, 15–19
contanti (cash), 226, 228
conto (bill), 125
conto corrente (checking account), 223
contorni (side dishes), 127
controlli l'olio (check the oil), 245
controllo passaporti (passport control), 239
conventions, explained, 1–2
cooking, 98–99
coppetta (cup), 131
coprire (to cover), 335
corriera (bus), 249
corsia di emergenza (emergency lane), 286
corta/e/o/i (short), 148, 284
cosa (what), 294
cosa le fa male (what hurts you), 275
costa di più (it costs more), 90
costa meno (it costs less), 90
costa poco (it costs little), 90
costruire (to build), 344
costume da bagno (bathing suit), 142
cotone (cotton), 146
counting, 63–66
countries, 56–58
cozze (mussels), 133
cravatta (tie), 147
credenza (credenza), 94
credit cards, 226–228
crema (custard), 126
crema solare (sun protection lotion), 296
crepi il lupo (may the wolf die), 327
cucchiaio/chucchiai (spoon/s), 97
cucina (kitchen), 88, 93–94
cucinare (to cook), 98, 333
culla (crib), 258

cuocere (to cook), 345
cuore (heart), 16
currencies, 228–231
cuscini (pillows), 94
customer care, 360
customs, 240–241

• D •

da morire (deadly), 75
da quanto tempo (how long), 300
d'accordo (agreed, okay), 12, 40
dai (you give), 15
dal giornalaio (at newspaper stands), 249
danno (damage), 288
dare (to give), 15, 32, 34, 337
dat tabaccaio (tobacco shop), 249
dates, making, 68–72
davanti a (in front of), 95, 106
days of the week, 66–68
decidere (to decide), 345
definite articles
    relationship with gender, 24–25
    when clothes shopping, 144
demonstrative adjectives, 263
dentifricio (toothpaste), 296
dentista (dentist), 277
dentists, 279
dentro (inside), 95, 106
denunciare (to report), 283, 288
department stores, 139–142
desidera (can I be of help, can I
    help you), 141
destinazione (destination), 240
destro/a (right), 274
di fronte a (opposite), 106
di lato (on its side), 95
di mattina (in the morning), 70
di media statura (of medium build), 283
di pomeriggio (in the afternoon), 70
di sera (in the evening), 70
dichiarare (to declare), 243

diciannove (nineteen), 64
diciassette (seventeen), 64
diciotto (eighteen), 64
dietro a (behind), 95, 106
dietro l'angolo (around the corner), 106
digitare (to enter), 228
dining out
    about, 123–124
    making reservations, 124–125
    paying for meals, 125–126
    sales slips, 126
dinner, 129–132
dire (to say, tell), 32, 33, 337
directions, asking for
    Fun and Games, 118
    locations, 113–117
    specific places, 103–109
    Talkin' the Talk, 105, 107, 108–109,
        111–112, 114, 115
    verbs, 109–113
direttore (manager, director), 309, 311
disegnare (to draw), 333
distance, 78
ditta (company), 186, 300, 307
diva (diva), 15
divano (couch), 93
divertente (fun), 153
divertirsi (to enoy oneself, to have a
    good time), 195, 305, 336
doccia (shower), 88, 94
doctors, talking to, 272–277
documento (identification), 174
dodici (twelve), 64
dogana (customs), 243
dolce/i (sweet/s), 14, 127, 134
dollaro/dollari (dollar/dollars), 230
domanda (question), 40
domanda d'assunzione (job
    application), 189
domani (tomorrow), 14, 67, 125, 231
dopo (after), 106
dopodomani (day after tomorrow), 67

doppiati (dubbed), 154
dormire (to sleep), 335
dottore (doctor), 277
double consonants, 18–19
dove (where), 40, 153, 294
dov'è (where is), 261
dove sono (where are), 261
dovere (to have to, must, need to),
37, 338
drinking, 119–123, 120–121
dritto (straight), 106
due (two), 63
duemila (two thousand), 64
duomo (cathedral), 109

• E •

e chi se ne importa (who cares), 12, 20
È lo stesso (It's all the same, It doesn't
matter), 12
È rotto (It's broken), 189
eating, 119
ecco (here you go, here it is), 32
eccome (very), 329
economico (cheap), 90
elenco telefonico (phone book), 176
elettrodomestici (household
appliances), 95
emergencies
about, 271–272
car trouble, 285–286
dentist, 279
doctors, 272–277
Fun & Games, 291
lawyers, 287–288
lost or stolen passports, 288–290
pharmacy, 277–279
repoting accidents to police, 280–281
robberies, 281–284
Talkin' the Talk, 275, 278–279, 280, 282,
285–286, 289–290

emergenza (emergency), 281
English words, in Italian language, 9–10
entrata (entrance), 140, 240
esame (exam), 26
esaurito (sold out), 163
espresso, 120–121
essere (to be)
about, 30, 295, 335
passato prossimo with, 183, 185
past participles using, 186
est (east), 105
estate (summer), 73, 121
estratto conto (bank statement), 223
etto (100 grams), 135
ettogrammo (hectogram), 78
euro, 228-230
Euro City (EC) trains, 246
Euro Star train, 246
excess baggage, 236
expressions, favorite, 323–325

• F •

fabbrica (factory), 309, 311
faccia il pieno (fill it up), 245
"false friends," 320, 321
famiglia (family), 19, 300-301
fantastico (fanstastic), 12
fare (to do, to make), 15, 32, 33, 198, 338
fare benzina (to gas up), 245
fare male (to hurt), 273, 276
farmacia (pharmacy), 277
fazzolettino di carta (tissue), 260
febbre (fever), 276
ferito (injured person), 281
fermare (to stop), 286
fermata (bus stop), 113
festa (party), 164, 170
Festival dei due mondi, 162
festivals, going to, 161–162
fettuccine (narrow, flat noodles), 128
fine settimana (weekend/s), 191

finestra (window), 88
finiamo (let's finish), 267
finire (to end), 153, 267, 344
finisca/i/ite (finish), 267
fino a (to, up to), 106
fiore (flower), 192
fiume (river), 193, 212
flauto (flute), 205
fodera (lining), 146
fon (blow dryer), 259
food
  breakfast, 126–127
  dining out, 123–126
  dinner, 129–132
  drinking, 119–123
  eating, 119
  faux pas, 321
  Fun & Games, 137
  lunch, 127–129
  ordering in Italian, 316
  shopping for, 132–136
  Talkin' the Talk, 122, 123, 124–125,
    126–127, 130, 131–132, 134–135
food labels, reading, 315
forchetta/e (fork/s), 97
formal, compared with friendly, 45
Formula 1 (Formula One car racing), 198
fornelli (stove-top), 95
forno (oven), 95
fotocopia (photocopy), 187
fotocopiatrice (photocopier), 187
francese (French), 25
francobolli (stamps), 218
frappé (fruit milk shake, frozen
    fruit shake), 132
friendly, compared with formal, 45
frigorifero (refrigerator), 93, 95, 259
frullati (mixed fruit juice), 132
frullatore (blender), 95
frutta (fruit), 15
frutta fresca (fresh fruit), 127
frutti di mare (shell fish), 133

Fun & Games
  accommodations, 269
  Answer Key, 361–367
  basics, 41
  business and telecommuting, 190
  clothes shopping, 150
  directions, asking for, 118
  emergencies, 291
  food, 137
  home, 102
  money, 232
  nightlife, 171
  numbers and time, 81
  recreation and the outdoors, 206
  salutations, 61
  small talk, 312
  transportation, 254
  trip planning, 219
funghi porcini (porcini mushrooms), 78
funzionare (to work, function), 228
fuori (outside), 95, 106
furnishings, 92–95
furto (theft), 283
fusili (spiral-shaped pasta), 128
future tense, 37
futuro semplice (simple future), 217–218

• **G** •

gallima (chicken), 194
gallo (rooster), 194
gamba (leg), 17
gamberetti (small shrimp), 133
gamberi (prawns), 133
garage (garage, car park), 88, 266
gatto (cat), 194
gelateria (ice cream shop), 131
gelato (ice-cream), 40, 131
gelato artigianale (homemade
    ice cream), 131
gelosia (jealousy), 17, 18
gemello/a (twin), 300

gendered words, 22–26
gentile (kind), 17
gestures, 20
ghiaccio (ice), 17, 121
ghirlanda (wreath), 17
giacca (jacket), 17, 142
giallo (yellow), 145
giocare (to play), 29, 197, 198, 205, 321, 333
gioco (game), 17
giornale (newspaper), 316
giorni feriali (weekdays), 252
giorni festivi (Sundays and holidays), 252
giorno (day), 17, 80
gira/giri/girate/girino (turn), 110
girare (to endorse), 223
girare a destra/a sinistra (to turn right/ left), 109
gita (tour), 212
gita orgaanizzata (organized tour), 211
giudice (judge), 17
gli (the), 19
gli inquilini (tenants), 88
gomma (rubber), 17
gomma a terra (flat tire), 286
gonfia/o (swollen), 276
gonna (skirt), 142
good-byes, common, 43–46
gradi (degrees), 77
grammo/i (gram, grams), 78
grande (big), 25, 142
grandi magazzini (department stores), 139
grassa (fat), 283
greetings
  common, 43–46
  replying to, 45–46
grembiule (apron), 93
grigi/io (gray), 145, 284
guanti (gloves), 147
Guardia di Finanza (Financial Guard), 126

guerra (war), 17
guida (guide), 212
gusto (flavor), 131

● *H* ●

ho bisogno di (I need), 141
ho fame (I'm hungry), 20
home
  appliances, 95–98
  cooking and cleaning, 98–99
  directions to, 85–86
  finding apartments, 87–91
  Fun and Games, 102
  furnishing apartments, 92–95
  household chores, 100–101
  Talkin' the Talk, 89, 90–91, 92, 96–97, 98–99, 100
  types, 87

● *I* ●

i mobili (furniture), 93
i padroni di casa (landlords), 88
i palchi (box seats), 156
i pensili (cabinets), 94
icons, explained, 4–5
ieri (yesterday), 67
il bagno (bar/beach/club/restaurant), 217
il (platto) fondo (bowl for soup or pasta), 97
il mio (mine), 264
il mio babbo/il mio papa (my dad), 310
Il Museo della Scienza e della Tecnica, 160
il (il piatto) piano (flat dish), 97
il più presto possible (as soon as possible), 286
il secondo (second course), 127
imbarco (boarding), 236
imparare (to learn), 333
imperatives, 267–268

impermeabile (raincoat), 142
imporre (to impose), 339
importante (important), 11
in bocca al lupo (in the wolf's
    mouth), 327
in orario (on time), 237
in padella (in the skillet), 133
in piazza (on the public square), 151
in ritardo (late, delayed), 237
in treno (by train), 215
incidente (accident), 281
incidente stradale (traffic accident), 288
incredibile (incredible), 11
indefinite articles
    relationship with gender, 23–24
    when clothes shopping, 144
indirizzo (address), 261
infermiera (female nurse), 277
infermiere (male nurse), 277
informazione (information), 182
infusi (herbal tea), 121
innamorarsi (to fall in love), 336
insegnante (teacher), 40, 311
insieme (together), 163
Inter City (IC) trains, 246
interferire (to interfere), 344
Internet, 174–175, 318
interprete (interpreter), 272
interrogative pronouns, 293–300
intimo donna (ladies' intimate
    apparel), 140
intimo uomo (men's intimate
    apparel), 140
introductions, making, 47–52
inverno (winter), 73
investire (to invest), 222
invitare (to invite), 164
invitations, 60
invito (invitation), 164, 169–170
io (I), 27
irregular past participles, 345
irregular verbs, 30–37, 336–343

Italia (Italy), 318
Italian films, 153, 316
Italian language tapes, listening to, 317
Italian publications, reading, 316
Italian radio, 317
Italian Verbs For Dummies (Picarazzi), 345
Italian words, in English language, 10–11
Italianfoodnet.com, 318
italiano (Italian), 25

• J •

jeans (jeans), 142

• L •

La dolce vita (film), 153
La festa dell'Unita, 161
La sagra del cinghiale (the wild board
    festival), 161
La sagra del pesce azzurro (the Blue
    Fish Fair), 161
La Scala, 159
la spiaggia (the beach), 209
La strada (film), 153
La vita è bella (film), 153
Ladri di biciclette (film), 153
ladro (thief), 15
lago (lake), 193, 212
lampada (lamp), 94
lana (wool), 146
lunga/ghe/go/ghi (long), 148
larga/ghe/go/ghi (loose), 148
largo (wide square), 107
lascia perdere (let it go, forget
    about it), 329
lastre (x-rays), 276
latte (milk), 132
lavandino (sink), 94
lavare i pavimenti (to wash the
    floors), 101

lavarsi (to wash oneself), 196, 336

lavastoviglie (dishwasher), 94, 95

lavatrice (washing machine), 95

lavello (sink), 94

lavero (job), 187

lavorare (to work), 307, 333

lavoro (work), 189, 311

lawyers, 287–288

leggere (to read), 334, 345

lei (she, you), 15, 27, 28, 45

length, 78

lentamente (slowly), 113

lenti a contatto (contact lenses), 281

lenzuolo/lenzuola (sheet/sheets), 94

Leonardo da Vinci airport, 215

lettere (letters), 218

letters, sending, 218

lettino (cot, lounge chair), 217, 260

letto (bed), 94

letto supplementare (extra bed), 258

libero professionista (self-employed), 187

libretto (registration), 288

libretto degli assegni (checkbook), 223

libro (book), 26

lino (linen), 146

lira/e sterlina/e (pound/pounds), 230

lisci (straight), 284

listening to Italian language tapes, 317

literal, being, 320

litro (liter), 78

lo sci alpino (downhill ski racing), 198

lo yogurt (frozen yogurt), 132

loggione (gallery), 156

loro (they), 27

lost luggage, 241–243

luggage, lost, 241–243

lui (he), 27

luna (moon), 15

lunch, 127–129

lunedì (Monday), 19

lunghi (long), 284

lupo (wolf), 194

● M ●

macché (of course not, certainly not), 328

macchina (car, machine), 113, 189, 286, 288

macedonia (fruit salad), 127

madre (mother), 15

magari (if only, I'd love it), 324

maglia (sweater), 142

maglietta (T-shirt), 142

magra (thin), 283

maiale (pig, pork), 132, 194

Malpensa airport, 215

mamma mia (my goodness), 323

mandare (to send), 267

mandiamo (let's send), 267

mandi/manda/mandate (send), 267

mangiare (to eat), 29, 333

mansarda (attic), 88

manzo (beef), 132

maps, public transportation, 251–252

marciapiede (sidewalk), 107

mare (sea), 193, 212

marmellata (jam), 14, 126

marrone/i (brown), 145, 285

me ne vado (I'm leaving), 20

meccanico (mechanic), 286

medicina (medicine), 277

medico (doctor), 272, 277, 311

merenda (snack-time), 119

merluzzo (cod), 133

mese (month), 80

messaggino (text message), 174, 178, 189

messaggio (message), 266

mezzo litro (half liter), 78

metric system, 77–80

metro (meter), 78

mettere (to put), 334, 345

mettere in ordine (to straighten up), 101

mettersi (to put on/to wear), 196, 336

mettete in ordine le vostre camere
(clean up your rooms), 267

mezza pensione (half board), 255, 258

mezz'etto (50 grams), 135

mezzo (half), 135

mezzo chilo (half a kilo), 135

mi (me), 275

mi aiuti, per favore (help me,
please), 271

mi gira la testa (I'm dizzy), 276

mi placciono (I like [something
plural]), 40

mi piace (I like [something singular]), 40

mi può aiutare, per favore (can you
help me, please), 141

mi raccomando (please, I beg you), 325

mi scusi, non ho capito (I'm sorry, I
didn't understand), 112

mi scusi/ino (excuse me), 103

mi sento male (I feel sick), 274

mi sento svenire (I'm about to faint), 276

mi sono persa (I'm lost), 40

mia mamma (my mom), 310

mia sorella (my sister), 301

microonde (microwave oven), 95

mila (one thousand), 64

mille grazie (thank you very much), 112

milligrammo (milligram), 78

millilitro (millileter), 78

millimetro (millimeter), 78

minuto (minute), 113

misura (size), 148

mite (mild), 77

moda (fashion), 139

modulo (form), 243

money
  banks, 221–223
  changing, 224–226
  credit cards, 226–228
  currencies, 228–231
  Fun & Games, 232

Talkin' the Talk, 222–223, 224–225,
  226–227, 227–228, 229, 230–231

monolocali (studio apartments), 87

montagna (mountain), 193, 209, 212

morire (to die), 338, 345

moto GP (motorcycle racing), 198

motorino (moped), 283

movies, going to, 154–156

mucca (cow), 194

multisala (multiplex), 155

muscolo (muscle), 276

Musei Vaticani, 160

museo (museum), 163

museums, going to, 160–161

musica (music), 163

musicisti (musicians), 162

• N •

nascere (to be born), 345

naso corto (short nose), 284

naso lungo (long nose), 284

nationalities, 56–57

nazione (nation), 18

neanche per sogno (no way), 328

nebbia (fog), 77

negozio di regali (gift shop), 260

neorealismo (neorealism), 316

neri/o (black, dark), 145, 284

niente (nothing), 243

nightlife
  culture, 151–152
  Fun & Games, 171
  going to a concert, 162–164
  going to a local festival, 161–162
  going to a museum, 160–161
  going to the movies, 154–155
  going to the theater, 156–159
  Italian films, 153
  suggesting activities, 164–171
  Talkin' the Talk, 152–153, 154–155,
    155–156, 157, 158–159, 160–161,
    161–162, 162–163, 165, 166, 168

no (no), 15
noi (we), 15, 27
non capisco (I don't understand), 297
non c'è di che (You're welcome), 12
non è caro (it's not expensive), 90
non fa niente (Don't worry about it, It doesn't matter), 12
non lo so (I don't know), 297, 300
non mi sento bene (I don't feel well), 274
non mi va (I don't feel like it), 325
non te la prendere (Don't get so upset), 324
nonno (grandfather), 18
nono (ninth), 18
nord (north), 105
nouns, relationship with gender, 22–23
numbers and time
  calendar, 68–72
  days of the week, 66–68
  making dates, 68–72
  metric system, 77–80
  numbers, 63–66
  ordinals, 85–87
  times of day, 66–68, 70–72
  weather, 72–77
numeri ordinali (ordinal numbers), 85
numero (number), 80, 113, 148
numero di telefono (telephone number), 176

● *O* ●

occhio (eye), 19
office equipment, 187
oggi (today), 67
ognuno (each person), 101
ombrello (umbrella), 147
ombrellone (beach umbrella), 217
ondulati (wavy), 284
opporsi (to oppose), 339
orario (timetable), 252
orario di apertura (business hours), 140

orata (sea bream), 133
ordering food in Italian, 316
organization of this book, 3–4
ospedale (hospital), 117, 272, 276
otto (eight), 63
outdoors and recreation
  Fun & Games, 206
  hobbies and interests, 200–205
  reflexive verbs, 195–196
  sports, 196–200
  taking tours, 191–194
  Talkin' the Talk, 193–194, 196, 199–200, 202, 203, 204
ovest (west), 106

● *P* ●

padre (father), 15
padrone (boss, owner), 309
pagare (to pay), 243
pagine gialle (yellow page), 176
paio di scarpe (pair of shoes), 148
pallacanestro (basketball), 191
pallavolo (volleyball), 191
palline (scoops), 131
pane (bread), 134
pane e coperto (cover/service charge), 125
panetteria (breadshop), 134–135
panorama (view), 192
pantaloni (pants), 142
pantofole (slippers), 148
parla/i inglese (do you speak English), 53
parla/i italiano (do you speak Italian), 53
parlare (to speak), 27, 29, 333
parlo un po' (I speak a little bit), 53
parrucchiere (hairdresser), 260
partenza/e (departure/s), 240, 252
partire (to leave), 27, 29, 216, 305, 334
partita (game), 300
passaporto (passport), 215, 236, 239

passare la scopa (to sweep), 101
passare l'aspirapolvere (to vaccum), 101
passato prossimo (compound past
   tense), 182–183
passports, 215, 288–290
past participles, irregular, 345
past tense, 37
pasta (pasta, pastry), 18, 126, 127
pasta all'uovo (egg noodles), 128
pasta fatta in casa (home-made
   pasta), 128
pasta fresca (fresh pasta), 128
pastore (shepherd), 80
patente (driver's license), 243, 288
pattinare (to skate), 197
pausa (break), 40
pecora (sheep), 194
pedalò (paddle boat), 217
peggio per te (too bad for you,
   tough luck), 328
pelle (leather), 146
penne (short, cylinder-shaped
   pasta), 128
pensione completa (full board), 255, 258
pensioni (small hotels), 255
per favore (please), 18, 103, 259
per quando (for when), 246
perché (why), 19, 165, 170, 294
perdere (to lose), 345
periferia (suburbs), 87
permesso (may I pass, come in), 12
permettersi (to afford), 336
però (but), 19
personal pronouns, 27
pesce (fish), 127, 133
pesce spada (swordfish), 133
peseta/pesetas (peseta/pesetas), 230
peso (weight), 14
pharmacies, 277–279
phones, 171–179
phrases, favorite, 327–329
piacere (to like), 201, 338–339
piano (floor), 85
pianoforte (piano), 163, 205

pianta (plant), 192
piantala (stop it, cut it out), 329
piatto/i (dish/dishes), 97
piazza (square), 107, 109
Picarazzi, Teresa (author)
   Italian Verbs For Dummies, 345
piccionaia (pigeonhouse), 156
piccolo (little, small), 14, 142
pino (pine), 192
piove (it's raining), 77
piscina (pool), 88, 260
pizza al taglio (slices of pizza), 134
piantina (map), 40
platea (orchestra), 156
pollo (chicken), 132
polpo/polipo (octopus), 133
poltrona (arm-chair), 93
pomata (cream), 281
ponte (bridge), 107, 109, 117
popular expressions, 11–12
porre (to put), 339
portacenere (ashtray), 260
portare fuori la spazzatura (to take
   out the garbage), 101
portiere (doorman), 266
possessives, 263–266, 300–304
posso dare un'occhiata (Is it all right
   if I just look), 141
postcards, sending, 218
potere (can, to be able to), 37, 339
pranzo (lunch), 119, 127
prato (meadow, lawn), 192
preferire (to prefer), 344
prego (you're welcome, thank you,
   can I help you, please, here you
   are sir), 18, 129
prelevare (to withdraw), 228
prelevare contanti (to withdraw
   money), 221
prendere (to take), 29, 110, 127, 231,
   267, 334, 345
prendiamo (let's take/have), 267
prendi/prenda/prendete/prendano
   (take), 110, 267

prenotare/fare una prenotazione
(to make a reservation), 256
prenotazione (reservation), 125
present tense, 37
preservativi (condoms), 320
presto (early, soon), 298, 300
prezzo (price), 140
prima (before), 106
prima colazione (breakfast), 119, 126
primavera (spring), 73
primo piatto (first course), 127
profumeria (perfumery), 140, 278
pronouns
  demonstrative adjectives and, 263
  formal and informal 'you', 27–28
  interrogative, 293–300
  personal, 27
  possessive, 263–266, 300–304
pronto (hello, ready), 173, 182, 298, 300
pronto soccorso (emergency room),
  276, 298
pronunciation, basic
  about, 12–13
  alphabet, 13
  consonants, 15–19
  vowels, 13–15
proporre (to propose, suggest), 339
proseguire/prosegui/prosegua/
  proseguite/proseguano (continue
  on), 110
prova (test), 26
public transportation
  bus or tram, 249–251
  maps and schedules, 251–252
  taxis, 245–246
  train, 246–249
pugilato (boxing), 198
pulire (to clean), 101, 344
pullman/pulmino (bus), 249
può ripetere per favore (would you
  repeat that please), 261

può ripetere più lentamente, per favore
(would you please repeat it more
slowly), 112

• Q •

quadro (picture), 17
quale/i (which, what), 294
quando (when), 80, 153, 294
quanti anni ha (how old is...), 40
quanti/e (how many), 80, 294
quanto (how much), 80, 294
quanto vengono (how much is it), 135
quattordici (fourteen), 64
quattro (four), 17
quattro stagioni (four seasons), 72
quercia (oak), 192
questo (this), 17, 263
questura (police headquarters), 283
quindici (fifteen), 64
quintale (quintal), 78

• R •

racchettone (beach tennis), 217
radio (radio), 18
ragazze (girls), 199
ragazzo/a/i (boy/boys), 26, 199
rasato (clean-shaven), 284
reading
  food labels, 315
  Italian publications, 316
recreation and the outdoors
  Fun & Games, 206
  hobbies and interests, 200–205
  reflexive verbs, 195–196
  sports, 196–200
  taking tours, 191–194
  Talkin' the Talk, 193–194, 196,
    199–200, 202, 203, 204
reflexive verbs, 195–196, 305–311, 336
regista (director), 156

regular verbs, 28–30
reparti (departments), 140
reserving rooms, 256–258
responsabile (responsible), 189
ricci (curly), 284
ricetta (prescription and recipe), 281
ricevuta/e (receipt/s), 232, 243
rifugi (mountain huts), 255
rigatoni (short-cylinder-shaped, and
    grooved pasta), 128
rimanere (to stay, to remain), 215, 339
ripetere (to repeat), 29, 334
riposarsi (to rest), 195, 305
riscuotere (to cash), 223, 226
riscuotere un assegno (to cash a
    check), 221
risotto (risotto), 127
rispondere (to reply, respond, answer),
    345
ritorno (return trip), 249
robberies, 281–284
Roma, città aperta (film), 153
rooms, reserving, 256–258
rosa (pink), 145
rossi/o (red), 145, 284
rotonda (rotary), 109

• S •

sagre (town celebrations relating to
    harvest, wild boar, or saints), 151,
    161
sala di pranzo (dining room), 88
salata (savory), 126
saldare il conto (to check out), 261
saldi (sales), 140
saldi alla cassa (reduction at cash
    register), 140
sale (salt), 14
salire (to go up), 340
salutations
    body language, 46

common greetings and good-byes,
    43–46
Fun and Games, 61
getting acquainted, 53–60
introductions, 47–52
invitations, 60
Talkin' the Talk, 48, 49–50, 51, 52, 53–54,
    54–55, 55–56, 59, 60
salute (bless you, health), 328
salve (hello, goodbye), 44
San Carlo, 159
sandali (sandals), 148
santo patrono (patron saint), 151
sapere (to know), 340
sassofono (saxophone), 205
scaffale (bookshelf), 93
scala (scale), 19
scala mobile (escalator), 140
scarpe (shoes), 148
scegliere (to choose), 340
scena (scene), 19, 156
scesa (descent), 19
scheda telefonica (phone card), 174
schedules, public transportation,
    251–252
sciarpa (scarf), 147
scimmia (monkey), 19
sciopero (strike), 309, 311
scippare (to snatch a handbag), 283
scippo (theft of a handbag), 283
scogliere (to melt), 345
sconto (discount), 19
scontrino (sales slip), 121, 126
scopa (broom), 97
scrivere (to write), 334, 345
scuola (school), 19
scuri (dark), 284
scusi/scusa/scusate (excuse me, sorry),
    11, 103, 259
sedersi (to sit), 341
sedici (sixteen), 64
sedie (chairs), 94

seguire (to follow), 110
segui/segua/seguite/seguano (follow), 110
semaforo (traffic light), 109
semplice (plain, simple), 126
sempre dritto (straight ahead), 106
sending letters and postcards, 218
señorita (miss, Spanish), 19
sentences, simple, 21
sentire (to hear, feel, taste, touch), 335
sentirsi (to feel), 336
seppia (cuttlefish), 133
servizio in camera (room service), 258
servizio sveglia (wake-up call), 258
seta (silk), 146
shoe sizes, 148
shopping, for clothing
  accessorizing, 147
  color, 145
  definite and indefinite articles, 144
  department store and boutiques, 139–142
  Fun & Games, 150
  sizes, 143, 148
  Talkin' the Talk, 141, 143–144, 145–146, 147–148, 149
shopping for food, 132–136
siamo arrivati presto (we arrived early), 298
simple future tense, 217–218
sinistro/a (left), 274, 276
sizes (clothing), 143, 148
Skype, 174–175
small talk
  Fun & Games, 312
  interrogative pronouns, 293–300
  possessives, 300–304
  reflexive verbs, 305–311
  Talkin' the Talk, 297–299, 302–304, 309–310
soccorso stradale (roadside assistance), 286

società (company), 186, 307
soggiorno (living room), 88, 93
sogliola (sole), 133
sole (sun), 14
solo (only), 18
soluzione (solution), 281
songs, listening to in Italian, 316
sono americano (I'm American), 58
sopra (on top of), 95, 106
sorpresa (surprise), 182
sotto (under), 95, 106
sottopassaggio (underpass), 107
spa, 217
spaghetti (spaghetti), 17, 128
sparecchiare (to clear the table), 97
specialista (specialist), 277
spettacolo (show), 153
spiaggia (beach), 19, 209
spiccioli (small change), 226
spigola (snapper), 133
spingere (to push), 140
spolverare (to dust), 101
sports, 196–200
spremuta (fresh-squeezed fruit juice), 121
stanza (room), 88, 256, 258
stare (to stay, to be), 341
stasera (this evening, tonight), 40, 125
stazione (station), 109, 117
sterlina/e (pound/pounds), 230
stilisti (designers), 139
stipendio (salary), 309, 311
stivali (boots), 148
stomaco (stomach), 276
strada (street), 85, 107
strada principale (main street), 109
stressing words, 19–20
stretta/e/o/i (tight), 148
studente (male student), 26
studentessa (female student), 26
studiare (to study), 333
studio (office, study), 88

stupendo (wonderful, fabulous), 12
subaffittare (sublet), 88
succhi di frutta (fruit juice), 121
sud (south), 106
suonare (to play [a musical
    instrument]), 170, 203, 205, 321
supermercato (supermarket), 132
supplemento (supplement, surcharge),
    237, 246, 249
svegliarsi (to wake up), 195, 196, 305
svendite (sales), 140

• *T* •

tabaccaio (tobacconist), 174, 218
tacchino (turkey), 194
tacere (to be silent), 341
taglia (size), 148
tagliatelle (flat noodles), 128
tailleur (skirt or pants and jacket), 142
Talkin' the Talk
    accommodations, 255, 257–258,
        260–261, 265–266
    basics, 31, 35–36, 37–38
    business and telecommunicating, 175,
        176–177, 178–179, 180, 181,
        184–185, 188
    days of the week, 67
    directions, asking for, 105, 107, 108–109,
        111–112, 114, 115
    emergencies, 275, 278–279, 280, 282,
        285–286, 289–290
    food, 122, 123, 124–125, 126–127, 130,
        131–132, 134–135
    home, 89, 90–91, 92, 96–97, 98–99, 100
    metric system, 78–80
    money, 222–223, 224–225, 226–227,
        227–228, 229, 230–231
    nightlife, 152–153, 154–155, 155–156,
        157, 158–159, 160–161, 161–162,
        162–163, 165, 166, 168
    numbers, 78–80

    recreaton and the outdoors, 193–194,
        196, 199–200, 202, 203, 204
    Salutations, 48, 49–50, 51, 52, 53–54,
        54–55, 55–56, 59, 60
    shopping, for clothing, 141, 143–144,
        145–146, 147–148, 149
    small talk, 297–299, 302–304, 309–310
    times of day, 72
    transportation, 234–235, 237, 238–239,
        241–242, 244–245, 247, 248, 249–250,
        250–251
    trip planning, 210, 211–212, 213–214, 216
    weather, 73–74, 74–75, 76
tamponi (tampons), 297
tappeto (rug), 93
tardi (late), 189
targa (license plate), 288
tartufi (truffles), 78
tasse (taxes, tuition), 311
tasso d'interesse (interest rate), 223
tavolino (small table), 122
tavolo (table), 94, 125
taxi (taxi), 245
taxis, 245–246
tazza (cup, mug, toilet bowl), 18, 94
tè (tea), 121
tè freddo (iced tea), 121
teatro (theater), 117
telecommunicating and business
    asking for people, 173–190
    discussing your job, 186–189
    Fun & Games, 190
    getting messages, 179–182
    making arrangements over phones,
        178–179
    past tense, 182–186
    phones, 173–178
    Talkin' the Talk, 175, 176–177, 178–179,
        180, 181, 184–185, 188
telefonino (cellphone), 174, 178
telefono pubblico (public phone), 178
tempo (time), 189

tempo incerto (uncertain weather), 77
tempo libero (free time), 200
tende (curtains), 94
tendine (tendon), 276
tenere (to hold), 342
tennis (tennis), 191
tense
  future, 37
  past, 37
  present, 37
  simple future tense, 217–218
terme (thermal springs), 217
text messaging, 174
theater, going to, 156–159
ti godi (you enjoy), 192
ti interessa/mi interessa (you're
    interested in/I'm interested in), 311
ti sta bene (serves you right, it looks
    good on you), 324
times of day, 70–72
tirare (to pull), 140
togliere (to take away), 342
tonnarelli (tubular noodles), 128
tonnellata (ton), 78
tonno fresco (fresh tuna), 133
tornare indietro (to go back), 110
torna/torni/tornate/tornino
    (go back), 110
tostapane (toaster), 95
tours, taking, 191–194, 211–212
tovaglia (table-cloth), 97
tovagliolo/i (napkin/s), 97
traffico (traffic), 286
traghetto (ferry), 215
trains, 246–249
tram (tram), 249
trama (plot), 156
tramonto (sunset), 192
trams, 249–251
transportation
  airports, 233–240
  car rentals, 243–245

customs, 240–241
  early or late, 253
  Fun & Games, 254
  lost luggage, 241–243
  public, navigating, 245–252
  Talkin' the Talk, 234–235, 237, 238–239,
    241–242, 244–245, 247, 248, 249–250,
    250–251
trasferisi (to move from one city to
    another), 88
traslocare (change houses), 88
trattoria (little restaurant), 124
trecentoventidue (three hundred and
    twenty-two), 63
tredici (thirteen), 64
treno (train), 15
treno rapido (express train), 246
trip planning
  arrivare (to arrive), 216
  beach and spa, 217
  booking trips, 213–215
  Fun & Games, 219
  partire (to leave), 27, 29, 216, 305, 334
  sending letters and postcards, 218
  simple future tense, 217–218
  taking tours, 211–212
  Talkin' the Talk, 210, 211–212,
    213–214, 216
  when and where, 209–210
tromba (trumpet), 205
tu (you), 15, 27, 28, 47
TV programs, 317
24-hour clock, 71

• **U** •

uccello (bird), 194
uffa (showing annoyance), 324
ufficio di cambio (exchange office), 224
ufficio postale (post office), 109, 218
ufficio/i (office/offices), 186, 307
Uffizi, 160

Umbria Jazz Festival, 162
umido (humid), 77
undici (eleven), 64
università (university), 20
uno (one), 63
uno sputino (a snack), 119
uscire (to go out), 32, 35, 342
uscita (exit, gate), 140, 236
uscita di sicurezza (emergency exit), 140
uso personale (personal use), 243

• V •

va bene (okay), 12, 40
vacanza (vacation), 240
vacci piano (slow down), 329
valigia (suitcase), 236, 266
vasca da bagno (bath tub), 88, 94
va/vada/vadano (go), 110
vedere (to see), 334, 345
velluto (velvet), 146
vendere (to sell), 334
vendesi (for sale), 93
Venezia (Venice), 318
venga nel mio ufficio (come in my office), 267
vengo dall'America (I'm from America), 58
venire (to come), 32, 33, 343
venti (twenty), 63
ventidue (twenty-two), 63
verbs. *See also specific verbs*
  directional, 109–111
  -ire with special patterns, 343–344
  irregular, 30, 32, 336–343
  reflexive, 195–196, 305–311, 336
  regular, 28–30
verde/i (green), 25, 145, 284
versare soldi sul tuo conto (to deposit money into your account), 221
vestirsi (get dressed, to dress oneself), 305

vestiti (clothes), 142
vestito (dress), 142
via (street), 85, 107
via principale (main street), 107
viaggiare (to travel), 215
viaggio (trip), 231
viaggio organizzato (organized trip), 215
viale (parkway, avenue), 107
vicino a (beside, next to), 106
vicolo (alley, lane), 107
villaggi turistici (resorts), 255
vino/i (wine/wines), 15, 121
viola (purple), 145
violino (violin), 205
violoncello (cello), 205
virtù (virtue), 20
visas, 215
viscosa (rayon), 146
visibilità (visibility), 77
visto (visa), 215
vita (life), 14
vitello (veal), 132
vivere (to live), 27, 29, 334, 345
voce (voice), 205
voi (you), 27
volere (to want), 37, 343
volo (flight), 215, 237
vongole (clams), 133
vorrei (I would like), 297, 300
vowels, 13–15

• W •

watching Italian movies, 316
weather, 72–77
weight, 78

• X •

xenofobia (xenophobia), 16
xilofono (xylophone), 16

le & Macs

d For Dummies
-0-470-58027-1

one For Dummies,
Edition
-0-470-87870-5

cBook For Dummies, 3rd
tion
-0-470-76918-8

c OS X Snow Leopard For
mmies
-0-470-43543-4

siness

okkeeping For Dummies
-0-7645-9848-7

b Interviews
r Dummies,
d Edition
-0-470-17748-8

sumes For Dummies,
Edition
-0-470-08037-5

arting an
line Business
r Dummies,
h Edition
8-0-470-60210-2

ock Investing
r Dummies,
d Edition
8-0-470-40114-9

uccessful
me Management
r Dummies
8-0-470-29034-7

Computer Hardware

BlackBerry
For Dummies,
4th Edition
978-0-470-60700-8

Computers For Seniors
For Dummies,
2nd Edition
978-0-470-53483-0

PCs For Dummies,
Windows
7 Edition
978-0-470-46542-4

Laptops For Dummies,
4th Edition
978-0-470-57829-2

Cooking & Entertaining

Cooking Basics
For Dummies,
3rd Edition
978-0-7645-7206-7

Wine For Dummies,
4th Edition
978-0-470-04579-4

Diet & Nutrition

Dieting For Dummies,
2nd Edition
978-0-7645-4149-0

Nutrition For Dummies,
4th Edition
978-0-471-79868-2

Weight Training
For Dummies,
3rd Edition
978-0-471-76845-6

Digital Photography

Digital SLR Cameras &
Photography For Dummies,
3rd Edition
978-0-470-46606-3

Photoshop Elements 8
For Dummies
978-0-470-52967-6

Gardening

Gardening Basics
For Dummies
978-0-470-03749-2

Organic Gardening
For Dummies,
2nd Edition
978-0-470-43067-5

Green/Sustainable

Raising Chickens
For Dummies
978-0-470-46544-8

Green Cleaning
For Dummies
978-0-470-39106-8

Health

Diabetes For Dummies,
3rd Edition
978-0-470-27086-8

Food Allergies
For Dummies
978-0-470-09584-3

Living Gluten-Free
For Dummies,
2nd Edition
978-0-470-58589-4

Hobbies/General

Chess For Dummies,
2nd Edition
978-0-7645-8404-6

Drawing
Cartoons & Comics
For Dummies
978-0-470-42683-8

Knitting For Dummies,
2nd Edition
978-0-470-28747-7

Organizing
For Dummies
978-0-7645-5300-4

Su Doku For Dummies
978-0-470-01892-7

Home Improvement

Home Maintenance
For Dummies,
2nd Edition
978-0-470-43063-7

Home Theater
For Dummies,
3rd Edition
978-0-470-41189-6

Living the
Country Lifestyle
All-in-One
For Dummies
978-0-470-43061-3

Solar Power Your Home
For Dummies,
2nd Edition
978-0-470-59678-4

available wherever books are sold. For more information or to order direct: U.S. customers visit www.dummies.com or call 1-877-762-2974.
.K. customers visit www.wileyeurope.com or call (0) 1243 843291. Canadian customers visit www.wiley.ca or call 1-800-567-4797.

Internet

Blogging For Dummies,
3rd Edition
978-0-470-61996-4

eBay For Dummies,
6th Edition
978-0-470-49741-8

Facebook For Dummies,
3rd Edition
978-0-470-87804-0

Web Marketing
For Dummies,
2nd Edition
978-0-470-37181-7

WordPress
For Dummies,
3rd Edition
978-0-470-59274-8

Language & Foreign Language

French For Dummies
978-0-7645-5193-2

Italian Phrases
For Dummies
978-0-7645-7203-6

Spanish For Dummies,
2nd Edition
978-0-470-87855-2

Spanish
For Dummies,
Audio Set
978-0-470-09585-0

Math & Science

Algebra I
For Dummies,
2nd Edition
978-0-470-55964-2

Biology For Dummies,
2nd Edition
978-0-470-59875-7

Calculus For Dummies
978-0-7645-2498-1

Chemistry For Dummies
978-0-7645-5430-8

Microsoft Office

Excel 2010 For Dummies
978-0-470-48953-6

Office 2010 All-in-One
For Dummies
978-0-470-49748-7

Office 2010 For Dummies,
Book + DVD Bundle
978-0-470-62698-6

Word 2010 For Dummies
978-0-470-48772-3

Music

Guitar For Dummies,
2nd Edition
978-0-7645-9904-0

iPod & iTunes For
Dummies, 8th Edition
978-0-470-87871-2

Piano Exercises
For Dummies
978-0-470-38765-8

Parenting & Education

Parenting For Dummies,
2nd Edition
978-0-7645-5418-6

Type 1 Diabetes
For Dummies
978-0-470-17811-9

Pets

Cats For Dummies,
2nd Edition
978-0-7645-5275-5

Dog Training For Dummies,
3rd Edition
978-0-470-60029-0

Puppies For Dummies,
2nd Edition
978-0-470-03717-1

Religion & Inspiration

The Bible For Dummies
978-0-7645-5296-0

Catholicism For Dummies
978-0-7645-5391-2

Women in the Bible
For Dummies
978-0-7645-8475-6

Self-Help & Relationship

Anger Management
For Dummies
978-0-470-03715-7

Overcoming Anxiety
For Dummies,
2nd Edition
978-0-470-57441-6

Sports

Baseball
For Dummies,
3rd Edition
978-0-7645-7537-2

Basketball
For Dummies,
2nd Edition
978-0-7645-5248-9

Golf For Dummies,
3rd Edition
978-0-471-76871-5

Web Development

Web Design
All-in-One
For Dummies
978-0-470-41796-6

Web Sites
Do-It-Yourself
For Dummies,
2nd Edition
978-0-470-56520-9

Windows 7

Windows 7
For Dummies
978-0-470-49743-2

Windows 7
For Dummies,
Book + DVD Bundle
978-0-470-52398-8

Windows 7 All-in-One
For Dummies
978-0-470-48763-1